Charitable Incorporated Organisations

Gareth G. Morgan

DIRECTORY OF SOCIAL CHANGE

Published by the Directory of Social Change (Registered Charity in England and Wales no. 800517)
Head office: 24 Stephenson Way, London NW1 2DP; tel: 08450 77 77 07
Northern office: Federation House, Hope Street, Liverpool L1 9BW
Visit www.dsc.org.uk to find out more about our books, subscription funding websites and training events. You can also sign up for e-newsletters so that you're always the first to hear about what's new.

The publisher welcomes suggestions and comments that will help to inform and improve future versions of this and all of our titles. Please give us your feedback by emailing publications@dsc.org.uk.

This book seeks to explain the principles and legal framework for Charitable Incorporated Organisations (CIOs) but it is not a full statement of the law. References to legislation are provided in many places and readers are urged to refer to the legislation directly whenever possible, but there will often be further legal issues beyond those directly mentioned in the text or cited in the references. With regard to CIO provisions in force, the law is stated as at 1 April 2013. However, some of the content (especially in chapters 10 and 14) deals with provisions which are not yet implemented, and details could be subject to change. Many issues are covered at an overview level only. No responsibility therefore can be accepted by the publisher, author or reviewers for loss occasioned as a result of any person acting or refraining from acting on the basis of this publication.

First published 2013

ISBN 978 1 906294 2 67

British Library Cataloguing in Publication Data
A catalogue record for this book is available from the British Library

Cover design by Kate Bass
Original text design by Sarah Nicholson
Typeset by Marlinzo Services, Frome
Printed and bound by Page Bros, Norwich

What they said about the book...

The Charitable Incorporated Organisation ('CIO') will, I am sure, become an increasingly popular charitable form because it remedies one of the key weaknesses in the charitable sector – the legal vulnerability of trustees.

It is often said that we live in an increasingly litigious age – all too often we read in the newspapers of apparently counter-intuitive outcomes to court cases; but whether litigation is actually on the rise does not matter, what matters is that people think litigation is becoming more prevalent.

In the two Reviews which I have carried out for the Government – Unshackling Good Neighbours (which looked at the red tape burdens on charities and voluntary groups) and the Official Review of the Charities Act 2006 – this apparently increased risk of being sued deterred people not only from volunteering but, more especially, from acting as a Trustee of a Charitable Trust or Association – a post which carries with it unlimited personal liability.

The proposal in the 2006 Charities Act to create the CIO was designed to remedy this deficiency. It has been a long time maturing! In my Charities Act Review I urged the Government to inject some urgency into the process. Six and a quarter years later, the necessary Statutory Instruments have been passed and the CIO has arrived. This guide is an important step in the development of CIOs. I therefore warmly commend it.

Lord Hodgson of Astley Abbotts, CBE, Official Reviewer of the Charities Act 2006

The combination of a straightforward approach, together with sufficient level of detail on the increasingly important CIO structure, means that guidance of the kind provided in this book will be most welcome for charities, their advisors and students of the charitable sector.

Debra Morris, Director, Charity Law and Policy Unit, University of Liverpool

Gareth combines a detailed overview of the Charitable Incorporated Organisation with a clear and accessible style. This guide will be invaluable to anyone contemplating setting up a CIO or advising organisations on setting one up. It provides an assessment of the advantages and disadvantages of the CIO structure and the issues that will need to be considered and the steps that will need to be taken in the lifecycle of a CIO, including setting up, conversion, record keeping, reporting and winding up. This comprehensive treatment will be essential reading for people who want to gain a full understanding of this long-awaited new legal form for charities.

Peter Horner, NAVCA

This book provides a thorough and objective analysis of the key legal, regulatory and accounting considerations relating to charitable incorporated organisations (CIOs). It contains helpful and clear explanations of the accounting, filing and external scrutiny requirements for CIOs which will be of interest to treasurers, trustees and senior management in charities as well as charity advisors. The publication of this book is timely and very welcome since CIOs are a new legal development which are likely to be of interest to many involved in the sector.
Anne Davis, Head of Charity and Voluntary Sector, Institute of Chartered Accountants in England and Wales (ICAEW)

Community Matters endorses the publication as a helpful explanation of the CIO structure and its application to community organisations.
Graham Willmington, Chief Executive, Community Matters

Gareth's work on the CIO covers an extensive range and is erudite but written in an accessible way both for professionals and for charity trustees. As legal adviser to many community associations, village halls and other community-based organisations, I heartily recommend this publication as an essential guide to CIOs for the voluntary and community sector.
Jonathan Dawson, solicitor and consultant in the voluntary and community sector

Contents

About the author

Gareth G. Morgan is Professor of Charity Studies at Sheffield Hallam University. He is course leader of the MSc in Charity Resource Management and he leads the University's Centre for Voluntary Sector Research which brings together sixteen staff in various faculties with specific interests in the sector.

He has published research on various issues of charity regulation and accounting, particularly in relation to small and medium-sized charities. He has prepared many policy proposals for consultations regarding issues of charity regulation, including submissions on the Draft Bill which became the Charities Act 2006 and for Lord Hodgson's Review of the Act, published in 2012. He has led or co-led several research projects with the Charity Commission and he serves on a number of working parties concerned with issues of charity structures, accounting and regulation.

Outside the University he is also part-time Senior Partner of the York-based charity consultants, The Kubernesis Partnership LLP, which supports a wide range of organisations in areas such as establishing new charities, charity mergers, changes of legal form, accounting, reporting, independent examinations, governance and tax issues in fundraising. He has supported several organisations through the processes of forming a CIO or SCIO and conversion of existing charities.

About the series

This series of key guides is designed for people involved with not-for-profit organisations of any size, no matter how you define your organisation: voluntary, community, non-governmental or social enterprise. All the titles offer practical, comprehensive, yet accessible advice to enable readers to get the most out of their roles and responsibilities.

Other titles in the series

Also available in this series: *Charitable Status*, Julian Blake, 2008; *The Charity Treasurer's Handbook*, Gareth G. Morgan, 2010; *The Charity Trustee's Handbook*, Mike Eastwood, 2010; *Effective Fundraising*, Luke Fitzherbert, 2004; *Minute Taking*, Paul Ticher and Lee Comer, 2012

For further information, please contact DSC (see overleaf for details).

Foreword

Like the author, I am an enthusiast for anything which simplifies the lot of those seeking to run charities. I also passionately believe that those who give their time as trustees should be given the best possible protection should things go wrong or money run out. CIOs promise to address this and other significant issues, making them attractive for trustees and their organisations by providing a structure which gives corporate status and limited liability in a simple package.

For established charities, especially those which are already incorporated, changing to a CIO structure won't always be appropriate. But for many new charities, and for unincorporated charities which need to convert to a corporate structure there are some obvious advantages. CIOs seek to overcome some of the disadvantages of other organisational forms and do so partly by simplifying the rules (which may be why about a third of all new charities in Scotland are now being set up as SCIOs).

Of course, the simplification of rules can and does bring with it new issues. CIOs are no exception and Gareth Morgan eloquently outlines both the pros and cons of CIOs in the book. With these issues in mind, lawyers and advisors in England and Wales may be cautious about this new structure. Until we see how effective the Charity Commission is at administering its new responsibilities for CIOs with its limited budget, we will be keeping an eye on administrative effectiveness and response times. If any teething troubles are addressed, as I hope they will be, in time CIOs could become an established part of the landscape alongside other more familiar organisational structures.

Regardless of these issues (which structure doesn't have some?), for many new, small and medium-sized charities, the new CIO structure will be a great relief from the daunting prospect of having to become company directors.

Whilst the concepts of CIOs are straightforward, there are many important issues to consider in establishing a CIO or converting an existing charity: this book offers a useful route map through those issues. The author has done an impressively thorough job of capturing the broad concepts of CIOs as well as the detailed provisions of the statutes and regulations. The subject is made both lucid and accessible. Importantly, the author also deals with the framework for CIOs across the UK, including the significant differences between the legal forms in England and Wales, Scotland and Northern Ireland.

This book, which is the first to focus exclusively on CIOs, will certainly help those treading the path to CIO status to do so with much greater confidence.

James Sinclair Taylor, Partner, Russell-Cooke Solicitors

About the Directory of Social Change

DSC has a vision of an independent voluntary sector at the heart of social change. The activities of independent charities, voluntary organisations and community groups are fundamental to achieve social change. We exist to help these organisations and the people who support them to achieve their goals.

We do this by:

- providing practical tools that organisations and activists need, including online and printed publications, training courses, and conferences on a huge range of topics;
- acting as a 'concerned citizen' in public policy debates, often on behalf of smaller charities, voluntary organisations and community groups;
- leading campaigns and stimulating debate on key policy issues that affect those groups;
- carrying out research and providing information to influence policymakers.

DSC is the leading provider of information and training for the voluntary sector and publishes an extensive range of guides and handbooks covering subjects such as fundraising, management, communication, finance and law. We have a range of subscription-based websites containing a wealth of information on funding from trusts, companies and government sources. We run more than 300 training courses each year, including bespoke in-house training provided at the client's location. DSC conferences, many of which run on an annual basis, include the Charity Management Conference, the Charity Accountants' Conference and the Charity Law Conference. DSC's major annual event is Charityfair, which provides low-cost training on a wide variety of subjects.

For details of all our activities, and to order publications and book courses, go to www.dsc.org.uk, call 08450 777707 or email publications@dsc.org.uk.

Preface

Any charity begins not with a legal structure, but with individuals who have a passion for a cause. But most causes require funds to be raised or income to be generated, and if the cause is charitable, there are enormous advantages in setting up an organisation as a charity – in terms of tax concessions, reputation, and the protection of donors who support the cause.

But, until recently, most charitable organisations had to make do with legal structures which were never specifically designed for charities. The advent of Charitable Incorporated Organisations (CIOs) thus marks a massive change. They were first enacted in 2005 in Scotland (the SCIO) and then for England and Wales in the Charities Act 2006. SCIOs were implemented from April 2011 and the regulations for English/Welsh CIOs finally took effect from January 2013. The CIO now offers a legal structure specifically for charities, which allows charities to operate as legal entities with limited liability, but without all the complications of company law.

My prediction is that very soon the CIO will become the most popular form for establishing new charities, especially for moderate-sized organisations which are at the heart of the development of the third sector. In addition, many existing charities are looking closely at whether it would make sense to convert to become CIOs.

Yet, whilst the concept of a CIO is very simple, it is underpinned by several layers of legislation. Anyone wanting to establish a new CIO or considering the conversion of an existing charity needs to understand, at least in outline, the principles behind the CIO structure, the requirements for its constitution, the process of registering a CIO, the issues for trustees in operating a CIO, and some appreciation of what happens if things go wrong and a CIO cannot meet its liabilities. The book also seeks to provide an overview of various aspects of charity law and regulation as they apply to CIOs.

These issues matter not only to those seeking to form a CIO – they affect anyone working with third sector organisations, whether professional advisors, funders, suppliers, bankers, or, most of all, those who become charity trustees of CIOs once they are formed. A clear understanding of CIOs is also vital for those in voluntary sector infrastructure organisations.

For students on academic courses concerned with the sector, a sound appreciation of charitable structures is a starting point for all other issues.

This book seeks to explain the principles, constitutional requirements, and regulatory basis for CIOs throughout the UK, for readers in all these categories. It aims to cover CIOs in sufficient detail to explain the process of setting up and registering a new CIO, and to outline the principles for taking an existing charity through a conversion to a CIO. For readers who need to understand the full legal background, there are footnotes throughout referring to the relevant provisions in the legislation. However, in many cases there are additional issues which cannot be covered here, especially where there is interaction with other areas of law (employment, premises, contracts, etc.): professional advice will often be needed to cover issues outside the scope of this book.

Of necessity, some of the content remains speculative (for example, at the time of writing no CIOs have yet been dissolved and some provisions are not yet implemented; also it is likely that the processes and procedures of charity regulators will change as experience of CIOs grows). Any comments or feedback would be gratefully received: please use the email address cio@kubernesis.co.uk.

I am an unashamed enthusiast for the CIO, from when it was first proposed back in the mid-1990s through to its final implementation. Although it has taken longer than expected to come to fruition, and the framework is certainly not perfect in all respects, I believe that the CIO offers one area where one can genuinely say that things are becoming more straightforward for the voluntary sector.

The CIO is not the right structure for *every* charity (as discussed in chapter 4) but where the CIO form *is* appropriate, I believe it will enable organisations to operate very effectively, with greater confidence for trustees, and greater clarity for other stakeholders. Of the various issues in the Charities Act 2006 (now consolidated in the Charities Act 2011), great attention has been given to the new definition of 'charity' and the new emphasis on public benefit. But whilst these issues are important, I believe the advent of the CIO will be at least as significant for the effectiveness of the sector. I hope this book will help.

Acknowledgements

From the initial proposals for CIOs in the 1990s and support by Government from 2002 (see chapter 18 for more on the origins), I felt that the CIO structure would be valuable to many of the organisations with which I work and to others starting new charities. From 2004, when I began presenting seminars on the Draft Charities Bill, I found great enthusiasm – with many participants wanting to understand all the details on CIOs – and likewise with my students at Sheffield Hallam University.

It was the appetite of these people which led me to approach the Directory of Social Change (DSC) soon after CIOs were enacted for England and Wales with the idea of a book on the subject, as a parallel to my *Charity Treasurer's Handbook*. That was in 2007 (with the Cabinet Office then expecting CIOs to be implemented by autumn 2008). But even with no firm date, DSC generously accepted my proposal, and we signed a contract with the idea that the book would be published within the early months of CIOs becoming a reality.

Over the years, with the delays in the implementation of CIOs, DSC generously agreed my repeated requests to postpone the book. Moreover, as time moved on (and with SCIOs implemented before CIOs in England and Wales) it became clear that the book needed to address many more issues than initially envisaged, in order to be useful to a wide range of readers. Consequently, the final book contains much more content than envisaged at the outset. I am enormously grateful to John Martin (Commissioning Editor) and Lucy Muir-Smith (Books Editor) for all their support and patience over the period of almost six years from concept to publication.

One cannot write a book like this in isolation, and beyond study of the legislation and documentation from charity regulators, much of the content has come from debating CIO concepts with others. I was privileged to serve on the CIO Working Party established by the Charity Law Association (CLA) in 2008/09 (commenting on the draft regulations published at that stage) and to have been involved in CLA and Scottish Executive consultations on the SCIO regulations. I have been honoured to speak about CIOs at a wide range of conferences and seminars, both for charity practitioners and for professional advisors: the questions and comments at those events have done much to shape the book. I would pay particular tribute to the voluntary sector in Hartlepool for the huge interest shown in CIOs over the years.

Nevertheless, when writing about a new concept like CIOs there is a real risk of error or confusion, and I am grateful to a wide range of people who made comments on the book in draft: their input has led to numerous improvements. James Sinclair Taylor of Russell Cooke Solicitors reviewed the entire manuscript in agreement with DSC: his input has prompted clarification of many issues. I also had feedback from a number of people with particular expertise, including Jonathan Dawson (solicitor and advisor to Community Matters) on various chapters, Prof Stefan Enchelmaier (University of York) on chapter 1; Dr Rory Ridley-Duff (Sheffield Hallam University) on chapter 3; Ian Oakley-Smith (PricewaterhouseCoopers) on chapters 12 and 17; Gavin McEwan (Turcan Connell, Edinburgh) on chapter 13; Dr Oonagh Breen (University College, Dublin), Jenny Ebbage (Edwards & Co, Belfast), and Jill Steele (CCNI) on chapter 14; and Francesca Quint (Radcliffe Chambers) on chapter 16. I am also very grateful to civil servants at the Cabinet Office and Scottish Executive, and to key members of staff at the CCEW, OSCR and CCNI for responding helpfully to a wide range of queries, in some cases over several years. However, the final content, and all opinions expressed, remain very much my own: I take full responsibility for all remaining errors.

I owe a huge debt of gratitude to my wife and business partner, Sharon, who proofread all the early drafts, identified points where explanations needed clarification, and did a huge amount to free me up to focus on the book: her support was truly amazing.

Ultimately, the value or otherwise of a book like this can only be judged by those who find themselves setting up and running CIOs, or advising others to do so. It is to all of you – the 'CIO community' – that the book is dedicated.

Gareth G. Morgan, May 2013

List of abbreviations

2005 Act	Charities and Trustee Investment (Scotland) Act 2005
2008 Act	Charities Act (Northern Ireland) 2008
2011 Act	Charities Act 2011 (applies to England and Wales)
AGM	Annual General Meeting
AIB	Accountant in Bankruptcy (Scotland)
CASC	Community Amateur Sports Club
CBS	Community Benefit Society (a type of IPS established to benefit the community – often, but not always, a charity)
CCEW	Charity Commission for England and Wales
CCNI	Charity Commission for Northern Ireland
Charities Act	Unless otherwise stated, this means the Charities Act 2011 (applicable to England and Wales)
Charities & TI (Scotland) Act 2005	Charities and Trustee Investment (Scotland) Act 2005
Charities Act (NI) 2008	Charities Act (Northern Ireland) 2008
CIC	Community Interest Company
CIO	Charitable Incorporated Organisation (unless otherwise stated at the start of the chapter or in the section concerned, use of the term 'CIO' includes CIOs established in E&W, SCIOs, and CIOs established in Northern Ireland).
CIO General Regulations	The Charitable Incorporated Organisations (General) Regulations 2012 (SI 2012/3012)
CIO (I&D) Regulations	The Charitable Incorporated Organisations (Insolvency and Dissolution) Regulations 2012 (SI 2012/3013)
CLG	Company Limited by Guarantee
CSO	Civil Society Organisation
CVA	CIO voluntary arrangement
CVL	creditors' voluntary liquidation
DRC	Designated Religious Charity (in Scotland or Northern Ireland)
E&W	England and Wales
E&W CIO	A CIO established under the law of England and Wales (formed under the Charities Act 2011 and registered with the CCEW)
EGM	Extraordinary General Meeting
FCA	Financial Conduct Authority
FSA	Financial Services Authority (the former name of the FCA)

HMRC	Her Majesty's Revenue and Customs
IE	Independent Examination (chapter 8)
IP	Insolvency Practitioner
IPS	Industrial and Provident Society
MVL	members' voluntary liquidation
NI	Northern Ireland
NI CIO	A CIO established under the laws of Northern Ireland (formed under the Charities Act (Northern Ireland) 2008 and registered with the CCNI) – see chapter 14
NISR	Northern Ireland Statutory Rules
OR	Official Receiver
para.	paragraph (a subdivision within a schedule or regulation)
PCC	Parochial Church Council (a legal structure used in the Church of England)
PDF	Portable Document Format (electronic file format, widely used for documents – needed, for example, when registering a charity)
OSCR	Office of the Scottish Charity Regulator
reg.	regulation
R&P	Receipts and Payments accounts
s.	section (of an Act of Parliament)
Sch.	Schedule (of an Act of Parliament)
SCIO	Scottish Charitable Incorporated Organisation (a CIO former under the Charities & TI (Scotland) Act 2005 and registered with OSCR) – see chapter 13
SCIO Regulations	The Scottish Charitable Incorporated Organisations Regulations 2011 (SSI 2011/44)
SCIO (RRD) Regulations	The Scottish Charitable Incorporated Organisations (Removal from Register and Dissolution) Regulations 2011 (SSI 2011/237)
SOAL	Statement of Assets and Liabilities (as used with R&P accounts)
SOFA	Statement of Financial Activities (in a charity's accounts prepared under SORP) – the acronym is also used by banks for Standing Order File Amendment – see chapter 9
SORP	Statement of Recommended Practice on Accounting and Reporting by Charities
ss.	sections
SI	Statutory Instrument (for E&W or UK-wide)
SSI	Scottish Statutory Instrument
TSO	Third Sector Organisation
TUPE	Transfer of Undertakings (Protection of Employment) Regulations 2006

Table of legislation and cases

Statutes

Statutory Instruments

Cases

1 What are CIOs and why are they useful?

Charitable organisations (or voluntary organisations with charitable status) have existed in the UK for centuries without any special legal structure. Over time, a system of charity law developed over many centuries. In fact, modern charity law still owes much to the 1601 Statute of Charitable Uses passed in the time of Elizabeth I (for more on the definition of 'charity' see page 21). But charity law has been mainly concerned with protecting charitable funds and property, and with the regulation of charities, rather than with specific legal structures. So, until recently, charities were normally set up using structures which are also used for many other types of organisations, rather than a specific form for charities.

Structures for charities – why CIOs?

In the earliest days, all charities were trusts: where individuals (trustees) came together on a personal basis to hold property or funds for charitable purposes. In due course, other structures developed such as charitable associations: bodies with members, governed by a constitution, where members elect a committee to govern the association. Many larger charities are formed as charitable companies – not-for-profit companies which are also registered as charities. There are also other possibilities such as charities established by Act of Parliament or by Royal Charter.

Nowadays, few people wanting to establish new charities are in a position to petition for Royal Charters or are able to seek private Acts of Parliament. So in practice, until the advent of charitable incorporated organisations (CIOs) the vast majority of charities have been established using one of the three well-proven legal forms:

- the charitable trust (usually governed by a trust deed);
- the charitable association (usually governed by a constitution); or
- the charitable company (governed by articles of association).

A few charities are set up using other structures, in particular the Industrial and Provident Society (IPS): a corporate structure often used by mutual organisations (such as clubs, credit unions, or co-operative businesses which are owned by the members). An IPS established for purposes which benefit the community (which includes charitable IPSs) is called a Community Benefit Society (CBS).[1]

Each of these forms – trusts, associations, companies, CBSs – has existed for many years, but none is specific to charities (they are discussed in more detail in chapter 4). But whilst each has some advantages they also have significant disadvantages.

Charitable trusts and associations are simple to set up and like CIOs have only one regulator, but have two major limitations: firstly that they are not corporate bodies and secondly that they do not offer limited liability. These terms and issues are explored below.

Charitable companies do not have these limitations – a company is a corporate body and normally has limited liability – but for a charity to be a company it has to comply with various requirements under company law (as well as charity law) including registration with Companies House. A CBS has some similarities to a company in that it is a corporate body with limited liability, but as with all IPSs, it is registered with the Financial Conduct Authority (FCA) rather than Companies House, and IPS law has a number of differences from company law.

To get round these difficulties it has long been suggested that a completely new legal structure would make things much simpler for charitable organisations, their trustees and anyone who deals with charities. The idea was to have a structure which would be:

- specific to charities, so there was no uncertainty about charitable status;
- a corporate body;
- with limited liability;
- *not* a company and so *not* subject to company law or registration with Companies House;
- where the organisation is registered *only* with a charity regulator and therefore is subject to only one regulator in terms of accounts and returns.

The obvious choice of name was to call it a 'charitable incorporated organisation'. A CIO is an incorporated body; it is a charity; and it is a specific kind of organisation – a legal structure used only for charities.

[1] The new name arises from the Co-operatives and Community Benefit Societies Act 2003.

Three jurisdictions of CIOs in the UK

There are three forms of CIO, corresponding to the three systems of charity law in the UK (or three legal jurisdictions):

- a CIO established under the laws of England and Wales is registered and regulated by the Charity Commission for England and Wales (CCEW);[2]
- a CIO established under the laws of Scotland is called a SCIO (generally pronounced 'ski-oh') – it is registered and regulated by the Office of the Scottish Charity Regulator (OSCR);[3]
- a CIO established under the laws of Northern Ireland will be registered and regulated by the Charity Commission for Northern Ireland (CCNI).[4]

The CIO structure was first implemented in Scotland (SCIOs) from April 2011, then CIOs in England and Wales from January 2013. At the time of writing, CIOs cannot yet be formed in Northern Ireland, but implementation is expected around 2015.

This book considers all three forms of CIOs but, up to chapter 12, each chapter introduces the principles and then considers the detailed requirements for CIOs in England and Wales. The differences for Scotland and Northern Ireland are then explained in chapters 13 and 14. To refer collectively to these three jurisdictions in the book the term 'charity regulator' is used. And, unless otherwise stated, the acronym 'CIO' is used to refer to all three forms.

Principles of a CIO

The main features of a CIO are as shown in table 1.1.

The rest of this chapter explores what these features mean in practice. It focuses on the legal principles for CIOs in England and Wales, but most of these principles are very similar for SCIOs and (when available) Northern Irish CIOs.

[2] Charities Act 2011, ss. 204–250.

[3] Charities & TI (Scotland) Act 2005, ss. 49–64.

[4] Charities Act (NI) 2008, ss. 105–122 & Sch. 7.

Table 1.1 Main features of a Charitable Incorporated Organisation

A corporate body	– Can hold its own property – Can sue and be sued in the name of the charity (rather than trustees personally)
Limited liability	– A major claim could lead to the charity being liquidated, but no claim can be made against the personal assets of members or trustees provided they act properly
Governing document	– Has a constitution
Registration	– Done entirely by the charity regulator (the registration *creates* the CIO and *confirms* its charitable status) – every CIO is a registered charity
Governance	– Has charity trustees (similar to trustees/directors of a charitable company, but no obligations under company law)
Accounting	– As for other non-company charities; special rules for charitable companies *do not* apply
Name	– Normally ends with 'CIO' ('SCIO' in Scotland) unless the status is otherwise disclosed on documents
Members	– Always has a membership but it can have a two-level structure of members electing trustees or single level where the only members are the trustees
Insolvency	– Regulations create a similar framework to the insolvency arrangements for limited companies (though differences apply in Scotland)

Legislation for CIOs in England and Wales

The CIO structure in England and Wales originally came into law in the Charities Act 2006: the requirements were expressed by way of numerous amendments to the Charities Act 1993 which made them hard to follow. But before CIOs were actually enacted, most of the provisions in the 2006 and 1993 Acts were consolidated into the Charities Act 2011 (making the CIO legislation much more readable). So the 2011 Act is the primary legislation under which CIOs are established.

However, the Act does not spell out all the requirements for CIOs in detail. As is common with much legislation, the Act allows the relevant Minister to make regulations for CIOs – this comes under the Office for Civil Society in the Cabinet Office. (The main reason why CIOs were not implemented until 2013 was due to the finalisation of these regulations.)

Two sets of regulations have been made: one concerning constitutional and operational issues and the other concerning dissolution and insolvency of CIOs. A third set of regulations will follow shortly, setting out the details for conversion of charitable companies to CIOs (see chapter 10).

So the legal framework for the structure and operation of CIOs in England and Wales currently comprises:

- The Charities Act 2011: sections 204–250 (Part 11 of the Act)
- The Charitable Incorporated Organisations (General) Regulations 2012[5]
- The Charitable Incorporated Organisations (Insolvency and Dissolution) Regulations 2012.[6]

In addition, the Charity Commission is empowered to make further regulations, in particular regarding the form of a CIO's constitution. These comprise The Charities Act 2011 (Charitable Incorporated Organisations) (Constitutions) Regulations 2012, which state that the specified form for CIO constitutions is to use one of the Commission's models. However, the Act only requires that constitutions have to be in this form or 'as near that form as circumstances permit'[7] so there is a measure of flexibility (see the Appendix and discussion in chapter 6).

However, like any charity, the operation of a CIO and the duties of its trustees are also governed by the rest of charity legislation, case law and the Commission's guidance.

---

[5] SI 2012/3012 – subsequently referred to as the 'CIO General Regulations'.

[6] SI 2012/3013 – subsequently referred to as the 'CIO (I&D) Regulations'.

[7] Charities Act 2011, s. 206(5).

Corporate status

The law makes a crucial difference between types of organisations:

- trusts and associations are *unincorporated bodies*;
- companies, IPSs and CIOs are *corporate bodies* (or, we can say, the organisation is *incorporated*).

In order to understand the possible benefits of a CIO – but also some of the complications – it is vital to understand this issue of incorporation. An organisation which is recognised in law as a corporate body is considered to be a 'person' in law, able to hold property in its own right, able to enter into its own legal agreements, and capable of suing or being sued in the courts, separately from the individuals behind the organisation. (If you are already familiar with this, skip to the next section, but if not the following points and examples may help.)

Natural and legal persons

The law recognises two types of persons or legal entities:

- natural persons (individual human beings)
- corporations (bodies or organisations which, under the law, are incorporated; that is, the organisation is established as a legal person in its own right).

Each of these can own property and/or enter into binding legal agreements. For many charities, it is very helpful for the charity to be a legal entity in its own right and the CIO is now one of the simplest ways of achieving this.

Unincorporated bodies

Many organisations are not incorporated; they are just formed by people coming together for common aims. This includes charitable trusts and charitable associations. It is only by going through a specific legal process, such as registering a company or a CIO, that a corporate body is formed. All other organisations are thus unincorporated bodies.

It is perfectly possible to run an organisation – even a charity – on an unincorporated basis. Around three quarters of registered charities in England and Wales are unincorporated. But for anyone else dealing with an unincorporated charity the issues can be complex, because the external party is making an agreement with a group of people, rather than a single person. If something goes wrong with the agreement, action would have to be taken against all the trustees.

For example, if an unincorporated charity needs to employ staff, then in law the employers would be the trustees who made the appointment. So, any employment dispute would have to be pursued against individual trustees. Moreover, every time the trustees change, contracts of employment should be updated, but this rarely happens, so it is not always clear whether the employer is the current trustees or the trustees who were in post when the appointment was made.

Lack of corporate status can also be a problem with ownership. If an unincorporated charity needs a building for its work and so it buys some freehold land, that land has to be registered in the names of the individual trustees. In the Land Registry's records a note must be added to show that the land is held in trust for the purposes of a specific charity, but the legal owners are still the individual trustees because only persons can own anything. If, as happens over time, the trustees change, the land needs to be re-registered in the names of new trustees. Alternatively, a small number of individuals could be appointed as 'holding trustees' to hold the property on behalf of the charity trustees, or a suitable corporate body – such as a larger incorporated charity or a nominee trust corporation – could hold title to the property as a 'custodian trustee'. Other arrangements are possible. Trustees who hold property for a charity, but without being involved in day-to-day governance are called 'trustees *for* the charity' as opposed to the charity trustees who make the decisions. But this can be hard to explain to those unfamiliar with the details of charity structures.

However, being unincorporated is not a problem for all charities. A grant-making charity with no staff and no premises or substantial investments can often operate quite simply as a charitable trust. A charity which provides self-help to people with a certain medical condition, but which has no staff and which only ever rents rooms for meetings may be able to operate effectively as a charitable association. Unincorporated charities are simpler to close down (they do not have to be formally dissolved) and so may suit low-risk projects of short duration.

When incorporation is needed

Once a charity reaches one of the following stages there are strong grounds for it to be incorporated:

- entering into substantial contracts with third parties to buy goods or services; or
- taking on substantial contracts with third parties for services to be provided by the charity (procurement of services from the charity, rather than grant funding); or

- employing staff; or
- owning freehold property or taking on leases.

In these cases it becomes much simpler if the charity is a corporate body: a legal entity able to make these agreements or hold property in its own right, rather than in the names of its trustees. If the charity is incorporated it means:

- contracts with third parties can be made in the name of the charity itself (rather than in the names of individual trustees);
- similarly, contracts of employment can specify that the charity itself is the employer (rather than individual trustees);
- the charity itself can formally own the title to any freehold property or investments;
- if the charity takes on a loan, the charity itself, rather than the trustees, is the legal entity responsible for making the repayments (though see the next section for more on what happens where the charity has insufficient funds to repay).

A few charities have long had corporate status under Royal Charters or Acts of Parliament. For example, in the Church of England, each Parochial Church Council (PCC) is a corporate body under church legislation approved by Parliament. It is also possible in some cases for a body of charity trustees to be incorporated in their own right (see page 52) but this does not offer limited liability.[8]

But until CIOs, the simplest way of establishing a new charity as a corporate body was to use the structure of a *charitable company*. Charitable companies are considered further in chapter 4 – in some instances they may be more suitable than a CIO – but they have to comply with company law as well as charity law.

CIOs as a means of incorporation

Once it is clear that a charity needs its own legal personality, the CIO offers a very straightforward alternative to the complexities of a charitable company or CBS. The law states that a CIO is a corporate body, and a CIO takes on its corporate form from the moment it is registered by the Charity Commission.[9]

A CIO thus offers a means of establishing a charity as a corporate body from the outset, so it can hold property and enter into contracts in its own

[8] Charities Act 2011, s. 251.

[9] Charities Act 2011, ss. 205 & 209.

right, but (for a CIO operating in England and Wales) it is registered only with the Charity Commission and regulated solely by charity law.

Limited liability

One of the major issues which often concerns charity trustees is: what happens if something goes wrong? In particular, what happens if a charity takes on financial commitments which it cannot fulfil? For example, what if it takes on a loan in the expectation of repaying it from future income, but then it loses a vital contract and no longer has the income to repay the loan?

In such cases a lender is entitled to take action through the courts to recover the amount due. The same applies to any other creditor; for example, a supplier who has not been paid for work done for the charity, or employees who have not been paid their salaries or redundancy pay, or someone who is making a claim against the charity for damages (such as a service user who was injured when the charity was meant to be looking after them).

In the case of an unincorporated charity – such as a trust or association – because it is not a legal entity in its own right, such a claim would be made against the trustees as individuals. Even if the charity has sufficient funds to settle the claim, it is still quite distressing for a trustee who just volunteered to serve on the committee of a charity to find a court summons being served on them at their home address! However, with an incorporated charity – whether a charitable company or a CBS or a CIO – the claim would be made against the charity itself, and a summons would be served on the charity itself at its registered office (for a company or CBS) or principal office (for a CIO).

In the first instance, anyone pursuing a valid claim against the charity or its trustees would be entitled to be paid out of the charity's own funds; this applies whatever the legal form. But often when things go badly wrong the charity may not have enough funds to settle all amounts due, and in some cases a creditor could then seek to recover the balance from the members or trustees.

The mere fact that an organisation is established as a corporate body does not necessarily solve this, as, without limited liability, a really determined creditor who exhausted the corporate assets could potentially take further actions against individual members or trustees. The members of the corporate body could then be required to make a financial contribution to settle a claim. But this can be resolved if the corporate body has limited liability.

Limited liability companies

The law has long recognised that there are reasons to allow those setting up businesses to be protected from creditors pursuing them personally; otherwise no one would ever take the risk of becoming a shareholder in big businesses which are vital to the economy. In fact, charities themselves often hold shares in major companies as part of their investment portfolios and so benefit from this: a charity could never risk investing in a commercial business with unlimited liabilities.

Since 1855 it has, therefore, been possible to establish companies with limited liability,[10] which means that under normal circumstances a creditor can only pursue a claim against the company itself – not against the members, nor against the directors (provided they have complied with all relevant legal requirements). The liability of any member of the company is limited to the amount paid for their shares. Shareholders could lose the entire value of their shareholding (very often, when a company fails, the claims of external creditors take all the funds and there is nothing left for shareholders). But losing what they paid for their shares is the *limit* of the members' liability.

By using the structure of a company limited by guarantee (CLG) – rather than a company with shares – the same principle is available to not-for-profit companies, including charities. In this case, rather than paying for shares, the members just give a guarantee that they would each contribute a small amount (such as £1 or £5) towards the liabilities if the company had to be wound up. A creditor could pursue the members for these amounts but no more (though in practice, the cost of chasing up members for small sums means that it is very rare for members of a CLG to be asked to pay the guarantee amounts, even when a company fails).

Limited liability CIOs

CIOs work on the same principle: the law states that liability of their members is limited.[11] However, the arrangement for a CIO is even simpler than with companies. In a company, the members have to subscribe for shares, or give a small financial guarantee (in a CLG).

[10] Limited Liability Act 1855. However, the full impact of incorporation with limited liability was only confirmed in the case of Saloman v. A Saloman & Co Ltd [1897] AC 22.

[11] Charities Act 2011, s. 205(3).

Although a CIO *can* be formed where the members give a guarantee, this will be very much the exception and the vast majority of CIOs will *not* require a members' guarantee. This means the members will have no obligation to contribute to the assets of the charity if it is wound up.

Nevertheless, limited liability only provides protection for financial claims against the corporate body. In law, an individual remains personally liable for a tort (a civil wrong which causes harm, such as an injury) and the person responsible could be sued for damages. For example, if a CIO trustee hits a pedestrian while driving home from a trustees' meeting, the trustee cannot avoid responsibility and claim the injury was caused by the CIO! There are also situations where charity trustees could face criminal charges such as for breaches of health and safety law. So limited liability does not mean trustees can act irresponsibly; they are still liable for their actions. But any formal agreements with funders, service users, and others will normally be made with the CIO, not with individual trustees, so if the CIO fails to deliver under the agreement, any claim would be against the CIO itself.

Limited liability and disclosure to others

Whilst limited liability is clearly attractive for the members and the directors or trustees of a company or organisation, it is important to realise that it is much less attractive to third parties. If a loan is needed to buy a vehicle, it is much more risky for a bank to lend this to a small organisation with limited liability (knowing that if something goes wrong its only claim will be against the assets of the organisation) than to lend it to an individual who owns a valuable house. Similarly, when renting a property on a long lease, the landlord has to consider whether or not to take the risk of granting a lease to a small limited liability organisation. If the organisation fails to pay the rent, the landlord will have a lot of expense to evict them and find a new tenant. This applies equally to a limited company or a CIO.

Banks will often only lend to small private companies in return for a personal guarantee from one or more of the directors. This effectively wipes out any benefits of limited liability for the director(s) concerned. But few charity trustees would consider giving personal guarantees to lenders. Without guarantees, a lender has to be able to decide whether to accept the risks of lending to a body with limited liability.

Over the years, as company law has developed, a great deal of attention has been paid to the development of limited liability, in order to ensure a fair balance of risk between the owners of a business and its creditors. Many of these features also apply to CIOs.

So that third parties know they are dealing with a limited liability body, the law requires this status to be disclosed, in most cases, as part of the name. So, a company's name must normally end with 'Limited' or 'Ltd' (or 'plc' in the case of a public limited company) so everyone is clear they are dealing with a limited liability body. Similarly, the name of a CIO normally ends with the letters 'CIO' (or 'charitable incorporated organisation' in full) showing the nature of the body.

In the case of charitable and other not-for-profit companies, it is possible to register a limited company without the word 'limited' as part of its name, but in such cases the limited status *must* still be disclosed at the bottom of letterheads, orders, emails, and other official documents. The same principle applies with CIOs if you particularly want to omit 'CIO' from the legal name (see page 91), but since a CIO is always a charity there is no risk of confusion with commercial businesses.

Advantages and disadvantages of limited liability: acting properly

The whole framework of limited liability is, however, subject to the requirement that the organisation must be run properly in accordance with relevant legislation.

In the most serious cases, trustees who ran a CIO with the intent to defraud others could face prosecution. In other cases, a trustee could be ordered by a court to make a contribution to the creditors if a CIO goes into liquidation and cannot pay its debts. But this only applies if the trustee knew at the time, or should have known, that the CIO was running up debts which it would be unable to meet (see page 226 for more on these issues).

So, limited liability never means absolute protection for trustees against any kind of liabilities: they must still run the charity properly with the normal duties of care. Actions amounting to fraud or dishonesty or certain breaches of statutory duties could lead to prosecution in any type of organisation. But it must be stressed that only in the most exceptional cases will the courts take action against charity trustees who were not seeking personal benefit.

The structure of a CIO does not, of course, prevent trustees from acting improperly. But because the legal framework for CIOs is specifically designed for charities (rather than the company law framework which is designed primarily for profit-making entities) many of the obligations under company law do not arise, so there is perhaps less scope for getting things wrong.

Incorporated and unincorporated charities: summary

A CIO is not a form of company

Although a CIO is an incorporated body with limited liability, it is crucial to remember that it is *not* a company of any kind. If you get involved in establishing a CIO while the concept is still new you may find that you have to explain this to funders, suppliers and possibly even bankers because, to many people, if any organisation is incorporated they assume that it is a company. There are in fact many different kinds of incorporated bodies in the UK (such as local authorities, NHS trusts, limited liability partnerships, IPSs), but many people forget all these other possibilities.

A CIO is governed entirely by charity law. Company law does *not* apply to CIOs except in a few areas (particularly in relation to insolvency) where the Charities Act or CIO regulations directly mirror provisions that are applicable to companies.

CIOs, CICs and other forms

Many people involved in the third sector are familiar with the structure of a Community Interest Company (CIC),[12] which is used for a wide range of non-charitable social enterprises. The differences between CICs and CIOs are discussed further on page 46. But, as the name suggests, a community interest company is a form of company, and whilst it has to meet a 'community interest test', the normal provisions of company law also apply.

With this in mind, take care with the terminology of companies and other abbreviations. Table 1.2 may provide some help with this.

[12] Under the Companies (Audit, Investigations and Community Enterprise) Act 2004.

Table 1.2 Key abbreviations for third sector legal forms

CIO	**Charitable incorporated organisation.** A CIO is *always* a charity. It is governed by charity law.
CIC	**Community interest company.** A CIC is *never* a charity. It is governed by company law.
CLG	**Company limited by guarantee.** A CLG *may be* a charity. Most CLGs are not-for-profit organisations but they do not have to be charities. A CLG that is a charity is described as a 'charitable company'[13] – it is subject to company law *and* charity law.
CBS	**Community benefit society.** An industrial and provident society with community aims; also known as a 'BenCom'. Many CBSs are charities (in which case they are also subject to charity law) but this is by no means essential.

So, if someone goes to the register of companies (available at www.companieshouse.gov.uk) they will find charitable companies and CICs listed. But they will not find any record of CIOs, just as Companies House does not list details of unincorporated charities. CIOs in England and Wales are registered solely with the Charity Commission, and to find details online it is necessary to look at the Register of Charities (at www.charitycommission.gov.uk).

Terminology of incorporated charities

In the past, there has been a tendency to talk about the different rules (particularly in relation to accounting) for 'incorporated charities' and 'unincorporated charities' with the assumption that incorporated charities are charitable companies, and hence subject to the additional accounting requirements of company law.

CIOs *are*, of course, incorporated charities, but they are *not* companies and so are not subject to the special accounting rules for charitable companies. In most respects, the accounting and reporting requirements for CIOs are the same as for unincorporated charities (see chapter 8 for details). This can be a significant advantage of CIOs, especially for smaller charities which need a corporate structure.

[13] Charities Act 2011, s. 193.

So it is much clearer to refer to 'company charities' (or charitable companies) and 'non-company charities' if discussing the different accounting rules. CIOs, though incorporated, are clearly in the category of non-company charities. Table 1.3 shows the principles.

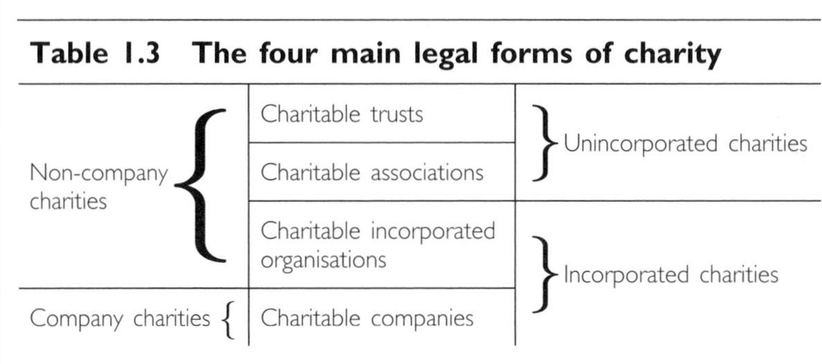

Table 1.3 The four main legal forms of charity

Non-company charities	Charitable trusts	Unincorporated charities
	Charitable associations	
	Charitable incorporated organisations	Incorporated charities
Company charities	Charitable companies	

Membership, governance and constitutions of CIOs

CIOs essentially have a two-level structure: members and trustees (as in a charitable association or a charitable company).

A CIO is formed as a body of one or more members, and in most CIOs the members have the right to elect the charity trustees who are responsible for the day-to-day governance of the organisation. The details of these arrangements are set out in the CIO's governing document which is simply called a constitution. Any changes to a CIO's constitution always require members' approval. The requirements for a CIO constitution are explained in chapter 6.

The members of the CIO can be individuals or corporate bodies. Membership can effectively be extended to other (unincorporated) organisations by allowing them to have an appointed representative who votes on the organisation's behalf. So it is quite possible to establish a CIO as an umbrella body whose members are other charities and voluntary organisations.

However, there is an important difference between membership of a CIO and membership of other types of organisations, as the Charities Act states that 'it is the duty of each member of a CIO to seek to advance the purposes of the CIO'.[14] (In particular, company law is based on the assumption that members of a company are primarily concerned with

[14] Charities Act 2011, s. 220.

their own personal interests.) In charities other than CIOs, the duty to advance the purposes normally only applies to trustees.

The CIO's constitution will state how people become members, and any other criteria for membership (such as approval by the trustees, the payment of subscriptions, a requirement to live in a certain area, etc.). Every member has a right to vote at members' meetings. (If necessary, a CIO can also establish non-voting associate membership arrangements, but such persons would not then be members of the CIO in the formal sense.)

Some CIOs may be established with just a single member; for example, where a charity sets up a new charity as a CIO, the original charity might wish to be the sole member, and hence be able to control the appointment of all the trustees. At the other end of the scale, some CIOs may be national organisations with many thousands of members. A CIO with a wide membership is referred to in the regulations as an 'association CIO'.

Between these two extremes is a form of CIO where all the members are trustees and all the trustees are members, giving a similar structure to a charitable trust or foundation (but with the benefits of corporate status and limited liability). Such an arrangement is called a 'foundation CIO'. In this case, the trustees (as members) have the right to appoint their own successors.

Those charged with governance of a CIO – the board of the CIO – are simply called 'the charity trustees of the CIO'[15] or 'the trustees' for short. However, they are not trustees in the sense of personally holding the property or funds of the CIO. The CIO is a corporate body, so the formal title to the charity's assets is held by the CIO itself. In this sense, the role of CIO trustees is similar to that of the trustees/directors of a charitable company (but *without* the specific duties of company directors). This fits with the Charities Act definition of charity trustees as 'the persons having the general control and management of the administration of a charity'[16].

For more on the duties of CIO members and trustees, including their roles when a CIO is being formed, see chapter 5.

[15] Charities Act 2011, s. 206(2)(b).

[16] Charities Act 2011, s. 177.

Registration

A CIO is formed by being registered with the Charity Commission. This is quite different from all other forms of registered charities: with charitable trusts, associations and companies the organisation is first established and only subsequently is an application made to register it as a charity (and, as explained in chapter 2, some charities do not have to be registered at all). When a CIO is registered by the Charity Commission, two events happen simultaneously:

- the CIO comes into being as a new corporate body; and
- it is registered as a charity.

At the point of formation, those who made the application (called 'the applicants' in the legislation) become the first members of the CIO, and the persons specified in the constitution as the first trustees immediately take on their duties as charity trustees of the CIO.

With a CIO, the date of formation and the date of charity registration will be the same, so there is no period when the organisation was formed but was not yet recognised as a charity. However, this does mean that work cannot start until the CIO has been registered which will usually take several weeks (see chapter 5). So a CIO may not be the most suitable legal structure for situations such as urgent disaster appeals where a new charity must be formed without any delay. But once a CIO is formed, it is definitively a charity. A CIO avoids the complications of establishing an organisation, applying for charity registration, and then perhaps having to agree constitutional changes if the Charity Commission considers that it is it not demonstrably charitable under its existing governing document. Because a CIO constitution is only a draft document until the CIO is registered, it is simple to amend the draft if needed during the application process.

Also, with other legal structures, some charities are excepted or exempted from registration (see page 24), but this never applies with a CIO: every CIO is a registered charity. If the Charity Commission does not feel able to agree an application to register a CIO – for example if the Commission is not satisfied that the proposed purposes are exclusively charitable – the organisation will not come into existence. It won't exist as an unregistered charity, or as an organisation of any kind: it will have no existence whatsoever. (See page 85 and chapter 16 for possible strategies if an application to register a CIO is refused.)

For those who have experience of applying to register charities under the existing structures, this requires a new way of thinking. Although the registration of new charities in straightforward cases is a good deal faster than it used to be, it takes considerably longer to register a charity than the time required to incorporate a company. But avoidance of a period when an organisation is formed but not yet confirmed as a charity can be a major advantage of the CIO. For example, if you have been promised a donation on condition that the organisation is a charity, or if a CIO is being formed to take over the work of an existing charity, it is no help to have the organisation formed and then find it does not meet the conditions for recognition as a charity. Also, in the past, when a new charity was formed it was often necessary to open a bank account initially on the terms for a non-charitable voluntary organisation, and only later to ask the bank to convert it to a charity account. When opening a bank account for a CIO, it will already be established as a charity.

However, where a CIO is being formed, it is important for everyone involved to appreciate that the new organisation does not come into being – it does not acquire its legal personality – until it is registered, and you will never know in advance the exact date when it will be formed. If, for example, the prospective trustees start raising funds before that date, they will be doing so in their own names and will have no protection of limited liability and separate banking arrangements would be needed. Likewise, if they were to offer a position to a new employee, they would be doing so on a personal basis.

Note that, in some cases, a CIO established in England and Wales may *also* need to register with OSCR if its work extends to Scotland, and potentially also in Northern Ireland (see chapter 15 for details).

CIOs in summary

This chapter has introduced the main features of CIOs: every CIO is a corporate body, with limited liability and registered as a charity. It is governed by a constitution with members and trustees.

Subsequent chapters explore these features in practice. Chapter 2 considers the details of charitable status, and chapters 3 and 4 compare CIOs with other legal forms for third sector organisations (non-charitable and charitable). Chapters 5 to 10 explain how to set up a CIO, how to convert an existing charity to a CIO, and issues in running a CIO. Chapters 11 and 12 look at issues in dissolving or merging a CIO. Chapters 13 to 15 explore the specifics for Scotland and Northern Ireland and the requirements for CIOs working across more than one jurisdiction. Chapters 16 to 18 look at CIOs from the perspective of other parties, disagreements with regulators, and the future of the CIO.

When setting up a new charity, a CIO will not be the right solution in every case (see chapter 4 for more on the alternatives). When an existing charity is exploring whether to convert to become a CIO, there are many issues to consider before going ahead (see chapters 9 and 10).

But the simplicity of the CIO in providing a corporate form with registered charity status, subject largely to one regulator and one legal framework, makes it a clear and effective structure for a wide range of charitable work.

2 Charitable status and public benefit

A CIO is first and foremost a *charitable* incorporated organisation. A CIO cannot be formed unless the relevant regulator (CCEW, OSCR or CCNI) is satisfied that once established, it will be, in law, a charity under the jurisdiction concerned.[1] Once formed it must then be governed and operated in accordance with charity law.

So, if you are looking to establish a new organisation, there is little point in considering the suitability of the CIO as a legal structure unless the resulting organisation will clearly meet the definition of a charity: that must be the first consideration. If you have a good idea for a third sector organisation but decide after reading this chapter that it will probably not qualify as a charity, then it is worth considering one of the other structures outlined in chapter 3.

The concept of charity

The concept of charity is rooted in love and concern for others. The word 'charity' derives from the Latin 'caritas' which is a translation of 'love'. Therefore, every charity exists in some sense for the sake of other people: for the beneficiaries (not for the trustees, or the members, or the staff).

To form a charity there has to be a vision, an aim, which seeks in some way to make the world a better place, whether by addressing issues of poverty, sharing a religious faith, providing artistic enjoyment, creating recreational opportunities, or in many other ways (see table 2.1 on page 27 for a full list of headings).

The notion of public benefit

This vision to do something which will benefit others is the heart of the 'public benefit' principle. A charity exists to benefit a wide range of people. In some cases the beneficiaries can include everyone on the planet, and others not yet born. In other cases the beneficiaries are a section of

[1] Charities Act 2011, s. 208(1)(a); Charities & TI (Scotland) Act 2005, s. 54(3); Charities Act (NI) 2008, s. 110(3)(a).

the public, such as people living in a certain locality, people with a certain medical need, or students attending a certain school or university (now or in the future).

In some cases beneficiaries may also be members or trustees, or even paid workers (in a charity providing therapeutic work). But the beneficiaries should never be *limited* to those who have a direct interest in the charity. The class of potential beneficiaries should always be wide. An organisation with a fixed list of beneficiaries could never be a charity.

A major element in making the case for a CIO to be registered is to demonstrate that the pool of beneficiaries is wide enough to show that it is established for public benefit.

Members and beneficiaries

Because a CIO has members, there can sometimes be a tendency to confuse members and beneficiaries, especially in a CIO with a wide membership. But usually this is a mistake, even if it is the members who are most involved on a day-to-day basis.

Often the members will simply be those who support the cause, rather than the beneficiaries. Or members may be the volunteers who carry out the CIO's services to benefit others. In a professional body established for charitable purposes, the members will be subject to rules regarding professional conduct and standards which enables their work to benefit society more generally. So, in most cases, the members are *not* the beneficiaries – or at most they are only a small proportion of the potential beneficiaries. For example, in a mountain rescue charity, the members are likely to be volunteers who provide the rescue service, rather than those in need of rescue who are the direct beneficiaries. But the roles may overlap: on occasion a member might him/herself be injured and need rescuing, or a beneficiary who was helped by the charity may subsequently become a member and help to rescue others.

In some cases it may be necessary to require potential beneficiaries to become members in order to use the charity's service; for example a sports charity may for safety reasons need to specify that only members can use certain equipment. But, if so, the CIO must seek to engage with all potential beneficiaries, and make it easy for someone to become a member. (A rule, for example, that new members can only be proposed by existing members would make it a private club, not a charity, if the organisation's services are only available to members. But there is no problem with a membership restriction of this kind if membership is about demonstrating support for the charity, rather than receiving benefits.)

Four definitions of 'charity'

The issue of what is and is not a charity is defined slightly differently in the three jurisdictions in the United Kingdom, under three separate pieces of legislation:

- the Charities Act 2011 (for England and Wales);
- the Charities and Trustee Investment (Scotland) Act 2005;
- the Charities Act (Northern Ireland) 2008 (as amended in 2013).

Moreover, there is a fourth definition of charity for tax purposes which is based on the English definition, but it also includes a so-called 'management test' that the charity must be managed by 'fit and proper persons'.[2] This is because a body established in another European country could be recognised as a charity in the UK for tax purposes. However, whilst some other countries have special legal forms for non-profit organisations, CIOs as described in this book only exist under UK laws.

A CIO may, of course, operate across the whole of the UK (or even internationally), in which case it may have to meet more than one of these definitions (see chapter 15). However, every CIO must be established in a specific country of the UK – in England, in Wales, in Scotland, or in Northern Ireland. So, when considering whether a proposed organisation could be a CIO, start from the definition of charity in the 'home jurisdiction' where it will be established.

In each jurisdiction the definition of 'charity' focuses on two principles: a charity is an organisation which:

- has exclusively charitable purposes; *and*
- is established for public benefit.

Note that in each jurisdiction new definitions of 'charity' have come into effect in recent years under the Acts above (the respective definitions were implemented from 2006 in Scotland, 2008 in England and Wales[3], and 2009 in Northern Ireland). So when considering other sources of guidance on charitable status, make sure they are dealing with the latest definitions.

The rest of this chapter summarises the legal definition of 'charity' and what it means in practice for a CIO established in England or Wales. For the differences in Scotland and Northern Ireland, see chapters 13 and 14.

---

[2] Finance Act 2010, Sch. 6.

[3] Originally under the Charities Act 2006, now consolidated in the Charities Act 2011.

Nevertheless the precise boundaries of what is and is not a charity have been the subject of numerous cases over the years, and large books have been devoted to this issue alone: what follows is only an overview. If you are considering setting up an organisation whose aims are close to the boundaries of what is charitable, it would certainly be wise to seek professional advice before proceeding.

Charitable status in England and Wales

In England and Wales, charitable status is *not* the same as charity registration. Unlike Scotland, where charity registration is compulsory (and this will soon be the case in Northern Ireland) many organisations in England and Wales are charities in law – they meet the English definition of 'charity' – but they do not have to be registered with the Charity Commission and so they do not have a registered charity number.

Moreover, in most cases charity registration confirms that an organisation is a charity – it doesn't become a charity at the point of registration. However, CIOs are an important exception to this, because a CIO does not exist until it is registered as a charity.

There are two main categories of 'unregistered' charities in England and Wales.

First, a number of charities are 'excepted' from charity registration by virtue of the 2011 Act or regulations, but they are still subject to the Charity Commission's normal powers. This includes most charities with less than £5,000 annual income, and a wide range of bodies connected to the armed forces and to the main Protestant churches, if they have less than £100,000 income.[4] (The £100,000 limit is likely to be reduced over time.)

Second, there are various *exempt* charities which fall outside the day-to-day oversight of the Charity Commission – largely because they are deemed to be regulated in other ways. They are listed in a schedule to the 2011 Act.[5] Many are major museums, galleries or educational bodies. Most exempt charities are being brought under 'principal regulators' other than the Charity Commission; for example, foundation schools and academy schools are regulated for charitable purposes by the Secretary of State for Education. Others will eventually lose their exempt status and will then become excepted charities, which means they will have to register with the Charity Commission if their income is over £100,000: this includes

[4] Charities Act 2011, s. 30(2)(b)–(d).

[5] Charities Act 2011, ss. 22–28 and Sch. 3.

CBSs which are charities (i.e. industrial and provident societies established for charitable purposes).

Any organisation established in England and Wales for charitable purposes which falls outside the exempt and excepted categories is required to be registered.[6] However, there is no such thing as an excepted or exempt CIO. Every CIO is a registered charity.

Also, there is no income requirement for registration of a CIO. Because a CIO does not exist at the point of applying for it to be registered, one can only discuss expected income. Even if it expects to have an income of less than £5,000 per year, a CIO can be registered (though the Charity Commission has said that such applications will not be considered until after 1 January 2014, to allow larger CIOs to register first). But from 2014 this means that even very small organisations can register as CIOs and hence get a registered charity number if they meet the definition of charity – though the members and trustees must still be able to comply with other requirements of being a CIO.

Because a CIO cannot be exempt or excepted, it is not possible for an organisation which would meet the definition of an exempt charity to be formed as a CIO.[7] So, the CIO structure cannot be used, for example, for an academy school.

In the case of a charity which would otherwise be excepted, the exception does not apply if it is a CIO. So, for example, Baptist churches are currently excepted from registration if the church has an income of less than £100,000, but if a Baptist church restructured as a CIO it would be a registered charity whatever its income may be. As a CIO it would have to meet all the other requirements of registered charity status such as completing an Annual Return for the Charity Commission.

It is also worth noting that a CIO must file its trustees' report and accounts with the Charity Commission each year, whatever its income (see page 140).

Charitable purposes

The Charities Act 2011 defines a charity as a body subject to the laws of England and Wales which is established for 'exclusively charitable purposes'.[8]

[6] Charities Act 2011, s. 30(1).

[7] CIO General Regulations 2012, reg. 5.

[8] Charities Act 2011, s. 1(1).

In the case of a CIO, the charitable purposes will be specified in its constitution in an 'objects' clause – normally worded as follows:

- The objects of the CIO are:
  (a) to . . . . ;
  (b) to . . . . ; and
  (c) to . . . .

Objects are often worded to fit with the descriptions of purposes in the Act (see below), using phrases such as 'to advance...', 'to promote...', 'to relieve the needs of...', etc.

A charity can have one object or many; however, if a CIO has several objects they must all be charitable, because of the requirement for exclusively charitable purposes. Drafting the objects in order to make sure that they are clearly charitable requires some understanding of charity law (see chapter 6 for more on preparing a constitution for a CIO).

When considering an application for a CIO to be registered, the Charity Commission is required to consider whether it would be established for exclusively charitable *purposes*, as expressed in the objects. The definition of charity in England and Wales is not directly concerned with the proposed *activities*, although the Commission always asks about the intended activities, in order to clarify the applicants' interpretation of the objects (see page 80 for more on the application process).

The Act goes on to state that a purpose is only charitable if it meets two requirements:[9]

- it must fall within the charitable headings in the Act; and
- it must be for the public benefit.

The following sections expand on each of these.

If the purposes (all of them, if more than one) meet both these requirements then the proposed CIO will be a charity, and provided there are no problems with the name or constitution, the Charity Commission will register it.[10]

---

[9] Charities Act 2011, s. 2(1).

[10] Charities Act 2011, ss. 207–209.

Descriptions of charitable purposes

The 2011 Act lists 13 headings or descriptions of purposes that are charitable in law,[11] as summarised in table 2.1.

Table 2.1 Headings of charity in section 3 of the Charities Act 2011 (slightly paraphrased)

(a) The prevention and relief of poverty
(b) The advancement of education
(c) The advancement of religion
(d) The advancement of health or the saving of lives
(e) The advancement of citizenship or community development (including rural or urban regeneration, and the promotion of civic responsibility, volunteering, the voluntary sector or the effectiveness or efficiency of charities)
(f) The advancement of arts, heritage, culture or science
(g) The advancement of amateur sport
(h) The advancement of environmental protection or improvement
(i) The relief of those in need by reason of youth, age, ill-health, disability, financial hardship or other disadvantage
(j) The advancement of human rights, conflict resolution or reconciliation or promotion of religious or racial harmony or equality or diversity
(k) The advancement of animal welfare
(l) The promotion of the efficiency of the armed forces of the Crown or emergency services
(m) Any other purpose which was recognised as charitable prior to 1 April 2008 (including recreational charities[12]) or which may reasonably be regarded as analogous to another charitable purpose.

It is not possible to discuss each of these in detail, but it is clear that a very wide range of worthwhile aims can fall into one or more of these headings.

Remember these are only 'descriptions of purposes' – there is no need for the objects of a CIO to use these phrases explicitly, and in any case the Charity Commission considers that many of the descriptions on their own may be too broad to demonstrate an exclusively charitable purpose without more clarification. See page 26 for more on wording the objects.

[11] Charities Act 2011, s. 3(1).

[12] Charities Act 2011, s. 5 – this incorporates provisions formerly in the Recreational Charities Act 1958.

The public benefit requirement

It is not enough for the purposes of a CIO to fall within one or more of the headings above; the purposes must also be 'for the public benefit'.

The broad concept of public benefit was introduced above, but unravelling the precise legal meaning of the term requires delving into case law, including two major tribunal hearings in 2011 which sought to clarify the requirement.[13]

The Charities Act simply states that a purpose is for the public benefit if it meets the 'public benefit requirement'. But it offers no definition except by referring to the term as understood in charity law (from past cases) and by saying that no purpose is to be 'presumed' to be for public benefit (so the public benefit must always be explicit).[14]

However, the Act required the Charity Commission to issue guidance on the public benefit requirement,[15] and in practice that is the best place to turn for clarification. In particular, charity trustees must by law 'have regard' to this guidance, so there is not much point in seeking to form a CIO unless the guidance has been considered. The Commission's initial guidance was published in 2008 and revised in 2011,[16] but new guidance is expected during 2013.

The guidance explains a wide range of issues, showing how the public benefit requirement applies in relation to different charitable objects – but at the heart of the requirement are two principles:

- the purpose itself must lead to a clearly identifiable benefit (sometimes called 'public benefit in the first sense'); and
- the benefit must be to the public at large or to a sufficiently wide section of the public (sometimes called 'public benefit in the second sense').

---

[13] Independent Schools Council and Charity Commission and others [2011] UKUT 421 (TCC); HM Attorney General and Charity Commission and others – Upper Tribunal (Tax and Chancery) case FTC/84/2011.

[14] Charities Act 2011, s. 4.

[15] Charities Act 2011, s. 17.

[16] *Charities and Public Benefit: The Charity Commission's general guidance on public benefit*, ref. PB1 amended December 2011 – supplementary guidance also applies for charities operating in specific fields.

Public benefit in the first sense: an inherently beneficial purpose

Public benefit in the first sense does not require measurable benefits which the government would accept for deciding social policy – it simply means that the purpose must deliver something which society regards as worthwhile.

So, for example, the law considers that society benefits when people are educated (so long as the education is worthwhile), when animal welfare is respected, when action is taken to alleviate poverty and disadvantage, and when those who are ill receive healthcare. It considers that society benefits when religious faith is taught and practised (as people are brought together for moral and spiritual purposes) – though the law does not distinguish between one faith and another.

However, there are cases where a purpose could fall within the headings in the Act but *not* be for the public benefit, often because it leads to harm: the classic case is Fagan's famous 'school for pickpockets'. Such a school might be established for the advancement of education, but the nature of the education would not benefit the public.

It is a fundamental principle that a purpose cannot be for the public benefit if it leads to significant *detriment* or *harm* which more than outweighs the benefit. So, for example, an organisation promoting a dangerous sport may come within 'the advancement of amateur sport' but if the risk of injury is very high this could well outweigh the health-related benefits of sport and exercise.

Public benefit in the second sense: the range of beneficiaries

For most new charities, however, the focus is more on demonstrating that public benefit is met in the second sense.

The purpose must benefit at least a section of the public – not a small, closed group. So in deciding whether a proposed organisation will be a charity, it is important to consider:

- who will be able to benefit; and
- any barriers or limitations which will restrict the pool of beneficiaries.

This does not mean a charity has to have a vast number of beneficiaries at any one time. For example, a charity providing grants to enable students to undertake specialist courses may decide that it is better to make one large grant each year, rather than many small grants. But it would not be a charity if grants were only ever made to people personally known to the trustees: there must be a wide pool of *potential* beneficiaries, and the trustees should be able to justify an application process for someone who will benefit most from receiving a grant.

Where the range of beneficiaries is to be restricted in any way, the Charity Commission's public benefit guidance will need careful consideration – although for charities whose sole purpose is the relief of poverty, case law indicates that a more limited class of beneficiaries is permissible.[17]

The barrier which has created the most discussion is fee charging. For example, if a charity offers services which can only be accessed on payment of large fees, or hefty ticket prices which most people could not afford, the pool of beneficiaries is likely to be heavily restricted.

This does not mean CIOs are prevented from charging fees. On the contrary, a great deal of charitable work is funded by fees and contracts. Also, there is no problem in charging fees if they are simply a means of raising funds and do not restrict who can access the services. But any CIO which plans to fund its work largely by charging fees needs to consider carefully whether they would create barriers to the point that few people could benefit. If so, it may be necessary to consider bursaries, subsidised tickets, or other means for poorer people to benefit from its services. Provision must always take account of the needs of the poor in ways that are more than tokenistic.

However, other barriers are important; for example an organisation which only benefited people in a tiny geographical area such as a single road or estate (such as a tenants association) cannot normally be a charity.

Private benefit and payments to trustees

Any benefit to the people who are not the beneficiaries of a charity is classed as private benefit, rather than public benefit. There are particular issues with payments or other benefits to trustees or people closely connected with them such as close relatives or business partners, known as 'connected persons'[18] (see the following section).

This does not mean private benefit is never allowed – there are many times when private benefits are accepted in law as being 'incidental' to the wider public benefit. However, private benefit is much broader than the

[17] HM Attorney General and Charity Commission and others, Upper Tribunal (Tax and Chancery) – often called the 'Benevolent Funds Case' ref FTC/84/2011: Decision 20 Feb 2012.

[18] The main definition of 'connected persons' is in s. 188 of the Charities Act 2011, though slightly different definitions apply in certain cases – e.g. s. 118 in relation to land disposals.

issue of benefits to trustees. For example, the work of most charities will involve paying salaries to staff or purchasing goods from commercial businesses: all of these payments will benefit people who are not the charity's beneficiaries. But provided these payments are reasonable and justified in order to carry out activities which further the charity's objects, and provided those receiving the payments are not trustees or connected persons, these do not usually present a problem.

If the purposes of an organisation will lead to significant private benefits as part of its overall aims, then the organisation is no longer considered to be established for public benefit, and cannot be a charity. For example, a private sector healthcare company may deliver benefits to the public through the services it provides, and the services may even be free of charge to the patients if it works under a contract with the NHS. But, because it is established for private profit, then even if the profit is in practice very small, it is still part of the overall aim and so it cannot be a charity.

Sometimes private benefits arise naturally from the work of a charity: for example the work of regeneration charities may lead to increased sales for local businesses, or a publishing charity may produce materials which, though educational, also benefit fee-earning professionals. But provided that the overall aim is charitable (rather than the provision of benefits to businesses or professionals) these benefits will frequently be accepted in law as being incidental.

Payments to charity trustees (and connected persons)

The normal principle is that in a charity the trustees should serve voluntarily. In the case of a CIO, the Charities Act states specifically that trustees cannot benefit personally unless very specific conditions are met.[19] They can be reimbursed their expenses (and it is good practice to do so) but they normally cannot be paid fees or wages for acting as trustees. Moreover, this limitation extends to close relatives of trustees ('connected persons') and to businesses where trustees or their relatives have significant interests. The normal wording of a CIO constitution makes this limitation clear (see clause 6(1)(c) of the model constitution in the Appendix).

Occasionally, the nature of a particular charity may mean that there is a need for someone to be a paid employee *and* a trustee. For example, in a religious organisation it may be felt essential for the minister to be a

[19] Charities Act 2011, s. 222.

voting member of the governing body (charity trustees). Similar issues sometimes arise with learned and scientific charities, or specialist arts organisations. If the organisation were structured as a CIO this would be possible if a specific provision was included in the CIO's constitution authorising certain trustees to receive salaries or stipends. However, the Charity Commission will only register the CIO with such provisions in its constitution if it is convinced that it is in the interests of the CIO to have a salaried trustee and that the benefit is genuinely incidental. Otherwise it will conclude that the CIO would not be established for public benefit.

For other cases involving fees for specific tasks, the Charities Act includes a provision enabling the other trustees to authorise specific payments to a trustee (or connected person) for other duties unrelated to the trustee role.[20] However, this provision only relates to fees paid on a freelance basis – a trustee cannot become an employee of the charity on this basis.

This can be used by a CIO if all the conditions in the Act are met. For example, sometimes a charity needs to run a training event which is too big to expect anyone to do on a voluntary basis, and the only suitable trainer is a trustee (or a close relative of a trustee). In such cases, the other trustees of the CIO could agree to pay a fee to that trustee to be a trainer. However, four conditions must be met:

- **Condition A:** The maximum amount of remuneration must be set out in a written agreement which is reasonable in the circumstances, and the trustees must consider the Charity Commission guidance on such arrangements.[21]
- **Condition B:** The (other) trustees must be satisfied beforehand that it was in the interests of the charity for services to be provided by the trustee concerned (bearing in mind that the trustee will no longer be able to vote as a trustee on any issue related to the work for which he or she is paid).
- **Condition C:** The total number of trustees benefiting at any time must be a minority (so the majority of trustees must agree to serve on a voluntary basis). If a connected person such as a trustee's relative is receiving payments, the trustee concerned is counted as benefiting for this purpose.
- **Condition D:** The governing document of the charity does not contain any express prohibition of such payments. (This is not a problem if using the Charity Commission's CIO models – see clause 6(2)(b) in the Appendix.)

[20] Charities Act 2011, s. 185.

[21] See *Trustee expenses and payments* (Charity Commission 2012, ref. CC11).

If this provision is used, any trustees benefiting are disqualified from acting on any issue related to the agreement (so cannot vote or count towards a quorum on such issues). So it is essential that the remaining trustees can still form a quorum to take decisions.

But any intended private benefits must be disclosed to the Charity Commission when applying to register a charity; so if there any plans to use these provisions when the CIO is formed, this should be declared in the application (see page 82).

Summary: charitable status and CIOs

The definition of charity in England and Wales has developed over more than 400 years. The new definition which took effect from 2008 gives many more headings for charitable purposes, but it places much greater emphasis on the public benefit requirement.

However, a huge range of aims and activities which are worthwhile to society can be expressed as charitable objects which fall within the definitions outlined above. Provided this is the case, there is no reason why the organisation cannot be established as a CIO.

But before committing to setting up a CIO it may be helpful to contrast the CIO with some of the non-charitable alternatives: these are considered in the next chapter.

3 Third sector organisations: charities, social enterprises, clubs and CICs

Whilst the CIO may seem an attractive structure for a wide range of voluntary activities, it is crucial to remember that an organisation can only be formed as a CIO if it will meet the legal definition of a charity, as explained in chapter 2.

This chapter looks briefly at some of the other structures for third sector organisations (TSOs) or civil society organisations (CSOs) as they are sometimes called. In particular, it looks at the important comparison between CIOs and CICs (community interest companies).

The term 'TSO' is used in this chapter to refer to any kind of organisation which is not established primarily for private profit (first sector) and which is not part of the state (the public sector or second sector). On this definition, charities are TSOs, whether they are structured as CIOs or using any of the other forms described in chapter 4. But the third sector also includes many other organisations including clubs and societies, trade unions, political parties, co-operatives, CICs, and other non-charitable social enterprises.

Some TSOs have paid board members or generate profits for members, but where TSOs are established on a not-for-profit basis and governed by volunteers it is usual to describe them as 'voluntary organisations'. Most charities fit this definition. CIOs are one possible form of charity. Charities are part of the wider class of voluntary organisations which are themselves part of the wider class of third sector organisations. See figure 3.1.

The issues in this chapter generally apply throughout the UK unless otherwise stated.

Figure 3.1 The landscape of third sector organisations

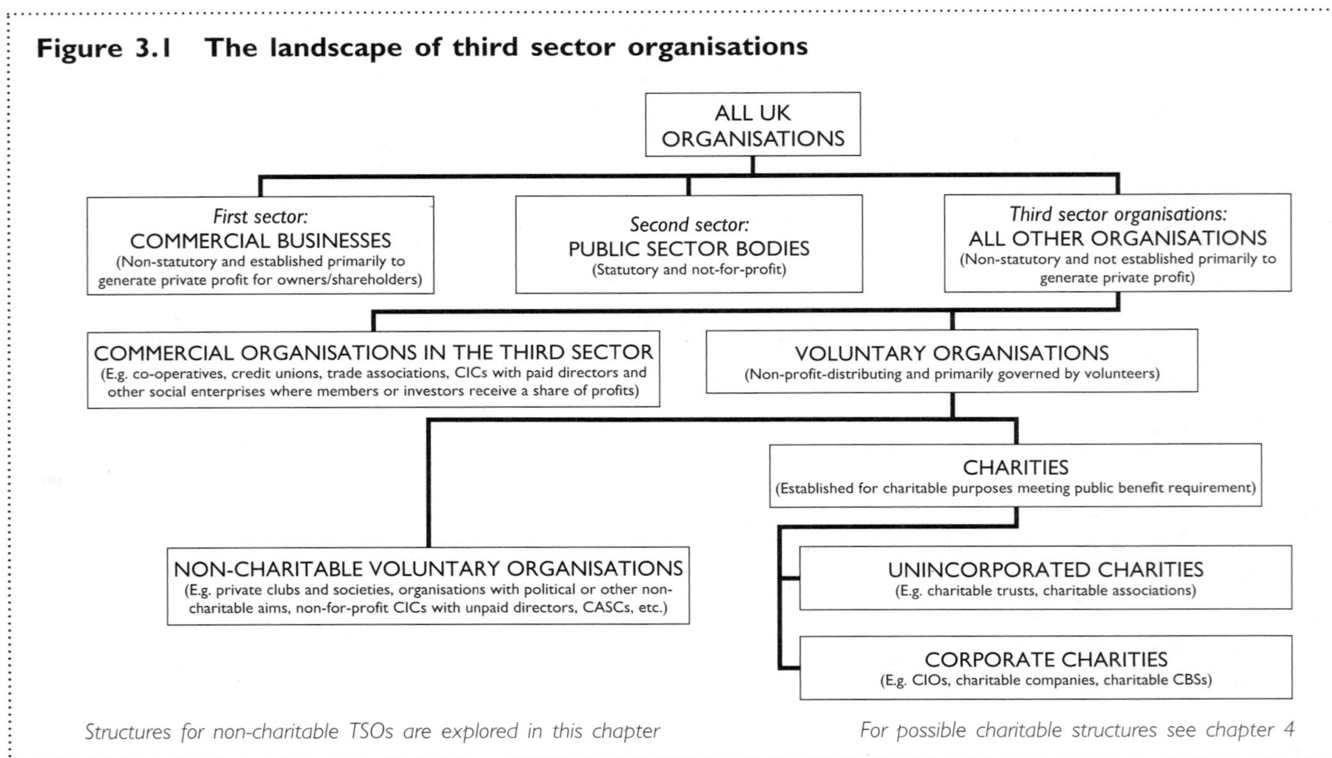

A charitable or non-charitable organisation?

When a new TSO is to be formed, one of the most important questions at the outset is to consider whether or not it should be a charity. Only if it will be a charity is there any possibility of forming it as a CIO.

As we saw in chapter 2, the definition of 'charity' has a precise legal meaning, though that meaning is slightly different between England and Wales, Scotland, and Northern Ireland. In England and Wales, an organisation is a charity if it has exclusively charitable purposes as defined in the Charities Act 2011.

However, the precise *purposes* of an organisation are not always clear when ideas are first raised. Often the initial thinking is more about activities than purposes. Many activities – for example the provision of medical care – can be undertaken either for a charitable purpose (the advancement of health for public benefit) or for a non-charitable purpose (such as trading to deliver a return for shareholders) or as an activity provided by the state (in the National Health Service).

Advantages and disadvantages of charitable status

If the activity can be undertaken for charitable purposes there are many advantages to forming the organisation as a charity. These include the ability to attract donations, the reputational benefits of charitable status, and the tax benefits which are available to charities.

But there are also many constraints to charitable status, in particular the fact that board members (charity trustees) cannot be paid, except in the limited circumstances explained in chapter 2 (see page 31). So, for example, if you are looking to set up a new social enterprise and want to have the authority as a board member but you also want to be paid a salary, a charity is unlikely to be possible, other than in the rare case of a charity where there are exceptional reasons for salaried trustees and where this amounts to no more than an incidental private benefit.

Charitable status also means all decisions must be taken on the basis of what will best advance the charity's purposes: personal considerations must be set aside. It also means accepting all the requirements of charity law, many of which are outlined in this book (at least in terms of how they affect CIOs). A charity has to make returns to a charity regulator, and has to meet more demanding accounting and reporting requirements than those which apply to non-charitable organisations. In particular, a private club could keep its accounts confidential to its members, but a charity is established for public benefit, and its end-of-year financial statements are available to anyone. Moreover, if charity trustees act improperly, charity regulators have the power to suspend them and to force the charity to take specific actions.

Charities must also take care with campaigning. It is perfectly permissible for a charity to spend a proportion of its funds on campaigning that is directly linked to its charitable objects – for example, an environmental charity campaigning for greater protection of the environment. But charities must take care not to stray into party political campaigning or into issues which fall outside their objects. For more information on this see *Speaking Out – Campaigning and Political Activity by Charities* (Charity Commission ref. CC9, March 2008).

So it is only worth establishing an organisation as a charity if the advantages outweigh the constraints.

Tax issues

It is important, however, to remember that the tax concessions for charities only apply to organisations which are legally charities, apart from some concessions to Community Amateur Sports Clubs (see page 39).

So an organisation which is *not* a charity – even if it is widely seen as a voluntary organisation – could be liable for tax on its activities. This means that there are no special tax concessions for CICs: if they make a profit, they are taxed in the same way as commercial companies, and if they occupy premises they must pay business rates on the same basis as other businesses.

Any non-charitable organisation undertaking trading activities – for example, selling publications or tickets for events – needs to make a tax return to HMRC and in most cases if it makes a profit, corporation tax is payable (there is an exception for 'mutual trading' where the only sales are to members, but not to non-members). If it occupies premises it will have to pay full business rates (unless the local authority agrees discretionary relief). Any investment income will be subject to tax. If it manages to attract legacies they would not qualify for relief from inheritance tax (except in the case of legacies to political parties).

Mixed charitable and non-charitable arrangements

These distinctions do not, however, mean there can be no interplay between charitable and non-charitable organisations in the third sector. A single organisation must be a charity or non-charity. But in some cases it is appropriate to establish two (or more) organisations working closely together, some charitable and some not. Common examples include:

(a) a charity (which could be a CIO) with a non-charitable trading subsidiary company (which could be a CIC) to undertake trading activities for fundraising purposes which fall outside the limits allowed for charities (see page 153);

(b) a private business (or a CIC) which establishes a charity (which could be a CIO) – it then transfers a proportion of its profits each year to the charity to make grants for charitable purposes (all employees of the business could be members of the CIO if desired);

(c) a non-charitable campaigning organisation whose work may include political campaigns working alongside a charity (which could be a CIO) that focuses on advice and welfare issues in the same field.

In situations of this kind where a mix of charitable and non-charitable work is planned, there may be a strong case for establishing two organisations, though, of course, only the charitable organisation could be a CIO. If so, it is worth thinking carefully about the *members* of the CIO, not just the trustees. In cases (b) and (c) above it may be appropriate for the non-charitable body (or persons it nominates) to be a member of the CIO (sometimes the sole member). However, as noted in chapter 1, remember that all members must then comply with the duties of CIO members: each member must seek to advance the CIO's purposes, for example when taking decisions at CIO general meetings (see page 68 for more details on CIO members).

In all these cases, if the two organisations work from the same premises and share facilities (and possibly staff) great care is needed to maintain the boundaries. Proper accounting arrangements are needed, with all policies clearly documented, to ensure that a charity does not in any way subsidise the aims of a non-charitable organisation. (There are some instances where a charity may agree a grant or investment to a non-charitable organisation where the aim is to advance the charitable purpose rather than simply to subsidise the non-charity, but any such arrangements with closely related organisations need to be very carefully documented, and professional advice will often be needed.)

Community amateur sports clubs

For organisations in the sports field, it may be worth considering the option of establishing a community amateur sports club (CASC). Although a CASC is *not* a charity, CASCs are entitled to a number of the tax benefits available to charities, so from a tax perspective they sit midway between charitable and non-charitable organisations.

A CASC is not accountable to a charity regulator, it is only accountable to HMRC (and to any governing bodies to which it is affiliated for the sports concerned). The key conditions are that the club's main purpose must be to provide facilities for eligible sports (as defined in the legislation), and to encourage people to take part in them; the club must be open to the whole community; and the club must be organised on an amateur basis.[1] A list of registered CASCs is published on the HMRC website (www.hmrc.gov.uk/casc/clubs.htm). There are currently over 6,000 (but this is small compared to over 200,000 bodies recognised as charities in the UK.)[2]

The tax benefits of CASC status include the ability to accept gift aid donations, no capital gains tax, no tax on interest received, mandatory 80% relief from business rates (all as for charities) and some concessions on trading profits. But a CASC does not benefit from the charity-specific concessions linked to VAT, nor to those on legacies.

A CASC is not a legal structure. Any type of organisation in the amateur sports field could be recognised as a CASC if it meets the criteria; this includes unincorporated associations, CLGs and CICs.

Possible structures for non-charitable organisations

Given that the CIO form is not available for non-charitable organisations, this section briefly summarises some of the possible structures that might be considered instead. Refer to other sources for more details on these (such as *The Russell-Cooke Voluntary Sector Legal Handbook* published by the Directory of Social Change).

Non-charitable trusts

A trust can be established for a wide range of purposes, not just for charitable aims. Many trusts relate to private family purposes (often to minimise inheritance tax – though it is worth noting that there is no inheritance tax in any case on bequests to charities). However, some appeals for particular campaigns are organised as trusts with political aims. Trusts are unincorporated, so any agreements are made by trustees personally.

---

[1] Corporation Tax Act 2010, ss. 658–661.

[2] On 4 March 2013, in a Written Ministerial Statement, the government announced a review of some of the eligibility conditions for CASCs, which may lead to some changes to the regime.

As with charitable trusts (see page 49), they are generally unsuitable for organisations with a membership: there is normally no democratic structure to allow members to elect trustees. Also, non-charitable trusts cannot last indefinitely as a result of the 'rule against perpetuities' established in common law (for most newly formed trusts in England and Wales the perpetuity period is 125 years).[3] This prevents people from tying up assets for excessive periods, unless they are made available for public benefit under a charitable trust.

Unincorporated organisations

The majority of voluntary organisations are formed as unincorporated associations where the members agree to be bound by a set of rules (normally called a constitution). Usually the constitution allows the members to elect a committee (often called the 'management committee') who have the responsibilities of governance and financial decision-making. The principles are similar to a charitable association (see page 52) but without charitable aims, so the organisation is not constrained by charity law. Many private clubs and societies, campaigning organisations, interest groups and political organisations are structured this way.

For most non-charitable TSOs, this is the simplest structure, but an unincorporated association does not have corporate status or limited liability.

Companies limited by guarantee

For a non-charitable TSO which wants the benefits of corporate status or limited liability, the most convenient form is usually a company limited by guarantee (CLG). All companies are bodies with members: in most cases the members are shareholders. CLGs are formed under the Companies Act 2006 (and so are subject to all the requirements of company law) but instead of having shareholders, the members all pledge a small guarantee (often only £1 or £5) towards possible wind-up costs. The members elect directors who form the board, though if no wider membership is needed, the members and directors can be the same people. The principles are similar to a charitable company (see page 54) but without charitable aims. The Companies Act 2006 established a common framework for company law across the UK.

---

[3] Perpetuities and Accumulations Act 2009, s. 5.

For larger and more complex TSOs which need to hold property, enter into contracts, or employ staff, or which face other risks, CLGs are widely used. However, a company cannot keep its affairs completely confidential: the company's articles, details of directors, and annual accounts must be filed at Companies House and anyone can inspect them (the current fee is just £1). Similar principles apply to the other corporate forms below.

However, in many cases a TSO structured as a CLG would meet the 'community interest test' and hence could be formed as a CIC (see next page) rather than just as a normal company.

Co-operatives and credit unions

An alternative to a company is a corporate body formed as an industrial and provident society (IPS). IPSs are corporate bodies with limited liability, but they are not subject to company law. The term IPS is somewhat outdated, but nowadays the law divides IPSs into two types: co-operatives and community benefit societies.[4] An IPS is governed by rules under which the members elect a board (usually referred to as 'directors' as in company law). IPS legislation comes under HM Treasury, with regulation by the Financial Conduct Authority (FCA) – formerly the Financial Services Authority (FSA).[5]

A co-operative is a business where members share the profits (so it cannot be a charity) but it is normally established with a wider vision than simply making a profit. The umbrella body, Co-operatives UK, gives the following definition: 'Co-operative businesses are owned and run by and for their members, whether they are customers, employees or residents. As well as giving members an equal say and share of the profits, co-operatives act together to build a better world.'[6]

---

[4] Industrial and Provident Societies Act 1965, as amended by the Credit Unions Act 1979, the Co-operatives and Community Benefit Societies Act 2003, the Co-operative and Community Benefit Societies and Credit Unions Act 2010 (and other amendments). This legal framework applies in England, Wales and Scotland – there are differences in Northern Ireland.

[5] The FSA became the FCA from 1 April 2013 under s. 6 of the Financial Services Act 2012. However, s. 50 of the Act gives power to the Treasury to transfer appropriate responsibility for mutual societies to the Prudential Regulation Authority (PRA) so further changes may follow.

[6] 'About co-operatives' [web page], www.uk.coop, Co-operatives UK, accessed April 2013.

Co-operatives can be established using many possible legal structures, but a bona fide co-operative under the IPS legislation is one possibility. The name will end with the word 'limited' but its legal form is an IPS, not a company. The members invest in the organisation as shareholders (sometimes a significant amount is required to provide working capital – for example to establish community-owned businesses – but in many co-operatives only a nominal investment of £1 is needed).

A particular form of co-operative is a credit union which provides deposit and lending facilities for members. Because of the provision of financial services it is subject to much more extensive regulation by the FCA: in particular a credit union has to belong to the Financial Services Compensation Scheme so that members' deposits are protected even if the credit union fails.

Community benefit societies

A community benefit society (CBS) – also known sometimes as 'BenCom' – is a different type of IPS that undertakes a business that is intended to benefit the community – in popular terms, a social enterprise (see page 45).

The law does not define in detail what is meant by 'benefit to the community'. However, it is much broader than public benefit requirement in charity law (see chapter 2), so a CBS can, for example, have paid board members. The community which benefits could be the customers (who receive goods or services which would otherwise be hard to obtain) or the workers (for example a CBS providing therapeutic work for people with disabilities). A CBS is normally established with an 'asset lock' (see 'Community Interest Companies' below for more details) so that profits cannot be distributed to members or used for purposes that are not linked to the community benefit aims. Although a CBS may receive grants and donations its main activity is normally some kind of trading: selling goods or services.

It is possible for a CBS (but not a co-operative) to be a charity if it has charitable objects, a suitable asset lock, and no more than incidental private benefits (see page 57) – but if so, all its trading activities would have to be either primary purpose trading, or fall within the limited exemptions allowed for non-charitable trading by charities (see page 153).

Community interest companies

Since 2005 it has been possible to establish a wide range of non-charitable TSOs requiring corporate status and limited liability using the form of a community interest company (CIC). A CIC does not allow members to share in profits to the same extent as a co-operative, but the legislation is more modern and easier to follow than IPS law and in most cases a CIC is more flexible than a non-charitable CBS. There are currently over 6,000 CICs registered.[7]

A CIC must have an object which is concerned with benefit to the community – the 'community interest test'. This is met if:

> *a reasonable person might consider that the carrying on of activities in furtherance of the object is for the benefit of the community.*[8]

A CIC can be formed as a company limited by shares (to attract external investment) or as a CLG – the CLG format is appropriate if the CIC is to be a not-for-profit organisation. Most CICs are formed to operate social enterprises (see below) though they can be used for other purposes.

The name must end with 'CIC' (or the Welsh equivalent 'CBC'), or it is even possible to have a public company which is a CIC, which in English has a name ending 'community interest plc'.[9]

A CIC is always required to have an 'asset lock' so that if it is wound up the assets must be transferred to another asset-locked body: a charity, another CIC, or an asset-locked CBS. Also a CIC cannot distribute profits or other assets to members (other than another asset-locked body) except up to specified limits as follows.

The definition of community interest is much broader than the definition of a charity (see page 21). A CIC can generate considerable private benefit – it can have paid directors (so long as the salaries are reasonable) and it can distribute up to 35% of its profits to shareholders if agreed.[10] (There are also limits on the percentages of dividend payable to shareholders and on payment of performance-related interest on loans, but following consultations, the current limits are likely to change.)

The concept of a CIC sits in some senses between a charity (which cannot distribute profits for private benefit at all) and a normal commercial company (which is not subject to any specific limits on the amount of profits that can be distributed).

A CIC is a company (unlike a CIO which is formed under charity law) – so a CIC is subject to all the normal requirements of company law. However, CICs are also subject to the Regulator of Community Interest Companies

---

[7] www.bis.gov.uk/cicregulator, accessed March 2013.

[8] Companies (Audit, Investigations and Community Enterprise) Act 2004, s. 35.

[9] Companies (Audit, Investigations and Community Enterprise) Act 2004, s. 33.

[10] Community Interest Company Regulations 2005, reg. 22(1)(b) (SI 2005/1788).

(the CIC Regulator) who oversees the community interest requirements. The CIC Regulator is an independent officer with a small staff, based at Companies House.

In most respects a CIC is only subject to the same financial reporting and auditing requirements as other companies; so, for example, a CIC with under £6.5 million income will not usually need an audit,[11] whereas for a charity an audit is required in all cases over £0.5 million income (see page 138). However, at the end of each year, as well as filing normal company accounts, it must file a 'community interest report' with the CIC Regulator.

In many cases a CIC will be the most appropriate form for TSOs which require corporate status and limited liability but which cannot meet the definition of a charity.

Moreover, the legislation states specifically that a CIC is *never* a charity[12] (so even if it has charitable aims it is not a charity). This can be advantageous for organisations which have aims which could be considered charitable but which specifically do not wish to find themselves subject to charity law. (Because the definition of a charity is based on purposes rather than a particular structure, there have occasionally been cases where the Charity Commission has registered an organisation as a charity against its wishes in order to protect charitable funds – a CIC rules out this possibility.)

Whilst there is no direct non-charitable equivalent of a CIO, a CIC probably comes closest, but there are fundamental differences because a CIC is formed under company law whereas a CIO is formed under charity law. See table 3.1 for a comparison of CICs and CIOs.

Social enterprise

Many TSOs which are involved mainly in trading activities, where the trade is undertaken for a social purpose, are described as social enterprises.

However, there is much debate about use of the term, and it is widely accepted that many different types of organisations can be social enterprises. Except in relation to a few specific government programmes, the term 'social enterprise' is not defined in law and it does not refer to a particular legal form of organisation. Also, it is possible

---

[11] In exceptional cases a CIC under £6.5 million income could require an audit if it had more than £3.26 million in assets (Companies Act 2006, s. 477, as amended).

[12] Companies (Audit, Investigations and Community Enterprise Act) 2004, s. 26(3).

for both charitable and non-charitable organisations to undertake trading for social purposes.

So, whilst a CIC could be a social enterprise, so could a CIO, or a subsidiary company owned by a CIO. Indeed, most of the organisational forms covered here and in chapter 4 can be considered as social enterprises if the majority of their activity relates to trading for a social purpose. Also, in some cases it is possible to distinguish different activities within one organisation, so it could be that a specific project within a CIO is identified as a social enterprise.

Because the term 'social enterprise' does not have a legal definition in this sense, it is not used in the rest of this book but it is worth bearing in mind that many resources and programmes aimed at social enterprises could be accessed by a CIO which engaged in social enterprise activities (in the sense of trading activities undertaken for a social purpose) as well as by CICs, co-operatives, CBSs and others.

CICs and CIOs compared

For a TSO which needs to be established as a corporate body, often the main choice will be between a CIO if it will be a charity, and a CIC if not. Table 3.1 summarises the differences.

Table 3.1 Comparison of CICs and CIOs

Community interest companies	**Charitable incorporated organisations**
Corporate entity with limited liability but *not* charitable	Corporate entity with limited liability *and* charitable status
Two-tier structure with members/ shareholders and directors	Two-tier structure with members and charity trustees
Governed by company law (with additions for CIC Regulator)	Governed solely by charity law – always focused on charitable objects
Asset-locked body subject to community interest test	Asset-locked body subject to charitable purposes only
Can have *paid directors* (as long as remuneration is reasonable), so key staff can be board members	Normally governed by *unpaid trustees* (payment to trustees only allowed in exceptional circumstances)

Community interest companies	**Charitable incorporated organisations**
No special tax concessions; a CIC is taxed like a commercial company: • Must pay corporation tax on profits • No access to charity VAT concessions • Any reduction on rates only at local authority discretion for voluntary organisations	Wide range of charity tax concessions; e.g.: • No tax on primary purpose trading • No tax on capital gains or investment income • Automatic 80% relief from business rates • No inheritance tax on legacies • Some VAT concessions; e.g. charitable premises, adverts, fundraising events
Not very attractive for grants and donations • Can usually only attract grants for business purposes • Many grant-making trusts will only fund charities, not CICs • No gift aid on donations	Charitable status is very important for attracting grants and donations • Individual donations can be made under gift aid • Charitable trusts are keen to support • For public sector funders, charity regulation sometimes seen as offering better protection
Members must give a small financial guarantee towards wind-up costs, or they can be shareholders if desired (subject to strict limits on distribution of profits)	Has members but *no* members' guarantee required, and no distribution of profits
Governed by Memorandum (on formation) and Articles	Governed by a Constitution
Accounts must comply with company law and a community interest report must be filed	Accounts comply only with charity law: but with charity rules on independent examination/audit
Available UK-wide	Different forms in England & Wales, Scotland and Northern Ireland

Conversion of non-charitable organisations to CIOs

In most cases it is possible for a non-charitable organisation to decide that in future its work should be restricted to charitable purposes and hence it could become a charity. This can be achieved either by amending its existing governing document to adopt charitable aims, or by winding up and transferring all its assets and activities to a new charity, such as a CIO.

If the existing organisation is already incorporated as a CLG, a CIC or a CBS it will soon be possible to convert directly to a CIO in England and Wales without winding up the existing organisation (see chapter 10). In Scotland, conversion of incorporated organisations (except for CICs) to become SCIOs is already possible (see page 268).

In other cases, a new CIO must be formed and the existing organisation must be wound up and all its assets and activities transferred to the CIO (assuming there is no restriction on such a transfer in its existing governing document). The general principles of this are as explained in chapter 9 for converting unincorporated charities to CIOs, but if a non-charitable organisation is becoming a CIO, the existing organisation will not be subject to charity law.

4 Structures for charities: the CIO and other legal forms

In chapter 1 the concept of CIOs was introduced. Chapter 2 explained the requirements of charitable status and chapter 3 considered some non-charitable alternatives. So for anyone who is definitely looking to establish a charity, this chapter compares CIOs with other legal forms for charities. It also includes some options not mentioned previously, such as incorporation of charity trustees without forming a CIO or a charitable company.

The broad principles in this chapter apply throughout the UK, although the points of detail relate to new charities formed in England and Wales. Where major differences apply in Scotland and Northern Ireland, these are mentioned briefly, but refer to chapters 13 and 14 for further details.

Charitable trusts

In the earliest days, all charities were trusts, or, in a few cases, bodies established by authority of the Sovereign under Royal Charters or occasionally under special Acts of Parliament (though the latter options are not considered in this book).

The governing document of a charitable trust is a 'trust deed' or 'declaration of trust'. A charitable trust can be established simply by an initial donor (often referred to as the 'settlor') setting aside some money or property and declaring a trust over it and appointing initial trustees (often a nominal gift such as £10 is used to establish the trust and the settlor may be one of the initial trustees). If the terms of the trust (as specified in the trust deed) indicate that the trust is formed for exclusively charitable purposes, a charitable trust is created.

The trust deed is signed by the settlor and the initial trustees, and their signatures must be witnessed. An application can then be made to register the trust as a charity, though in England and Wales charitable trusts will not normally be registered by the Charity Commission unless there is evidence that they will have at least £5,000 annual income, so many small charitable trusts remain excepted from registration (see page 24). However, even if the income is under £5,000, the trust can still be recognised as a charity for tax purposes, by HMRC.

Advantages

The advantages of a charitable trust include the simplicity: in urgent situations a trust deed can be drawn up very quickly and executed by the settlor and initial trustees: there is no need for external registration to establish the trust. It can start operating as a charity immediately – although it can be hard to persuade others that it is definitely a charity until it is registered as a charity (or recognised as a charity for tax purposes in the case of a charitable trust in England and Wales whose income is too small for charity registration).

When establishing a charity which will not enter into major contracts or run services (typically a grant-making charity), or if the charity will have major reserves to insulate the trustees from external risks, the simplicity of a charitable trust is attractive.

Also, there is a slight concession in the rules on charity accounting in England and Wales which in some cases may attract a settlor to use a charitable trust rather than a CIO or any other form. Normally a charity with an income of more than £250,000 must prepare its accounts in accordance with the Charities SORP[1] (see chapter 8) which requires that the accounts must show details of grants made. Sometimes philanthropists establishing new charities are reluctant to have to publish the precise causes which they support. In the case of a charitable trust (but not other types of charities) there is an exemption from this requirement during the lifetime of the settlor (or the settlor's spouse/civil partner).[2]

Disadvantages

First, a charitable trust has only a single-level structure: in most cases future trustees are appointed by the existing trustees or settlor – there is normally no accountability to a wider body of members. Therefore, it is not generally used for a charity which needs a democratic structure.

---

1 *Accounting and Reporting by Charities: Statement of Recommended Practice* (Charity Commission, 2005).

2 Charities Act 2011, s. 132(4).

The second disadvantage is that a charitable trust is not recognised as a corporate body, unless the trustees apply to be incorporated (see page 52) and it does not have the protection of limited liability. (See chapter 1 for more on these principles.) So any property must be held directly by the charity trustees (or a nominee or separate trustees *for* the charity) and all contracts and agreements are made by the trustees personally.

Corporate trustees

Sometimes a charitable trust is formed with a sole trustee which is a corporate body such as a company or local authority, rather than having individual trustees. (This is distinct from appointing an external body as a trustee *for* the charity, as mentioned in chapter 1, page 7.) The identity of a corporate trustee does not change over time, so it is a convenient way to hold assets, and a corporate body will usually have limited liability. But the charity remains legally a charitable trust.

However, a corporate trustee cannot take decisions without human involvement, so there has to be a process of decision-making. Sometimes the trust deed states that the trust must act in accordance with the directions of a committee or advisory board (so the members of the advisory board are then regarded in law as the charity trustees).[3] In other cases, the board of the corporate body takes the decisions – but this can cause confusion. For example, there are many charitable trusts with a local authority as trustee, and the members of the local authority must distinguish carefully between decisions they take as elected members of an authority, and decisions they take on behalf of the charity. Also, since the charity itself is not incorporated (only the trustee is) the protections of limited liability do not apply to the charity as a whole. So, a charitable company or CIO is nowadays widely regarded as a clearer structure than a charitable trust with a corporate trustee.

[3] As defined by Charities Act 2011, s. 177.

Charitable associations

By the middle of the nineteenth century it became clear that the structure of a charitable trust wasn't always the most suitable, especially for organisations with a large membership, or where there were frequent changes in the trustees. As a result, charities began to be formed using the structure of an unincorporated association (a membership organisation, governed by 'rules' or a 'constitution'). In most associations, a committee is elected whose members have the duties of charity trustees if the association is formed for charitable purposes. If the aims set out in the constitution are charitable, and if there are proper restrictions to ensure that the trustees cannot receive payment or other benefits, except within strict limits (see page 31), the association can be registered as a charity.

For charitable associations in England and Wales, this is subject, as with charitable trusts, to demonstrating that the charity has or will have at least £5,000 income in its first year, but where this is not possible an association could still be recognised as a charity for tax purposes by HMRC.

Advantages

Charitable associations normally have the benefits of a two-tier structure and so wider accountability for trustees. Many smaller charitable voluntary organisations which do not particularly need to incorporate are structured this way. As with a charitable trust, a new charitable association can be established very quickly.

Disadvantages

As with a charitable trust, an association is not recognised as a corporate body (unless the trustees apply to be incorporated, as outlined in the following section) and it does not have the protection of limited liability.

Incorporation of trustees of an unincorporated charity

One option, which is often overlooked in considering legal forms for charities, is a provision for incorporation of the existing trustee body of an unincorporated charity under the Charities Act 2011, for charities in England and Wales.[4] Similar provisions apply in Northern Ireland,[5] though there is no equivalent in Scotland. This is sometimes called

[4] Charities Act 2011, ss. 251–266.

[5] Charities Act (NI) 2008, ss. 73–85.

'section 251 incorporation' (referring to the provision in the 2011 Act)[6] to distinguish it from incorporation as a CIO.

It is possible in principle for the trustees of almost any unincorporated charity (normally a charitable trust or association) to apply to the Charity Commission to grant a 'certificate of incorporation' for the existing body of trustees. The charity remains governed by the same governing document (a trust deed or constitution) but the body of trustees becomes a corporate body which continues indefinitely. Any property, rights or liabilities held in the names of the trustees as individuals is automatically vested in the incorporated body[7] (so there is no need for the processes described in chapter 9 for transferring assets from an unincorporated charity to a CIO).

When applying for incorporation under section 251, the trustees should request a new name for the corporate body of trustees – for example 'The Incorporated Trustees of the XYZ Association'. Unless the Commission specifies otherwise, changes in the individual charity trustees can still take place from time to time in accordance with the charity's existing governing document.[8] A note of incorporation is added to the Register of Charities (but there is no change to the registered charity number).

The Charity Commission's guidance on this option (updated in 2012)[9] states that the Commission will only consider such requests where it is satisfied that 'incorporation is in the best interests of the charity,' and where the trustees have 'adequately informed themselves of other forms of incorporation (such as the CIO structure)'.

Advantages and disadvantages

Section 251 incorporation can sometimes be useful when a charity needs corporate status to hold freehold property or enter into contracts. However, it does *not* offer limited liability: the Act states specifically that the liability of individual charity trustees remains unaffected.

As a result, only a few charities have made use of section 251 incorporation – the CIO (or charitable company) offers much more. Nevertheless, in cases where transferring assets to a CIO would create major difficulties (see chapter 9) this can be an attractive alternative: the transfer process is more like the CIO merger process as explained in

[6] Previously known as 'section 50 incorporation' under the Charities Act 1993.

[7] Charities Act 2011, s. 252 & s. 251(4)(b).

[8] Charities Act 2011, s. 259.

[9] *Incorporation of Charity Trustees* (Charity Commission 2012, ref. CC43).

chapter 11. Also, the governing document of the charity remains unchanged, which can sometimes be an advantage (for example in a charity with a large membership where it is difficult to get members' approval).

Charitable companies

As charity law and corporate law developed, it became clear by the 20th century that if a company was established with charitable objects, the company itself could be a charity (rather than trying to use a corporate trustee for a charitable trust). This provided a convenient means for an entire charity to be a corporate body with limited liability.

A company is a legal entity formed when several people (the members) come together for a common purpose, but rather than just operating as an association along the lines described above, it is relatively simple to apply for the company to be incorporated as a legal entity in its own right. This is achieved by registration at Companies House (the office of the Registrar of Companies). Once Companies House issues a certificate of incorporation, a new legal entity is created, which is separate from the individuals who founded the company. (Nowadays, a company can also be formed with just one member; for example a one-person business could be established as a limited company to keep the business assets legally separate from those of the owner.)

Most companies are established for profit-making businesses, and the members are shareholders, but since 1862 it has been possible to form companies limited by guarantee (CLGs) where the members do not share in the profits. This CLG structure is used for charitable companies. Instead of taking shares in the company, each member gives a financial guarantee (usually a nominal amount such as £1, or £5) towards possible costs if the company has to be wound up while he or she is a member.

In the past, the governing documents of a company were called 'the memorandum and articles'. But since 2009, the memorandum is only a document signed by the initial members: all provisions governing the company, including its charitable objects, are contained in the articles. (In the case of an older company, provisions in the memorandum are now deemed to be part of the articles.)

Advantages

The principles of charitable companies are well established, and most larger UK charities use this form. The framework of company law is also well understood by other bodies, which can help when negotiating major contracts or investments.

Where the charity is run by professional staff who understand company law, or where the trustees have this expertise, it presents few problems, and the additional requirements of complying with company law are not a major burden. Increasingly, many moderate-sized organisations have adopted the form of a charitable company if they employ significant numbers of staff or do work under contracts or own freehold property.

Disadvantages

For smaller and medium-sized organisations, the complexities of complying with company law can be demanding, especially if there is no member of staff or trustee with previous experience of running a company.

Every board member is both a director under company law and a charity trustee under charity law and so both Companies House and the relevant charity regulator have to be notified, using different procedures, of any changes. The term 'trustee/director' is sometimes used to clarify the status, but it can be hard to ensure that the individuals concerned fully understand their duties.

In a CLG charity, there can also be problems with requiring a members' guarantee, particularly for a charity with a wide membership. Any membership form should clearly explain the guarantee, as it is a legal obligation (even though the likelihood of members being requested to pay the guarantee is minimal, because even if the company became insolvent it would rarely be worth a liquidator contacting members for small sums). Members can sometimes be confused between the guarantee and a membership subscription. Also, sometimes members do not understand that the guarantee is the *limit* of their liability and are concerned that they could be asked for more.

Any amendments to the articles of a charitable company require a number of steps. For example, with a charitable company in England and Wales, anything which is classed as a 'regulated alteration'[10] – such as a change to the wording of the objects, the trustee benefits clause, or the dissolution clause – typically requires at least four stages (once the wording has been agreed in principle by the trustees):

(a) obtaining permission from the Charity Commission to make the proposed amendment;
(b) calling a general meeting under company law to pass a resolution to amend the articles (or passing a written resolution);
(c) submitting the resolution to Companies House, together with a copy of the Charity Commission authorisation, to be registered on the company's files;
(d) once the change is registered at Companies House, advising the Charity Commission so that the amendment to the charity's governing document is recorded on the Register of Charities.

If these steps are not all completed correctly, there can be serious doubts as to whether amendments have taken effect, or whether the previous articles still apply.

A company also has to pay annual fees to Companies House, and though they are relatively small (currently £13 if everything is done electronically) some smaller charitable companies run mainly by volunteers find such costs frustrating.

A more serious issue is that some features of company law which are mainly intended for profit-making bodies can get in the way of how many charities would prefer to work. Many provisions of company law are designed to protect shareholders making commercial investments in a company.

For example, companies are required to follow strict accounting standards in their published accounts. This means that, regardless of income, the accounts of a charitable company must be prepared on the accruals basis (rather than the receipts and payments basis allowed for smaller charities such as CIOs and other charities which are not companies). This means even a very small charitable company must follow the Charities SORP[11] (see chapter 8) in the preparation of its accounts, so support from a

---

[10] Charities Act 2011, s. 197–200.

[11] *Accounting and Reporting by Charities: Statement of Recommended Practice* (Charity Commission, 2005). A new SORP is expected to take effect in 2014.

professional accountant or qualified independent examiner is likely to be needed at year end.

Charitable community benefit societies

A few charities are set up using other structures, in particular as an industrial and provident society (IPS). A body formed under IPS law has corporate status and limited liability, but the legislation is designed for societies (especially those nowadays seen as social enterprises) rather than for commercial companies.

As explained in chapter 3, a co-operative IPS, where members share in the profits cannot be a charity. But an IPS formed as a community benefit society (CBS)[12] will often meet all the requirements of charitable status if it is established for charitable purposes and has rules to exclude remuneration or other private benefits to its board members. If so, a CBS can be recognised as a charity.

Advantages and disadvantages

At present a CBS cannot be registered as a charity in England and Wales because IPS charities are classed as exempt charities (see page 24), so they do not appear on the Charity Commission's Register and they do not have a registered charity number: a CBS can only be recognised as a charity for tax purposes by HMRC. This is due to change, as the government has agreed that all exempt charities will either be brought under 'principal regulators' (which will not apply to CBSs) or required to register with the Charity Commission, and the Charities Act 2011 includes provisions for this.[13] But, as yet, no definite date has been announced for CBSs to register as charities.

In the past some CBSs saw the exempt charity status as an advantage, in that they were not subject to direct regulation by the Charity Commission. But increasingly the lack of a registered charity number makes it harder to attract charitable funding. Also, it is widely believed that some of the CBSs in England and Wales, recognised as charities by HMRC, may not actually meet the legal definition of a charity under the Charities Act 2011. This might be, for example, because of objects which are not clearly charitable or because of wide-ranging provisions in their rules allowing remunerated board members, to an extent which

[12] The new name arises from the Co-operatives and Community Benefit Societies Act 2003.

[13] Charities Act 2011, s. 23.

amounts to more than 'incidental' private benefit (see page 31). At one time it was considered that the rules on trading by charities were more flexible for a CBS than for other types of charities, but following clarifications of the rules on charity trading in the Finance Act 2000 this is no longer the case. However, CBSs remain popular in certain sectors where umbrella bodies provide well-developed model constitutions and support.

In Scotland, a charitable CBS needs to register with OSCR in the same way as other charities, and the same will apply in Northern Ireland once CCNI begins registering charities. (Note that IPSs in Northern Ireland are subject to different legislation from those in Britain.)

Many aspects of IPS law are designed for financial institutions: a CBS is formed and regulated by the FCA (rather than with Companies House). Registration and annual fees are higher than for companies.

For all these reasons, it would be rare to choose the CBS as a form to establish a new charity: in almost all cases a charitable company or CIO will be more suitable.

Charitable incorporated organisations

A CIO offers a means of establishing a charity as a corporate body from the outset, so it can hold property and enter into contracts in its own right, but it is registered only with a charity regulator and subject to one legal framework. In England and Wales, the law states clearly that a CIO is a corporate body, and it takes on its corporate form from the moment it is registered by the Charity Commission.[14] It also has the protection of limited liability, and whilst it is possible to have a members' guarantee there is no requirement for this. So most CIOs are formed *without* requiring a guarantee from members.[15] (Similar principles apply for SCIOs and for CIOs in Northern Ireland – see chapters 13 and 14.)

The basic features of CIOs were summarised in table 1.1 on page 4. Chapters 5 to 12 explain the principles of CIOs in more detail, including the constitutional and accounting issues, implications for other charities wishing to convert to CIOs, mergers, wind-ups, and the processes which apply if a CIO becomes insolvent. Chapters 13 to 17 consider the position of CIOs across the UK, the processes of challenging regulators' decisions, and the rights of others dealing with CIOs. Where applicable, each of these

[14] Charities Act 2011, s. 205(1) and s. 210(1).

[15] Charities Act 2011, s. 205(3).

chapters examines the advantages and possible limitations of CIOs in more detail.

Advantages and disadvantages

In summary, a CIO offers an attractive alternative to all the other forms of charity described above, for the following reasons.

- Compared to unincorporated charitable trusts and associations, a CIO offers the benefits of corporate status and limited liability.
- Compared to purely incorporating the trustees of the existing unincorporated charity (not available in Scotland) a CIO offers limited liability, not just corporate status. It also offers a modern legal structure designed specifically for charities.
- Compared to charitable companies and CBSs, a CIO offers a means of establishing an incorporated charity with limited liability, but with one regulator and a legal framework based solely on charity law.

In general it is no more work to form and register a new charity as a CIO than as a charitable trust or association (and it is less work than a charitable company, because there is no need for the incorporation at Companies House). So, unless there is a particular reason for choosing one of the other forms, the CIO will be the obvious choice in many cases when establishing a new charity.

In England and Wales, it can also be advantageous that there will be no lower income limit for registration of CIOs, whereas other charities cannot normally be registered with the Charity Commission unless they have evidence of at least £5,000 income.[16] Every CIO has to file accounts with the Commission, regardless of income, which will demonstrate a measure of accountability (for other registered charities in England and Wales this only applies if its income is more than £25,000).

However, it must be remembered that a CIO does not come into being until it is registered, so this is a significant disadvantage when a charity must be formed urgently (see chapter 5 for more on fundraising for a new CIO). If major fundraising opportunities would be lost in this way, it may be better to use one of the other charity structures mentioned in this

[16] Charities Act 2011, s. 30. However, the normal rules on charity registration do *not* apply to CIOs by virtue of reg. 6 of the CIO General Regulations 2012. Under s. 209 of the Act, all CIOs are registered charities. (However, under transitional provisions announced to manage workload in the first year of CIOs in England & Wales, applications for registration of CIOs with expected income under £5,000 cannot be considered prior to 1 January 2014.)

chapter where the organisation can be formed quickly and then charity registration can follow later. (For larger projects, one option would be to form a charitable company and then convert the company to a CIO in due course, as explained in chapter 10.)

But in other cases, the fact that a CIO is not formed until its charitable status has been established may be an advantage: with other structures there is always a period of uncertainty in the time between the formation of the organisation and the confirmation of its charitable status by a charity regulator or HMRC. Fundraising during this period can be hard: individual donors wishing to make donations under gift aid, or grant-making trusts which only support other charities are unlikely to give support to a new organisation until its charitable status is confirmed, and similar issues arise when a CIO is formed to take over the work of an existing charity. So, in these cases, there are few, if any, benefits in forming the organisation before it is registered as a charity.

A separate potential disadvantage in the early stages of setting up is that CIOs remain relatively new, and it may take time explaining the status to other parties such as banks and funders (see chapter 17), especially if a CIO needs to borrow funds at an early stage. Some may also consider CIOs more risky, because the framework is relatively unproven. But at the time of writing, SCIOs have been available for around two years and are proving very popular. Even in England and Wales a wide range of CIOs were registered in the first few months and many others are in the pipeline.

Unincorporated charities may continue to be attractive for those establishing modest charitable grant-making funds and for smaller voluntary associations with charitable aims, especially those without staff or premises and not undertaking contract-funded services. But in other cases, corporate status and limited liability will be highly desirable for a new charity. So the choice for many will be between a CIO and a charitable company. The final section of this chapter considers that comparison.

Charitable companies versus CIOs

Where it is clear that a new charity needs to be established as a corporate body with limited liability, then, barring Royal Charters, private Acts of Parliament and IPS charities, the choice will normally be between:

- a charitable company, formed under company law but also registered as a charity; or
- a charitable incorporated organisation (CIO), formed and registered under charity law.

Table 4.1 summarises the main differences.

Deciding which is most appropriate is not always an easy decision. On the one hand, charitable companies have existed for many years and are well proven. The framework of company law has been well-tested by the courts. The options in terms of secured loan finance are broader for companies than for CIOs (see chapter 17).

On the other hand, the convenience of a CIO in terms of being subject only to charity law, and only one regulator,[17] and not having to prepare accounts complying with company law means many attractions in terms of simplicity, especially for smaller charities needing corporate status. Moreover, in the case of charities working in sensitive fields where trustees' names need to be kept confidential, this is much more easily achieved with a CIO. Also the very simple processes for CIO mergers which allow a CIO to transfer its undertakings directly to another CIO without dissolution (see page 209) make CIOs very flexible.

Other differences to consider include the arrangements for constitutional amendments (see pages 210–214) and for registers and their access (see chapter 7).

However, different principles apply for exempt charities, as explained in chapter 2. An exempt charity cannot be a CIO, so in these cases – for example if the charity is to be an academy school – a charitable company is the only option.

[17] A CIO operating in more than one country of the UK may need to register with more than one charity regulator – see chapter 15 – but it never has to register with Companies House.

Table 4.1 Comparison of charitable companies and CIOs

CHARITABLE COMPANIES (COMPANY LIMITED BY GUARANTEE)	**CHARITABLE INCORPORATED ORGANISATIONS**
Corporate entity with limited liability and charitable status	Corporate entity with limited liability and charitable status
Governed by company law *and* charity law	Governed solely by charity law
Members must give a small financial guarantee towards wind-up costs	Has a membership but *no* requirement for a members' guarantee.
Governed by Articles of Association (and Memorandum signed by initial members)	Governed by a Constitution which is normally simpler than the articles of a company
Accounts must comply with company law and Charities SORP	Accounts comply only with charity law (as applied to CIOs)
Can form a company quite quickly (in 1–7 days max.) and apply later for charity registration (but then have a period with uncertain charitable status)	Formation of a CIO and charity registration take place simultaneously (but is likely to take 1–3 months from application)
Cannot be registered as a charity in England and Wales without evidence of at least £5,000 income (no lower limit in Scotland and Northern Ireland)	All CIOs are registered charities; there is no requirement for minimum income
No requirement in England and Wales to file an annual report and accounts with the Charity Commission if income is less than £25,000 (but must still file with Companies House)	Annual report and accounts must always be filed with CCEW/OSCR/CCNI
Well established and understood	New
Can convert to a CIO (or to a CBS) if needed	CIOs cannot directly convert to any other legal form
Can wind up or merge with other charities	Can wind up or merge with other charities (very simple process for CIO mergers which directly transfers all property, rights and liabilities)

CHARITABLE COMPANIES (COMPANY LIMITED BY GUARANTEE)	**CHARITABLE INCORPORATED ORGANISATIONS**
External registration of charges at Companies House gives additional security for lenders, especially if a floating charge is needed. Well understood by banks and other lenders.	Loans to a CIO can be secured on freehold property (and all lending must be disclosed in the CIO's accounts) but no external registration of charges (see page 330).
Articles can be amended by vote of members, but regulated alterations (e.g. changes of objects) require approval by the charity regulator	Constitution can be amended by a vote of members, but regulated alterations (e.g. changes of objects) require approval by the charity regulator
Changes to articles require a minimum of 75% of members in favour at a meeting or 75% for a decision by written resolution	Changes to a constitution require a minimum of 75% of members in favour at a meeting (67% in Scotland) or 100% for a decision by written resolution
Changes to articles involve various stages with charity regulator *and* Companies House, but unregulated alterations can take effect from date of the vote	Changes to constitution only have to be registered with charity regulator, but for CIOs in England and Wales and Northern Ireland (but not with SCIOs) they only take effect when registered by the regulator
Common legal structure UK-wide (though with different systems of charity regulation).	Separate legal frameworks for CIOs in England and Wales, Scotland (SCIOs) and Northern Ireland (however, CIOs in Northern Ireland not expected before 2015)
Registers of company directors (trustees) and members must be maintained with access as specified in company law	Registers of trustees and members must be maintained with access as specified in CIO regulations (less access for third parties)
Registered office of a company must be a physical address	Principal office of a CIO can be a PO box address
Difficult to establish without disclosing the identity of trustees	Can be established with trustees' names not in the public domain if agreed by the charity regulator (e.g. in sensitive fields like domestic violence)

Note: All points in this table are listed at an overview level only and may not cover all cases: refer to the appropriate chapter for details. Provisions relating to CIOs in Northern Ireland will only apply when the legislation is fully implemented.

In general, for larger and more complex organisations, the burdens of complying with company law may not be onerous compared with other requirements, and the benefits of being a company may be attractive in terms of dealing, for example, with major public sector bodies or providers of loan finance. This is especially likely in the early days when only a few charities have been formed as CIOs, though bear in mind that CIOs have been established in Scotland (SCIOs) since April 2011 and now account for a sizable proportion of new charity registrations (see page 334). However, other new corporate forms such as limited liability partnerships (LLPs) rapidly gained acceptance within a relatively short time after becoming law and CIOs will most likely progress in the same way.

Where the specific features of company law are not needed – particularly for smaller and medium-sized charities which need corporate status – the CIO offers an effective way to establish new charities without those running the charity having to work with two regulators, and two separate legal frameworks.

Moreover, for existing unincorporated charities which need to incorporate, conversion to a CIO will generally be simpler than converting to a charitable company, especially if they are governed by older trust deeds without dissolution clauses (see page 168) or where the charity has permanent endowment (see page 174). For charities which have been previously formed as charitable companies but where the challenges of complying with company law have proved demanding, the option of converting to a CIO (see chapter 10) may be an attractive way forward.

5 Forming a CIO: the steps

One of the attractions of the CIO structure is that CIOs are relatively easy to establish – and once established the legal status is very clear. As explained in chapter 1, every CIO is a corporate body with limited liability and is also a registered charity. The CIO comes into being as a corporate body at the point when it is registered as a charity.

It follows, therefore, that an organisation cannot be established as a CIO unless it will, when formed, meet the criteria to be a charity, as explored in chapter 2. In England and Wales, it must be established for one or more exclusively charitable purposes and those purposes must be for the public benefit (there are slight differences in Scotland and Northern Ireland – see chapters 13 and 14).

Stages and timescales

There is a fundamental difference between forming a CIO and forming a charity using any of the other structures discussed in the last chapter. For *non-CIO charities*, there is a two-stage process. Firstly, the organisation is established (typically as a trust, an association, or a company). At that stage a bank account can be opened and the organisation can start accepting funds and carrying out any activities which don't depend on having a registered charity number. Then, secondly, if it is to be a registered charity, an application is made for charity registration: if this is successful, the organisation is registered as a charity.

For non-CIO charities there is always a delay between the date the organisation is formed and the date of charity registration. Sometimes the gap between the two dates is only around a month, but in cases where the application for charity registration is complex, or where the organisation's income is initially below the registration threshold (normally an income of at least £5,000 a year is needed for charity registration in England and Wales)[1] the gap can be several years. During

[1] Under s. 30(3) of the Charities Act 2011, the trustees of any non-exempt charity will ultimately be able to apply for registration, even if its income is under £5,000, but at the time of writing that provision has yet to be implemented. However, this constraint does *not* apply to CIOs because every CIO is a registered charity under s. 209 of the 2011 Act and s. 30 does not apply to registration of CIOs (CIO General Regulations 2012, reg. 6).

that period between formation and charity registration, the trustees may tell people that they consider the organisation is 'established for charitable purposes' but without a charity registration number it can be hard to persuade people that it is a charity.

In some cases, the organisation may also have gone through the process of recognition as a charity for tax purposes, and charity registration may only be the third stage in a process lasting many years. For example, in England and Wales, many charities linked to the main Protestant Christian churches are currently excepted from charity registration until their income reaches £100,000 a year.[2] If a new church is set up as a charitable trust, for example, the first stage would typically be the execution of a trust deed so that property can be held for religious charitable purposes, then a year or two later the trustees may decide that they need to operate a gift aid scheme, and the charitable trust becomes recognised as a charity for tax purposes. But it may be many more years before the income exceeds £100,000 and the church becomes a registered charity.

With CIOs, these time gaps do not apply, because the CIO does not come into being until the time of charity registration. Once registered by the relevant regulator (CCEW, OSCR or CCNI) the CIO is formed as a corporate body and it is a registered charity from day one.

However, this does not mean that CIOs are much faster to set up than other charities: the charity regulator still has to go through the normal processes of considering whether the proposed CIO meets the requirement of charitable status. The CCEW aims to process most CIO applications in 40 days where the objects are relatively standard and where one of its model constitutions is used and timescales are similar with OSCR. However, in complex cases an application for charity registration can take months or even years. However, where a number of similar CIOs will be formed – for example local charities in a national federation – it can be worth approaching the regulator to agree a specific model constitution for CIOs in that field. This will take time initially, but will greatly speed up subsequent registrations of individual CIOs using the federation model. In England and Wales, the Charity Commission is increasingly seeking to work with umbrella bodies in ways such as this.

---

[2] Charities Act 2011, s. 30(2)(c).

But if the regulator is not satisfied with an application, the CIO will not be formed. Unlike trusts, associations and companies, a CIO can never fail to meet the criteria for charity registration. Rather, if an application is made to set up a CIO and the regulator is not satisfied that it would be a charity, the application is refused and the CIO is not created.[3] If this happens the applicants will need to start afresh from square one: if they decide that the best way forward is to operate the proposed body as a non-charitable organisation they will need to start again and adopt a suitable non-charitable governing document. On the other hand if they conclude that with certain changes to the application the organisation would be charitable they may decide to make a fresh application to form a CIO. (Occasionally, a charity regulator may reject an application to establish a CIO for reasons which appear to be incorrect in law. In such cases it may be possible to appeal to the relevant charity tribunal – see chapter 16 – but this is a major step which would take considerable time and resources.)

Bear in mind that until the CIO is formed, the trustees cannot open bank accounts for the CIO, or enter into formal agreements such as employing staff or taking on premises. So if a new charity is to be established as a CIO, it is vital to start the registration process well ahead of when the charity needs to be operational.

Sometimes with a new charity, activities move faster than the formal processes, but this has dangers. If those applying to form a CIO have already started raising funds for the charitable purposes of the CIO before the CIO is registered, the law states that any such funds automatically belong to the CIO once it is formed.[4] But it could be very confusing to ask people to give to a charity which does not yet exist, and those holding funds in the meantime would have all the liabilities of charity trustees with none of the legal protection of the CIO structure. So it is wise to avoid accepting grants or donations or organising fundraising events until the CIO is formed – any advance fundraising should focus purely on seeking support in principle, rather than actually accepting gifts. For example, communications with prospective donors or funders could say:

> We are looking to set up a new charity to do...... and we wanted to ask in principle if this is something you would be willing to support once the charity is formed (as a CIO)?

Even in straightforward cases, the time taken by regulators to consider an application for charity registration is rarely less than a month, and to

---

[3] Charities Act 2011, s. 208(1); Charities & TI (Scotland) Act 2005, s. 54(4); Charities Act (NI) 2008, s. 110(3).

[4] Charities Act 2011, s. 210(2).

allow for queries, it would be wise to submit the application at least three to four months before the CIO needs to be operational. (If this timescale would present huge problems, it could be beneficial to consider a non-CIO structure – see chapter 4 – so that bank accounts can be opened and agreements made while the charity registration is in progress.)

But, assuming that the CIO is the chosen structure, the one-stage process is a good deal simpler than with some of the alternative charity structures (which are evaluated in chapter 4). With a CIO there is only one regulator to consider, and for donors who will only give to a registered charity, it can be quite helpful that the organisation does not come into being until it has a registered charity number. Moreover, the total time for getting to the stage of being a corporate registered charity will usually be slightly shorter with a CIO than when establishing a charitable company, because there is no separate process at the start of incorporating the company at Companies House before applying for charity registration.

The rest of this chapter considers the main steps for forming a CIO in England and Wales, where the application is made to the Charity Commission, apart from the detailed issues regarding the constitution which are considered in chapter 6. In terms of the process, there are many similarities in Scotland and Northern Ireland, but also some important differences: see chapters 13 and 14 for details.

CIO members and trustees

The applicants (initial members of the CIO)

Every charity starts its life with people (or sometimes, existing organisations) who believe in a cause and want to set up a charity to do something about it. But whilst the day-to-day governance of a CIO will fall to its charity trustees, a CIO does not start with trustees – the starting point lies with those who will be its initial members.

As explained in chapter 1, every CIO is a corporate body with members. There can be one member or many, and a member does not have to be an individual (corporate members are possible). See page 98 for a detailed outline of membership structures in a CIO's constitution and page 127 for details of possible criteria for membership of a CIO.

Strictly speaking, it is the initial members who make the application for the CIO to be formed and registered as a charity (not the initial trustees, although in many cases the members and trustees may be the same people). But since the CIO does not exist at the time the application is made, the law describes them as 'the applicants'[5] – they only become members if and when the CIO is formed.[6]

The Charity Commission's registration process for establishing a new CIO does not currently require any documentation to be signed by the applicants, even though the application is made on their behalf (signatures are only needed by the initial trustees). But since the CIO, once formed, must keep a register of members[7] (see chapter 7) it is obviously essential to identify the members from the outset. Otherwise, it will be impossible to start a proper register of members when the CIO comes into being, and disputes as to who is a member, and hence who can vote, are likely to arise at the first general meeting!

So, no application should be made to register the CIO unless it is clear who the applicants are. In particular, the Charities Act states that the applicants are applying for the CIO to be registered with the constitution they provide[8], so whoever physically submits the application must be confident that all the applicants are willing to become members under the terms of the constitution if the CIO is registered. In practice, the simplest way to do this would be either:

- to call a meeting of the applicants (the prospective members) to agree the constitution, and to keep a record (minutes) of that meeting; or
- to ask each applicant to confirm in a document that he/she/it is happy to become a member of the CIO on the basis of the draft constitution proposed.

Note that if a meeting of the applicants is held on these lines, they could pass a resolution to agree the draft constitution, but it would not make sense for them to 'adopt' the constitution as happens when an unincorporated association is formed (see page 52). They are simply agreeing to apply for a CIO to be formed, and to accept the proposed constitution as a basis for the application.

CIOs will generally be constituted either as a 'foundation CIO' where the members and trustees are the same people or as an 'association CIO' with a wider membership (see page 98 for more on these constitutional options).

---

[5] Charities Act 2011, s. 207(1).

[6] Charities Act 2011, s. 210(1)(c).

[7] CIO General Regulations 2012, reg. 26(1).

[8] Charities Act 2011, s. 210(1)(a).

With a foundation CIO the initial trustees will also be the initial members, and hence the applicants must always be the same as the proposed initial trustees listed in the constitution.

In the case of a CIO which is likely to have a large membership, there is often no need to get all members signed up as applicants – the CIO could be formed with just a few members, and others could be enrolled once the CIO is formed. So, even if following the association CIO style of constitution it will often be sufficient for the applicants to be the initial trustees. However, where a CIO is formed to take over the work of a charitable association, the existing members may want a clause in the CIO constitution to state that all those who are members of the existing association on the date the CIO is formed are initial members of the CIO. If so, the applicants will be the entire membership of the existing association.

The initial trustees

Whilst the members come together to form the CIO as a body, they do not necessarily have to be involved on a day-to-day basis. As explained in previous chapters, the day-to-day governance of a CIO rests with its charity trustees. Every charity needs enthusiastic people committed to the cause, who are willing to serve as the charity trustees. Without committed trustees the charity is unlikely to succeed in its mission, so identifying good initial trustees is the first step for anyone wanting to set up a CIO.

Strictly speaking, the legislation always refers to those who govern a CIO as 'the charity trustees of the CIO'[9] because they are trustees in the sense that they have the authority to take decisions for the charity, but they are *not* trustees in the traditional sense of holding property on behalf of others. One of the major advantages of a CIO is that the CIO itself is a corporate body, so all assets can be held directly in the name of the CIO (rather than needing to be held in the names of individual trustees) and, in the case of endowment funds, the CIO itself can be trustee of the fund. The same principle applies to any corporate charity (including charitable companies). Nevertheless, it is normal to describe the charity trustees of any type of charity simply as 'the trustees' and that terminology is followed in this book. (However, charity trustees of a CIO are *not* directors of a company, so it is best to avoid any use of the term 'director' when referring to CIO trustees.)

[9] For example, Charities Act 2011, s. 206(2)(b).

Sometimes the applicants who become founding members of a CIO may not wish to be trustees. For example, the leading applicant may be someone who is planning to make a large donation to the charity once formed but who has business commitments involving considerable periods overseas, and is unable to commit the time to being a trustee. Such an applicant would no doubt still wish to be a member and have the right to vote at AGMs of the CIO when future trustees are elected (the founder could even be the sole member of the CIO). Sometimes the founding member is not an individual but an existing charity or company: but individuals will normally be chosen as the first trustees. However, in many cases (and certainly in a foundation CIO) the first trustees will be the applicants.

One of the factors that the Charity Commission will consider when reviewing an application to register a CIO is whether the people listed in the application to be the initial charity trustees of the CIO are suitable for the task (some people, such as those with unspent convictions for fraud or dishonesty and undischarged bankrupts, are automatically excluded,[10] but having trustees with skills relevant to the proposed field of work for the CIO will help to strengthen the application).

Normally the trustees' roles must be voluntary, as paid charity trustees are only allowed in special circumstances (see page 31). So someone who is hoping to become a paid worker with the CIO would not generally be able to be a trustee; likewise anyone with major interests in a firm which hopes to benefit from business with the CIO could not normally be a trustee. There is no specific advantage to using a CIO if there are issues of trustees' remuneration: CIOs are subject to the same rules as other charities regarding payments to trustees. This is a major difference from a CIC where paid board members are very common (see page 43).

This does not mean that a CIO could never have salaried trustees: there are certain types of charity where this may be very important (for the principles see page 30). Aside from this, occasional fees to trustees can be authorised for services outside their trustee duties if the four specified conditions are met – appropriate provisions are included in the model constitutions (see page 102). But it must be understood that these are exceptions: the norm is a CIO where all trustees serve voluntarily. Any form of payment to trustees or their close relatives, or benefits to businesses where trustees have an interest, will need to be disclosed in the 'private benefits' section of the application for charity registration,

[10] Charities Act 2011, s. 178.

and the Charity Commission will only register a charity with such provisions if it is satisfied that they are essential for the effective working of the charity.

The legislation for CIOs established in England and Wales allows for trustees which are corporate bodies rather than individuals. The possibility of a charity with a corporate trustee was mentioned in relation to charitable trusts on page 51. But there are few situations where this could be beneficial, as the CIO is itself a corporate body with limited liability and so such an arrangement does not offer any additional protection. The Charity Commission model constitutions only allow for natural persons as trustees (see clause 12(2)(a) in the Appendix). In the case of a CIO which is part of a group structure with charities as subsidiaries of other charities (see page 153), it might simplify administration to have one unchanging corporate trustee for the group. But for most CIOs, there are good reasons to allow corporate *members* (see page 15) but few arguments for corporate *trustees* (see page 51), so this book assumes that all CIO trustees will be individuals.

A key question when setting up any new charity is to decide how many trustees are needed. The Charities Act simply states that a CIO must have 'one or more' trustees, so in theory a CIO could be formed with just one trustee.[11] But the Charity Commission will not register a charity with fewer than two individual trustees (or one corporate trustee) and in practice it is normally very cautious about any application which proposes to register a new charity with fewer than three individual trustees, as it must be sure that there are arrangements for effective governance. However, it is often clear from the outset that a new charity will need a board with considerably more than three members in order to have sufficient breadth of expertise, and to provide continuity if a trustee is suddenly unable to act. ('Seven, plus or minus two' is often considered a good size for the board of a voluntary organisation – i.e. between five and nine trustees in all.) If it is possible to identify all the initial trustees at the time of making the application, it is much better for them all to be involved from the outset.

Everyone who serves as a trustee of the CIO must understand the responsibilities involved but it is not necessary for all trustees to be over the age of 18: the regulations set a minimum age of 16 years.[12] Particularly for a CIO involved in work with young people, it could be really valuable to have some trustees aged 16 or 17.

[11] Charities Act 2011, s. 206(2).

[12] CIO General Regulations, reg. 31.

The regulations do not specify any limits to the numbers of trustees under 18 years old, but the Charity Commission model requires at least one trustee to be over the age of 18 and effective charity governance will normally mean that at least 50% of trustees should be 18 years old or over. Indeed there is no requirement to allow for trustees who are under the age of 18 at all: unless the nature of the charity's work makes it important to include young trustees, it will normally be simpler to specify in the constitution that all trustees of the CIO must be adults. However, careful consideration is needed before making any provision for trustees who are under the age of 18 (or indeed for trustees over 18 who may have special needs which make it hard to them to exercise the normal duties of trustees as indicated below) – the Charity Commission's guidance should be considered.[13]

The Charities Act includes a very specific statement of the duties of CIO trustees.[14] It states:

> **(1)** *Each charity trustee of a CIO must exercise the powers and perform the functions that the charity trustee has in that capacity in the way that the charity trustee decides, in good faith, would be most likely to further the purposes of the CIO.*
>
> **(2)** *Each charity trustee of a CIO must in the performance of functions in that capacity exercise such care and skill as is reasonable in the circumstances, having regard in particular—*
>
> *(a) to any special knowledge or experience that the charity trustee has or purports to have, and*
>
> *(b) if the charity trustee acts as such in the course of a business or profession, to any special knowledge or experience that it is reasonable to expect of a person acting in the course of that kind of business or profession.*

The level of capacity needed by trustees will vary between a small CIO with simple affairs and a larger more complex one, but all trustees must exercise a reasonable level of care and those appointed because of specific business or professional skills must exercise a higher level of skill where relevant. It will be no excuse for a trustee to say he or she was too young, or was unable to discharge his or her duties because of a disability

---

[13] See *Finding New Trustees: What Charities Need to Know* (Charity Commission 2013, ref. CC30).

[14] Charities Act 2011, s. 221. These duties could be relaxed by regulations under s. 221(3) but following consultation the government agreed that it was *not* appropriate to allow for any relaxation of these duties.

(though the CIO should provide appropriate support to enable trustees with disabilities to perform their duties effectively).

The regulations add to the duties by stressing the independence of CIO trustees and prohibiting them from accepting inducements from third parties to act in a particular way.[15]

> **(1)** *A charity trustee ('T') of a CIO must not accept a benefit from a third party conferred by reason of—*
>
> *(a) T being a charity trustee; or*
>
> *(b) T doing (or not doing) anything as a charity trustee.*
>
> **(2)** *Benefits received by T from a person by whom T's services (as charity trustee or otherwise) are provided to the CIO are not regarded as conferred by a third party.*
>
> **(3)** *This duty is not infringed if the acceptance of the benefit cannot reasonably be regarded as likely to give rise to a conflict of interest.*
>
> **(4)** *In this regulation 'third party' means a person other than the CIO, an associated body corporate, or a person acting on behalf of the CIO or an associated body corporate.*

It is vital, therefore, that anyone agreeing to be a CIO trustee accepts these duties and obligations. Prospective trustees are also strongly encouraged to read the Charity Commission's guidance on duties of trustees.[16] More detailed guidance can be found in *The Charity Trustee's Handbook*, also published in this series (see page vi).

As part of applying to register a CIO (as with any charity) the trustees must submit a signed declaration where each prospective trustee confirms that he or she understands the duties of being a charity trustee.

Activities and public benefit

In addition to the declaration by trustees and the proposed constitution of the CIO (see chapter 6), a further key document is needed to register a CIO: this is a statement of the activities of the charity, and how those activities will lead to furthering the charitable purposes for public benefit.

These statements apply to all charity registrations, not just CIOs. They provide essential information to enable the staff in the Charity Commission's registration team to consider whether the organisation (or the proposed organisation in the case of a CIO) will be established for exclusively charitable purposes.

---

[15] CIO General Regulations 2012, reg. 34.

[16] *The Essential Trustee: What you need to know* (Charity Commission 2012, ref. CC3).

The Charity Commission's online registration system has two separate boxes: one to describe the activities and another to explain how the activities will lead to public benefit. However, if there are several proposed activities, it can be clearer to attach a separate document describing each activity and how it will lead to public benefit before going on to the next.

As explained in chapter 2, to be a charity an organisation must be established for exclusively charitable purposes, and those purposes must be for the public benefit. The formal statement of the purposes of a charity is set out in the 'objects clause' (see page 26) in its governing document. In the case of a CIO, it is set out in its constitution (see chapter 6). The statements of activities and public benefit spell out:

- *how* the objects will be fulfilled, by explaining the proposed activities;
- *who* will benefit from these activities and why this amounts to 'public benefit' in the sense used in charity law.

See the example in table 5.1. (The objects are stated elsewhere in the application, but it can help to repeat them in a document of this kind, as all the discussion of activities and public benefit must focus on the proposed objects.)

It is worth remembering, however, that under the laws of England and Wales, the definition of 'charity' is based on purposes, not activities. The Charity Commission's role is not to assess the merits of the proposed activities – it is up to the trustees, not the Commission, to decide how the charity is to be run. So long as the activities will be charitable in law and will relate to the stated purposes, the Commission should avoid judging the operational plans. But the Commission takes the view that it is necessary to consider the proposed activities in detail to understand fully the nature of the purposes as expressed in the objects clause of the constitution, so in practice considerable scrutiny of the proposed activities is likely when applying to register a CIO. This is especially important when the wording of the objects is very broad and could be interpreted in different ways. (Sometimes, however, the activities are made clear in the objects clause itself.)

Example of a statement of activities and public benefit

Upperton Health Forum CIO – Application for charity registration

Explanation of proposed activities and how they will advance the purposes of the charity for public benefit

Objects (as in proposed constitution):

The CIO is established for the advancement of health of the public in Upperton and surrounding areas

Proposed activities

The CIO will undertake a wide range of health-related activities and health education projects including: smoking cessation groups, healthy eating classes, walking groups, and diabetes support. Projects will be publicised through GP surgeries, clinics, libraries, and local supermarkets, with a particular focus on residents in wards with high unemployment or large numbers of persons over retirement age. Although the forum will be independent of the NHS, close liaison with a variety of NHS services is planned; however, the CIO will not undertake any activities classed as medical treatment.

It is anticipated that the CIO will employ a qualified healthcare professional as project leader, and two of the five proposed trustees of the CIO are medically qualified.

Public benefit

The direct beneficiaries will be the individuals supported through the health programmes who will gain from improved health, longer life expectancy, and better chances of securing work where health problems have prevented this. Even where little or no improvements to physical health are achieved, engagement with activities such as those proposed are known to bring psychological benefits (improved mental health). These changes will lead to indirect benefits for the wider community.

All service users will be aged 18 or over, but in other respects activities will be offered to all members of the community. Most services will be provided free of charge. In some cases a small charge will be made to cover materials or refreshments, but these will be set at a nominal level affordable by even the poorest members of the community.

Note: This example shows the possible structure of such an explanation, but in most cases considerably more detail will be needed.

Before drafting such statements, read the Charity Commission's guidance on the public benefit requirement (available on its website).[17] This is statutory guidance which all trustees need to consider each year.[18] Supplementary guidance is also available for charities working in specific fields. In explaining how the activities lead to public benefit it may be helpful to refer directly to particular sections of the Commission's guidance.

These statements are not part of the CIO's constitution, they are simply statements of the *intentions* of the initial trustees. They are not fixed in stone: over time, the trustees of a charity are free to adopt new activities and methods of working. Moreover, many activities may be conditional on securing sufficient funding so it may be necessary to make this clear. It is an offence to give false information to the Charity Commission,[19] so these statements need to spell out as far as possible what the trustees plan to do at least (say) in the first year or so of the CIO's life. It is not, however, necessary to provide full business plans: if documents of this kind are available they can be attached to the application, but often they are too broad to highlight the key explanations of activities to be undertaken for public benefit.

It will often be necessary to go through several drafts of such statements before the initial trustees are happy that they are ready to submit the final version. But try to keep them reasonably brief: except in the most complex or unusual charities, two pages is normally quite sufficient to cover both the proposed activities and the explanation of how they will lead to public benefit.

Statement of proposed activities

All the explanations of activities must relate to the charity's objects as stated in the proposed CIO constitution. For example, if the CIO is being established for the advancement of education, the activities must be educational (such as provision of lectures, workshops or publications). If the CIO will be formed for the advancement of health, the activities will need to have obvious health-related outcomes (such as provision of medical treatment or advice). In a CIO with religious objects the

---

[17] The guidance is on the 'Public Benefit' pages of the Charity Commission website. See Home > Charity requirements & guidance > Charity essentials > Public benefit on www.charitycommission.gov.uk.

[18] Charities Act 2011, s. 17(5).

[19] Charities Act 2011, s. 60.

activities may include provision of public worship, teaching the faith and other outreach work.

Don't waste space explaining fundraising activities, or how the charity will operate internally – these are not activities carried out to fulfil the charity's purposes. (Fundraising may be very necessary, but it is only when the funds raised are actually spent on the charity's work that it can carry out activities to advance the stated objects. So if finances are mentioned, the focus will be on how funds are to be *spent* rather than how they are raised.) Sometimes it is necessary to explain practical issues such as the premises which the trustees hope to acquire or the staff they plan to employ in order to undertake the proposed activities, but, if so, make clear that these are only the means to an end. For example, a religious charity may have to raise considerable funds to maintain and improve a historic building, but maintaining the building is not itself a charitable activity: rather the focus needs to be on the activities which will take place in the building which will enable the faith to be advanced. A charity working with young people may need to employ youth workers, but focus on the activities which the youth workers will undertake with the young people, rather than the workers themselves.

Make sure that the explanations are clear to someone who has no knowledge of a charity, and avoid use of jargon such as 'therapy sessions' or 'action workshops' without describing exactly what takes place and who is involved.

A charity does not have to undertake all its work directly. For example, if the CIO will be a grant-making body, the explanation of activities will explain the sort of grants which the trustees expect to make. Such explanation will need to include likely grant recipients, and how the trustees plan to seek grant applications or otherwise identify the groups or individuals who will receive grants.

Because an application to register a CIO is always about a *proposed* charity, the explanation of activities needs to be expressed in the future tense; for example 'The trustees intend to provide...' or 'A building has been identified that the CIO will seek to acquire, which will be used for...'. Even if some activities are already in progress under other auspices, they will need to be transferred to the CIO, so they are still proposed activities in relation to the CIO itself. For example: 'Volunteers in the community are already supporting children with their reading – the CIO will take over this work, and funds raised will be used to pay for travel expenses, reading materials and a part-time manager to allow more children to be supported.'

Public benefit explanation

As considered in chapter 2 (see page 28), the public benefit requirement is the central feature of the definition of 'charity'. Explaining how a CIO's proposed activities will enable the intended purposes to be carried out for public benefit is usually the most critical element in the application: unless this is clear, the Charity Commission will be unable to conclude that the proposed CIO will be a charity. The explanation will normally focus on:

- *why* the activities will be beneficial;
- *who* will benefit – i.e. the proposed *beneficiaries*;
- *how* the activities will lead to benefit for the beneficiaries.

Sometimes these are obvious from the objects themselves or the explanation of activities but not always – so it is best to give an explanation of who is involved and how the activities lead to public benefit. Here are some examples of situations where further explanation is needed on each of the points above.

For activities such as education, people often assume that there is no need to explain *why* they are beneficial to the public, and certainly in the case of a school teaching a full range of subjects there is little doubt. But a proposal to undertake education in a very narrow field may need much more justification – simply promoting a particular view is unlikely to be educational as understood in charity law. For example, the courts have ruled that training of spiritualist mediums does not offer sufficient public benefit to be charitable.[20]

Identifying *who* will benefit may be obvious in some cases; for example if a charity is established to provide pre-school education of children in a certain community, then the beneficiaries are clearly the children in the relevant age group in that community. But you still need to explain how participants will be selected – will pre-school education be offered to every child in the community whose parents want them to attend? Or will fees be charged? If so, give an indication of likely charges, and unless the fees are very low, the statement needs to explain what the trustees plan to do for those children whose parents cannot afford them. Will there be any other limitations? For example, if preference will be given to those with links to a particular faith-based organisation, this will need to be explained and justified.

---

[20] *Re Hummultenberg* [1923] 1 Ch. 237.

In other cases, you may need to work carefully to identify the beneficiaries from the outset. For example, if a charity's main activity will be training and professional regulation for health professionals, the health professionals are almost certainly *not* the main beneficiaries – the beneficiaries are the wider public who will have the benefits of improved healthcare, and this would need to be very clearly explained.

This notion of who will benefit – or in legal terms, the 'beneficial class' – is a very important issue in charity law, which the Charity Commission considers very carefully in assessing applications for charity registration. In some cases – for instance in a charity working on climate change issues – the beneficiaries may be everyone on the planet (both those currently alive and others to be born in future). This is called 'universal public benefit'. But at the other extreme, a charity which only supports people in a certain occupation who also have a specific medical condition and live in a specific city may only have a very narrow group of beneficiaries. In this case the beneficial class may be too small to be regarded as a 'section of the public' and hence the Commission may conclude that the proposed charity would not be established for public benefit.

However, the issues involved in demonstrating that a given organisation will be established for the public benefit can sometimes raise complex issues of charity law – this section has only highlighted a few key points to consider when drafting the statement. As explained, it is important to refer to the Charity Commission's guidance on the public benefit requirement, and in complex cases you may well need professional advice.

The application process

So, as explained, before seeking to register a CIO, you need to have agreed or identified:

- the applicant(s) – who will become initial member(s) of the CIO;
- the initial trustees;
- the proposed constitution of the CIO (see chapter 6); and
- clear statements of the proposed activities and how they will lead to public benefit.

Once these are ready, the application to register the CIO can be entered using the Charity Commission's online registration system.

The registration must be submitted by a named individual using an email address which acts as your user-ID. The person submitting the application can be an applicant, a prospective trustee, or a professional advisor (the latter could include an advisor based in a voluntary sector infrastructure organisation).

If you have not previously used the online registration system, you first need to register and then wait to receive a password by email.

To begin the process using the Charity Commission website as arranged at the time of writing, select 'Start up a charity' then 'Register a new charity' and then at the bottom of that page under 'Apply to register a charity' click 'Login' and on the next page click 'Enter this service'. (However, this structure may change from time to time). You can then 'Apply for an account' or login with your email and password if already registered.

Once logged in, there are two options:

- *Apply to register a new charity.*
- *Continue with an application you have started.*

For a new application select the first option, but as explained below it is rarely possible to complete everything in one session, as you will need to generate a declaration to be signed by the trustees before you can complete the process. As such, you may well need to save it and come back at a later stage. (Note that incomplete applications are only kept for 90 days – after that you will need to start afresh.)

You are asked first to enter your own contact information, and then you begin entering details for the CIO itself, beginning with its name. Remember to include 'CIO' on the end of the name, unless this is to be omitted from the legal name (see page 91 for more details).

Click the button to say that you are registering a CIO. The box asking for the date of the governing document disappears (because a CIO's governing document does not take effect until it is registered) and instead you are asked to select the type of registration – a completely new CIO, an incorporation of an existing charity (see chapter 9), or an amalgamation of existing CIOs (see chapter 11).

You will also be asked whether you are using one of the Charity Commission's model constitutions, and if so whether it is the 'foundation CIO' or 'association CIO' model (see page 98 for more on these models).

The remainder of the application process is largely the same as for other types of charity – there is a series of screens to complete, covering information under three main headings.

Your organisation

This includes details of the constitution, principal office of the CIO (see next chapter), the proposed financial year end (see chapter 8) and details of proposed funding. (On the funding, remember that with a CIO you can only discuss *anticipated* funding.)

What you do

This section includes the proposed objects of the CIO (which must be copied exactly from the constitution) and the proposed activities and how they will be carried out for public benefit. See above regarding preparation of these statements – unless they are straightforward it is often easier to put 'See attached' in the boxes of the online form, and attach the statements as a supplementary document at the end. You will also be asked to select the categories in which the charity will be working and the types of beneficiaries – these are used as part of the online register to enable identification of charities in different fields. You also identify here the location of the charity's work, including specific local authority areas in England and Wales, Scotland, Northern Ireland, and countries outside the UK. (Note that these categories should relate to the beneficiaries and activities as described, rather than where the charity raises funds. So, if you raise funds in the UK exclusively to fund work in (say) Kenya, you would select 'Kenya' as the place where the charity carries out its activities.)

Who is involved

In this section you enter the overall contact person for the charity (this could be a particular trustee or proposed member of staff, but the address should be the same as the principal office) and then full details must be entered for every person who will be an initial trustee of the CIO (full name, address, telephone number, date of birth, details of any former names, and email address if desired). Getting all this information together in advance is crucial to completing the application successfully. This section also includes vital information on whether the charity will work with children or vulnerable adults, and details of any private benefit issues (see page 30).

Once all these stages are complete you come to a final screen where you can print off a declaration which must be signed by all trustees. At this stage the application will need to be saved and arrangements made for each trustee to sign the printed declaration. Note that in the case of a charity working with children or vulnerable adults, the trustees' declaration must deal with whether or not the trustees have carried out eligibility checks (commonly called 'CRB checks') on each other.

Once every trustee has signed, a scanned copy of the document is made and this will then need to be uploaded. (If you do not have access to a scanner you can send this separately by post, but it is clearly simpler if everything is uploaded together.)

When you are ready to continue with the application, log in again and check all the details from start to finish. At this point you can attach appropriate documents which must be saved in the form of PDFs. You must attach:

- the proposed constitution of the CIO;
- a scanned copy of the signed trustees declaration (unless this is being sent separately by post);
- any supplementary documents needed such as a statement of activities and public benefit, if this was too detailed to enter in the boxes provided. (If necessary, you could attach other documents such as business plans or details of proposed premises, but only if they are vital to the application.)

Once you think all is ready, take time to review all the details correctly as it will cause considerable delays if you have to advise the Commission of corrections at a later stage. The system allows you to create a PDF to print off with all the details entered. Double check the trustees' addresses, the wording of the objects and everything else. When you are ready, click 'Submit', and the application will go to the Charity Commission's registration department for consideration.

Next steps

Once the application has been submitted you should receive an automatic acknowledgement from the Charity Commission.

The application then goes for an initial check simply to ensure that the required documents were submitted and that there are no obvious gaps, and assuming that there are no problems you will get a further acknowledgement a few days later giving the name of the case officer in the Commission's registration team who is dealing with your application and a timetable for an initial response (generally around three weeks later).

It is worth noting that the Commission uses a 'triage' process at this stage to distinguish between applications which are very straightforward, those which require some further issues to be resolved, and those which raise major issues.

Queries

Close to the three-week deadline, you are likely to receive the first communication which relates to the specifics of the application. Except in the most straightforward applications, the registration officer will have identified certain issues which need clarification. This can range from basic queries about a trustee's address or former name to requests for more detail about proposed activities. More serious concerns could relate to the wording of the objects or there could be queries or requests for changes to other parts of the constitution.

Sometimes the queries can raise complex issues in relation to other legislation such as the Equality Act 2010, or in a charity working with children, for example, you could be asked for more detail about the vetting of prospective trustees. The Commission may ask for additional documents such as leaflets or business plans (if created) or even statements from prospective service users explaining how they would benefit from the proposed activities. If the application includes any information about possible private benefits – for instance if it is planned that the CIO will use premises owned by a trustee – the Commission may well ask to see a draft lease.

If the Commission is unhappy with some part of the CIO's constitution, any change should be agreed by the applicants. But, as there is no formal document signed by the applicants, it is normally sufficient if you (as the person handling the application) can confirm that the applicants have agreed the change. You will then submit a revised constitution simply as an attachment to your email reply. (This is one area where CIO registrations are simpler than other charities – because the constitution is only a *draft* constitution at the time the application is submitted, you do not need to call special meetings to agree changes at this stage. However, see 'Amending the constitution' on page 107 if you need to change the constitution once the CIO is formed.)

Bear in mind that the Charity Commission staff do not rely solely on the information submitted; they may look for other relevant information, especially if the charity has a website. Clearly the CIO itself cannot have a website at the time of applying to be registered, but if there is an existing website mentioned in the application which the CIO proposes to take over, make sure that what it states about aims and proposed activities ties up with the formal application.

However, it is rarely possible to anticipate with confidence what queries will be raised on a specific application. It is best to respond as clearly as you can when they arise. Don't include vast amounts of additional documentation with the application just in case it is needed; this will simply slow the process down. Often queries will relate to how the trustees intend to manage certain aspects of the work, so nearly all queries will need discussion with the prospective trustees. Do make sure, therefore, that relevant people can be contacted quickly at all stages in the application process. On complex issues, it may be necessary to hold a meeting of the prospective trustees to agree a policy before a response can be made (and professional advice may well be needed in preparing a response, especially if issues are raised regarding the CIO's proposed charitable purposes).

Once a query has been raised, the registration process stops until the Commission receives your response, so try to reply as soon as you are in a position to give a clear response which is endorsed by those who will be the CIO's initial trustees. (Normally all such communication will take place by email.) As with the initial application, make sure that any further information is clearly explained in terms that will make sense to an officer who may have no direct experience of charities in the specific field concerned.

Every time you respond it may be up to a further three weeks before the registration officer is able to consider your reply, so in complex applications the delays both at the Commission's end, and at your end (gathering information, checking thoughts of prospective trustees) means an application for charity registration can sometimes take many months. But according to the Charity Commission's website at the time of writing, the Commission aims to avoid prolonged registrations, and in reasonably straightforward cases it anticipates that most CIO registrations will be determined in around 40 days from the initial application.

The decision

In due course, the registration officer will give you a decision. It will either be:

- yes – the Charity Commission is satisfied that the proposed CIO meets all the legal requirements and will be a charity and that it can therefore be registered; or
- no – the Charity Commission is unable to approve the application. This could be either for an administrative reason, such as a key omission in the constitution or concerns about a prospective trustee, or it could be because the Commission has been unable to conclude that the proposed CIO would be established for exclusively charitable purposes for public benefit.

A rejection is, of course, disappointing, but it may not be the end of the road. If the applicants feel that the Commission has made an error it is possible to appeal to the charity tribunal (see chapter 16). However, you can also request an internal review by a more senior member of the Commission's staff (this may be helpful if you feel there was a simple misunderstanding by the registration officer).

In most cases, however, if the application is rejected, it is worth taking a clear look at the grounds for rejection: it may be worth seeking external advice. If the issues can be addressed, get everyone together to review all the decisions made leading up to the application, especially the wording of the objects and the proposed activities, and start again with a fresh application. If not, and you accept the Commission's conclusions that the organisation would not be a charity, the applicants may wish to consider moving forward by establishing a non-charitable organisation such as a CIC (see chapter 3).

Registration of the CIO

Assuming the application is approved, the initial message will simply say that the registration officer has approved the CIO for registration, but it then goes to another team for formal addition to the Register of Charities. Typically this will be a day or two later.

At that point you will get a further message confirming that the CIO has been registered and given its registered charity number. The CIO now exists as a corporate body.

Another 24 to 48 hours has to pass before a new charity appears on the online Register of Charities; at that point, check that all the details have been recorded correctly and print off a copy. In due course a registration code and password will be received (by post) which allows amendment of the details held on the Register (for example if new trustees are appointed) and a facility to download a charity registration certificate. Note that the password for the online system is sent to the named contact (at the CIO's Principal Office), not to the person who was handling the application.

The CIO now exists! The first trustees' meeting can be held, bank accounts can be opened, accounting records can be set up, staff can be employed (subject to appropriate recruitment processes) and the work of the charity can proceed.

6 The constitution of a CIO

Charitable organisations need to have a governing document which sets out the purposes for which the charity is established and how it is governed. Some of the different types of governing documents were discussed in chapter 4.

The governing document of a charity formed as a CIO is simply called the 'Constitution' of the CIO. This chapter explores the legal requirements for CIO constitutions and discusses the practical issues involved in preparing a constitution for a new CIO.

You may find it useful to refer to the Appendix, which includes one of the model CIO constitutions provided by the Charity Commission. Other models are being produced for CIOs in specific sectors such as churches, pre-schools and community associations.[1] But, as we will see, preparing an effective constitution for a specific CIO requires considerable thought: it is much more than just a matter of filling in the blanks in a model.

CIO constitutions: general principles

Form and presentation

It is sometimes suggested that because a CIO is a corporate body with limited liability it needs a governing document similar to the articles which govern a charitable company. But, in fact, the constitution of a CIO is normally much simpler than the articles of a company. This is because much of the content of a company's articles is needed to comply with requirements under company law, but CIOs are not companies and are not subject to company law. In principle, the constitution of a CIO does not

[1] An adaptation of the Commission's Association CIO model approved by the Charity Commission specifically for use by community associations is published by Community Matters and can be downloaded for a small charge (with separate notes which should also be purchased) from www.communitymatters.org.uk/legalstructures. The Pre-School Learning Alliance is also producing a Charity Commission-approved model in its publication *Charitable Incorporated Organisations: Registering a childcare provider as a CIO*, available for a small charge from https://shop.pre-school.org.uk.

need to be much more complex than the constitution of an unincorporated charitable association.

The law requires that the constitutions of all CIOs must include certain elements, and there are also other features which are strongly recommended to enable the CIO to operate effectively. (However, many of these provisions are also included in the latest model documents for unincorporated charities, so this does not mean that CIOs are necessarily more complex.) In order to ensure that these key elements are included it will normally be easiest to start from a suitable model, except for cases where the CIO is very specialised and where the person preparing the constitution has considerable experience of drafting legal documents. In any case, the Charity Commission models have a specific status under the regulations, as explained on page 106. But before considering the use of models, it is vital to understand the legal requirements.

The role of a CIO constitution

The governing document of a charity – in this case the constitution of a CIO – serves many roles. These include:

- identifying the charity with a name to distinguish it from other bodies;
- setting out the objects or purposes of the charity;
- indicating the legal structure and hence the laws by which it is governed;
- specifying how trustees are appointed (and identifying those who will be the first trustees when the CIO is formed);
- specifying how people become members (if the CIO has a wide membership);
- making rules for meetings of trustees and members – so that decisions are properly authorised – including rules to deal with conflicts of interest so that trustees do not take part in a decision which could benefit them personally;
- specifying what will happen to the assets if the charity is wound up.

The governing document is central to the life of the charity. When people become members of a CIO, they are agreeing to be bound by the constitution in terms of how they work with other members and make decisions. Trustees are bound by the constitution more directly – as a charity, a CIO holds funds and other resources which are given in trust to advance the charity's objects – so the trustees are always dealing with resources which are not their own. All the trustees' decisions must be taken in accordance with the constitution – acting otherwise could mean that a trustee was committing a breach of trust, and the trustee could then lose the benefit of limited liability through the CIO. A trustee who acted in ways which were contrary to the CIO's constitution would become personally liable for his or her actions.

It is thus essential that those becoming members of a CIO have access to a copy of its constitution so that they know what they are joining. If the charity has a website, it is normally sensible to make the constitution available on the website, and to provide printed copies when requested. In the case of trustees, it is vital that each trustee of the CIO has a personal copy of the constitution and refers to it regularly: an induction pack for new trustees should always include a copy of the charity's constitution, along with recent accounts, minutes and other documents. For new trustees who are unfamiliar with reading constitutions, someone should take time to explain the document so that they understand its significance and the importance of referring to the constitution when taking decisions.

The constitution is also important to third parties (see chapter 17). Any funders offering significant resources to a charity will frequently ask to see the constitution so that they understand the basis of the organisation which they are considering supporting. In the case of a CIO which needs to borrow, the constitution will almost certainly be required by banks or other lenders. Occasionally even normal suppliers may want to see the constitution if they are offering to supply goods on credit.

For all these reasons it is vital that the constitution is clearly drafted, well presented and kept up to date (see page 107 regarding constitutional changes).

Legal requirements for CIO constitutions

Whilst the term 'constitution' is used to describe the governing documents of CIOs in all parts of the UK, the requirements for the constitution of a SCIO are somewhat different from an English or Welsh CIO (see page 249 for more on SCIO constitutions) and similarly there will be a some constitutional differences for Northern Irish CIOs (see page 287). The rest of this chapter focuses on the constitution of CIOs established under the Charities Act 2011; i.e. a CIO established in England or Wales. Most of the following sections also assume that the constitution is to be written in English (see page 105 regarding CIO constitutions in Welsh).

The 2011 Act includes certain requirements for the constitution of a CIO[2] and further requirements are added by the CIO General Regulations.[3] Together these set out the legal requirements for CIO constitutions. A CIO cannot be formed if the proposed constitution does not include these requirements.[4]

The Charity Commission is given the power to make further regulations regarding the 'form' of a CIO's constitution: the Act states that the constitution must be in the form specified or 'as near to that form as the circumstances admit'[5] For example it could make rules regarding the order of clauses, or font sizes to be used. The Commission is using this provision to encourage use of its model documents (see page 106 for more on these) and has specified its own models (or Welsh translations of them) as the prescribed form.[6] However, this does not mean the models can only be varied to the extent of choosing options and filling in blanks: many charities will need significant additions for their own circumstances, and it may sometimes be appropriate to delete non-statutory parts of the models if they will never apply. So, before considering the Commission's models, it is best to start from the fundamental constitutional requirements in the Act and regulations.

Heading of the constitution

Although there is no specific legal requirement for an overall heading on a CIO constitution, it is important to leave no doubt that the document is intended as a constitution of a CIO established under the Charities Act 2011 (rather than under any other jurisdiction). It is also good practice to show the date on which it was adopted or last amended.

---

[2] Charities Act 2011, s. 206.

[3] CIO General Regulations 2012, regs 13–18.

[4] Charities Act 2011, s. 208(1)(b).

[5] Charities Act 2011, s. 206(5).

[6] The Charities Act 2011 (Charitable Incorporated Organisations) (Constitutions) Regulations 2012 (regulations made by the Charity Commission under ss. 206(5) & 347(3) of the Charities Act 2011).

For a new CIO, it is therefore essential to include some sort of heading on the following lines:

> **Constitution of Charitable Incorporated Organisation**
>
> [Name of CIO]
>
> Charities Act 2011
>
> Agreed by the applicants on: [date]

Note that the initial date will simply be the date on which the applicants (the initial members) agreed *to apply* for a CIO to be registered – the actual registration date of the CIO (if the application is successful) will, of necessity, be some weeks later, once the Charity Commission has considered the application.

Once the CIO is registered, it would help to add onto working copies of the constitution:

> Incorporated and registered as a charity on: [date]
>
> Registered charity number: [#######]

If the constitution is subsequently amended (see page 107 for the steps involved) the heading 'Agreed by the applicants' should be changed to show the date when the latest amendments were registered by the Commission:

> Last amended on: [date].

Name

The constitution must specify the name of the CIO,[7] and this will normally be the first clause.

Care is needed when choosing a name for a charity: it needs to be as clear as possible to prospective supporters and to beneficiaries. The normal rules on choosing a charity name are important when setting up a CIO. Some terms are trademarks of existing organisations and cannot be used by new charities without permission (for example, to prevent local charities appearing to be affiliated to a national body if this is not the case). Take care also to avoid infringing any commercial names, including internet domain names: if in doubt, seek professional advice.

The Charity Commission has the power to refuse to register a CIO if it considers that the proposed name is too similar to another charity,

---

[7] Charities Act 2011, s. 206(1)(a).

misleading as to the true nature of its purposes or activities, infringes other regulations, or implies connection with government (national or local).[8]

In order to identify the organisation as a CIO, the name of a CIO will normally end with the letters 'CIO' (or, if preferred, the words 'Charitable Incorporated Organisation' in full).[9] This tells external parties that they are dealing with a charitable body with limited liability. This is similar to other corporate entities with limited liability where the last part of the name shows the legal structure – for example, the following are used under other legislation:

- Ltd – private limited company;
- LLP – limited liability partnership;
- CIC – community interest company.

It is possible to dispense with 'CIO' on the end of the name if it would cause difficulty or if it would make the name too long or complex, so long as the status of the organisation as a CIO is clearly stated 'in legible characters'[10] on all official documents (letters, emails, contracts, fundraising materials, cheques, conveyances, etc.). However, the benefits of doing so may be limited. Charitable companies are often keen to avoid using 'Ltd' as part of their name as it can make them look like commercial businesses, but the CIO designation can *only* be used by charities that are formed as CIOs (in fact, anyone holding out that an organisation is a CIO when it is not is committing a serious offence which could lead to substantial fines).[11] The use of 'CIO' as part of the name makes it clear to everyone that (a) the organisation is a registered charity, and that (b) it is an incorporated body. In this way, having 'CIO' as part of the charity's name may be beneficial. Moreover, if the name ends with 'CIO' this only has to be used wherever the full legal name of the charity is shown; there is no need to include 'CIO' in working names and logos, so long as the full name is clearly shown somewhere on every document.[12]

---

[8] Charities Act 2011, s. 208(2) and s. 42(2).

[9] Charities Act 2011, s. 211.

[10] Charities Act 2011, s. 212.

[11] Charities Act 2011, s. 215.

[12] Charities Act 2011, s. 211(1).

Location of the principal office

Every CIO must have a 'principal office' (similar in concept to the registered office of a company) where the charity can receive official correspondence. This will appear on the Register of Charities.

The CIO's constitution does not give the actual address (the trustees are free to change the principal office from time to time) but for a CIO to be formed and registered with the Charity Commission for England and Wales the principal office must be in England or Wales. (For a principal office in Scotland the charity would be formed as a SCIO, or as a Northern Ireland CIO if the principal office is there.)

The CIO constitution must specify either 'the principal office is to be in England' or 'the principal office is to be in Wales'.[13] This is because slightly different rules apply to English and Welsh CIOs – in particular, a CIO with its principal office in Wales can have documents in Welsh (see page 105).

If the charity has an obvious central office, it is usually best for this to be the principal office, so that correspondence comes directly to the key officers, but the principal office does not have to be the same as the address where the CIO carries out its work. In some cases it may be preferred for the principal office to be the home address of the trustee who deals with the Charity Commission and other official documents, or it could be with professional advisors. But arrangements must be made to ensure that all correspondence that comes to the principal office is dealt with promptly; for example if the Commission has concerns about a CIO it will write to the principal office and may require a reply within 14 days or less.

Some charities working in sensitive fields do not wish to reveal their operational address, and in some cases it may be better to use a trustee or professional advisor to provide the principal office. But if a PO box address is used for the charity's normal correspondence, there is no reason why this cannot be used as the principal office address: unlike the equivalent provisions in company law, there is nothing in the Charities Act to say the principal office must be a physical address, so long as the address is clearly in England or Wales as indicated by the postcode. (Alternatively, it is possible to apply to the Commission to withhold the principal office address from publication,[14] but this would make it very difficult for anyone to contact the charity.)

---

[13] Charities Act 2011, s. 206(1)(c).

[14] Under the Charities (Accounts and Reports) Regulations 2008, reg. 40(4).

Purposes

The most important part of any charity governing document is the statement of the charity's purposes. The clause explaining the purposes is normally called the 'objects clause' because it spells out the object or objects for which the charity is established.

CIOs, like other charities, can be established for any purposes which fall within the thirteen heads (or headings) in the Charities Act 2011.[15] However, remember that to be a charity, it is not sufficient just to have purposes which fall within these headings – the purposes must be 'for the public benefit'[16] (see page 21 for the principles, and for a more detailed discussion see *Charitable Status* by Julian Blake, published in the same series).

A charity will often have several objects, but each object must identify a purpose which is charitable (to be a charity, an organisation must have *exclusively* charitable purposes). So whilst it is often helpful to have two or three purposes in order to allow some for different strands of the CIO's work, it is best to avoid very long lists of objects as you will have to satisfy the Charity Commission on *each* object.

It is possible for a charity to be established for a particular purpose or for 'general charitable purposes' – the latter term embraces *all* the heads of charity. It is worth ensuring the objects are broad enough to allow for development of a charity's work, and sometimes grant-making charities, for example, may need objects that are wide enough to allow grants to be made for any kind of charitable purpose. But for operational charities it is often clearer to have objects which directly express the field of work. When applying for the CIO to be registered (see page 80) it is often much easier to explain how the charity will advance its objects for public benefit if the objects are not too broad. It is usually best to keep to a small number of objects (often a single object will suffice) – if there are many objects a case has to be made under each one to show the public benefit that will result. Also, in many cases supporters are influenced by a charity's precise field of work as expressed in its objects: if the objects are very broad it becomes harder to solicit unrestricted donations.

The drafting of the objects clause needs considerable care: it is this clause which will receive the most attention by the Charity Commission when the application is made to register the CIO (see page 74). Remember that a CIO can only be formed and registered if the Charity Commission is

[15] Charities Act 2011, s. 3.

[16] Charities Act 2011, s. 4

satisfied that it will be a charity.[17] In deciding this, the main issues which the Commission's registration team has to consider are the wording of the objects clause and the explanation of the activities to be undertaken to carry out those purposes for public benefit.

It is thus essential that the proposed object(s) tie up with the proposed activities. However, the objects must be worded in such a way that they fall within the headings in the 2011 Act. The objects are expressed primarily in terms of the purpose for which the charity is established, rather than how it will carry out its work (although sometimes the 'how' aspect is included as an addition to clarify the purpose and make the objects more precise). For example, if you are proposing to establish a CIO to run a community theatre, consider an objects clause which stated:

> The objects of the CIO are to operate a theatre in Upperton.

This would almost certainly *not* be accepted as a charity, because the Charity Commission would argue that not all theatres are charities (some are established for private profit, and even some non-profit theatres may be little more than private clubs putting on shows with little or no artistic merit). A more helpful wording could be:

> The object of the CIO is the advancement of the arts for the benefit of the public in Upperton and the surrounding area, in particular (but not exclusively) by the operation of a theatre.

But even this wording will not succeed in achieving registration of the CIO unless the section of the online registration form regarding the charity's activities spells out clearly the sort of performances to be provided and how they will be accessed (see 'Activities and public benefit' on page 74 for more on this). In order to show that the CIO will advance the arts for public benefit (in the way that is understood in charity law) the performances will need to be educational and have a quality of artistic merit, and be accessible to a wide range of people to attend (so it will help to explain how shows will be publicised and how ticket prices will be set to ensure that poorer people are not excluded).

The objects cannot normally be expressed in terms so that only members of the CIO will benefit – the beneficiaries must be the public or a section of the public. An organisation which only benefits its own members cannot be a charity, unless membership is open to anyone who may be able to benefit (but not if there is a closed arrangement such as requiring new members to be proposed by an existing member). In some cases, such as a

---

[17] Charities Act 2011, s. 206(1)(a).

charity providing sporting activities, it may be appropriate to require that users must become members of the CIO before they can use the equipment or facilities, but if so, membership must be accessible and affordable.

Sometimes those establishing charities wish to spell out in great detail the basis on which the objects will be advanced; for instance a religious charity may want to include a detailed doctrinal statement. In such cases it is usually easiest to include the detail in a separate schedule rather than as part of the main objects clause (for example 'the object of the charity is the advancement of the Christian faith in accordance with the doctrinal statement in Schedule 1'). However, beware of making such statements too restricting for the future.

Drafting the objects clause for a new charity requires considerable skill and experience in charity law. Some examples of possible wordings are provided on the Charity Commission's website, but in general if you are new to drafting charity governing documents it would be wise to seek guidance from a suitable specialist.

Powers

Prior to CIOs, any charity governing document has generally included a long section of 'powers' available to the charity or its trustees. The objects clause specifies *why* the charity is established and the powers spell out *how* charitable funds can be spent.

Traditionally, the powers clause authorises the trustees to commit charitable funds to a wide range of expenditure and to agree other actions which may not be directly supporting the charity's beneficiaries, but which may be necessary in order for the charity to carry out its work. Sometimes this clause begins with a very specific power related to the work of the charity (for instance, 'power to operate a residential home for retired sailors') and then a list of much more general powers such as employing staff, paying for premises, incurring fundraising costs, paying for insurance, affiliating to other bodies. However, to be sure nothing has been missed, it is usual for a powers clause to end with a power 'to do anything else within the law which promotes or helps to promote the objects'.

The powers clause normally begins 'In furtherance of the above objects but not otherwise…' – in other words the power can only be exercised in such a way that it enables the objects to be advanced. For example, a power to pay staff cannot be used simply to award additional staff bonuses which go beyond the employee's contracts, unless the payments are part of an incentive scheme to enhance the charity's work.

It is important to remember that paying employees or paying a landlord for premises will result in private benefits to those concerned (see page 30 for a reminder of the distinctions between public benefit and private benefit). Even if the employees and landlord have no connections with trustees so there is no conflict of interest, such expenditure is not *directly* benefiting the charity's beneficiaries. But if such expenditure enables the charity to provide services to beneficiaries and those services advance the charitable purposes, it is a reasonable use of the trustees' powers, providing the governing document gives authorisation.

The good news for CIO constitutions is that the Charities Act states:

> *Subject to anything in its constitution, a CIO may do anything which is calculated to further its purposes or is conducive or incidental to doing so.*[18]

That standard provision is broad enough to cover every power which a CIO may need. So unless it is desired to *limit* those powers – because they are seen to be too broad – it is not necessary for a CIO constitution to include a powers clause at all! (This may well save at least a page compared to other charity governing documents.)

Limiting the powers would be rare but could be done for ethical reasons: for example, the constitution could say that 'the CIO shall not have the power to supply alcohol from any premises under its control'. However, it is worth bearing in mind that future members could vote to amend the constitution to alter the powers and remove such a provision. If you want to prevent this it would be necessary to include an 'entrenchment' of such a restriction (see page 103). But it is not permissible to add any restriction which would prevent the CIO disposing of property;[19] for example the constitution cannot prevent the CIO from selling land or buildings (so long as it complies with the normal charity law requirements[20] when doing so).

Whilst there is no statutory *requirement* for a powers clause in the constitution of a CIO, it can help to include a clause which restates the power from the Act. It may also be helpful to add one or two other powers for the avoidance of doubt. For example, even though the standard powers in the Act would include taking out loans if needed to advance the objects, banks and other lenders often like to see an explicit 'power to borrow' before they will lend funds to a charity. The Charity Commission model includes a powers clause on these lines (see the Appendix to this book,

[18] Charities Act 2011, s. 216(1).

[19] CIO General Regulations 2012, reg. 14.

[20] See Charities Act 2011, ss. 117–129.

clause 4). It also reminds anyone reading the constitution that whilst the CIO has the power to sell, mortgage or lease out property, it can only do so subject to the normal processes in the Charities Act 2011 which apply to almost all charities.

Members

It is important to remember that a CIO (like a company) is first and foremost a body of members who are brought together in a corporate entity (although the CIO itself is a legal person in its own right – its assets and liabilities are separate from those of the members). Whilst charity trustees will be appointed to *govern* the CIO, the CIO's members retain key powers.

CIOs can be formed with many possible membership structures, but in most cases trustees are elected by the members. Other methods of appointment are possible, including nominated and ex officio trustees.

Structure 1: an association CIO

The most obvious arrangement (in terms of understanding the CIO) is where there are many members – too many for them all to be trustees. The members come together at the AGM to elect the trustees. The members have a vote on major issues such as changes to the constitution, but the ongoing day-to-day governance and financial decisions are taken by the trustees. In the regulations this is called an 'association CIO'[21] because the governance is similar to a charitable association. On this basis a CIO could have thousands of members or more. It is very appropriate for any kind of charitable organisation where people commit to being members and want a formal vote in major decisions, such as community associations, professional bodies, sports charities, campaigning charities or umbrella organisations. Some charities have arrangements under which all supporters are encouraged to become members so that they have a formal stake in the organisation through a right to vote at the AGM.

Structure 2: a foundation CIO

A second option is where the members and trustees are the same people – i.e. everyone who is appointed a trustee becomes a member, and if someone ceases to be a trustee he or she also ceases to be a member. The trustees therefore appoint their own successors, with no accountability to

[21] CIO General Regulations 2012, reg. 2.

a wider membership. The regulations call this a 'foundation CIO' because it is similar to the governance of a charitable foundation. Many charities which do not need any wider accountability are structured on this basis. It is often the simplest approach for grant-making charities, and for service-providing charities which see themselves as agencies providing a particular service on behalf of funders and commissioners. However, CIOs of this kind still technically have the two-tier structure, as outlined in 'Structure 1' above, even though the members and trustees are the same people. The constitution must distinguish decisions taken by trustees (such as approving the annual accounts) and decisions by members (such as amending the constitution).

Structure 3: a single-member CIO

A third option is a CIO with just a single member – where that member elects all the trustees. This may be useful in the case of a new CIO set up by an existing charity where the existing charity wishes to retain control by appointing all the trustees (not just initially, but also for the longer term). It could also be appropriate for a major donor setting up a new grant-making charity where the original donor wishes to control all future appointments of trustees. However, if there is only one member who is a natural person (as opposed to a corporate body) the constitution must make provision for other members to be appointed when he or she dies, as a CIO must always have at least one member.[22] There are specific regulations concerning decision-making by a sole member.[23]

Membership: other issues

Other membership structures are possible. The members can be individuals or corporate bodies (such as companies, local authorities, other CIOs, or other kinds of incorporated charities such as PCCs in the Church of England). The Charity Commission models do not allow for unincorporated bodies to be members of a CIO, although they do allow for an individual to be a member as an appointed representative of an unincorporated organisation. However, there is nothing explicit in the legislation stating that a member of a CIO has to be a single legal person, and the Commission has accepted CIO constitutions which allow for unincorporated organisations to be members in their own right[24], but any

---

[22] Charities Act 2011, s. 205(2)(c).

[23] CIO General Regulations 2012, reg. 43.

[24] For example, the model constitution produced by Community Matters (see footnote on page 87).

such provision requires amendment of the Commission's models. It is worth noting that many charitable companies allow unincorporated bodies to be members. (However, such arrangements could theoretically lead to challenges if, for example, different trustees of an unincorporated charity which was a member of a CIO had different views on how to exercise the membership.)

A key element which distinguishes CIOs from other types of charity is that members (not just trustees) have an active duty to support the CIO. The Charities Act states:

> *Each member of a CIO must exercise the powers that the member has in that capacity in the way that the member decides, in good faith, would be most likely to further the purposes of the CIO.*[25]

The Charity Commission model constitution makes clear that membership is only open to those who accept this duty (see the Appendix, clause 9(1)(a)), but the requirement applies under the 2011 Act in any case.

Where the members are individuals there is no lower age limit (unless the CIO's constitution sets a limit) so it is perfectly possible to allow children of any age to be members (whereas trustees must be at least 16 years old). However, in the event of a dispute between the CIO and its members it is important to remember that contracts with children cannot be enforced at law and young children may find it hard to accept the duty set out above. However, if membership is mainly a form of support for the charity, it may be fully appropriate to allow children to become members. If this is not intended, it may be wise to put a provision in the constitution that members must be 18 years old or over (although this is *not* included in the Charity Commission models).

The constitution must say whether or not the members are liable to contribute to the assets of the CIO if it is wound up[26] – i.e. it is possible to have a 'members' guarantee' similar to a company limited by guarantee. But, as explained in chapter 4, one of the key advantages of a CIO compared with a charitable company is that a CIO does *not* need its members to give a guarantee, so very few CIOs will want this. The recommended Charity Commission wording in the constitution in such cases is:

> *If the CIO is wound up, the members of the CIO have no liability to contribute to its assets and no personal responsibility for settling its debts and liabilities.*

---

[25] Charities Act 2011, s. 220.

[26] Charities Act 2011, s. 206(1)(d).

The legislation requires that the CIO's constitution must also contain the following provisions about membership:

- who is eligible for membership and how a person becomes a member;[27]
- how a member retires from membership of the CIO;[28]
- other circumstances in which membership may be terminated;[29] (such as non-payment of subscriptions, breach of rules for use of the charity's premises, etc.).

The constitution must also make provision for 'general meetings' of members – normally an AGM and other general meetings as required. In particular, it must specify issues such as the procedure for calling meetings (the notice required, methods of communication, etc.), the quorum for such meetings, and the procedures for decision-making.[30] The decision-making processes can allow for postal votes,[31] and for members to appoint proxies[32] to vote on their behalf, and potentially also for a poll of members to be demanded at a meeting (i.e. using written voting papers) as under company law. The provisions can also allow for electronic communications. Postal (or electronic) voting may be useful in a CIO with members widely separated geographically, though most CIOs will wish to avoid the complications of proxy voting and polls.

If necessary, a CIO can have different classes of members with different voting rights. All would be members of the CIO, but it might be helpful to say that only members who are over the age of 18, for example, could vote in the election of trustees. Similarly, a religious charity might wish to say that only members who signed a particular doctrinal statement were eligible to vote on certain issues.

Trustees

The constitution must give the names of the first charity trustees of the CIO[33] (though their addresses are not required) and must specify how trustees are

[27] Charities Act 2011, s. 206(2)(a)

[28] CIO General Regulations 2012, reg. 13(3) 'standard member provisions' para (a).

[29] CIO General Regulations 2012, reg. 13(3) 'standard member provisions' para (b).

[30] CIO General Regulations 2012, reg. 13(3) 'standard member provisions' para. (c) and 13(5)–(11).

[31] CO General Regulations 2012, reg. 13(6). This explicit provision for CIOs to hold postal votes is helpful, because whilst many charitable companies use postal votes, they may be open to challenge.

[32] CIO General Regulations 2012, reg. 13(5).

[33] CIO General Regulations 2012, reg. 13(1).

appointed thereafter[34] (including any conditions on eligibility to be a trustee) and how they retire or may otherwise be removed from office.[35]

It seems a little odd to include the names of the first trustees in the middle of the constitution as in the Charity Commission models, especially as after a few years the initial trustees may well have stepped down. It may be clearer for this clause to refer to a schedule, and then list the initial trustees in a schedule at the end of the constitution (but the schedule would still be part of the constitution itself).

The initial trustees must sign a declaration submitted as part of the registration process, but it is important to remember that the 'applicants' who apply for formation of the CIO are the initial members who may not be the same people as the initial trustees. But there is no requirement to name the applicants in the constitution.

The constitution must include the rules for holding of trustees' meetings including similar issues to members' meetings (calling of meetings, appointment of a chair, quorum)[36] – but because the trustees will normally meet much more frequently than the members it is particularly important to ensure the arrangements are effective and workable for the specific CIO concerned.

Benefits to trustees and conflicts of interest

Trustees of a CIO are entitled to be reimbursed for expenses which they have legitimately incurred.[37]

But beyond this, if there are any circumstances in which it is intended that trustees may receive benefits from the CIO this must be stated explicitly in the constitution (see page 30 for more on payments to trustees). For example, if the trustees want to be able to use the provisions in sections 185 to 188 of the Charities Act 2011 under which the other trustees can, in exceptional cases, agree to pay a fee to a trustee for work outside his or her trustee duties (see page 31) this must be stated explicitly.[38]

---

[34] Charities Act 2011, s. 206(2)(b).

[35] CIO General Regulations 2012, reg. 13(3) 'standard trustee provisions' paras (a)–(b).

[36] CIO General Regulations 2012, reg. 13(3) 'standard trustee provisions' para. (c).

[37] Charities Act 2011, s. 222(3).

[38] Any such arrangement benefiting a trustee of a CIO is also subject to the conflict of interest provisions in s. 222 of the Charities Act 2011 and reg. 36 of the CIO General Regulations 2012.

Even with such a provision, trustees must disclose to other trustees if any issues arise where they could be subject to a conflict of interest, even if the conflict is non-financial. Where this arises, the trustee(s) concerned must withdraw and would not count towards the quorum for the meeting. The Charity Commission model (clause 7) includes a suitable provision in the constitution to make this clear. In cases of very severe conflict a CIO may need to take further steps, such as ensuring conflicted trustees do not receive papers for agenda items where they are required to withdraw.

Dissolution

A CIO's constitution must contain directions about the 'application of its property on dissolution'[39] – in other words, what will happen to the CIO's remaining assets if it is wound up. The assets will need to be used for charitable purposes that are as similar as possible to those of the CIO. The Charity Commission's model wording will be suitable in most cases.

Procedures, records, etc.

It is normal for a charity constitution to contain many other provisions to ensure that it is properly run, and the Charity Commission models illustrate this in some detail. For example, they include provisions to remind the trustees about record-keeping, annual accounts, annual returns, execution of documents, minutes, disputes, etc.

None of this is *required* to be in a CIO's constitution under the regulations, although many of these provisions confirm other legal requirements such as the keeping of registers for the CIO (under the CIO General Regulations 2012) and filing accounts (under the Charities Act 2011). So it is helpful to include these provisions in the constitution as a reminder of many of the basic responsibilities of running a charity (and a CIO in particular). See chapter 7 for more on CIO registers and communications.

'Entrenchment' or restricting future changes to the constitution

In general, the members of a CIO could at a later date vote to make changes to the constitution (see page 107). Some changes require Charity Commission consent, but any provision in the constitution could generally be changed if the relevant processes are followed, so long as it remains a valid CIO constitution.

[39] Charities Act 2011, s. 206(2)(c).

However, sometimes those setting up a charity wish to include provisions that cannot be changed without some external consent (i.e. not just the approval of the members and the Charity Commission). Where this is done, the relevant constitutional provisions are said to be 'entrenched'.[40]

Common reasons for entrenchment including protecting the interests of founder members (so that future members cannot change the rules to exclude them) or to protect doctrinal statements in religious charities (so that the doctrines could not be changed purely by a 75% vote of members) or to ensure that a local charity adheres to the values and standards laid down by a national umbrella body. For example, the constitution could include a provision that no constitutional change could be agreed without the consent of the founder member, or that changes to the doctrinal statement can only be made with the consent of a specific national body.

However, it isn't possible to prevent changes *ever* being made – the entrenchment provisions simply impose additional processes that must be followed before the relevant provisions of the constitution can be made. Moreover, if 100% of the CIO members agree, even entrenched provisions can be changed.[41] So, in practice, if you wish to ensure that changes cannot be made without the consent of a specific person or organisation, that person or corporate body needs to be a permanent member of the CIO. Entrenched provisions can also be changed by the courts, or by a formal order of the Charity Commission[42] (this is analogous to the Commission's power to make 'schemes' – when a charity needs to be reorganised but does not have the relevant powers in its governing document, the Commission can achieve this by making a scheme).[43]

The model CIO constitutions provided by the Charity Commission do not include any entrenched provisions: any such restrictions would need to be added specifically (normally by adding more detail to the clause on constitutional amendments). However, it is best to avoid entrenching the whole constitution, as even minor changes could then only be made by following the specified process. Entrenchment (if needed at all) should be restricted to major provisions which are fundamental to the nature of the charity.

Where a CIO has a single member it is not normally necessary to include entrenchment, as the constitution could in any case only be amended if

[40] CIO General Regulations 2012, reg. 15.

[41] CIO General Regulations 2012, reg. 15(3)(a).

[42] CIO General Regulations 2012, reg. 15(3)(b).

[43] Charities Act 2011, ss. 67–73

the member agrees. The constitution simply needs to specify that no other members can be admitted (or, at least, not without the consent of the founder member).

Where an application is made to register a CIO which includes entrenched provisions, the Charity Commission must be advised accordingly, for example by means of a supplementary letter uploaded as an additional document at the final stage in the online registration system (see page 83).

Other provisions for specific charities

The legislation and the Charity Commission models are only intended to address constitutional provisions that will apply to virtually all CIOs. But it is perfectly possible to include additional material if needed. For example, some CIOs may wish to write into the constitution details of specific committees of trustees, codes of ethics for members or the process for agreeing membership subscriptions. Others may want clauses setting out details of the disciplinary procedures to be followed before someone's membership can be terminated. Especially if a CIO is being formed to take over the work of a long-established existing charity, provisions of this kind may need to be incorporated and updated from the existing governing document.

So, whilst the models are a helpful starting point, preparing an effective CIO constitution that will allow an organisation to advance its charitable purposes as well as preserving any established culture, values and methods of working may take some care.

Nevertheless, it is important to avoid going into too much detail in the constitution of the CIO. The constitution should only cover major issues on which the members as a whole would want a vote if changes are considered – but amending the constitution will always involve considerable effort (see page 107). More detailed issues are better dealt with in separate documents or 'rules' that can be approved and amended purely by the trustees. The Charity Commission model CIO constitutions allow the trustees to make rules on these lines.

Welsh constitutions

If a CIO's constitution states that its principal office is to be in Wales, the constitution may be *either* in English *or* Welsh (for CIOs with a principal office in England, the constitution must always be in English).[44]

[44] Charities Act 2011, s. 206(4).

If the constitution is in Welsh, the title 'Charitable Incorporated Organisation' becomes 'Sefydliad Elusennol Corfforedig' and the name of the CIO will normally end with 'SEC'.[45] The abbreviation 'SEC' is subject to the same protection as 'CIO' – an organisation must not claim to be an SEC unless it is so constituted. However, at the time of writing the Charity Commission's model constitutions are only available in English.

It is important not to confuse an SEC (i.e. a Welsh CIO) with an SCE which is a *Societas Cooperativa Europaea* or European Co-operative Society[46] – a form of third sector organisation with members from at least two European countries. An SCE would *not* generally be able to be a charity in the UK, because the idea of a co-operative is that the members share in the profits (see page 42).

Using the Charity Commission's model constitutions

The Appendix to this book includes the text of the Charity Commission's model constitution for a CIO with 'voting members other than its charity trustees' (i.e. an association CIO as discussed on page 98). This is appropriate for a CIO with a wide membership.

As this is the more complex model, and as it clearly distinguishes the roles of members on the one hand and trustees on the other, it helps to illustrate practical wordings for the constitutional issues discussed in this chapter.

The Commission also produces a slightly simpler model for a CIO whose only members are its trustees – the foundation CIO. Both models are available from the Commission's website as PDF documents with a wide range of supporting notes.

It does not seem that the Commission intends to produce a model for a single-member CIO (or a CIO with only a small number of fixed members) but this could easily be produced by adapting the association model.

Shorter and simpler CIO constitutions are certainly possible, but the Charity Commission models are fairly comprehensive, and the Commission strongly encourages their use. Moreover, regulations state that a CIO's constitution must follow the form of one of the Commission's models or be 'as near that form as circumstances permit'.[47] Using one of

---

[45] Charities Act 2011, s. 212(2).

[46] SCEs are established under Council Regulation (EC) No 1435/2003.

[47] Charities Act 2011, s. 206(5) and The Charities Act 2011 (Charitable Incorporated Organisations) (Constitutions) Regulations 2012 made by the Commission.

the Commission models will typically lead to a final constitution of at least 5,000 words, or around twelve pages if printed in a typical font (the association CIO model is longer than the version for foundation CIOs).

Nevertheless, there will clearly be cases where considerable additions or variation from the Commission models will be needed for charities in particular fields. Other CIO model constitutions are being developed, in particular by umbrella bodies (though, of course, any umbrella body seeking to develop such models is strongly advised to seek Charity Commission approval before promoting their use).

However, it is never wise to draft a constitution simply by filling in the blanks in the model. Options need to be considered carefully. Sometimes text in a model is irrelevant to a particular CIO and if it is not legally required it is best deleted – but, equally, provisions may need to be added for a specific CIO which are not in the models. All the issues considered in this chapter will need careful discussion with the applicants, initial trustees and possibly major donors and funders, to ensure that the end result will be an effective CIO structure with good workable arrangements for the longer term.

Amending a CIO's constitution

Once a CIO is formed and registered by the Charity Commission, its constitution is finalised. It becomes binding on the CIO's members and it must be followed by its trustees if they are to fulfil their duties.

However, the constitution is not fixed in stone, and the legislation includes fairly straightforward procedures for making subsequent amendments to the constitution. One of the attractions of the CIO structure is that the constitution can be amended relatively easily. The process is very similar to amending the constitution of an unincorporated charitable association.

Common reasons for amending a CIO's constitution may include:

- changing rules such as the minimum and maximum number of trustees;
- altering quorums for meetings;
- adding postal voting if not previously allowed;
- altering membership criteria;
- altering the charitable objects, for example to widen the area of benefit;
- altering the name of the CIO.

Regulated and unregulated alteration to the constitution

In all cases amendments, once agreed, must be communicated to the Charity Commission, but it is important to distinguish between changes which require the Commission's *consent* (i.e. they cannot come into effect unless the Charity Commission agrees) and changes which simply require *notification* to the Commission.

Under the Charities Act,[48] any of the following changes are 'regulated alterations':

- any change to the CIO's charitable purposes (i.e. changes to the wording of the objects);
- any alterations regarding the application of the CIO's assets when it is dissolved (i.e. changes to the dissolution clause);
- any changes to the rules on trustee benefits (for example if a CIO had exceptional reasons for wanting to allow a trustee to be an employee then, if there was no existing provision, it would be necessary to seek Charity Commission approval to add a new clause allowing this).

On the last point it is worth noting that the Charity Commission's model constitutions already allow approval of fees to trustees for services beyond normal trustee duties, provided all the conditions are followed (see clause 6(2)(b) of the model in the Appendix and see page 30 for more on trustee benefits). It is also worth noting that in a one-off situation, the Commission could give approval under other provisions in the Charities Act,[49] so amendment of the CIO's constitution would only be needed for ongoing arrangements.

For any regulated amendments, the Charity Commission's 'prior consent' must be obtained.[50] So, in practice, the trustees (or anyone else proposing a regulated change) will want to contact the Commission well before the meeting at which it is to be considered. (When contacting the Commission it would help to stress that the charity is a CIO, and that consent is being sought under section 226 of the Charities Act 2011. Applications can be made through the Charity Commission website.)

Any amendment which does not fall into the above three areas is an unregulated alteration – it does not require Charity Commission consent, because other matters are seen as purely administrative. However, all

[48] Charities Act 2011, s. 226(2).

[49] By an Order under s. 105 of the Charities Act 2011.

[50] Charities Act 2011, s. 226(1).

changes must be approved by the members and notified to the Commission and only take effect when registered by the Commission (see page 114).

Amending or adding entrenched provisions

If the existing constitution included entrenched provisions (see page 103), any constitutional amendment which would affect such a provision can only proceed if the relevant processes or consents are followed. This will need planning from the outset to ensure that the relevant approvals are obtained, and the processes explained below may need to be revised to take account of these requirements (for example, a 75% approval by members at a general meeting may not be sufficient). However, it is worth remembering that *any* change – even to an entrenched provision – can be passed if 100% of members agreed (and with Charity Commission consent where needed).

A change to *add* entrenched provisions to the constitution of an existing CIO can only be agreed by 100% of members.[51] This is because such provisions may well restrict the rights of existing members.

Preparing constitutional amendments

Any proposed amendment to the constitution of a CIO needs to be drafted as a resolution of some kind, which will be put to the members for consideration. The trustees may well draw up the resolution, but because a CIO is a membership body, the constitution cannot be amended by the trustees – only by the members.

A resolution may propose amendments to wording, insertions or deletions. If whole clauses, sub-clauses or paragraphs are inserted or deleted it is best to propose that subsequent sections are renumbered accordingly. It is often helpful to provide explanation for the changes, but make clear that any points of explanation are not part of the actual resolution. See the wording in the example overleaf. (In the case of a regulated alteration, it would help to confirm that the Charity Commission has consented to the change, as without this, there is no point in presenting the resolution for members to vote.)

[51] CIO General Regulations 2012, reg. 15(2)(b).

Example of a constitutional amendment resolution

Upperton Health Forum CIO

Proposed constitutional amendment to be considered at the AGM on 13 October 2014. (Note that points in italics are for explanation only and do not form part of the resolution.)

(I) **Add** at the end of clause 9(1)(a):

'No person may become a member unless he or she lives or regularly works in the Borough of Upperton.'

Explanation: This is to address the recommendation that the voting membership of the charity (those who can vote at the AGM when trustees are elected) should be restricted to people with a permanent link to the local community. Visitors from outside the area will still be able to benefit from the work of the Forum but they will not be voting members.

(II) In clause 19(3) **delete** the second sentence and **replace** with:

'The quorum is three trustees or half the trustees if greater'.

Explanation: This is to ensure that no decisions are taken at trustees' meetings unless half the trustees are present (or three trustees if we ever got down to four trustees or fewer) – rather than the present arrangement where decisions can be taken with only a third of trustees present.

Proposed by: The trustees.

If the amendments are very extensive, it may be better to propose that the entire constitution be deleted and replaced by a new draft constitution attached to the resolution.

Meetings and decisions on constitutional amendments

Usually decisions on constitutional amendments are taken by members at a meeting; although a written resolution can be used if easier (see page 113).

A meeting of members is called a 'general meeting' in CIO constitutions. Votes on constitutional amendments could be made at the Annual General Meeting (AGM) or at a specially convened general meeting – often charities call this an Extraordinary General Meeting (EGM), though the term is not used in the CIO model constitutions. Separate minutes should be kept for general meetings as opposed to trustees' meetings.

Even in a foundation CIO – where the trustees and members are the same people – if the decision is to be taken at a meeting, it is necessary to hold a general meeting of members rather than a trustees' meeting, even though the same people are involved. In practice the general meeting is normally held on the same date as a trustees' meeting. Usually it is best to hold it immediately before the trustees' meeting so that the trustees are clear that the constitutional change is agreed before they hold their normal meeting – but remember that changes still have to be registered with the Charity Commission before they take effect.

In a single-member CIO, the member (or the member's representative if the member is a corporate body) could meet on his or her own, consider the issues and then decide whether or not to approve the resolution! Possibly trustees or advisors may be in attendance, but the decision rests with the member alone – though the member must tell the CIO (i.e. advise the trustees) what he/she/it decided.[52] However, in practice it may be easier to use a written resolution (see page 113) if there are only one or two members.

It is important to give sufficient notice of a general meeting. The Charity Commission models require at least 14 clear days' notice, though in a CIO with a large membership spread across the country it may be fairer to make the notice period much longer – possibly as much as 60 or 90 days. The phrase 'clear days' notice' excludes the day of the meeting and the day notice is given; so, if notice is given on the 1st of a month, the earliest possible date for the meeting is 16th of the month. But that timetable would only apply if messages are physically handed to recipients. Under the regulations,[53] a notice from a CIO sent by post or by email (where the member has agreed to receive communications by email) is deemed to be received 48 hours after it was sent (excluding Saturdays, Sundays and bank holidays). So if the 1st of a month is a Friday, the recipient would only be considered to have received notice on Tuesday 5th. Therefore, allowing 14 clear days, the earliest date for the meeting would be Wednesday 20th. The notice of the meeting must include the text of any proposed alteration to the constitution (see clause 11(3)(c)(iv) in the Charity Commission model).

At the general meeting itself, the provisions of the constitution must be carefully followed: in particular, the constitutional amendment cannot be considered unless sufficient members are present to form a quorum as specified in the CIO constitution. (In most CIOs, trustees are likely to be members as well as trustees, so the trustees can usually count towards the quorum. Although, as with trustee meetings, trustees cannot vote or be

[52] CIO General Regulations 2012, reg. 43.

[53] CIO General Regulations 2012, reg. 53.

counted towards the quorum on any issues where they are set to benefit personally.)[54]

After there has been time for debate, the chair of the meeting will put the resolution to the vote, and it must be carried by at least 75% of the members present and voting in order to be carried.[55] (Note that the 75% majority is a higher threshold than applies for constitutional amendments in many other charities which are not CIOs.) Voting can normally be done on a show of hands but unless the voting is clearly unanimous it is always wise to count the votes to be certain whether the 75% majority was achieved. Alternatively, members can be asked to vote in writing (sometimes called a 'poll'). The constitution can include provisions allowing members to 'demand' a poll – in the Charity Commission model it is possible for 10% of members at the meeting to demand a poll (but if so they must make the request before the show of hands result is declared). However, this is optional – many CIOs may find it simpler to omit the provisions for members to demand a poll and leave it to the chair to decide if a poll should take place.

If the constitution allows for proxy voting (i.e. a member who appoints someone else to vote on his or her behalf) or postal voting, then those voting by proxy or by post count towards the figures for the quorum and the resolution. (Possible wording for each of these options is available in the full Charity Commission model constitutions, but it is not reproduced in the Appendix to this book.)

Members who abstain in the vote do not count for the 75% rule, but they do count towards the quorum. For example, consider a CIO with 300 members whose constitution specifies that at least 50 members must be present at a general meeting (with no provision for postal or proxy votes).

- **Case I:** 48 members present. No constitutional amendment can be passed, whatever the voting. An informal discussion could take place, but it is not a formal general meeting, so no votes should be taken.
- **Case II:** 53 members present. 40 vote in favour, 13 against, no abstentions. The constitutional amendment is passed (but only just): with 53 members voting, anything over 39.75 in favour gives a 75% majority, so 40 in favour is just sufficient.
- **Case III:** 53 members present, 30 vote in favour, 3 against, 20 abstain. The constitutional amendment is passed: a quorum is present, and of the 33 members voting, anything over 24.75 votes in favour will give a 75% majority.

---

[54] CIO General Regulations 2012, reg. 36.

[55] Charities Act 2011, s. 224(2)(a).

- **Case IV:** 53 members present, 30 vote in favour, 23 against, no abstentions. The constitutional amendment is lost: a quorum is present, but as indicated in case II, with 53 voting, a 75% majority needs at least 39.75 votes in favour. Even though a majority are in favour, 30 out of 53 is not a 75% majority – so the resolution is defeated and the constitution remains unchanged.

Agreeing constitutional amendments by written resolutions and postal votes

Sometimes, rather than calling a general meeting, it is more convenient to take a decision by means of a written resolution. This often works well for relatively uncontroversial decisions where there is no convenient general meeting and there are not too many members. However, unlike votes taken at general meetings which can be passed with a 75% majority, a written resolution is only passed if it is unanimous, i.e. 100% of members have to agree,[56] and because of this there can be no abstentions if the amendment is to be passed. The requirement for 100% agreement is because if members do not go to a meeting there is no chance for those opposed to the proposal to persuade others to vote against it – so the requirement protects CIO members from passing inappropriate constitutional amendments just because someone proposes a change. (Note that this 100% rule for written resolutions is higher than for companies where a special resolution can be passed with written agreement by 75% of the members.)[57]

In the past when an organisation required a written resolution, a document was physically passed from one member to another, and the resolution was only agreed when every member had signed. But the Charities Act simply states that it must have 'unanimous agreement' by members and this could be signified in various ways. For example, if there are five members and each signs a copy of the resolution and returns it to the CIO it is passed on the date when the last member signs.[58] Or in cases where members have agreed to receive communications by email, an email from each member to the CIO confirming his or her agreement would suffice. However, proper records of all decisions taken by members must be kept, whether at a meeting or by other means.[59]

Even where everyone is happy to receive email communications, it is very hard to get 100% of members to confirm their agreement in a charity with a large membership. It may be better to call a general meeting, in which

[56] Charities Act 2011, s. 224(2)(b).

[57] Companies Act 2006, s. 283.

[58] CIO General Regulations 2012, reg. 16(1).

[59] CIO General Regulations 2012, regs 41–43.

case a 75% majority of those attending will suffice (so long as at least a quorum is present). If no quorum is present, the meeting must be adjourned; but under the Charity Commission model – see clause 11(5)(e) – a quorum is automatically achieved 15 minutes after the start of the adjourned meeting (even if only a handful of members are present).

If it is difficult to get people to attend meetings it is a good idea for the constitution to allow for postal voting for decisions that require a general meeting. In that case, so long as a meeting has been called which people can attend if they wish, only a 75% majority is needed. If the constitution allows for postal votes, anyone voting on that basis is treated as being present at the meeting. The full text of the Charity Commission model includes optional clauses which can be added to allow for postal voting (including email voting) and any CIO with a widely dispersed membership may wish to consider including this.

Registering amendments with the Charity Commission

As with all charities, constitutional amendments passed by a CIO must be communicated to the Charity Commission; but in the case of a CIO the Charities Act states that the changes 'do not take effect' until registered by the Commission.[60] This is an important way in which CIOs differ from other charities (but, as we saw in chapter 1, the Commission is responsible for the legal status of a CIO, not just its regulation as a charity).

Because of this process, it is not possible to pass a constitutional amendment at a CIO general meeting that takes effect immediately. So, for example, an amendment to the process of electing trustees passed at an AGM could not take effect until registered by the Charity Commission, and it would only therefore apply from the following year's AGM (even though a change of this kind is not a regulated alteration).

The CIO must send both the resolution itself, and a copy of the constitution as amended, so that the Charity Commission holds an up-to-date copy of the full constitution. (This is also useful for members and trustees, as it ensures that the constitution is kept up to date.) The notification must reach the Commission no later than 15 days after the resolution was passed (measured from the date of the general meeting, or when the last person agreed to a written resolution). If submitting a regulated alteration, be sure to attach a copy of the Commission's consent (or refer to the prior correspondence).

In the case of amendments to a CIO constitution containing entrenchment provisions, the CIO must also send a 'statement of compliance' to the

[60] Charities Act 2011, s. 227.

Charity Commission confirming that the amendment has been made in accordance with the entrenchment provision.[61] If the amendment does not affect anything covered by the entrenchment, the statement of compliance can simply confirm that no provisions were altered which required special approval under the entrenchment process and hence the amendment was passed under the normal procedures. But if, for example, the entrenchment clause required external approval for the change, the statement should confirm that this approval was obtained (and it would be wise to attach a copy of the relevant communication from the external authority concerned, although the Commission is allowed to accept the CIO's own assurances).

At the time of submitting the amendment to the Charity Commission, you will not know the actual date when the amendment will be registered, and hence exactly when the revised constitution takes effect. So it would wise to head the amended constitution with something like:

> Incorporating amendments agreed at a general meeting held on [date] to take effect from the date of registration of the amendments by the Charity Commission.

Then update the heading when you get the confirmation from the Commission that the amendment has been registered.

In straightforward cases, the Charity Commission is required to register the amendment, and the constitution as amended then takes effect. The Commission normally aims to respond to requests of this kind within 15 working days (though no specific time limit is written into the Charities Act). It follows that if an amendment needs to take effect by a certain date (such as by year end) it would be wise to pass it at least a month before the relevant deadline and notify the Commission immediately after the resolution is passed. (If it is vital for the amendment *not* to take effect until a specific date, the changes could be drafted so that within the constitution as amended – i.e. even when registered by the Commission – a particular provision only applies after a particular date, with the former arrangements applicable until then.)

[61] CIO General Regulations 2012, reg. 17.

However, the Charity Commission can refuse to register a constitutional amendment for a CIO (even if validly passed by the members) if:

- it is a regulated alteration and the Commission had not given prior consent;[62] or
- the amendment seeks to change the name of the CIO and the Commission has objections to the new name[63] (see page 91 regarding permissible names); or
- if the Commission considers that the CIO had no power to make the change[64] (for example, it can refuse amendments which would mean that the CIO was no longer a charity, or if the revised constitution would no longer meet the legal requirements).

It is, of course, possible that members who were unhappy with a decision could lobby the Commission not to register the amendment, but the Commission has no power to refuse to register an otherwise valid CIO constitutional amendment which was properly passed, simply because some members were unhappy.

If the CIO is registered with a constitution that includes entrenched provisions, the Charity Commission would also (it is hoped) refuse to register a change without the relevant 'statement of compliance'. Strictly speaking, it is the CIO which is at fault if it submits an amendment to an entrenched constitution without such a statement; but the Commission could then use its regulatory powers to require the trustees to obtain the necessary approvals and submit a statement of compliance.

[62] Charities Act 2011, s. 227(4).

[63] Charities Act 2011, s. 227(3)(b).

[64] Charities Act 2011, s. 227(3)(c).

7 CIO records, registers and communications

Once a CIO is formed and registered, the work of the charity needs to proceed, so that its charitable purposes can be carried out for public benefit. The charity trustees of the CIO will meet to take decisions, income will be raised, expenses will need to be paid, accounts will need to be kept and, except in the smallest charities, staff will need to be employed and premises will be required.

Many of these issues are not specific to CIOs, and will not be considered in detail in this book; however, see chapter 8 for more on the accounting issues, and chapter 17 on the rights of employees and third parties.

Why registers matter

The constitutional nature of a CIO means that the legislation requires certain procedures to be followed with regard to its members on the one hand, and its charity trustees on the other. If there is ever doubt as to who is a member and who is a trustee on a given date, it is a recipe for massive confusion, and if the issues cannot be resolved, expensive litigation can result.

In a foundation CIO the members and trustees will be the same people, but it is still important to keep the roles separate because when people meet as members they have different powers from when they meet as trustees. However, many CIOs will have a membership which is either wider or narrower than the trustees (as explained in chapters 5 and 6) and, in those cases, the distinction between members and trustees is critical.

This chapter focuses on the two registers which a CIO must maintain – the register of trustees and the register of members – and includes the all-important issue of confidentiality and who has access to the registers. It also considers the issues of membership applications, communications with members (and others) and the requirements for minutes.

Whilst the general principles in this chapter apply to all CIOs, the details below are specific to CIOs established in England and Wales. For differences in Scotland and Northern Ireland, see chapters 13 and 14 respectively. (Note, in particular, that the rules regarding registers of a SCIO differ somewhat from the requirements stated here.)

The terms 'association CIO' and 'foundation CIO' (as explained in chapter 5) are defined and used directly in the regulations regarding CIO registers,[1] so whilst those terms are not always helpful, they are used without quotes in this chapter.

Register of trustees

Every CIO must maintain a trustees' register,[2] which records the following details for each trustee:[3]

- name (forename and surname, including any former names – see below);
- address (this can be a service address – see further below);
- date of becoming a trustee;
- date of ceasing to be a trustee.

Former names only include names formerly used for 'business purposes' (this would include any charity roles, but a married woman who has changed her name, for example, and who always uses her birth name for business roles would not need to disclose her married name). Moreover, there is no need to record names which were changed before the age of 16, or former names last used more than 20 years ago.[4]

A trustee's service address could be a work address, for example, rather than the trustee's home address; however, it must be an address at which documents can be served by physical delivery and where acknowledgement of delivery can be obtained (i.e. a signature, so it cannot be a PO box). For individual trustees, it is permissible to put 'The principal office of the CIO' as the service address (provided it is a physical address) but this could have practical issues, as it means an official document for the trustee can just be left at the CIO's own office. So, where a CIO agrees to this, it is important to establish a clear arrangement for forwarding communications (unless trustees are regularly on the premises).

However, a trustee's home address must be disclosed on the Annual Return to the Charity Commission, so if the trustee wants to use a service address, it would be worth keeping a record of trustees' home addresses as an extra column on the register. The trustee's date of birth is also needed for this. Likewise, most CIOs will wish to record telephone numbers,

[1] CIO General Regulations 2012, reg. 2.

[2] CIO General Regulations 2012, reg. 26.

[3] CIO General Regulations 2012, Sch. 1 Part 2.

[4] CIO General Regulations 2012, Sch. 1 Part 4 para. 11.

email addresses, etc., for trustees. However, additional information of this kind would not be part of the statutory register of trustees.

In cases of serious problems with a charity, the Charity Commission has the power to suspend all the trustees and appoint an interim manager in their place (see page 237).[5] The interim manager then has all the normal powers of the charity trustees. If this happens with a CIO, the interim manager's details must be entered in the trustees' register (with a note that an interim manager has been appointed and the date).

Note that it is possible to have CIO trustees which are corporate bodies rather than natural persons (see page 72). In this case, the regulations require further information in the register – but in this book we only consider CIOs where the charity trustees are individuals.

In practice the trustees' register can be kept quite easily as a spreadsheet or word-processed document divided into columns (though paper records are fine if preferred). It would be wise to mark the columns clearly to distinguish statutory and non-statutory information in the event of an external party requesting access to the register (see page 125). But it would also be wise to make regular printouts, keep backups, and to ensure that the document remains usable as technological changes take place.

Note that the register must contain, in addition to the current trustees, the details of past charity trustees and the dates on which they ceased to be trustees. Unlike the position in Scotland (where records only have to go back six years), no time limit is specified in England and Wales and so this information should go back to the formation of the CIO. As such, over time, in a CIO with a rapidly changing trustee body, even the register of trustees may become a substantial document. A simple indicator to differentiate current from past trustees may be helpful. If a trustee steps down and is later reappointed it is best to create a completely new entry on the register, otherwise the former dates could be lost.

The register must be kept up to date as trustees join, leave or change address. Any change must be recorded within 28 days,[6] but there can be real problems if the information on trustees is out of date, so in practice changes should be recorded immediately.

In the case of a foundation CIO (where there is no separate register of members), in the rare event of members with different voting rights, the trustees' register must also record for each trustee the category of membership applicable. Whilst this will be very rare, it underlines the

[5] Charities Act 2011, s. 76.

[6] CIO General Regulations 2012, Sch. 1 Part 3, para. 5.

point that, even in a foundation CIO, membership and trusteeship involve different rights and powers.

Register of members

An association CIO must also keep a register of members.[7] An association CIO is defined as any CIO where the members and trustees are not the same – it does not have to have a large membership.[8]

The register of members must record the following details for each member:[9]

- name (but in the case of members there is no requirement for former names);
- address (this can be a service address – see below);
- category of membership (such as adult members or junior members, but this is only needed if the CIO has more than one class of members with different rights);
- date of becoming a member;
- date of ceasing to be a member.

Details of former members have to be kept for ten years from when the person ceased to be a member.

Even a single-member CIO is an association CIO and must therefore keep a register with details of the member. In fact, the regulations require a specific note that it is only a single-member CIO. If the number of members goes up from one (to have two or more members) or goes down to one, the dates on which it started or ceased to be a single-member CIO must be specifically recorded as additional notes in the register.[10] Because a CIO is defined in law as a corporate body with one or more members, if there is only one member that member should not resign unless a new member is appointed.

For members that are corporate bodies rather than individuals, it makes sense also to record details such as the legal form of the member and the company and/or charity registration information, where applicable. Curiously, however, the regulations only require this for corporate trustees of a CIO, rather than the much more common situation of a CIO with corporate members.

---

[7] CIO General Regulations 2012, reg. 26.

[8] CIO General Regulations 2012, reg. 2.

[9] CIO General Regulations 2012, Sch. 1 Part 1.

[10] CIO General Regulations 2012, Sch. 1 Part 1, para 2.

As with trustees, it is permissible for members to have service addresses (such as work addresses) rather than home addresses. The regulations also allow for the possibility of a member just putting 'The principal office of the CIO' as his or her service address. But for a CIO with a wide membership, this would mean keeping an entire supplementary list of members' normal addresses and it could mean that the CIO has the expense of sending on large numbers of communications from other members (see 'Access to the registers' on page 125). So, unless a CIO has a particular need to keep members' addresses secret even from other members, it may be sensible to make a rule in the conditions of membership to discourage this, for example by charging a much higher than normal subscription if a member wants to use the CIO's principal office as a service address.

The register of members must be kept up to date as members join or leave or change address and any change must be recorded within 28 days.[11] However, in the case of a request for access to the register you must be able to say whether any changes are outstanding,[12] so it is easier to make changes immediately.

If there are more than 50 members, the register of members must be kept in a form which creates a natural index, typically by keeping the names in alphabetical order (or, more helpfully, an alphabetical list of current members and a separate alphabetical list of past members).

Most CIOs with a wide membership will want to keep further information on members – typically, telephone numbers, email addresses, details of special interests, allocation to geographical sections and similar information. If members are required to pay a subscription, you will need to keep subscription records. Moreover, in many CIOs the members may be the main donors, and the information is likely to be combined with records of giving, bank details, status of gift aid claims, etc., using a suitable database system. However, in an association CIO with a more limited membership, a spreadsheet approach – as suggested for the trustees' register – may be sufficient.

All this information is additional to the statutory register of members, and does not have to be disclosed in response to an access request. Moreover, this additional information must not be disclosed unless members have agreed – it would amount to a breach of the Data Protection Act (see page 123) – except in cases such as crime prevention where the Data

[11] CIO General Regulations 2012, Sch. 1 Part 3, para. 5.

[12] CIO General Regulations 2012, Sch. 1 Part 3, para. 10.

Protection Act makes exceptions. If the CIO wants to be able to publish a full membership directory including telephone numbers, email addresses, etc., it would be worth making this clear on the membership form, so that new members give consent at the outset. In a CIO where members are primarily donors, it is likely that the members' register will be maintained by fundraising staff, so it is important that they understand the legal significance of the register for constitutional purposes, and the need to keep past members' details for ten years.

Uncertainty of membership: Charity Commission involvement

In a CIO (or any charity with a membership) disputes can arise as to who is or is not a member. For example, a crucial general meeting is called and people who thought they were members turn up to vote, but the trustees say that they are not eligible because they haven't renewed their subscriptions. But the (ex-)members concerned argue that they paid, but someone has mislaid the payment. Or perhaps a vote by the trustees was taken to exclude a disruptive member (after following the required procedures in the constitution) but the person argues that the decision was invalid because the relevant trustees' meeting was inquorate, and hence insists she is still a member.

These sorts of disputes can take up huge amounts of time and resources, and have sometimes even ended up in the courts. However, the Charities Act includes a simple power allowing the Charity Commission to determine who is and is not a member of a charity, and, in the case of a CIO, it can then require the register of members to be updated accordingly.[13] An application to the Commission to make such a determination can be requested by the charity itself (i.e. by a decision taken by a properly convened meeting of the CIO's trustees) or, in a serious situation where a charity is already subject to the Charity Commission inquiry, the Commission itself can decide it needs to clarify the membership. If necessary, the Commission can appoint an independent person to investigate the facts and make a decision on its behalf. (However, the Commission may need to be persuaded that the issue is important enough to justify its involvement.)

Of course, clear membership procedures and up-to-date registers should mean that it is only in the most exceptional situations that the Charity Commission is asked to get involved, but, for a CIO in difficulty, this power may be very helpful.

[13] Charities Act 2011, s. 111 and CIO General Regulations 2012, reg. 27.

Data Protection Act implications

The registers of members and trustees in a CIO will, of necessity, contain personal information (except in the special case of a CIO where all the members and trustees are corporate bodies rather than individuals). The registers must therefore be maintained in accordance with the Data Protection Act 1998. Even if the CIO does not hold any other personal records, it must comply with the Act with regard to the information held on these registers.

This means complying with the Data Protection Principles set down in the Act, as shown in the following box. The schedules referred to in principle 1 set out conditions for the processing of personal data, for example where the processing is necessary for a lawful purpose or where the data subject has given consent. If sensitive data is held – for example, racial origin, political opinions, religious beliefs, health – then additional conditions apply. The principles apply whether the information is held manually or on computer.

The Data Protection Principles[14]

1. *Personal data shall be processed fairly and lawfully and, in particular, shall not be processed unless –*
   - *(a) at least one of the conditions in Schedule 2 is met, and*
   - *(b) in the case of sensitive personal data, at least one of the conditions in Schedule 3 is also met.*
2. *Personal data shall be obtained only for one or more specified and lawful purposes, and shall not be further processed in any manner incompatible with that purpose or those purposes.*
3. *Personal data shall be adequate, relevant and not excessive in relation to the purpose or purposes for which they are processed.*
4. *Personal data shall be accurate and, where necessary, kept up to date.*
5. *Personal data processed for any purpose or purposes shall not be kept for longer than is necessary for that purpose or those purposes.*
6. *Personal data shall be processed in accordance with the rights of data subjects under this Act.*
7. *Appropriate technical and organisational measures shall be taken against unauthorised or unlawful processing of personal data and against accidental loss or destruction of, or damage to, personal data.*

[14] Data Protection Act 1998, s. 4 and Sch. 1 Part 1.

8 *Personal data shall not be transferred to a country or territory outside the European Economic Area unless that country or territory ensures an adequate level of protection for the rights and freedoms of data subjects in relation to the processing of personal data.*

In most cases the 'data controller' (i.e., the CIO in this case) must register with the Information Commissioner. This process is called 'notification' and involves payment of an annual fee (the fee is currently £35/year, except for very large organisations with more than 250 employees or more than £25.9 million turnover, for which the fee is £500/year).

Many charities hold a wide range of personal information and need to 'notify' under the Act. A CIO would not need to notify if it *only* holds the statutory information needed for the members' and trustees' registers,[15] but in practice almost all CIOs will want to hold more than the minimum information needed by law. However, there is also a broader exemption for not-for-profit bodies if information is held only for the purposes of:

- establishing or maintaining membership;
- supporting a not-for-profit body or association; or
- providing or administering activities for either the members or those who have regular contact with it.

To use this exemption there are also conditions on what processing can be undertaken (basically it must be limited to normal membership activities).[16] Also, bear in mind for a CIO where membership is limited to people of a particular faith, or to persons with a particular medical condition, the mere fact of recording someone's name as a member of the CIO means that you are recording 'sensitive personal data' relating to religion or health.

The not-for-profit exemption may be sufficient to cover certain CIO membership schemes, but for a CIO with a wide membership that provides a broad range of activities (and especially if data is also held on non-members) it will nearly always be necessary to notify under the Act. (The Information Commissioner's website www.ico.gov.uk provides a wide range of guidance on data protection issues, and for more specific guidance in the charity sector see *Data Protection for Voluntary Organisations* by Paul Ticher, published by Directory of Social Change.)

---

[15] Data Protection Act 1998, s. 34.

[16] See *The exemption from notification for 'not-for-profit' organisations* at www.ico.gov.uk.

Access to the registers

When the law allows a body to incorporate, a fundamental principle is that, subject to certain restrictions, external parties should have the right to know who is behind it. In particular, people normally have the right to know who the trustees are in a charity, and for a corporate body with members, who the members are. Understanding how these rights operate in a CIO is crucial.

Access to the register of trustees

Anyone is entitled to request access to the register of trustees (although the CIO can make a reasonable charge to cover copying and postage if the request comes from someone who is not a current member or trustee).[17] However, if a charity has been given dispensation by the Charity Commission not to publish trustees' names in its annual report,[18] the names of trustees covered by the dispensation (whether past or present) do not have to be disclosed[19] (see page 142 for more on the trustees' annual report – the TAR). This can be an important advantage of structuring the charity as a CIO (rather than as charitable company) if it has trustees involved in sensitive work whose identities should not be disclosed.

It is unlikely that someone will contact the CIO for access to the register if only the trustees' names are wanted, because these will normally be available from the Charity Commission website and disclosed in the TAR. But, because the Charity Commission does not maintain a public register with trustees' addresses, anyone wanting their addresses may make a formal request for access to the register.

If a valid request is received for the register of trustees, you must provide the trustees' names and their service addresses (and dates of starting/ceasing to be a trustee, including past trustees unless the request only relates to current trustees). If trustees do not want their personal addresses released, they may therefore wish to give their address on the register as a service address of the CIO's principal office (as outlined on page 121).

---

[17] CIO General Regulations 2012, Sch. 1 Part 3, para. 8.

[18] Such dispensations are given under the Charities (Accounts and Reports) Regulations 2008, regs 40 or 41.

[19] CIO General Regulations 2012, Sch. 1 Part 3, para. 9.

Access to the register of members

A much more significant issue for an association CIO with a wide membership is a request for access to the register of members, as this may mean providing information on hundreds or thousands of people. However, whilst the law generally allows access to the trustees' register, access to the members' register is more limited. Only someone who is currently a member or trustee can ask for a copy of the register of members. (There is an exception to this in the rare event of a CIO with a members' guarantee, but, as explained in earlier chapters, almost all CIOs will want to avoid members' guarantees.)

This right of access is, however, essential to the accountability of a CIO. If, for example, a number of members are unhappy with a key issue regarding the charity and wish to put a resolution to a general meeting of members, but the trustees refuse to call a meeting, the members concerned need to have the contact information for other members in order to circulate resolutions or to convene a meeting themselves (see clause 11(2) in the Charity Commission's model constitution in the Appendix).

It is important, therefore, when people become members of a CIO that they realise their names, addresses, and dates of joining and leaving (though no other details) can be made available to other members (and that this will apply for up to ten years after they cease to be a member if someone asks for details of ex-members as well as current members). But the notion of an association (on which an association CIO is based) is that people are coming together as members of the same charity and will be happy for their basic membership information to be shared with other members so that they can work together in exercising their rights and duties. Note that even if the CIO has a large membership, it cannot charge for access to the membership list by someone who is a current member.

If the principle of members having access to other members' addresses would cause difficulties, it would be possible for members to give the CIO's own address as their service address. However, as noted, this could leave the CIO with an expensive bill in forwarding letters sent by a member to all the other members. Alternatively, if the charity could potentially be established in Scotland and formed as a SCIO this may be better, as access to members' addresses can then be limited to the trustees (see chapter 13).

If access to the members' register would cause real problems which cannot be managed, it might be better to structure the CIO purely as a foundation CIO (where the only members are trustees) and to have a wider affiliation scheme whose participants are not legally members of the CIO with voting rights. Within a structure of this kind, it would be wise for all literature to describe those in the scheme as 'supporters' or 'friends' rather than 'members' because membership of a CIO has a legal meaning with rights and duties. This approach means that the CIO has no formal accountability to a wider body of members who have a direct role in electing trustees.

Starting the registers

When a new CIO is formed, it is easy to think that it is obvious who the initial members and trustees are and therefore to delay setting up registers. But as soon as one person joins or leaves, if the date is not noted, it becomes almost impossible to maintain a correct register.

So, as soon as confirmation is received that a CIO has been registered, it is strongly recommended that the registers are set up immediately (at this stage it may only take ten minutes with a spreadsheet). The initial members will be the applicants who asked for the CIO to be formed (see page 68) and the initial trustees will be the persons named in the constitution (though, for a foundation CIO, only a trustees' register is needed). In both cases the date of joining will be the date on which the CIO was formed.

The location of registers

The registers should be kept at the CIO's principal office, unless the trustees resolve to keep it at another address.[20] However, nowadays, the likelihood of anyone asking to inspect the register in person is remote – in most cases people will ask for an electronic copy. (You could, however, decide to provide a printed copy which is less easily used for generating mailings, if you foresee problems of that kind.)

Recruiting and registering new members

In a CIO with a wide membership it is important to be clear as to why people should become members. Are you encouraging everyone who supports the charity's aims to become a member? Or is membership only open to persons or organisations approved by the trustees? Is membership mainly about being a donor/supporter who receives regular communications and in return has the right to vote for trustees? Or is membership restricted to the specific client group (beneficiaries) that the

[20] CIO General Regulations 2012, Sch. 1 Part 3, para. 6.

charity will be working with? The CIO could be formed as an umbrella body where the members are other charities rather than individuals. In other CIOs, membership may be about having a commitment to a particular campaign, or it may be about a commitment to standards in a professional body. In the latter case, someone may have to complete a complex programme of training and assessment before becoming a member. However, remember that every charity must be established for public benefit, not for the benefit of its members (except in the case where beneficiaries have to become members for practical reasons, such as in a charitable sports club).

Whatever the approach, every CIO that is looking to enrol new members needs clear procedures to enable someone to join, and normally this will involve some kind of form (either paper-based or online) which a new member completes.

It is helpful if the form explains the charity's objects, the duties of members, details of subscriptions, and any other commitments. You may also want to point out the rule on access to members' addresses. If members will be donors, you may also wish to combine the membership form with a direct debit mandate or standing order and a gift aid declaration (membership subscriptions to a charity can be gift-aided if they do not lead to any personal benefits other than the right to receive information on a charity's work and the right to vote at an AGM). A possible form is shown in the following example; but this is only a starting point: each CIO will need to consider carefully what is needed for its own circumstances.

As membership forms come in, make sure that new members are promptly added to the register so that they receive appropriate communications (and of course, don't forget to thank them for their support!) Remember, too, that gift aid declarations must be kept for inspection when you have an HMRC gift aid audit (see *The Charity Treasurer's Handbook*, also published in this series, for more on gift aid).

A possible CIO Membership Form (for a CIO with a wide membership)

Upperton Health Forum CIO

A charitable incorporated organisation
Registered charity number #######
Principal office: 23 The High Street, Upperton UP1 1XW

Application to become a Member of the Charity

NAME: ....

ADDRESS: ....

....

EMAIL: ....

TEL: ....

- **I apply to become a Member of Upperton Health Forum CIO with immediate effect.**
- **I understand it is the duty of Members to use their powers, in good faith, to further the purposes of the charity.**
- **As a Member I understand that I will have the right to vote for Trustees at the AGM, and have other rights as specified in the Constitution, but that the day-to-day governance of the charity is in the hands of the Trustees.**
- **I understand that my details will be held on the charity's Register of Members, and that my name and address will be available to other Members if they wish to contact me.**
- **I may resign at any time, but as long as I remain a Member I undertake to support the charity by a donation/subscription of not less than £1 per year** (more if possible). If I resign, I understand that the charity will continue to hold details of past Members as required by law.

❑ I enclose an initial donation of £ ....

❑ Please send me a standing order form.

GIFT AID DECLARATION

If you are a taxpayer, we invite you to complete this declaration which will enable the charity to reclaim tax on your donations – please tick if applicable.

giftaid it

To: Upperton Health Forum CIO

❑ Please treat as Gift Aid donations all qualifying gifts of money I make today and in the future. I confirm I have paid or will pay an amount of Income Tax and/or Capital Gains Tax for each tax year (6 April to 5 April) that is at least equal to the amount of tax that all the Charities or Community Amateur Sports Clubs that I donate to will reclaim on my gifts for that tax year. I understand that other taxes such as VAT and Council Tax do not qualify. I understand the charity will reclaim 25p of tax on every £1 that I give.

Signed: .... Date: ....

Please return the completed form to [name] or to the charity's principal office as above.

Communication with members and trustees

Part of the reason for registers is not only to keep a legal record, but also to facilitate effective communication. Under the constitution of a CIO (see chapter 6) there are many situations where communications must be sent to members or trustees. It is important that these are handled correctly, in accordance with the constitution, to prevent later challenges.

One of the key issues is to ensure that communications are properly sent and, where necessary, documents are 'properly served' so that, in the event of a dispute, a member or trustee cannot complain that he or she didn't know about the meeting or resolution concerned.

Electronic communications

The CIO regulations allow for the possibility of electronic communications, but only if the person concerned (the member or trustee) has agreed to receive communications in that form.[21] However, if you are using a Charity Commission model constitution with the optional wording for electronic communication and someone gives an email address on a CIO membership form (for example), you are entitled to assume that they are consenting to receive any official CIO communications by email unless the person says otherwise (see clause 22(3)(a) in the Appendix).

It is possible in principle for members of the CIO to agree that communications can be sent purely by being posted on the CIO's website, but the details in the regulations regarding opt-outs from this, and minimum periods of providing information on a website, must be followed carefully.[22] Also it will not normally be appropriate to use websites for confidential announcements unless they are protected by suitable security, in which case you must be certain that members have been given the appropriate means of access. In most cases it will be safer to send emails whenever any communication needs to be circulated, though for non-confidential materials, you may wish to include a link to a website rather than sending huge attachments.

However, in all cases where information is sent electronically to a member (or where you do not send a document in full but only a link to a website) the member has the right to ask for the information in hard copy

[21] CIO General Regulations 2012, regs 49–52 & Sch. 3, paras 5–7.

[22] CIO General Regulations 2012, Sch. 3, paras 8–13.

form. In such a case, the printed version must be provided within 21 days, at no charge.[23]

The Charity Commission's model constitution includes provisions to clarify members' rights regarding electronic communications (see the Appendix, clause 22). However, it is acceptable for the constitution to prohibit or restrict the use of electronic communications.[24]

If the CIO sends out information by email, members are entitled to respond by the same means, so be sure to give a suitable address for replies.[25] It can be helpful to have a special email address for members to use for constitutional/voting issues so that such messages are not confused with general enquiries.

Valid communications

The most important issue in ensuring that communications are valid, on time, and (where necessary) properly served is, of course, to read the CIO's constitution and follow what it says! If the Charity Commission model has been used, provisions for proper communications with appropriate notice are clearly explained.

The Charity Commission's model (see clause 11(3)) requires a minimum of 14 days' notice to members if a general meeting is called (and many CIOs may wish to specify longer notice). The model does not specify a minimum notice period for trustees' meetings, but some CIOs may want to add this to prevent a few trustees from calling a meeting at short notice when others are unavailable.

The regulations state that information supplied by the CIO is deemed to be received 48 hours after posting (if sent by post to an address in the UK); or 48 hours after being sent by email (assuming it was properly addressed or emailed, with the correct postage if applicable). However, in calculating the 48-hour period, Saturdays, Sundays and public holidays are discounted.[26] See page 111 for some practical examples.

In most cases (for instance, calling meetings or circulating resolutions) it is sufficient to ensure that communications are sent on time following the required procedures. If a message was sent properly and the member didn't get it, it may be inconvenient or embarrassing, but it does not mean

---

[23] CIO General Regulations 2012, reg. 52.

[24] CIO General Regulations 2012, reg. 49.

[25] CIO General Regulations 2012, regs 50–51 & Sch. 2.

[26] CIO General Regulations 2012, reg. 53.

that any decision taken at the relevant meeting becomes invalid, so long as the CIO has records to show that it was sent properly.

However, if a communication is to be relied on as legally binding in terms of requiring action to be taken it must be 'served' on the CIO, the trustee, or member as appropriate. A document can only be served by delivering it in person or sending it by post to the specified address in hard copy form. In the case of communications to the CIO, this means sending it to the principal office, and in the case of communications to a member or trustee, it means sending to that person's address (this may be a service address) as shown in the register of members or trustees as applicable.[27] In order to be certain that a document was properly served, you will normally want to use recorded delivery if sending by post, or have an independent witness if the document was served by hand. (An exception applies if agreement is reached to accept service by email: in particular, formal documents can normally be served on the Charity Commission by email, if procedures given on the Commission's website are followed.)

Other records: minutes, accounts, etc.

Whilst the register of members and register of trustees have a particular significance, a CIO must, of course, keep proper records of *all* its affairs. The charity trustees are responsible for ensuring that the CIO keeps the required records.

Like all charities, a CIO must keep proper accounting records (see page 135), so as soon as a CIO is formed it is important to establish books, whether manual or computerised, to record all financial transactions.

A CIO must, by law, keep minutes of meetings. This includes minutes of trustees' meetings (and any other decisions taken by trustees such as by email, if the trustees agree to take decisions that way).[28]

A CIO must also keep minutes of general meetings and of resolutions passed by members without calling a meeting.[29] Even if the CIO only has a sole member, that member must tell the CIO any decisions which he, she or it takes as a member of the CIO, and these must be recorded.[30]

If the trustees have established sub-committees, minutes of these should also be kept, unless they are purely informal groups. But if the trustees have delegated certain decisions to a sub-committee, then decisions of a

[27] CIO General Regulations 2012, regs 47–48.

[28] CIO General Regulations 2012, reg. 37.

[29] CIO General Regulations 2012, reg. 41.

[30] CIO General Regulations 2012, reg. 43.

sub-committee would count as decisions made by trustees, and must therefore be recorded.

Remember that, even a foundation CIO will need to call a members' meeting for matters such as constitutional amendments, so in all CIOs separate minutes are needed for members' and trustees' meetings. Make sure that minutes are clearly labelled to show whether they relate to a members' meeting, a trustees' meeting, a sub-committee, or anything else. In particular, a member who is not a trustee has a right of access to minutes of general meetings (but not trustees' meetings) so, in an association CIO, it is vital that they are kept separate. If necessary, the CIO can charge the member a 'reasonable fee' for providing copies of minutes, for example, but you cannot charge the member just to look at them.[31]

For both members' meetings (general meeting) and trustees' meetings, the minutes must be kept for six years[32] (although many CIOs will want to keep a permanent record lasting indefinitely from the day on which the charity was formed – it can be really valuable to anyone writing a history of the organisation many years later).

In both cases, once the minutes are signed (either by the person who chaired the meeting, or the chair of the next trustees' meeting, or general meeting as appropriate) they are treated in law as formal evidence of decisions taken by trustees or members of the CIO (as applicable).[33]

Records may be kept electronically, but they must be capable of being printed in hard copy form.[34] They must be kept at the charity's principal office, unless the trustees resolve to use another specific address.[35] These rules apply to the registers, minutes, and any other records which must be kept in order to comply with the CIO regulations.

---

[31] CIO General Regulations 2012, reg. 41.

[32] CIO General Regulations 2012, regs 37(2) & 41(2).

[33] CIO General Regulations 2012, regs 38 & 42.

[34] CIO General Regulations 2012, reg. 46.

[35] CIO General Regulations 2012, reg. 44.

8 Accounting and reporting for CIOs

Financial statements at year end

As is the case for all charitable organisations, the trustees of a CIO must prepare financial statements at year end. Two separate documents are required:

- the trustees' annual report;
- the annual accounts.

However, most charities find it best to prepare them as one overall document, because the annual report and the accounts are closely related. The accounts of a charity make little sense without the trustees' report explaining the charity's objects and activities. Likewise, the trustees' report will include financial information such as the charity's reserves policy, which would be hard to understand without the accounts. Moreover, when filing the accounts with the appropriate charity regulator, it is considerably simpler if there is one overall document.

Except for the smallest charities (those with an income of not more than £25,000 in England and Wales) the accounts must include an independent scrutiny report by an independent examiner or auditor. Note that there is no lower limit for external scrutiny of the accounts in Scotland, nor in Northern Ireland (when implemented), so in these jurisdictions the accounts must always have at least an independent examiner's report attached (see chapters 13 and 14 for further details).

This chapter summarises some of the main issues in preparing annual reports and accounts for CIOs in England and Wales, especially where there are specific issues to consider for a CIO which would not apply to other charities. But what follows is only an overview; for more detailed guidance on charity finance and annual accounts (including more on Scotland and Northern Ireland) see *The Charity Treasurer's Handbook*, also published in this series.

Accounting records

As in all charities, the trustees of a CIO must keep proper books (or 'accounting records' to use the legal term) which are sufficient to show all the day-to-day transactions. No one – whether a treasurer or external accountant – can possibly produce year-end accounts without this information; and without financial information the trustees cannot take ongoing decisions.

Day-to-day records

In practice, the trustees will need to delegate the day-to-day financial management. In a small CIO run mainly by volunteers, the work may be done by one of the trustees acting as treasurer. A large CIO may have a finance department with several full-time staff. The law does not specify *how* the financial records are to be kept but they must be sufficient[1] to:

- record all amounts received and paid out, including the *reasons* for the payments and receipts;
- record the assets and liabilities of the charity (bank balances, cash in hand, fixed assets, amounts due to third parties, debts due to the charity, etc.);
- disclose the financial position of the charity with reasonably accuracy at any time; and
- enable the trustees to prepare the relevant year-end accounts.

The trustees must ensure that suitable arrangements are made for this – one of the key decisions when setting up a new charity as a CIO is to ensure that *someone* will take responsibility for the books from day one. In particular, most charities find themselves dealing with general (unrestricted) funds as well as funds that are held for specific purposes (restricted funds) and even endowment funds. Therefore, in most cases, whatever system is used needs to allow for fund accounting. See *The Charity Treasurer's Handbook* for more detailed guidance.

The accounting records (the books and supporting documents) and the annual report and accounts must be kept for six years after the relevant year end.[2] As such, a CIO which has been operating for some time will need at least seven years of records: for the current year and six prior years. In the event of a CIO being dissolved (see chapters 11 and 12) the last trustees are responsible for ensuring that records are kept for this

[1] Charities Act 2011, s. 130.

[2] Charities Act 2011, ss. 131 & 134.

time, even though the CIO itself no longer exists (unless permission is obtained from the Charity Commission to destroy them).

The books of a new CIO

Where a new CIO is established, the books need to start with a zero balance on the day it was incorporated and registered as a charity. Then, as funds are received, it will start to have some assets to show.

If there was a former unincorporated charity which is being wound up and transferred to the CIO (see chapter 9), the funds transferred will be one of the first receipts in the CIO's books, but the CIO's accounts still start from £nil. Moreover, when an unincorporated charity converts to a CIO, remember that the CIO is a completely new legal entity and needs its own set of accounts: it is best to start a complete new set of books, whether manual or computerised.

However, in the case of a charitable company or other corporate body which converts directly to a CIO (see chapter 10), no new entity is created and so there is no need to start a new set of books. The accounting records will continue as normal until the first year end as a CIO is reached.

Financial years

As with other charities, the trustees of a CIO are free to choose any year end which suits the charity's work. Charities that are heavily dependent on public sector funding often find it convenient to work to a 31 March year end. Those working in schools and other activities linked to the academic year often find an accounting year that ends 31 July or 31 August works best. Many charities, especially religious organisations, use a 31 December year end. The financial year does not even have to finish at the end of a month; for example, if a charity has much of its income through gift aid donations it may be easiest to work to a 5 April year end so that the accounts tie up exactly with the tax year.

The first financial year of a new CIO will often be for a period which is not exactly 12 months, because it must start from the date on which the CIO was formed.[3] For example, if a CIO is registered on 11 February 2014 and the trustees decide to work to a 31 March year end, the first accounts will cover a period of 13½ months from 11 February 2014 to 31 March 2015. This is the case even if the CIO does not receive any funds until 1 April 2014 – the first accounts must start from the date of incorporation.

[3] Charities (Accounts and Reports) Regulations 2008, reg. 3(2).

On the other hand, if the CIO is formed on 3 September 2014 and starts active work on 1 October 2014, but the trustees still want to use a 31 March year end, the first financial period will cover just less than 7 months from 3 September 2014 to 31 March 2015. In cases like this, the regulations allow a charity to prepare accounts for any period between 6 and 18 months.[4]

However, where a CIO is formed a long time before it starts work, it may be necessary to prepare accounts where all figures are nil until work begins. For example, consider a CIO which is registered on 24 July 2013, receives its first funds on 1 April 2014 and prepares accounts to a 31 March year end. The first accounts cannot run from 24 July 2013 to 31 March 2015 because that is more than 18 months. So it will be necessary to prepare an initial set of accounts with nil figures that cover just over 8 months from 24 July 2013 to 31 March 2014. Then the first active accounts will cover the 12 months from 1 April 2014 to 31 March 2015.

Sometimes accountants refer to accounts such as these with no financial movements as 'dormant accounts', but the legal concept of dormant accounts only applies under company law – there is no direct equivalent for CIOs and other non-company charities. Therefore, if a CIO has an accounting period in which all the figures are nil, accounts should still be produced in the normal way, showing the nil figures, and a trustees' report is still needed. In particular, the report will need to explain what plans the trustees are making for the future to advance the charity's purposes for public benefit.

Thresholds for accounts preparation, scrutiny and filing

The Charities Act 2011 includes a number of financial thresholds, mostly based on the gross income of the charity, which determine the minimum requirements for accounts preparation and scrutiny, as shown in table 8.1. Note that there are some differences in the case of a CIO with a subsidiary trading company (see page 153). Also, remember that this table is specific to CIOs established in England or Wales and registered with the Charity Commission (see chapters 13 and 14 for SCIOs and Northern Ireland CIOs).

Except in one respect (see page 140) the thresholds are exactly the same for CIOs as for other non-company charities: CIOs are *not* subject to any of the special accounting rules that are applicable to charitable companies. So it is perfectly possible for CIOs with an income of up to £250,000 to prepare their year-end accounts on the receipts and payments basis if the trustees consider this appropriate and if funders are happy with this.

[4] Charities (Accounts and Reports) Regulations 2008, reg. 3(4).

Table 8.1 Financial thresholds for CIOs in England & Wales (see text for an explanation of abbreviations)

Gross income of CIO	Minimum requirements for *presentation* of the accounts	Mininum requirements for *scrutiny* of the accounts
£0 to £25,000	Receipts and payments accounts with a statement of assets and liabilities	Approval by trustees
£25,000 to £250,000	Receipts and payments accounts with a statement of assets and liabilities	Independent examination (lay examiner)
£250,000 to £500,000	Accruals accounts (SOFA, balance sheet and notes) prepared in accordance with the Charities SORP,[5] subject to certain simplifications)	Independent examination (professionally qualified examiner)[6]
More than £500,000	Accruals accounts (SOFA, balance sheet and notes) prepared in accordance with the Charities SORP, applied in full)	Audit

These requirements are considered in the section starting on page 142, but remember that these are the *minimum* requirements in law. Donors, funders or members of a CIO, or anyone lending to the CIO or giving it credit, may well want more than this. For example, many funders prefer to see

[5] *Accounting and Reporting by Charities: Statement of Recommended Practice* (Charity Commission, 2005). A new SORP is expected to take effect in 2014.

[6] In the rare case of a charity in the £250,000 to £500,000 income band having more than £3.26 million of assets, an audit is needed even though the income is less than £500,000 (Charities Act 2011, s. 144(1)(b)). However, Lord Hodgson's review of the Charities Act 2006 has recommended dropping this and the government has agreed to consider this.

accounts prepared in accordance with the Charities SORP, especially for charities with an income of more than £100,000 (and in such cases the Charity Commission recommends use of a professionally qualified independent examiner) even though receipts and payments accounts scrutinised by a lay examiner are legally permissible for an income of up to £250,000. (In some cases, additional requirements of this kind could even be written into the constitution of a CIO, though there are no additional provisions of this kind in the Charity Commission models.)

When making choices on the presentation and scrutiny of accounts, it is important to remember that a CIO is a corporate body with limited liability. So, firms which are considering doing business with a CIO may want to make some kind of credit assessment, because they cannot pursue individual trustees for payment if the CIO does not meet its obligations. The published accounts are the key resource used for this purpose. This is especially important if a CIO is taking on major commitments (such as to a landlord). So the trustees of a CIO may wish to adopt higher standards for the accounts than they would for an unincorporated charity of the same size.

Filing of report and accounts with the Charity Commission

The rules for CIOs on the filing of accounts with the Charity Commission are different compared with other registered charities. With a CIO, the annual report and accounts must *always* be filed with the Charity Commission regardless of the income.[7] (With other charities, the annual report and accounts only have to be sent to the Charity Commission in years when the income is more than £25,000.) At one level this may seem as if it is an extra burden, but in practice the availability of every CIO's accounts from the Charity Commission website (regardless of income) may well promote greater confidence in the accountability of CIOs.

Make sure that everyone appreciates this point, because many treasurers and accountants, even those who work extensively with charities, may assume that no accounts have to be filed for charities with incomes of less than £25,000. However, as we have just outlined, this exemption does *not* apply to CIOs. The reason for requiring *all* CIOs to file accounts with the Charity Commission is because a CIO is a corporate body with limited liability, and so, as noted, it is vital for those who are dealing with a CIO, such as those providing goods and services on credit, to have an easy means of getting access to its accounts. (Most other limited liability bodies are companies, and their accounts are available from Companies House, but because a CIO is not a company, it has no accounts to file at Companies House.)

---

[7] Charities Act 2011, s. 163(3).

The annual report and accounts must reach the Commission within ten months of the CIO's year end,[8] otherwise the trustees are in breach of the Charities Act 2011 and the Commission will take steps, such as marking the CIO's entry on the Register of Charities with a red border, with links to any other charities with common trustees. Most funders also take serious note of overdue accounts. Moreover, the CIO's credit rating is likely to suffer seriously if accounts are overdue. So, whilst it is important for all charities to file their accounts promptly with the Charity Commission, it is doubly important for a CIO.

It is worth noting, however, that the ten-month time limit for filing accounts under charity law is longer than the corresponding period of nine months for private companies to file their accounts at Companies House.[9] Credit rating agencies may be unaware of this difference between company law and charity law, and may think that a CIO's accounts are overdue if they have not been filed with the Charity Commission by nine months after year end. Moreover, a nine-month time limit applies for charities that are registered in Scotland (including SCIOs) to file their accounts with OSCR.[10] So, in reputational terms, there is much to be said for CIOs in England and Wales getting their accounts filed with the Charity Commission, at the very latest, by nine months after year end.

Most CIOs will choose to file their accounts electronically by uploading a PDF to the Charity Commission website, using the logon details provided when the CIO was registered. However, a CIO could submit paper accounts by post to the Commission, if preferred.

If filing electronically, the Charity Commission does not require the PDF to contain original signatures, but it must show the date on which the report and accounts were approved by the trustees and the names of those who signed.[11] The same applies with the report of the auditor or independent examiner. A CIO will *not* have met its legal obligations if the electronic copy just shows 'Approved by the trustees on............... and signed by...............' with no details entered. Whilst all registered charities must file a copy of the report and accounts as signed, this is doubly important for CIOs because of their limited liability status and the consequent comparison with companies when it comes to credit rating issues.

---

[8] Charities Act 2011, s. 163(1)(a).

[9] Companies Act 2006, s. 442(2)(a).

[10] Charities Accounts (Scotland) Regulations 2006, reg. 5(1).

[11] Charities (Accounts and Reports) Regulations 2008, reg. 40(2)(c)(iii).

The format of the report and accounts

As explained in table 8.1, charities in England and Wales, including CIOs, have two possible formats for preparing their year-end accounts:

- receipts and payments accounts with a statement of assets and liabilities;[12] or
- accruals accounts complying with the Charities SORP;[13]

These are considered on pages 146 and 148, respectively. For all registered charities, including CIOs, a trustees' annual report (referred to in the rest of this chapter as a 'TAR') is required alongside. It is a matter of negotiation between the CIO trustees, staff (if applicable) and the auditor or independent examiner as to who does what in terms of preparing the documents. In many cases it is helpful to use the expertise of the auditor or examiner to help with the final presentation, but it is important to remember that the production of the report and accounts is the *trustees' responsibility*. Any input from an auditor or examiner at the preparation stage is purely to assist the trustees in their duty. The CIO trustees therefore need a clear understanding of the requirements and must take full responsibility for approving the report and accounts once drafted (and for seeking amendments if they are not happy).

The trustees' annual report

The TAR is a vital document which explains the constitutional basis of the charity and how it has carried out its work in the relevant year (the TAR should always be based on the same financial year as the accounts).

The legal requirements for the TAR are set out in regulations,[14] and explained more clearly in the initial pages of the *Statement of Recommended Practice: Accounting and Reporting by Charities*, known as the 'Charities SORP'. Many people think the SORP is only relevant with accruals accounts (see below) but the requirements for the TAR apply even if the accounts will be on the receipts and payments basis.

A common format for a TAR is as shown in the following example. Some of the key issues to bear in mind when preparing a TAR for a CIO (as opposed to other types of charity) are as follows.

[12] Charities Act 2011, s. 133.

[13] Charities Act 2011, ss. 132, 162, 163 and Charities (Accounts and Reports) Regulations 2008.

[14] Charities (Accounts and Reports) Regulations 2008, reg. 40.

A typical format for the TAR

<Name of Charity> CIO

Trustees' Annual Report for the Year Ending dd mmm yyyy

I: Legal and Administrative Details

- Official name, principal office, registered charity number etc.
- Trustees
- Details of governing document (CIO constitution and date last amended)
- Objects of charity

II: Explanation of the Work of the Charity

- Description of the work of the year (in relation to the public benefit requirement)
- Objectives and Activities*
- Achievements and Performance*
- Financial Review*
- Plans for Future Years*

(For small charities, it is permitted just to give a brief review of main activities and achievements, but the explanations should still link to the principle of public benefit.)

III: Organisation and Sources of Support

- Organisational Structure*
- Sources of Funding*
- Contribution of Volunteers*

IV: Policies

- Confirmation that the trustees have considered the Charity Commission guidance on public benefit
- Trustee induction policy*
- Grant-making policy*
- Investment policy* and review of investment performance*
- Reserves policy
- Risk assessment* and systems used to manage risk*
- Assets held for other charities [if applicable]

Trustees' approval and signature

**For smaller charities below the audit threshold (normally £500,000 income) these sections can be omitted.*

The legal and administrative details at the start of the TAR must make clear that the legal form of the charity is a charitable incorporated organisation (it would be helpful to spell this in full) and its governing document will be the latest version of its constitution. It is useful (though not compulsory) to give the date of incorporation. If the CIO was formed to replace a former unincorporated charity, make sure that the charity registration number is the new number given to the CIO. The charity address will be the CIO's principal office (see page 93).

The initial administrative section will include details of the charity trustees of the CIO (on the date when the TAR was approved, together with any changes in trustees since the beginning of the financial year). However, in the case of a CIO where trustees could be in danger if they were named in the report, it is possible to apply to the Charity Commission for authorisation[15] to allow the trustees' names to be omitted from the TAR. This is common, for example, in domestic violence charities. This ability to omit the trustees' names for sensitive charities (with Charity Commission consent) is a significant attraction of the CIO form (when compared with charitable companies). Under the regulations, a request could also be made to omit the principal office address, but since a CIO can have a PO box as its principal office, this will rarely be needed: a charity is likely to lose out on donations and other support if there is no means of sending postal communications.

The legal and administrative details must explain who has the right to appoint trustees. So if the CIO has members other than trustees, it will often make sense to explain the criteria for membership (if members have to be approved by trustees, make this clear). It will usually also help to say how many members there were at year end. The report should explain that trustees are elected by the members at the AGM (if some trustees are nominated or ex officio, make this clear). In the case of a foundation CIO where the trustees are also the members, a simple statement on those lines will suffice. In an association CIO, it is not necessary to list the individual CIO members (and in most cases it would be a breach of confidentiality to do so). But if the CIO has only a very small number of members who can thus control the appointments, they should be named; for example it might be appropriate to state:

> The CIO was formed by three existing charities ABC, PQR, and XYZ, and these charities are the members of the CIO who determine the election of trustees.

The explanation of the work of the charity must focus on how the CIO has carried out its charitable objects for public benefit – this is known as the requirement for 'public benefit reporting', which has applied to all registered charities since 2008. It is important to focus on the objects of the charity, the beneficiaries, the activities, explaining how the activities lead to benefit for the beneficiaries. As explained in chapter 2, a charity does not have to benefit

[15] Under the Charities (Accounts and Reports) Regulations 2008, reg. 40(4).

the entire public – for many charities the beneficiaries are a section of the public – but the TAR must explain clearly who benefits and how. If the CIO has a wide membership it is important to be clear whether the members are the beneficiaries. Often the members are the people most directly involved on a day-to-day basis, but the beneficiaries may be much wider.

In the case of a newly formed CIO taking over the work of an existing charity, the narrative section will need to explain this, for example:

> The CIO was formed on 11 February 2014 to take over the work of the former unincorporated charity [name and registered charity number]. The members/trustees of the former charity resolved that it should be wound up from 31 March 2014 and all work transferred to the CIO. Five of the CIO trustees were also trustees of the former charity, but two new trustees were appointed when the CIO was formed. The CIO trustees met regularly during this period to agree arrangements for the transfer, and all assets and staff of the former charity were transferred to the CIO from 1 April 2014.

The section of the TAR dealing with organisational structure is usually concerned with staffing, but it can also be used to explain the membership structure if appropriate, especially if there are committees on which members who are not trustees are represented.

Most of the TAR elements shown under 'Policies' in the typical TAR format on page 143 are only needed by larger charities over the audit threshold, but trustees of all registered charities need to confirm that they have considered the Charity Commission guidance on public benefit (this is a legal requirement under the Charities Act).[16] In addition, every TAR, whatever the size of the charity, must include details of the charity's reserves policy. Because a CIO is a limited liability body, the reserves policy is particularly important to show that the trustees are confident that the charity can meet its obligations and can continue as a going concern.

If you are preparing a TAR for a CIO which has taken over from another type of charity, take care with terminology. A CIO has a principal office, not a registered office, it is governed by its charity trustees (not a management committee or directors), and there should be no references to a 'company secretary' or any similar concepts under company law. Take care to talk about 'the charity' or 'the CIO' rather than 'the trust', 'the association' or 'the company' (unless any of the latter terms are part of the actual name for the CIO).

Some charities like to prepare a glossy report at year end which is separate from the trustees' annual report needed by law. A CIO is free to

[16] Charities Act 2011, s. 17(5).

do this if the trustees feel that it would be beneficial, but it is best to call this the *Annual Review* to avoid confusion with the trustees' annual report required by law. However, it is worth noting that there is nothing to prevent inclusion of pictures, case studies, etc. in the statutory TAR so long as it also includes all the information needed by law. In many cases it is simpler to prepare one document which contains *all* the information needed by external stakeholders. But if a CIO decides to prepare a separate annual review, take care that any financial information included is reviewed by your auditor or independent examiner. If the financial information amounts to a set of 'summary accounts', an additional report on this summary information is needed.

Annual accounts: receipts and payments basis (including additional requirement for CIOs)

The receipts and payments (R&P) basis for preparing the accounts is generally considered to be simpler and easier for smaller charities, and a potential advantage of the CIO structure (compared with charitable companies) is the option of providing year-end accounts on this basis for CIOs with an income of up to £250,000. However, as explained below, the CIO regulations make a small addition to the normal requirements for R&P accounts.

But before preparing CIO accounts on the R&P basis, make sure that trustees, members, funders and lenders (if applicable) will be happy: some funders and lenders may insist on accruals (SORP-based) accounts even for charities with an income of less than £250,000 income.

The main statement in a set of R&P accounts – the 'receipts and payments account' – just records money in and money out. Everything appears in the accounts in the year when the payment or receipt occurred (without considering amounts due in one year but paid in a different year). So, if the books are kept on a cash basis and are properly closed off at year end, it is relatively easy to convert them to the required format at year end.

However, the principles of fund accounting (see page 136) are an essential element of trust law, so if the CIO has restricted funds, these must be clearly separated in the R&P account.

Whilst a charity preparing R&P accounts does not have to produce a full balance sheet at year end, it must provide a 'statement of assets and liabilities' (SOAL) alongside the R&P account. The SOAL summarises the position at year end for all the assets (such as bank balances, investments, cash in hand, tangible assets such as equipment, debtors owing money to the charity such as gift aid tax refunds awaited) and the liabilities (for example year-end creditors where amounts are due to third parties, loans outstanding, fees due to the independent examiner). It is helpful (though not mandatory) to give monetary values for all the assets and liabilities, although some values may just be trustees' estimates. If values are provided, the SOAL can be totalled to give an overall figure for 'net assets' for the charity as a whole. However, unlike a balance sheet, the SOAL does not balance with anything else; it is simply a list of assets and liabilities.

Whilst funders and supporters may be interested mainly in the R&P account, the SOAL is very significant in the accounts of a CIO – even more so than for other small charities. Many small companies file abbreviated accounts at Companies House which contain no more than a simplified balance sheet, the contents of which are actually very similar to a SOAL. Banks and credit agencies make extensive use of these abbreviated balance sheets for assessing the credit-worthiness of small companies, and it is likely that the SOAL filed by a smaller CIO will have similar importance. It is certainly worth presenting the SOAL with clear headings, and giving figures (even if only estimates) for all assets and liabilities.

There are no formal regulations in England and Wales for R&P charity accounts and, apart from one small addition for CIOs (see below), no mandatory rules on notes to the accounts. So it is possible to prepare the R&P accounts and SOAL in any format that is felt to be suitable, although the Charity Commission provides recommendations as part of its publication, *CC16 – Receipts and Payments Accounts Pack*. This includes templates which can be downloaded to use as a basis if desired (including a template for the TAR). There is no reason why these cannot be used for smaller CIOs, although some people find the forms inflexible and prefer to prepare the report and accounts from scratch.

The CIO regulations do, however, stipulate that if R&P accounts are used for a CIO, two specific notes must be added to the SOAL where applicable:[17]

(a) the notes must include particulars of any guarantee given by the CIO (if still in force at year end): for instance if the CIO has agreed to underwrite the costs of an event or project run by another organisation or if has underwritten a commitment on behalf of a beneficiary or if it has given a guarantee to the trustees of a former unincorporated charity; and

[17] CIO General Regulations 2012, reg. 62.

(b) the notes must include any debt outstanding at year end which is a secured charge on an asset of the CIO, for example if it has a property with a mortgage outstanding, or in the rare event of a CIO with a floating charge (see page 330), the details must be given.

These are not necessarily extra requirements for a CIO, as a well-prepared SOAL for *any* charity using R&P accounts should include these disclosures if applicable. However, if they are omitted, readers may wonder if they have simply been overlooked. So, if neither of these is needed, it could help to add a note saying:

> The trustees confirm, in accordance with the Charitable Incorporated Organisations (General) Regulations 2012, that at year end the CIO did not have any outstanding guarantees to third parties nor any debts secured on assets of the CIO.

Further guidance on the presentation of an R&P account and SOAL is provided in *The Charity Treasurer's Handbook.*

Annual accounts – accruals/SORP basis

Charities with an income of more than £250,000, including CIOs, must prepare their accounts on an 'accruals basis' and the format and presentation must comply with *Accounting and Reporting by Charities Statement of Recommended Practice*, which, as noted, is known as the 'Charities SORP'.[18]

The accruals basis means that figures in the accounts show income earned and costs incurred for the relevant financial year. This will often give a different result from the R&P basis once provision is made for transactions which spread across more than one year. The differences between the R&P and accruals basis typically result from debtors and creditors (which may arise in one year but the physical payment occurs in the following year) and from depreciation where the cost of assets such as vehicles or equipment are spread across a number of years.

Accruals accounts are more complex to prepare, but they are generally seen to be more useful in assessing the financial strength of an organisation because they are prepared to give a 'true and fair view' of the income, expenses, and the assets and liabilities at year end, whereas R&P accounts only give a factual statement of money in and out (and a list of balances on the SOAL). With accruals accounts it is possible to make much more meaningful comparisons from year to year, and between different charities.

---

[18] The SORP is published by the Charity Commission on behalf of the SORP Committee. At the time of writing the current version is SORP 2005 (updated with a new introduction in 2008). However, a new Charities SORP is expected in 2014.

Accruals accounts require estimates and judgements (for example whether an asset should be depreciated over three years or five, or whether or not a promised donation should be recognised as a debtor). So there is not always a 'right answer' – different people preparing accruals accounts for a given charity might produce different results, but the notes to the accounts should explain any judgements made so that the reader can understand the basis for the decisions. Ultimately these issues of accounting policies are a matter for the trustees, but they will normally take guidance from the treasurer, finance officer, or the auditor or independent examiner.

To give a true and fair view, accruals accounts must follow relevant accounting standards, and in the case of a charity, the SORP is central to this. Although the SORP is called a statement of 'recommended' practice, many of its provisions are directly referred to in the regulations under the Charities Act 2011,[19] so most of the SORP is, in practice, compulsory for charity accounts on the accruals basis.

Charity accounts presented under the SORP comprise two main statements: a 'statement of financial activities' (SOFA) and a balance sheet. The SOFA is primarily an income and expenditure account divided into columns for different types of funds; it also shows movements due to revaluation of assets (such as changes in the values of investments), if applicable. The year end totals on the SOFA have to balance with the balance sheet.

Alongside the SOFA and balance sheet, a wide range of information has to be given in notes. These are listed in regulations[20] and amplified in the SORP. These include an explanation of accounting policies, details of the individual funds of the charity, staff costs, grants made, and details of any transactions with trustees or 'connected persons' (see page 31).

The SORP includes a number of simplifications which can be used by charities with incomes that fall below the audit threshold, which will be useful for CIOs with incomes of less than £500,000.[21] The main concession is that the figures on the SOFA for incoming resources and resources expended do not have to be broken down on a 'functional basis'. This means the resources expended do not have to be split between fundraising costs, expenditure on charitable activities and governance costs as normally required for SORP accounts. Rather, the resources expended can be split under natural headings (such as salaries, premises, travel and stationery) or on any basis which the trustees feel is appropriate.

[19] Charities (Accounts and Reports) Regulations 2008, reg. 8(5).

[20] Charities (Accounts and Reports) Regulations 2008, Sch. 2.

[21] SORP 2005 Appendix 5.

It is important to note that, apart from these concessions, the SORP must be applied in full by any charity preparing accruals accounts (if for some reason this is impossible, a note is needed to explain any departures from the SORP).[22] So, the SORP cannot be applied on an *ad hoc* basis – the accounts of a CIO must be prepared *either* on the R&P basis *or* fully in accordance with SORP. Apart from the point above, there is no half-way house.

Most accountants who specialise in charities are very familiar with the Charities SORP, and users of charity accounts (such as funders) are familiar with accounts prepared on this basis.

In the case of a CIO, the SORP will be applied in the same way as for other charities of the same size, so there are few significant differences to consider. However, it is worth noting that in the case of charitable companies, the SORP includes a number of additional issues which must be considered in order to ensure that the accounts comply with company law.[23] For example, if there are movements on endowment funds, a charitable company needs a separate income and expenditure account to comply with the Companies Act 2006 as well as the SOFA. But because a CIO is *not* a company, these provisions are not relevant even though the CIO is an incorporated charity. Similarly, a number of provisions which charitable companies have to include in the trustees' report, and additional declarations made by company directors on a balance sheet when 'small company' provisions are used, can be omitted by a CIO.

So, even when a CIO's accounts are prepared on the accruals basis following the SORP, they will generally be slightly simpler than accounts for a charitable company of the same size and more like those of an unincorporated charity.

External scrutiny of the accounts

As shown in table 8.1, there are potentially four levels of external scrutiny which can apply to the accounts of a charity,[24] including a CIO:

- approval of the accounts by the trustees only (with no external scrutiny) (this is allowed for charities with incomes of up to £25,000);
- review by a lay independent examiner (for charities with incomes of up to £250,000);
- review by a professionally-qualified independent examiner (for charities with incomes of up to £500,000)
- full professional audit (compulsory for those with incomes greater than £500,000).

---

[22] Charities (Accounts and Reports) Regulations 2008, Sch. 2, para. 1(1)(v).

[23] SORP 2005 paras 419–429.

[24] Charities Act 2011, ss. 144–145.

For more on these regimes, see chapter 8 in *The Charity Treasurer's Handbook*. An independent examination (IE) is a less demanding form of scrutiny than a full audit, and the IE gives a negative assurance which states 'no matter came to my attention...', rather than a positive assurance that in the auditor's opinion the accounts 'give a true and fair view'. However, the framework for IE is laid down in detail by regulations[25] and by Directions of the Charity Commission,[26] so it is a demanding process: the independent examiner can only give the assurance that no matters came to his or her attention if he or she is satisfied after following the ten stages in the Directions. Most funders are very happy for charities in the relevant bands to have an IE rather than an audit, and most trustees of CIOs whose incomes fall below the audit threshold will want to take advantage of this.

The financial thresholds are the same for CIOs as for other charities in England and Wales, but it is important to make sure that your auditor or independent examiner fully understands the status of the charity as a CIO, and conducts the audit or examination on that basis. The wording of an audit or IE report for a CIO is essentially the same as for an unincorporated charity and all legal references will be to the Charities Act 2011. (This is very different from the audit or IE of a charitable company, where the report will refer to various provisions of the Companies Act 2006.)

Whilst the audit and IE thresholds are the same, it is important to remember that, unlike other registered charities, the report and accounts of a CIO must be filed with the Charity Commission even if its income is less than £25,000. So whilst it is *permissible* in CIOs at this level for the trustees to approve the accounts themselves without any external scrutiny, it is worth bearing in mind that the accounts will be widely available, and the support of an independent examiner may be very helpful. Where an unincorporated charity has converted to a CIO, the trustees will often wish to continue with the same auditor or examiner as before; but as the CIO is a new charity, a fresh engagement letter will be needed.

The duties of an auditor or independent examiner are substantially the same whatever the charity's legal form, but there are important issues that the auditor or examiner will need to consider regarding the CIO as a

[25] Charities (Accounts and Reports) Regulations 2008, reg. 31.

[26] *Independent Examination of Charity Accounts: Examiners' Guide* (Charity Commission 2012, ref. CC32) – the Directions to independent examiners are made under the Charities Act 2011, s. 145(5)(b).

corporate body. In particular he or she will need to check that all assets of the charity are properly vested in the CIO. It is not unusual when unincorporated charities convert to a corporate form (whether a CIO or a charitable company) to find that some assets have not been transferred and are still held in the names of individual trustees of the former charity (see chapter 9 for more on such conversions). This is not just an issue with land and buildings – for example, if funders have not agreed to a charity converting to a CIO, it could be that a large sum outstanding on a funding agreement which is shown as a debtor in the CIO accounts is really a debt due to the trustees of the former charity. Sometimes a bank will agree to transfer an account, rather than requiring the CIO to open a new bank account, but if so the account name must be changed to that of the CIO. So, particularly when a conversion has taken place, there are important issues for auditors and independent examiners to look out for.

Where a professionally qualified independent examiner is needed, the examiner must be a member of a relevant professional body as specified in the Charities Act.[27] This includes members of the six chartered accountancy bodies in the UK, Fellows of the Association of Charity Independent Examiners, and members of three other bodies. The examiner must, of course, comply with regulations of the professional body concerned: some only allow members to conduct independent examinations if they hold a practising certificate or have achieved a certain level of membership.

Because of the CIO's status as a limited liability body, as part of the review process an auditor or independent examiner will need to consider whether it is able to meet its obligations – in particular, whether the CIO is able to continue as a going concern (see chapter 12 for issues of CIO insolvency).

The duties will include checking any secured debts or guarantees given in order to ensure that the additional CIO notes needed for R&P accounts have been included if applicable (see page 147). Whilst an auditor or independent examiner is unlikely to miss a secured loan, smaller charities do not always think to mention guarantees given to third parties.

It is worth noting that if auditors or independent examiners identify serious matters which they believe are of 'material significance' to the Charity Commission's regulatory powers, these must be reported directly to the Commission.[28] This duty overrides the normal duty of confidentiality. This applies to auditors and examiners acting for

[27] Charities Act 2011, s. 145(3)&(4).

[28] Charities Act 2011, s. 156.

charities of all kinds, but whilst the status of a CIO provides some legal protection to the trustees, it is important to remember that they could still be reported to the Commission in such cases.

However, for most CIOs, the relationship with the auditor or independent examiner will extend beyond the formal scrutiny of the year-end accounts, and will include a wide range of other support and advice on financial issues. In most cases, the auditor or examiner will be an important source of help as the work of the CIO grows and changes over the years.

CIOs with subsidiaries – group accounts

Many medium-sized and larger charities undertake trading activities which fall outside the charity's objects – for example, charities which run restaurants and coffee shops that are open to the public, or charities selling services to people who are not the charity's intended beneficiaries, or charities selling cards and other gifts by mail order.

If the income from such activities falls outside the exemptions allowed under tax law, it is often necessary to establish a separate company as a subsidiary of the charity, to carry out these activities. Generally a trading subsidiary is needed if the turnover from such non-charitable trading exceeds 25% of the charity's income or £50,000[29] (whichever is the least) although there are other exemptions to consider. For more information see chapter 11 of *The Charity Treasurer's Handbook*.

The subsidiary is usually formed as a normal private company limited by shares, or sometimes a community interest company (a CIC – see page 43) with the shares held by the charity. (The subsidiary is a non-charitable body so it cannot itself be a CIO.) The profit from the subsidiary is then given back to the charity as a company gift aid donation (see page 38 for more on mixed charitable and non-charitable arrangements). However, professional advice will normally be needed to establish a subsidiary of a CIO: there are many issues to consider.

This arrangement applies equally to CIOs and other types of charity: although the CIO itself is not a company, a CIO would have to pay corporation tax if its trading income exceeded the stated limits. But there is no reason why a charity *A CIO* cannot own shares in a trading company *B Ltd* if *B* is trading to generate funds for *A*. The company's registers should clearly show the CIO (under its full name) as the shareholder and the company's accounts should make clear that it is controlled by the CIO.

---

[29] Finance Act 2000, s. 46(4).

There are also cases where one charity can be a subsidiary of another. For example, if a charity, *C*, has a governing document which states that charity *A* can appoint more than half of the trustees of *C* (for example, if *C* were a CIO with *A* as its sole member) then *A* would normally be considered to have 'control' of *C* for accounting purposes. In other words, *C* would be regarded as a subsidiary charity under the control of *A*. This would apply whatever the legal structures of charities *A* and *C*. (If *A* and *C* were both CIOs, it is possible that one CIO could be a subsidiary of another CIO for accounting purposes, as illustrated in figure 8.1).

Group accounts

In these cases – where a charity has subsidiaries (whether the subsidiaries are charitable or non-charitable) – a 'charity group' is considered to exist. Therefore, under the Charities Act, the parent charity must prepare 'group accounts',[30] unless the consolidated group income (see definition below) is under £500,000. The group accounts are prepared under the Charities SORP: they will include a SOFA combining the incoming resources and resources expended of the parent charity and the subsidiaries, and a balance sheet showing the total assets of the group.

Figure 8.1 A CIO with subsidiaries

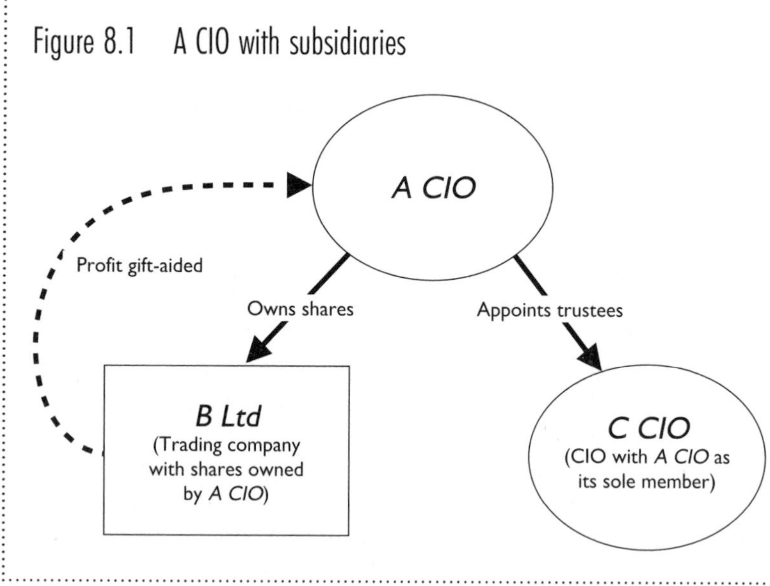

[30] Charities Act 2011, s. 138.

So, in the example above, if *A CIO* had subsidiaries *B Ltd* and *C CIO* the following sets of accounts would be needed:

- individual accounts for *A CIO* (charity accounts for the parent charity alone);
- group accounts for *A CIO* consolidated with *B Ltd* and *C CIO* (charity accounts prepared under the group accounting provisions);[31]
- individual accounts for *B Ltd* (normal commercial company accounts);
- individual accounts for *C CIO* (charity accounts).

In practice, the accounts for *A CIO* as a charity on its own, and the group with *A CIO* as parent are normally combined into one document, with columns headed 'Charity' and 'Group' respectively – so *A CIO* will only file one set of accounts with the Charity Commission.

Group accounts and exception for small groups

There is an exception to the requirement to prepare group accounts in the case of 'small groups' where the consolidated income is less than £500,000.[32] But this does not mean that all charities under the audit threshold are excepted from the group accounts rules, because sometimes a charity with a relatively small income can have a subsidiary with a large turnover.

The consolidated income (or technically the 'aggregate gross income' of the group)[33] is calculated by adding up the income of all members of the group, after taking out transfers within the group (so that no income is counted twice). Suppose that, in a given year, the following figures apply to the example above:

- the gross income of *A CIO* is £150,000 (including £70,000 from *B Ltd*);
- the turnover of *B Ltd* is £400,000 (generating a profit of £70,000 gift aided to *A CIO*);
- the gross income of *C CIO* is £90,000 (including a grant of £20,000 from *A CIO*).

The consolidated income in this case is: £150,000 – £70,000 + £400,000 + £90,000 – £20,000 = £550,000. This is over the £500,000 exemption, so group accounts are needed even though the income of *A CIO* is only £150,000.

[31] Charities (Accounts and Reports) Regulations 2008, regs 15–17.

[32] Charities Act 2011, s. 139(2) and Charities (Accounts and Reports) Regulations 2008 reg. 18.

[33] Charities (Accounts and Reports) Regulations 2008, reg. 9.

Moreover, once group accounts are needed, two further requirements take effect:

- the group accounts must be prepared on the accruals/SORP basis[34] (R&P accounts are not allowed, even though both charities in this example are CIOs and the total income of the charities in the group is less than £250,000);
- the group accounts must be audited[35] (even if the total charity income is within the normal band for independent examination).

So, in this example, the group accounts of *A CIO* would need to be audited. In addition, the accounts of *C CIO* would at least need an independent examination (as a charity in its own right), but no external scrutiny would be needed by statute for *B Ltd* as a small non-charitable company. However, in these circumstances the auditors of the parent body are often appointed to act for the subsidiaries as well, and they may conclude that in order to be confident of their audit assurances on the group accounts it is simplest to audit all entities in the group.

Practical implications

If a CIO has subsidiaries and group accounts are needed (because the consolidated income is greater than £500,000) it will be essential to use a firm of auditors with significant charity experience. But if you are responsible for the finances of a CIO with subsidiaries it is important to understand the basic principles of establishing whether group accounts are needed. In particular, bear in mind the definition of a subsidiary as outlined on page 154.

As shown in the example, even a relatively modest CIO can need group accounts if it has control of subsidiaries which lead to a consolidated income more than £500,000.

[34] Charities Act 2011, s. 138(3)(b).

[35] Charities Act 2011, s. 151(1).

9 Converting unincorporated charities to CIOs

So far we have focused on the processes of setting up a CIO as a new charity, and subsequent issues in running a CIO. However, the advantages of the CIO form – particularly in terms of corporate status and limited liability but without the complexities of company law – mean that many existing charities with other structures may wish to convert to become a CIO.

In this chapter we look at the issues for unincorporated charities where it is decided to become a CIO, particularly those which are currently structured as charitable trusts or charitable associations. In these cases, converting to a CIO involves winding up the existing charity. However, if the charity is already a corporate body – such as a charitable company – in many cases it is (or will be) possible to convert directly, without winding up the existing entity (see chapter 10 for details).

These conversion processes are available for charities which wish to become CIOs in all three UK jurisdictions, but the remainder of this chapter focuses on the provisions in England and Wales. For differences in Scotland and Northern Ireland, see chapters 13 and 14 respectively.

Converting an unincorporated charity: the principles

Although it is common for people to talk about 'converting' a charity to a new structure or 'incorporating' an existing charity, the process of transition always involves creating a completely new charity.

So, for an unincorporated charity to become a CIO, there are two separate elements to the process:

- forming the new charity as a CIO;
- winding up the existing charity, and transferring all its assets to the CIO.

Moreover, it is normally impossible to complete all of these at the same time, so there will usually be a period of time where the old and new charities exist in parallel. The CIO is a legally separate body from the old charity, and in England and Wales it will have a new charity registration number. (However, in Scotland, when converting to a SCIO it is possible in some cases for the conversion to happen in such a way that the same charity number is retained – see page 266.)

The process is largely the same as for converting an unincorporated charity to a charitable company. The only real difference is that the process of forming the CIO is handled purely with the Charity Commission (there is no involvement with Companies House). However, if the unincorporated charity has permanent endowment (see page 173) or has a governing document with no wind-up clause (see page 168) the legislation actually makes it easier to convert to a CIO than to a charitable company.

Remember that an unincorporated charity is normally formed as a trust – a body of individual trustees (see page 49) – or as an association, where members elect trustees under a constitution (see page 52). In each case the trustees come together to advance the charity's aims. But they are still individuals. If, as normal, they hold assets on behalf of the charity – whether cash in hand, funds in bank accounts, major investments, or freehold property – the assets are vested in those individuals as trustees (or sometimes assets are vested in holding trustees who may be different persons from the charity trustees, as discussed on page 7 in chapter 1). So, when converting such a charity to a CIO, a new corporate body is formed, and the assets are then transferred.

Issues to consider and specialist advice

This chapter outlines some of the issues to consider in that process, but it cannot allow for all possibilities. It is worth, therefore, considering at the start of the process if professional advice is needed. This will be essential if property is involved and professional help usually will be required for transfers of leases, staff contracts of employment, and agreements with third parties (such as funding agreements). In many cases you may need the CIO to take on liabilities, not just assets (some examples of this will be outlined in the chapter). Advice will be vital if the unincorporated charity faces financial difficulties, large or uncertain liabilities, or disputes.

Of course, there are many advantages to operating as an incorporated charity (whether a CIO or charitable company) but it is never a case of saying 'we will set up a CIO and just carry on from there'. In most cases, more work will go into the transfer process than into the formation of the new CIO. Unless the assets (and liabilities, if applicable) are properly transferred from the unincorporated charity to the CIO, the existing charity cannot be wound up and you end up with the complexities of running two charities side by side. It is not unknown for this to go on for several years if major problems arise. So, some careful planning of the whole process from the outset is vital.

Timescales and accounting issues

Because the CIO is a completely new legal entity, separate from the old charity, you cannot just continue an existing set of charity accounts. Final accounts should be prepared for the old charity up to the date of its wind-up, and new accounts for the CIO from its date of formation (see page 190 and chapter 8 for more on the accounts of a new CIO).

So, although a transfer can take place at any point in time, the accounting issues are much simpler if it is possible to arrange for the final transfer of assets to take place on the last day of the charity's normal accounting year. In order to achieve this, however, planning needs to start a long time ahead. Table 9.1 shows a possible conversion timescale for a fairly straightforward conversion in a charity with a 31 March year end.

Table 9.1 A possible timescale for converting an unincorporated charity to a CIO

April 2014	Trustees agree in principle to convert to a CIO at next year end (i.e. conversion to take place on 31 March 2015).
May–July 2014	Consult members, funders, staff and others about the principle of the conversion. Consider any changes to current governing document (objects, numbers of trustees, voting, etc.) to be included in the CIO's constitution. If the existing charity has members, fix date for a special members' meeting in October to approve wind-up of existing charity (this could be combined with a normal AGM in charities where an AGM is held).
Aug–Sept 2014	Drafting of the CIO Constitution (allow for several drafts until everyone is happy). Detailed planning for the conversion process – allocate responsibilities and take professional advice at this stage on any issues which may not be straightforward (do not bury problems until later).

October 2014	New CIO constitution agreed by the applicants (the people to be the initial members – often the same as the trustees). Resolution passed to wind up the existing charity and transfer to a CIO 'as at 31 March 2015 or such other date as the trustees may decide'.
November 2014	Application to register the CIO is submitted to the Charity Commission.
December 2014	Responding to Charity Commission queries
January 2015	CIO is formed and registered on 11 January. First meeting of the CIO trustees follows. Finalise transfer agreement between the old charity and the CIO (or pre-merger vesting declaration).
Feb–Mar 2015	Formally notify all parties that the transfer is proceeding. Open new bank accounts for the CIO if needed. Make sure all contracts are re-established with the CIO.
31 March 2015	Transfer date – all assets and liabilities of the old charity transferred to the CIO. Last accounts for the old charity will finish on this date.
1 April 2015	Work of the charity now undertaken through the CIO. All literature, website, emails, etc. should now show the details of the CIO (not the old charity).
July 2015	Trustees of the old charity hold a final meeting to approve the last set of accounts (year ending 31 March 2015) and file with the Charity Commission.
31 March 2016	First year end for the CIO. First CIO accounts prepared for the period 11 January 2015 to 31 March 2016. (Note that the first accounts must start from the date of incorporation, though in fact there were no transactions in the CIO's books from 11 January to 31 March 2015, so in practice the accounts cover 12 months of activity.)

Of course, it is not essential for the transfer date to tie in with a normal year end: sometimes this is impossible because of other factors. Accounting years can be adjusted if trustees consider it necessary (although a charity cannot keep adjusting its year end without permission from the Charity Commission[1] and financial periods of more or less than 12 months can be challenging for financial systems and for financial decision-making).

The simplest approach is if all aspects of the transfer are completed on one day – so whilst the CIO will be *formed* before the transfer date, there is no date when the old and new charities are both *operating*. But in complex cases this may not be possible, and there may be an overlap period of up to a year when both the old and new charities are active and two sets of accounts are needed. But, in terms of minimising accounting costs and avoiding confusion for staff, trustees and others, a clear transfer date that ties in with the normal year end is always simplest.

Be sure to allow sufficient time for registration of the CIO: although the Charity Commission aims to process straightforward applications in around 40 days, any case which leads to detailed queries can take considerably longer. If it is vital that the CIO is formed by a certain date, it would be wise to apply for registration at least three to four months beforehand. Also, time is needed for an orderly transfer. If you are looking to wind up the existing charity at 31 March, it is no use having a CIO registered on 29 March, as there is no time to make all the practical arrangements. In most cases you will need the CIO to be registered at least four to six weeks before the proposed transfer date, and sometimes much longer. (However, as explained in chapter 8, it is best if you can avoid the CIO being registered more than 18 months before its first financial year end because otherwise additional sets of accounts are needed.)

Forming the CIO

Once the basic steps are mapped out, the initial stage will focus on preparing a constitution for the CIO that will take over from the existing charity, and then applying for the CIO to be registered.

These steps are essentially as explained in chapters 5 and 6, so they will not be repeated here. However, bear in mind that even when you are applying to register a CIO that will take over from an existing charity, the process of charity registration is still as demanding as setting up a brand new charity. Take care with drafting the constitution and the explanation

[1] Charities (Accounts and Reports) Regulations 2008, reg. 3(4)–(7).

of how the CIO will advance its charitable purposes for public benefit. Be sure that the trustees' declaration for the Charity Commission is properly signed by all the initial trustees of the CIO.

Sometimes people assume that these processes are a mere formality, but important decisions are involved, particularly in drafting the constitution. Consider the following examples.

- Should the new charitable objects be exactly the same as before, or would a new wording be appropriate? Bear in mind the new headings of charitable purposes available in the Charities Act 2011 (see page 27). However, if choosing new wording take care that it is not so different from the old that there could be problems in transferring assets held for the former charitable purposes. Also, if the new objects are substantially broader than the old, assets transferred will have to become a restricted fund within the CIO, held exclusively for the former objects, so the CIO will start off with no unrestricted funds. (On the other hand, some widening of the objects may be essential to comply with the Equality Act 2010.)
- There are usually certain things in any charity governing document which are out of date and drawing up a new constitution as a CIO can be a chance to modernise. But take care – it is very easy to follow the Charity Commission model and omit a crucial element in the *existing* trust deed or constitution such as a statement of values, rules on different types of membership, or essential qualifications for someone to be a trustee. If any of these issues are so fundamental that they should not be changed, you may need to consider entrenchment of these provisions in the CIO constitution (see page 103).
- If the existing charity has a membership beyond the trustees, how will members transfer? You may need a clause defining the initial members of the CIO to be those persons who were members of the former charity as at a specific date.
- Will the initial trustees of the CIO be exactly the same people as the trustees of the old charity? Although this will often be the case, there can be advantages in making a slight change so that the old and new trustees are not exactly the same, particularly if negotiations are needed (see page 170). Sometimes there will be a new person in the wings who could sensibly be included as a trustee of the CIO even though he or she was not a trustee of the old charity. Likewise, an existing trustee looking to step down may continue with the wind-up arrangements of the old charity but may decline to become a trustee of the CIO.

Note that during the first year of implementation of CIOs in England and Wales, the Charity Commission (with the support of the government) indicated that applications to register a CIO to take over the work of an existing charity could normally be considered only on a phased basis according to the income of the existing charity – the timescales are as shown in table 9.2.

Table 9.2 Timescales for initial CIO registrations in England & Wales following implementation

First date for applications	*Applications to form CIOs eligible from:*
10 December 2012 (with first new CIOs formed from 2 January 2013)	Applicants seeking to register brand new CIOs not linked to an existing charity, provided the anticipated income of the CIO is at least £5,000
1 March 2013	Existing unincorporated charities with an annual income of more than £250,000
1 May 2013	Existing unincorporated charities with incomes of more than £100,000
1 July 2013	Existing unincorporated charities with incomes greater than £25,000
1 October 2013	Existing unincorporated charities with incomes of more than £5,000
1 January 2014	Existing unincorporated charities with annual incomes of less than £5,000. Also applications for brand new CIOs with anticipated annual incomes of less than £5,000.

Deciding on the wind-up process for the old charity

There are several alternative processes which may be considered firstly for winding up the old charity and secondly for transferring the assets from the old charity to the CIO.

In practice these decisions overlap, as the wind-up decision will always include a decision in principle to transfer the assets. But additional processes are usually needed to implement the transfer, especially as, in most cases, the trustees of the old charity will wish to transfer liabilities as well as assets. As well as the agreement to wind up the old charity, it is usually necessary to negotiate a 'transfer agreement' between the trustees of the old charity and the CIO. Alternatively, or in addition, especially where permanent endowment or designated land are involved, the trustees may need to make a 'vesting declaration'. These terms and the associated processes are discussed below, but first we consider the formal processes of agreeing to wind up a charity.

Agreeing to wind up the old charity

Broadly speaking, there are three main ways in which agreement can be reached that the old charity should be wound up and transferred to the CIO:

(a) a resolution under the governing document of the existing charity to wind up and transfer assets to a CIO (where there are suitable powers to do so); or

(b) where the governing document does not contain suitable powers, a resolution can be made under the Charities Act to transfer all property of an unincorporated charity to a CIO; or

(c) a 'scheme' of the Charity Commission could be sought.

One of the most important issues to consider at the outset is whether the existing charity has the power to wind up and transfer its assets to a CIO. Read the governing document and check if there is a dissolution clause – the wind-up process must comply with whatever is stated in that clause. It is also important to consider who can make the decision to wind up. In many cases, such decisions cannot be taken purely by the trustees of the existing charity.

In the rare cases where neither (a) nor (b) will achieve the outcome needed, it is possible to apply to the Charity Commission to make a 'scheme'[2] – a legal document which alters the administration of a charity. In this case, it would typically transfer all property, rights and liabilities of the existing charity to the CIO. However, legal advice will certainly be needed, and a considerable timescale will be involved. The use of schemes is not considered further in this book.

Charities established by Royal Charter or Act of Parliament

If the existing charity is established by a Royal Charter or Act of Parliament, the members and trustees of the charity do not usually have the power to wind up the whole body and transfer its assets to another

[2] Charities Act 2011, s. 69.

charity, so converting to a CIO may well be impossible. For a charity established by Royal Charter, a wind-up will generally need permission of Her Majesty (through the Privy Council). For a charity established by Act of Parliament, refer to the relevant legislation – sometimes a government minister can make an order to dissolve the charity (for example in the case of many educational charities, the Secretary of State for Education can give permission). In the case of church bodies, consent may be possible from the relevant church authorities (such as the Church Commissioners in the case of Church of England bodies, but they would not be able to authorise an Anglican PCC to wind up, except as part of parish reorganisations). But in other cases it could need a private Act of Parliament to change the legal form, or in some cases the Charity Commission may be prepared to make a scheme with similar effect.[3]

Charitable associations

If the existing charity is a membership body (a charitable association) any decision to change the constitution or wind up can normally be taken only by the members (not the trustees). If the charity has a large membership, considerable work may be needed in advance to explain to members what is proposed in order to get their support at the crucial meeting.

Unless the decision can be combined with a normal AGM, it may be necessary to plan for an extraordinary general meeting (EGM). If so, great care must be taken to follow all the procedures in the *existing* constitution to ensure that the EGM is properly called with sufficient notice, and with a clear resolution circulated in advance. Where the existing constitution allows for postal or proxy voting, these arrangements may be helpful. If the existing constitution requires a certain number of members to be present at an EGM in order for it to be quorate, you may need to consider making the EGM attractive to attend. For example, it could be combined with another event or a prestigious guest speaker.

In many cases, the existing constitution may not allow for electronic communications, so time is needed to send these notices by post. If the charity has members who take an interest in the constitution, it would be wise to have the full proposed constitution of the CIO available for circulation with the resolution (or at least available in advance).

A simple one-line resolution is acceptable but, if possible, the resolution should specify the timescales and clearly authorise the charity trustees to take the steps needed. A possible wording might be as follows.

[3] Charities Act 2011, s. 73.

Sample wording for a wind-up resolution in a charitable association

RESOLUTION PROPOSED FOR CONSIDERATION AT AN EXTRAORDINARY GENERAL MEETING TO BE HELD ON 23 OCTOBER 2014

That in accordance with clause xx of the constitution, the organisation known as [name of current charity] (registered charity number xxxxxxx) (the existing charity) be DISSOLVED on 31 March 2015 (or such other date as the trustees may decide) and all assets and liabilities held for the purposes of the charity be transferred on that date to a new Charitable Incorporated Organisation formed under the Charities Act 2011 to be known as [name of CIO] (the CIO):

- PROVIDED that the CIO shall be formed with objects as similar as possible to those of the existing charity (subject to any updating for present circumstances); and
- PROVIDED that the charity trustees of the CIO shall be the same persons as the trustees of the existing charity at the date of this meeting; and
- PROVIDED that the dissolution and transfer shall not proceed unless the CIO has been registered as a charity by the Charity Commission not later than 28 February 2015 (or by such other date as the trustees may agree, but not less than 21 days prior to the dissolution).

AND THIS RESOLUTION AUTHORISES THE CHARITY TRUSTEES OF THE EXISTING CHARITY

- to sign such agreements and execute such deeds as are necessary to give effect to this transfer

provided that, in the case of assets held for restricted purposes, they shall ensure that similar restrictions are imposed when the assets are transferred to the CIO.

If all the members of the existing charity will be members of the CIO from the outset, and hence will be the applicants seeking formation of the CIO (see chapter 5), the new constitution needs to be ready to attach to the resolution and the first bullet needs to be rather more specific. It might be adjusted to read:

> AND THE MEMBERS HEREBY RESOLVE to apply for registration of a CIO with the constitution as attached to this resolution, except that changes may be agreed in liaison with the Charity Commission provided that [named person; for example, the existing Chair] states that in his/her opinion they are not changes of a substantial nature.

Care is needed to ensure that the meeting is properly conducted and that members have a chance to speak before a vote is taken. Sometimes the decision can be controversial if members feel loyal to the existing charity and worry that the CIO is a part of a hidden agenda for wider changes. A good chair who is confident of procedures under the existing constitution can make a big difference. When the vote is taken, be sure to record the voting figures in the minutes, because the existing constitution may well require a dissolution resolution to be passed by a specific majority (typically by two-thirds of those present and voting).

As this will usually be the last general meeting of the old charity, the person who chaired the meeting should sign the minutes once satisfied that they are a correct record. These may be needed by the Charity Commission, banks, solicitors or others to ensure that the proper authority exists to transfer the assets.

Charitable trusts with wind-up powers

Most relatively modern trust deeds include a clause allowing the trustees to vote (sometimes by a specific majority such as two-thirds) to wind up and transfer all the assets to another charity with similar objects. For example, the latest model deed for a charitable trust produced by the Charity Law Association[4] includes the following provision.

- *The Trustees may at any time decide by resolution passed by [at least x proportion] of the Trustees that the Charity is to be dissolved. The Trustees will then be responsible for the orderly winding up of the Charity's affairs.*
- *After making provision for all outstanding liabilities of the Charity, the Trustees must apply the remaining property and funds in one or more of the following ways:*
  (1) by transfer to one or more other bodies established for exclusively charitable purposes within, the same as or similar to the Objects;
  (2) directly for the Objects or charitable purposes within or similar to the Objects; or
  (3) in such other manner consistent with charitable status as the Charity Commission approves in writing in advance.
- *A final report and statement of account relating to the Charity must be sent to the Commission.*

If such a clause in included in the existing trust deed, this is relatively straightforward and the wind-up decision can be taken at a normal trustees' meeting.

---

4 *Model Trust Deed/Declaration of Trust for a Charitable Trust* (Charity Law Association 3rd edn).

Where the Charity Commission's permission is mentioned in the trust deed, this is often needed only where the trustees are *unable* to find a suitable charitable body with similar objects. So the Commission's consent is not normally needed if transferring to a CIO with almost identical objects to the existing charity (although, when applying to register the CIO you will make clear that it is intended to replace an existing charity). However, some trust deeds may specify that Charity Commission permission is needed in any case.

Unincorporated charities without wind-up powers

Older charities may have governing documents which do not contain an explicit dissolution clause. However, the Charities Act 2011 includes helpful procedures allowing trustees of an unincorporated charity to vote to wind it up and transfer to a CIO, even when there is no explicit power in the existing deed.[5]

Normally these powers can only be used by charities with up to £10,000 income per year, but if the proposal is to transfer to a CIO, the £10,000 limit does not apply (so long as all the other conditions are met).[6] Note that this only applies if the resolution is to transfer to a CIO and not to other kinds of incorporation such as charitable companies.

The trustees of the existing charity must be satisfied that the proposed transfer 'is expedient in the interest of furthering its purposes' and that the purposes of the recipient charity (the CIO) are 'substantially similar' to the existing purposes.[7] The resolution must cover all assets of the existing charity,[8] including permanent endowment if applicable (though see page 174 on the processes involved in transferring permanent endowment). The resolution must be passed by a two-thirds majority of the existing trustees (i.e. those voting in favour must be at least two-thirds of those present and voting at a properly convened trustees' meeting – it does not require support from two-thirds of the total number of existing trustees).

In order to pass such a resolution, the CIO must already be formed (the trustees cannot authorise a transfer under this process to a charity which does not exist).

---

[5] Charities Act 2011, ss. 267–274.

[6] Charities Act 2011, s. 267(2).

[7] Charities Act 2011, s. 268(3)(b); or, if permanent endowment is involved, the similarity must extend to 'all' the existing purposes – s. 274(3).

[8] Charities Act 2011, s. 268.

Having passed the resolution, the trustees must send a copy to the Charity Commission with a note of their reasoning (make clear that it is a resolution under section 268 of the Charities Act 2011). The Commission can require the trustees to publicise the decision in whatever manner the Commission considers appropriate, and, if so, it must take account of any comments received within 28 days of the publicity appearing. It can also ask the trustees for further clarifications or assurances.

Unless the Commission raises objections, the resolution then takes effect 60 days after the Commission was first advised of it (or, if publicity was required, up to 102 days after the start of the publicity).[9] However, if the Commission raises further queries with the trustees, the clock stops while these are dealt with. In practice, the Commission will usually say 'yes' to such resolutions if there are no obvious problems, but as long as you have proof that notice was given to the Commission on a specific date, it can be helpful for the trustees to know that they can proceed if the Commission has not objected within the timescales specified.

Once the resolution takes effect, the trustees of the existing charity must arrange for all its property (i.e. all assets) to be transferred to the CIO, but they may negotiate timescales with the CIO's trustees.[10] In most cases they will want the CIO to accept liabilities, not just assets; in which case, a transfer agreement will be needed.

However, a section 268 resolution cannot be used to transfer 'designated land'[11] without separate Charity Commission authority. This term is defined as any land held on trusts which stipulate that it is to be used for charitable purposes: see page 186.

This procedure for transferring the property of an unincorporated charity to a CIO can save a great deal of complexity, which has been needed in the past when trustees of older charities wished to transfer assets to another charity.

In rare cases where neither the resolution itself nor a trustees' vesting declaration (see page 174) can achieve the transfer of assets – for example if investments are held in the names of trustees of the old charity who cannot be traced – the trustees of the CIO due to receive the assets (rather than the trustees of the old charity) can request the Charity Commission

[9] Charities Act 2011, s. 271. The wording of the timescales is complex, but up to 102 days (60 days + 42 days) could be needed in some cases.

[10] Charities Act 2011, s. 272(2).

[11] Charities Act 2011, s. 267(1)(b).

to make a 'vesting order'.[12] This has the effect of directly vesting the assets concerned in the CIO, and may provide a solution in otherwise very complex situations.

Organising the transfer

The practical issues for arranging the transfer of assets (and liabilities, if applicable) from the old charity to the CIO need care and considerable planning from the outset (some issues, such as pension deficits, could make the transfer practically impossible). This book cannot cover all the issues in detail, and unless the issues are very straightforward, professional advice will be needed, but the following points summarise key aspects to consider.

The following issues are discussed thematically rather than in chronological order. Many issues may need to be addressed at up to five stages:

(a) at the planning stage;
(b) once the decision has been made but before the CIO is registered;
(c) after the CIO is registered but before the transfer date;
(d) on the actual transfer day; and
(e) after the transfer, once everything is in the hands of the CIO.

Agreeing the transfer and 'due diligence' issues

For an existing charity to wind up and transfer its assets and liabilities to another charity (a CIO in this case) both bodies of charity trustees must be in agreement. There will almost always be issues which are not clear cut and which require negotiation. Even though the trustees may be the same or almost the same in each case, it is important to maintain the separate roles and consider the issues, especially the risks. Potentially complex issues of conflicting duties may arise, and professional advice may well be needed on how to manage these. This process of assessing the suitability of another organisation for a major agreement (such as a merger) is called 'due diligence': often professional advisors are instructed to give an independent view, especially if there will be changes of trustees between the old charity and the CIO.

In practice, if the two bodies of trustees are the same or almost the same they may decide that little or no due diligence work is needed, especially if they are confident that they properly understand the old charity and the CIO. But since the CIO's trustees will normally be taking on liabilities (as well as assets) from the old charity, they need to be sure that the CIO is

[12] Charities Act 2011, s. 272(4).

getting a net benefit – i.e. the assets must be worth more than the expected liabilities. Equally, the trustees of the old charity need to be sure that the CIO is properly established with compatible objects, and that it is set up with suitable trustees and has appropriate procedures in place to continue the work for the benefit of the intended beneficiaries. Particular care is needed with restricted and endowment funds, as explained on page 173.

Principles in transferring assets, liabilities and contractual agreements

Resolutions by the old charity can authorise the transfer of assets, but they cannot force the CIO to accept the transfer of liabilities. So in the case of an active charity with ongoing commitments, the trustees of the old charity will normally want some kind of indemnity that the CIO will meet outstanding liabilities: otherwise, even after the CIO takes over, they could still be personally liable to a third party for commitments made while they were trustees of the old charity. This can be provided under a transfer agreement (see the following section).

Similarly, contracts of employment will not automatically transfer without a specific agreement. Agreements with third parties will require 'novation' in the name of the CIO if the trustees of the old charity are to be released from their obligations. 'Novation' means the creation of a new contract with the CIO in place of the old contract with the trustees of the unincorporated charity, so early discussions should be held with funders, landlords, etc. to avoid problems at a later stage (this will be explored further in later sections of the chapter). As such there are many issues to consider at the outset beyond the initial agreement to wind up the old charity.

Transfer agreements

Once all the issues are agreed in principle, they should normally be set out in a written agreement between the old trustees and the CIO (once the CIO is formed). This can be a 'deed of transfer' (i.e. a formal gift from the old charity to the CIO) but if liabilities are to be transferred as well as assets, the arrangement may more easily be handled as a contract under which the CIO agrees to indemnify the old trustees for any liabilities, in return for receiving the assets.

See the following simple example although in complex cases much more may be needed. (The agreement could refer to 'the trust' or 'the association' as appropriate rather than 'the old charity', if preferred.) Remember that the old charity is an unincorporated body, so the charity itself cannot enter into an agreement – the agreement is made on behalf of the trustees – but the CIO, as a corporate body, can enter into a contract in its own right.

A simple agreement for transfer between an unincorporated charity and a CIO (where no land, buildings or pension funds are involved)

TRANSFER AGREEMENT

Made between AB, CD, EF, GH ('the old trustees') being the charity trustees of [Name of old charity] registered charity number xxxxxxx ('the old charity')

and [Name of CIO] registered charity number yyyyyyy ('the CIO').

Date of transfer: dd/mm/yyyyy

1. The old trustees agree to transfer all assets they hold for the charitable purposes of the old charity to the CIO on the date of transfer specified above. For the avoidance of doubt, this includes money held in cash or in bank accounts, investments, equipment, furniture, other tangible assets, and any debts due to them as trustees of the old charity at the date of transfer.
2. Any assets held as restricted funds or endowment funds shall, when transferred, be held on trust by the CIO for the same purposes as they are held by the old charity.
3. In consideration of receiving these assets, the CIO agrees to indemnify the old trustees against any liabilities properly incurred by them during their trusteeship of the old charity. *[In some cases the CIO trustees may feel this is too broad – for example if they have concerns about certain actions by former trustees a more limited wording should be used.]*
4. The contracts of employees in post with the old charity at the date of transfer shall transfer to the CIO, and both parties agree to observe the provisions of the Transfer of Undertakings (Protection of Employment) Regulations (TUPE). *[Give exceptions if any staff will not transfer, for example persons on fixed term contracts due to expire on the transfer date.]*
5. All records, documents and creative media held by the old charity, including any intellectual property they contain, shall transfer to the CIO on the date of transfer. Both parties agree to observe the requirements of the Data Protection Act 1998 in respect of any personal data. The CIO agrees to retain accounting records and other information for the periods required by law, and to allow reasonable access to the old trustees to enable them to complete the final accounts of the old charity and for any other purposes related to their duties as charity trustees.
6. In the case of contracts with third parties or other funding agreements in force at the date of transfer (and due to continue beyond that date) both parties undertake to use their best endeavours to ensure such agreements are transferred from the old trustees to the CIO and agree to execute such documents as are reasonably necessary to achieve this.
7. The old trustees assign to the CIO all rights relating to gifts, donations, legacies, grants, or other income which may become due to them as trustees of the old charity after the transfer date.

8 Both parties agree to ensure the continuity of insurance arrangements, and to ensure that any insurance policies held on behalf of the old charity are assigned to the CIO from the date of transfer.

9 Any reasonable administrative expenses incurred by the CIO prior to the date of transfer will be paid from the funds of the old charity.

10 [Add further details on any specific assets which require further detail, such as vehicles.]

Signed on behalf of
the old trustees: .... [Name of trustee]

.... [Name of trustee]

[Date]

Signed on behalf of
the CIO: .... [Name of CIO trustee]

.... [Name of CIO trustee]

[Date]

Restricted funds and endowment funds

There is an important difference between transferring unrestricted funds from the old charity – which will become the corporate property of the CIO – and transferring restricted and endowment funds, where the CIO itself will technically be *the trustee* of assets which are held on trust for specific purposes. (For more on restricted and endowment funds, see *The Charity Treasurer's Handbook*, also published in this series.)

The main issue is that the trustees of the old charity must ensure any assets which are subject to restrictions, or which constitute permanent endowment are transferred to the CIO and are to be used on the same terms as before. It is, of course, vital to identify and preserve documents which specify the terms of such funds and pass them to the CIO.

'Permanent endowment' means assets that are held on condition that they cannot be spent: the endowment must be held permanently and only the income can be applied to the charitable purposes.[13] Many grant-making charities hold permanent endowments which are invested to provide income which is used to make grants, and some service-providing charities hold endowment funds given by donors on similar terms. If permanent endowment is to be transferred to a CIO, special procedures

[13] Charities Act 2011, s. 353(3).

are needed as outlined in the next section (in which case professional advice will usually be needed).

However, whilst these distinctions between the different types of funds are important in law, and all restrictions must be carefully followed during the transfer, they do not necessarily create major problems in practice, as long as the trustees of the two charities clearly understand the different funds and the consequent requirements for charity accounts. If the CIO prepares accounts under the Charities SORP (see page 148), the statement of financial activities (SOFA) will clearly distinguish the three types of funds. Even with receipts and payments (R&P) accounts, restricted and endowment funds must be clearly identified as a matter of trust law.

Provided the terms of any restricted and endowment funds are clearly distinguished for accounting purposes and day-to-day decisions, the distinction only becomes important if the CIO is potentially insolvent (see chapter 12). If this happens, creditors will have a claim on the unrestricted funds of the CIO, but restricted funds and permanent endowment funds are usually protected under trust law.

In some cases, if the CIO has wider objects than the old charity it may be that *all* transferred assets are to be treated as restricted funds, as explained on page 162.

Transferring permanent endowment: use of pre-merger vesting declarations

In some cases with modest endowment funds that do not comprise land, it may be simpler for the trustees to resolve that the fund should be spent by way of a grant to the CIO if there is no significant reason for keeping the fund as an endowment. (If so, the grant when received becomes part of the CIO's unrestricted funds, or a restricted fund if the grant is made for specific purposes that are more limited than the CIO's objects.) As a result of changes originally made by the Charities Act 2006, the trustees do not need Charity Commission approval to take such a decision for endowment funds with incomes of less than £1,000 a year or less than £10,000 of assets.[14] Even for larger endowments there is a reasonably straightforward process for seeking the Commission's consent if the trustees take a clear decision that the endowment could be used better by being spent (though at least three months' notice must be given).

However, where permanent endowment is to be transferred to a CIO and remains as an endowment, one cannot technically speak of the existing charity being wound up because a permanent endowment is, by definition,

---

[14] Charities Act 2011, ss. 281–292

a charity with a permanent existence. Nevertheless, the transfer can still be achieved by the CIO, as a corporate body, becoming the trustee of the existing endowment. The same principle applies to any assets held on 'special trusts', including restricted funds.

Such arrangements used to require special Charity Commission orders, but they can now be achieved relatively simply by the trustees of the old charity making a 'pre-merger vesting declaration' under the Charities Act 2011, using provisions specific for transfers to CIOs.[15] The declaration takes the form of a deed made by the trustees of a charity which is being wound up and placed on the Charity Mergers Register (see page 188). The Commission provides a sample wording on its website.

The effect of the pre-merger vesting declaration, from the date it takes effect, is fourfold:

(a) the property of the old charity is vested in the CIO;

(b) the CIO is appointed as a 'trust corporation' (which is necessary for a corporate body to hold permanent endowment);

(c) in the case of property which was subject to special trusts (including permanent endowment), the CIO is appointed trustee;

(d) the permanent endowments, other property on special trusts (restricted funds) and the CIO itself are deemed to be a single charity. This means that all decisions are taken by the CIO's charity trustees in the normal way. Only one set of charity accounts is needed, with the restricted and endowments funds treated as funds of the CIO in the usual manner, as specified under the Charities SORP or in the R&P accounts.

A transfer agreement will usually still be needed to cover other issues, but the pre-merger vesting declaration is a very effective means of handling the transfer of permanent endowment (and all other property) in a way that leaves the CIO able to operate effectively.

Key issues for specific aspects of the transfer

Transferring bank balances

Often the most obvious assets to transfer will be money held in bank accounts. The implications of transferring bank deposits depend heavily on the procedures operated by particular banks.

---

[15] Charities Act 2011, ss. 310–313 as amended for CIOs by reg. 61 of the CIO General Regulations 2012.

It is worth speaking to the charity's bank at an early stage explaining the proposed conversion, and checking whether the bank will require a new account to be opened for the CIO (see page 327). Most banks will require this because the CIO is a legally separate body from the former trustees, and accounts for corporate bodies are normally operated under different mandates from accounts for unincorporated charities. Also, if there is an overlap period when the old charity and the CIO are both operating, separate accounts are essential. (Bear in mind that, in the early days, it may be necessary to explain the nature of a CIO if you are dealing with bank staff outside a specialist charity team, and you may need to adjust forms to fit the circumstances.) The bank will generally need a copy of the CIO's constitution and confirmation of its registration: i.e. a printout of the entry on the Register of Charities, or a downloaded 'certificate of charity registration' which can be obtained using the login details provided by the Charity Commission.

If new bank accounts are needed, they should be opened in good time so that any documentation showing account numbers can be amended. If the old charity had separate accounts for different purposes (such as current accounts and deposit accounts) a new account will usually be needed corresponding to each old account. On the day of transfer or just before, the new current account details should be advised to any customers, funders or donors who make payments directly to the charity's account.

On the day of transfer (or the last working day beforehand, if the transfer falls at a weekend), the bank should be requested to transfer the balance of the old charity's account(s) to the new accounts. If the old charity is being wound up immediately, the old accounts should then be closed to prevent further transactions. If there were uncleared cheques at the date of transfer, check whether the bank can transfer these automatically to the new account. If not, the balance transferred should be the reconciled figure in the charity's books (rather than the balance at the bank) with sufficient funds left in the old account to cover the uncleared cheques. The old current account will then need to stay open until all outstanding cheques have cleared.

However, if the charity has a large number of members or individual donors with standing orders paid directly to the charity, it is very difficult to get them all to change their instructions to their banks. In such cases it is worth asking if the bank will allow the CIO to take over the relevant account of the old charity. Many banks are prepared to agree this, subject to completion of a new mandate and suitable declarations by the old and new trustees.

Failing this, it is worth asking the bank to apply the 'Standing Order File Amendment' scheme (SOFA – not to be confused with a statement of financial activities in a charity's accounts). Under this scheme, the old charity can request its bank to contact all other banks which are members of SOFA and request them to amend any customers' standing orders with the old account details to the new account for the CIO. This is done electronically, so it is much less work than contacting donors individually.

The SOFA scheme currently covers 22 major UK banks, but it wouldn't affect incoming standing orders from some specialist or overseas banks. Also, the old account will need to be kept open until you are confident that all incoming standing orders are transferred, so if the bank is not prepared to let the CIO take over the old account, this may mean the old charity has to remain in existence for a further 12 months. However, the complexities of transferring standing orders is leading many charities with large numbers of supporters to switch to using direct debits

Transferring cash

If possible, it is worth trying to bank any cash in hand and cheques received on the day of the transfer (or the last working day beforehand) so that all moneys to be transferred are held in bank accounts. This makes the accounting simpler.

However, any petty cash, or floats that must be kept in hand should be counted on the day of the transfer with a note kept for the final accounts of the old charity, and petty cash containers should then be re-labelled to show that the cash belongs to the CIO.

If everything is in the hands of one treasurer or finance officer this is relatively simple, but in a charity where cash is held in several locations, you may need to send out clear instructions in advance. If cash is physically held by a treasurer who is not continuing in that role with the CIO, the cash must be physically handed to the new person (and a receipt should be requested).

Tangible assets

Physical assets such as furniture, office equipment, and medical equipment will pass to the CIO on the date of transfer. Usually no physical action is needed to move the equipment if the CIO will continue to operate from the same premises. However, all charities should have a fixed asset register, and this should be annotated to show the change of ownership of assets on the transfer date. If assets are physically marked –

for instance labels stating 'This equipment is the property of [name of charity]' – you should affix new labels stating that the asset is now the property of the CIO.

Motor vehicles may be registered with the former charity itself as the 'registered keeper' and, if so, the Driver and Vehicle Licensing Agency (DVLA) should be advised of a change of keeper to the CIO.

In the case of a charity with archive or heritage assets – for example pictures in an art gallery or artefacts in a museum – these will all transfer to the CIO. This may require extensive updating of records and re-registration with any relevant bodies.

Investments

If the old charity has investments – whether stocks and shares held directly, or an investment portfolio managed externally – the title must be transferred from the old trustees to the CIO. Usually this is just a matter of completing appropriate documentation. If the charity uses investment managers or stockbrokers, speak to them at an early stage.

Many charity investments are held on the charity's behalf in the name of a nominee company, so in that case it is simply necessary to ensure the nominee's records are suitably amended. However, if the charity holds shares directly, the former trustees will be shareholders (members) of a company, and title to the shares must be transferred to the CIO. Similarly with other investments held directly.

Investments held as permanent endowment should be clearly distinguished during the transfer process from investment of operational funds and the procedures explained on page 174 must be followed in order for the CIO to become the trustee of the endowment.

In the case of a charity with a large investment portfolio, great care is needed to ensure that *all* investments are properly transferred. If errors are made, substantial charitable assets could be lost which might only be recoverable through expensive litigation.

In other circumstances, transfers of investments from one party to another can be liable to stamp duty, but because both parties are charities no stamp duty is payable. However, make the charitable status clear from the outset.

Funding agreements

Where the old charity holds funding agreements lasting more than a year, it will be important to persuade the funder to transfer the agreement to the CIO from the date of transfer. So it is vital to contact them at an early stage (often before the CIO is actually formed) to explain what is planned and to establish what steps they will need to take to consent to transferring their support to the CIO. Failure to get consent could trigger a subsequent obligation on the CIO to repay funds even when they have been spent.

Some funders – for example, many grant-making charitable trusts – will usually have little difficulty agreeing this. Others, such as the Big Lottery Fund, may require forms to be completed, and you may have to go through an approval process. This is part of the funder's own 'due diligence' process to ensure that funding allocated to one charity is not transferred improperly to another body which cannot meet the original requirements.

The issues can be more demanding with contract funding, for example if a public sector body such as a local authority is procuring services from the charity. You will first need to persuade the funder that the CIO will be properly placed to continue the work, and seek consent for the old trustees to *assign the contract* to the CIO. However, this means that the local authority needs to enter into a new contract with the CIO – as explained, this is called 'novation' of the contract.

As always, make contact in good time to discuss this – the officer you are dealing with may need to contact the commissioner's contracts department or legal team. In case of difficulty, read the existing contract carefully. It will often contain a clause concerning subcontracting or assignment which will say something like:

> The Contractor may not assign or subcontract any of its obligations under this contract without the written agreement of the Council (which shall not be unreasonably withheld or delayed).

This means that whilst the trustees of the old charity cannot pass on the agreement to another party (the CIO) without the Council's agreement, the Council should not 'unreasonably' withhold or delay giving permission. If it is clear that the CIO will be run by the same people as before and will deliver the work to the same standard as before, it would usually be unreasonable for the Council to refuse the request.

Also, it is worth pointing out that in many cases public bodies would prefer to have contracts with a corporate body such as a CIO, rather than with an unincorporated charity. If there were serious failings requiring litigation, under the agreement with the old charity, the Council would have to sue trustees individually – suing a single corporate body is likely to be easier.

Any funding applications or tenders where you do not expect to receive any income until after the transfer date should be submitted in the name of the CIO (*not* the old charity), so there is no need to get the funders' consent for a transfer. You may, therefore, need letterheads, etc. for the CIO before the transfer date, but this is only possible once the CIO has been formed. For bids made further ahead, you will need to apply in the name of the old charity, but explain that plans are in hand for conversion to a CIO and hence that the grant or contract, if awarded, will be to the CIO.

Gift aid

If the CIO is to receive donations from individuals under gift aid, it will need to register afresh with HMRC to be able to submit gift aid claims as a new charity. It would be fraudulent for the CIO to make gift aid claims under the identity of the old charity. In particular, tax law operates quite differently for trusts as opposed to corporate bodies, even though the rules on gift aid are the same in both cases.

The CIO must first be registered with the Charity Commission (you cannot apply to HMRC to recognise a body which does not exist). You will then need to complete form ChA1 and return it by post to HMRC (see www.hmrc.gov.uk/charities for details). At the time of writing the form does not seem to be updated for CIOs, so add details to the form to make it clear that the charity is a CIO. There is space to enter details of the activities undertaken for public benefit – the same information can be used as provided to the Charity Commission to register the CIO (see page 74) – or a summary of this. Give the date of formation of the CIO as the date the constitution became effective. (Be sure to register with HMRC as a charity, not as a community amateur sports club.)

No gift aid claims can be made by the CIO until recognition as a charity for tax purposes has been completed, which will take several weeks, but the recognition will normally be backdated to an 'effective date' of when the CIO was formed. However, the fact that the CIO has been registered as a charity with the Charity Commission means that tax recognition by HMRC should follow automatically, unless HMRC has reason to suspect that it is being run for fraudulent purposes by persons who are not 'fit and proper' to be in charge of a charity.

Nevertheless, from the date of transfer, all literature, websites, donation envelopes, etc. (and gift aid declarations if separate) must be clearly updated so that they refer to the CIO and the new charity registration number. If the old charity received donations via external giving sites (Justgiving, Virgin Money Giving, Mydonate, etc.) check whether the charity's account with the external provider can be transferred to the CIO, or whether the provider requires the CIO to open a fresh account under the new registered charity number.

In the case of ongoing donors giving directly to the charity under gift aid declarations, remember that the existing declarations referred to the old charity and, strictly speaking, a new declaration is needed if a donor will continue to donate under gift aid to the CIO. However, if there are many donors and if the old and new charities have similar names and similar objects, HMRC will normally agree that gift aid declarations for existing donors will continue to be accepted for tax claims by the CIO. But a CIO which wants to rely on this is strongly advised to seek written confirmation from HMRC at the outset, rather than waiting until the next gift aid audit.

All donor records (whether manual or computerised) should be passed to the CIO under the transfer agreement.

Agreements with suppliers

Any ongoing agreements with suppliers will need to be transferred to the CIO. This includes suppliers of utilities (gas, water, electricity), suppliers of materials and stationery, insurance, maintenance contracts, ongoing agreements with freelance staff, etc.

In most cases these are not difficult to transfer because the supplier wants the charity to continue buying its services after the conversion, so all that may be needed is a letter on the old charity's letterhead about two weeks before the transfer saying something along these lines:

> Please note that as from [date] this charity is converting to the new legal form of a charitable incorporated organisation (CIO). The new name will be [Name of CIO] and the new charity registration number will be #######. On that date the existing charity will be wound up and all activities will transfer to the CIO from that date. Please would you transfer our agreement with yourselves to show it in the name of the CIO from this date, and please ensure future invoices are addressed to [Name of CIO].

However, some existing contracts with suppliers may state that the contract cannot be transferred to any other party – if so, you will need to seek the supplier's consent for novation of the agreement with the CIO (rather than simply advising them of the transfer).

Some agreements may need more discussion. In the case of insurance policies, for example, you are asking the insurers to accept a new policyholder, so you may need to complete a new proposal form, and often the trustees of the old charity will want continued cover for a time. Software licences also need to be transferred, although with mass-produced software the licence is usually linked to the particular computer rather than a named organisation. Agreements such as leases on vehicles or office equipment may require more negotiation, as the leasing company needs to be confident that the CIO will have the resources to commit to the remaining term of the lease.

Beneficiaries, members and service users

It is easy to focus on administrative issues and forget the beneficiaries and other users of the charity's services – but often the main reason for the conversion to a CIO is to give the charity a firmer basis which will benefit them in the long run.

If the charity has a defined beneficiary group, consider how best to contact them to explain the change. You will want to confirm that the CIO will continue to deliver the same support on the same terms as before. (But take care to word such a message in terms that will not cause alarm, especially if dealing with vulnerable beneficiaries.) However, where the charity has legal obligations to specific beneficiaries – for example a long-term commitment to support a disabled person – specialist advice will be needed.

If the charity which is converting is a grant-maker, it would be worth assuring grant recipients that future grant commitments made by the old charity will be honoured by the CIO.

Also, if the existing charity has members, do not overlook the need to communicate with them to explain what is happening. You may have sent out papers for an EGM at the start of the process in order to get their approval, but many will have ignored such documents or forgotten what was agreed many months before. Where former members are becoming members of the CIO, it may be appropriate to confirm their new status immediately after the conversion.

Care is needed to consider any other stakeholder groups that should be informed.

Employees

Staff serve under contracts of employment, and prior to the transfer, the employer will be the trustees of the old charity (though, unless contracts have been regularly updated, you may find that staff are technically employed by trustees who left some years ago – this is one of the reasons why a charity with staff is best structured as a corporate body).

These contracts need to be transferred to the CIO, which means that technically the staff will have a change of employer. Provided no changes are made to their terms and provided proper procedures are followed, they cannot refuse the change (unless they choose to resign) but you must comply with the 'TUPE' requirements: the Transfer of Undertakings (Protection of Employment) Regulations.[16] Breach of these requirements may allow employees to claim for unfair dismissal. A transfer of all the activities of an unincorporated charity to a CIO will automatically transfer all contracts of employment to the CIO under TUPE.

The details of TUPE are beyond the scope of this book, but the central issue is that employees' rights must be safeguarded when a service transfers from one entity (the old charity) to another one (the CIO). This means, for example, that if the CIO subsequently has to make staff redundant, their period of service for calculating redundancy will be counted from when they were employed by the old charity, not the date when they started working for the CIO. Also, they are protected from any change in contractual terms of service, such as offering staff new contracts with the CIO with reduced salaries or holiday entitlements. However, where an unincorporated charity is converting to a CIO, there is usually no intention to make any changes that would breach TUPE protected rights. Even if the legal requirement to consult staff does not arise, they should be informed in good time regarding what is planned and any concerns or queries dealt with. (If there is a recognised trade union, information must be provided to the union and it may need to be formally consulted, but a trade union is unlikely to have concerns if there are no plans for redundancies or worsening of conditions).

Then, shortly before the transfer date, you should write to each member of staff confirming that as from the transfer date, his or her contract of employment will transfer to the CIO, and confirming that all existing conditions of service will continue to apply and that his or her

[16] Transfer of Undertakings (Protection of Employment) Regulations 2006 (SI 2006/246). The regulations are made under the European Communities Act 1972, in order to comply with the UK's obligations under European law.

employment with the CIO will be treated as continuous from his or her service with the former charity.

The TUPE process does not apply to any member of staff whose contract was in any case due to terminate on or before the transfer date – for example, someone on a fixed-term contract – provided the existing employment was lawfully brought to an end. However, professional advice on staff transfer under TUPE should always be sought unless the implications of TUPE are fully understood.

Note that in all cases where there are staff, the CIO will be a new employer and will need to register afresh with HMRC for an employer's PAYE reference.

Pension schemes

A key complication may, however, arise in the case of pension schemes and it is vital to consider this at the outset. There is usually no problem with defined contribution schemes where financial contributions are made to a fund which is not managed by the employer (including stakeholder pensions, and the new workplace pensions provided under the auto-enrolment process as a result of the Pensions Act 2008).

But in the case of a charity with a defined benefit scheme (typically a final salary scheme) any deficit in the pension scheme would normally need to be settled by the old charity because it would then cease to have any employees in the scheme. It could not be transferred to a new entity. So, in a charity with a large pension deficit, winding up and converting to a CIO may simply be impossible. This could apply even if the old charity was simply one member of a multi-employer defined benefit scheme.

With this in mind, early consideration of pension implications is essential and specialist advice will almost always be needed.

Premises and loans

The transfer of premises may well be the most complex issue. If the old charity had freehold property, title to the land will need to be transferred to the CIO and re-registered accordingly at the Land Registry. If the land was held for the former charity for a long time, this can sometimes mean registering it for the first time. Any services involving transfers of freehold property can only be provided by a solicitor or licensed conveyancer.

Note that if the property was formerly held in the names of a number of individual trustees, each one will normally need to sign the deed of transfer (with a witness), so make sure that they can be contacted. If not, or if one or more of the former trustees has died and the charity has not appointed new holding trustees, the process outlined on page 175 using a pre-merger vesting declaration may help (see the following section in the case of designated land).

Ideally, the transfer of property will take place on the same day as all other transfers, but for this to be possible, solicitors will usually need to be instructed several months ahead in order to make the necessary arrangements.

Particular issues arise if the old charity had a secured loan (a mortgage) on the property, as the consent of the lender will be needed to transfer the charge to the CIO. This may take some time to agree and requires a reinvestigation of title. The lender may see it as increasing the risks of default to allow the loan to be assigned to a body with limited liability. Even unsecured loans can only be transferred if the lender agrees.

In the case of leasehold premises, complex negotiations with landlords may be needed to agree assignment of the lease to the CIO (and, as with banks, if the landlord has little experience of the charity sector, you will first need to explain the nature of a CIO). You may well have to cover the landlord's legal and surveyor's fees. If the negotiations would be difficult, it can be temping just to leave the agreement in the names of the old trustees, but they would typically then be in breach of a condition not to share possession of the premises with others (the CIO in this case). However, it is worth noting that in any case for leases granted prior to 1 January 1996, the original tenants will remain bound by the lease even after it has been transferred to the CIO, unless the landlord can be persuaded to release them from this (so if, for example, the CIO went into liquidation and rents were unpaid, the landlord could still pursue the old trustees). For leases granted after 1 January 1996, the original tenants will automatically be released from their obligations[17] once the lease is transferred to the CIO (unless the landlord requires guarantees from the old trustees as a condition of the transfer). Legal advice, therefore, will normally be essential.

However, in premises such as serviced units, the rental is more likely to be under a licence rather than a lease. In these cases it is usually not difficult for the old charity to terminate its licence, and a new licence is established with the CIO.

If the charity only rents premises on a sessional basis, there will be few difficulties as there is not normally any ongoing contract. But often room

[17] Landlord and Tenant (Covenants) Act 1995, s. 5.

bookings are made well ahead, so make sure that any bookings for sessions after the transfer date are clearly made in the name of the CIO.

Designated land

Designated land is defined as any land held on trusts which stipulate that it is to be used for charitable purposes[18] – i.e. where it is specifically referred to in the charity's governing document (sometimes called 'specie land'). It is a form of permanent endowment where the asset is in the form of a specific piece of land. Almshouses are a common example. Similarly, village hall charities or religious charities often hold designated land if the charity was established by someone who gave a specific plot of land to be held for the purposes of a village hall or a place of worship. But where an existing charity raised funds and bought land, or where land is simply held for investment purposes, it would not generally be designated land (for instance if a house had been left to the charity in someone's will, but with no condition that the house itself had to be used directly for the charitable purposes).

Even if land is designated, it can be transferred to a CIO as long as it remains held on the same trusts as previously (so it remains designated) and if the old charity has a power to dispose of assets (a wind-up provision). A pre-merger vesting declaration (see page 175) can be used.

But if the old charity is being wound up using a section 268 resolution because of no authority in the governing document, a scheme or order of the Charity Commission will be needed to vest designated land in the CIO. However, in all cases where land is involved, the Commission's guidance should be carefully considered[19] (and a solicitor will, in any case, be needed to handle transfers of land).

For the avoidance of doubt, if it is known from the outset that the CIO will hold designated land, it may help to add additional wording to the CIO constitution referring to the land and making clear that it is held on trust for the specific purposes. For example the powers clause could include an additional power:

> to hold on trust [give details of the land or property] as designated land under the terms of the Charities Act 2011 for the purposes specified in the trust deed of [date] namely for use as a [insert previous conditions on use etc.].

---

[18] Charities Act 2011, s. 267(1).

[19] *Sales, leases, transfers and mortgages: What trustees need to know about disposing of charity land* (Charity Commission 2012, ref. CC28).

Subsidiary companies

If the old charity had a trading subsidiary company (see 'CIOs with subsidiaries' on page 153 for more on this) it can normally be transferred directly to become a subsidiary of the CIO. It remains the same legal entity; so, for example, if the subsidiary had its own bank accounts, these will continue unchanged. Usually it will be a company limited by shares, and the shares need to be transferred from the old trustees to the CIO.

However, there should normally be an agreement in place between the subsidiary and the trustees of the old charity to cover services, sharing of staff, or apportionment of overheads, rents, etc. This will need to be replaced with a fresh agreement with the CIO.

Partnership agreements

If the old charity has formal agreements to work in partnership or collaboration with other charities or voluntary organisations (whether as a conventional partner or subcontractor) these agreements need to be re-established with the CIO.

External registrations

Any registrations or memberships held by the old charity with external bodies will need to be transferred to the CIO. These can include:

- statutory registrations such as notification under the Data Protection Act or registration for VAT (if needed);
- registration with regulatory bodies such as Care Quality Commission or with Ofsted for childcare provision;
- registration for service of food or for sale of alcohol or provision of entertainment under the Licensing Act 2003;
- registration of internet domain names (and trade marks or patents if applicable);
- membership of self-regulatory schemes such as the Fundraising Standards Board;
- membership of external organisations to which the older charity is affiliated (especially if they involve voting rights);
- etc.

It is impossible to produce a complete list of such issues: these are simply possibilities. It is best to go through every possible contact that the charity has with external parties and consider what to do. This needs to be done at an early stage to ensure that the transfer process does not create difficulties such as large fees or onerous new requirements.

Communications

From the transfer date, all external communications must clearly refer to the CIO (apart from issues specifically related to the wind-up of the old charity). Take care to ensure that all staff use new letterheads for the CIO, update email footers, amend websites, and ensure any literature which may have a contractual basis (such as order forms and donation forms) is amended.

This may seem bureaucratic or even wasteful (however, you could use stickers to avoid reprinting everything). But it is critical to get this right – if, for example, someone places an order after the transfer date and the documentation refers to the old charity and a dispute arises, the trustees of the old charity remain liable. They may be able to force the CIO to indemnify them, but it is much better for the CIO itself to make the commitment.

Practicalities in managing the transfer process

It is clear from the descriptions above that managing all these issues concerning the transfer may take considerable time and effort, depending on the size and scope of the charity's work. Once the trustees have agreed in principle to convert to a CIO, it is a good idea to put one member of staff in charge of the process (often this falls to the Finance Manager) but he or she will need considerable support from others. The tasks will certainly require additional time over and above the person's normal work.

Also, there will usually be costs for professional fees and for administrative expenses such as printing new letterheads, updating websites, and informing third parties. The scale of these costs can vary enormously, but it is vital to budget for them when the conversion to a CIO is first considered.

Dissolving the old charity (or not) and the Charity Mergers Register

In most cases when an unincorporated charity is wound up and all activities have been transferred to a CIO, the old charity can be dissolved once the final set of accounts has been prepared.

At that stage, it is straightforward to ask the Charity Commission to remove the old charity (if registered) from the Register of Charities. However, instead of simply asking for the old charity to be removed, a request should be made to record it on the Charity Mergers Register (this can be done even if the old charity was not a registered charity) showing details of the CIO to which its assets have been transferred.

The Charity Mergers Register (maintained by the Commission) was created by the Charities Act 2006 (now in the Charities Act 2011) to cover situations of this kind.[20] It records cases where one charity has closed and merged into another. Once a former charity is placed on the mergers register, any gift to the old charity after the date of registration of the merger takes effect is, in law, a gift to the charity into which it has merged (i.e. to the CIO in this case).

This means that if donations arrive with documentation clearly referring to the old charity, they can legally be paid to the CIO without requiring the donor's permission (though in the case of payments by cheque, you may need to ask the donor to amend the cheque if the account name has changed). More significantly, where someone has left a legacy to the old charity in a will, that bequest will transfer automatically to the new charity. (The personal representatives of the deceased cannot argue that the charity specified in the will no longer exists and hence that the bequest fails.)

Even if a charity rarely receives legacies, it is still better to ask for the old charity to be placed on the mergers register just in case a gift of this kind is received, rather than simply asking for it to be removed from the register.

However, there is an important limitation to consider. Quite often wills with charitable bequests include some alternative provision to allow for the possibility of a charity no longer existing at the time of the person's death. For example: 'I leave the sum of £20,000 to the XYZ Society (registered charity number #######) but if the Society no longer exists at the time of my death, I leave this sum to my nephew, Fred.' In this case, even if the XYZ Society was placed on the mergers register as having merged into the XYZ CIO, the XYZ Society itself would not exist at the date of death, and the gift would legally pass to Fred.

If the former charity is likely to receive future legacies, there may be a strong likelihood of donors who may have made bequests on these lines. If so, it can be better to keep the former charity in existence as a 'shell' so that it can receive any bequests of this kind and pass them on to the CIO.

It is possible that the law may be amended by a Law Commission review[21] to amend the operation of the Charity Mergers Register to remove this limitation, but any change is unlikely to take effect before 2017.

---

[20] Charities Act 2011, ss. 305–314.

[21] See lawcommission.justice.gov.uk/areas/charity-law.htm.

Nevertheless, keeping the old charity in existence as a shell will mean some work. It will still require clearly identified trustees who will need to meet at least once a year, and they will have to prepare a trustees annual report and annual accounts each year (even if the figures are nil) and complete the Charity Commission's Annual Update, otherwise the Commission is likely to conclude that the old charity is inactive and it will be deregistered (see chapter 12). It may be necessary to keep a bank account open, which could incur bank charges. It can cause confusion for newer donors to see two charities with almost identical names on the Register of Charities, and someone may erroneously look at the old charity rather than the CIO, see it has little or no income, and think the charity has folded. (The old charity could be kept in existence but deliberately de-registered once it has had a year with an income of less than £5,000, but it would then have to re-register if it receives a significant legacy.)

However, the option of keeping the old charity in existence indefinitely is not available if a pre-merger vesting declaration was used to transfer permanent endowment, as this can only be used as part of a merger (although some time could elapse between the vesting declaration and the final registration of the merger).

It is only worth keeping the old charity operating if the benefits in terms of possible legacies, for example, are likely to exceed the effort and disadvantages involved. In other cases, it is best to record the old charity on the Charity Mergers Register: the CIO will still get the benefit of any legacies left directly to the old charity. And in other instances it is often possible to make a case to the other beneficiaries under the will to abide by the spirit of the original legacy, if you can show that the work of the original charity is continuing in almost identical terms within the structure of a CIO.

Note that the Charity Mergers Register does not apply when one CIO transfers or amalgamates with another CIO[22] (see chapter 11) because, in those cases, any gifts to the old CIO automatically pass to the new CIO as a result of direct provisions in the Act.

Final accounts for the old charity

The final accounts for the old charity should show the transfer of all assets to the CIO (normally as an extraordinary item) and a final balance of £nil (and the trustees' report should explain the process and give details of the

[22] Charities Act 2011, s. 314.

CIO to which the assets were transferred). The first accounts of the CIO will start from £nil at the point of incorporation and show the incoming transfer (see chapter 8).

Even though the old charity is no longer operating once the transfer has taken place, the trustees of the old charity should hold a final meeting to approve the accounts for its last year. Normally this will be some months after the transfer. The Charity Commission's policy is not to require final accounts from a charity which has closed, unless the governing document requires this.[23] Nevertheless, most charity governing documents state that a final set of accounts must be sent to the Charity Commission if the charity is dissolved.

However, once a charity has been removed from the Register of Charities (whether through being placed on the Charity Mergers Register or otherwise) it is no longer possible to submit any information through the Charity Commission's online system, so the final set of accounts for the old charity (if its income is greater than £25,000) should be submitted to the Commission by post or email, with a suitable note of explanation, and they will then be recorded. Note that external parties will not be able to view these online, so when an unincorporated charity winds up and converts to a CIO, it can lead to an apparently missing year of accounts (and even the last year's accounts for the old charity which were previously available online will cease to appear.)

This can be problematic, as the first set of accounts for the CIO may not be available in some cases until as long as 28 months after the CIO was formed (if it has a first accounting period of 18 months and then takes the full 10 months after year end to file its accounts). So, where it is felt important to maintain a record of past accounts for funders and others, the CIO may wish to publish the last few years' accounts for the old charity on its own website, especially the final accounts leading to the transfer (but clearly labelled to distinguish them from the CIO's own accounts).

[23] Charity Commission Operational Guidance OG531-1, para. E1.3.

10 Converting charitable companies, CBSs and CICs to CIOs

From the days when CIOs were first proposed, it was recognised that because of their simplicity, charities which had been set up with other structures, even if they were already incorporated (most frequently as charitable companies), might wish to convert to CIOs. In such cases, the law allows a *direct conversion* of the existing body into a CIO, without needing to wind it up and transfer assets.

For the pros and cons of CIOs, charitable companies and other structures, see chapters 3 and 4. This chapter explains the processes involved if it is decided to convert a charitable company, a CBS, or a CIC to a CIO.

Direct conversions to CIOs: the concept

A direct conversion of this kind is possible because a company is already a corporate body, so the process involves taking an existing body and changing its constitutional basis from one based on company law, to one based on charity law. But, since it remains the same entity, many of the complications involved in converting unincorporated charities do not apply – there is no need to transfer staff or property, no need to set up new contracts, etc. (However, there are still legal issues to consider, which will be outlined later in this chapter.)

In all three UK jurisdictions (England and Wales, Scotland, and Northern Ireland) the primary legislation sets out procedures allowing a company to convert directly to a CIO – that is *without* winding up the company and creating a new entity.

Moreover, the same principles apply to conversion of some other types of third sector organisations which are already formed as corporate bodies, including charitable Community Benefit Societies (CBSs) and Community Interest Companies (CICs). (Note that direct conversion of CICs is not possible in Scotland.)

At the time of writing, as shown in table 10.1, regulations allowing direct conversions have only been implemented in Scotland (see chapter 13 for the details). It is anticipated that conversion of charitable companies and CICs to CIOs will be possible in England and Wales from early 2014 (subject to Parliamentary approval of the regulations). The conversion of CBSs is likely to follow from a later date once the registration of charitable CBSs by the Charity Commission has started (at present they are exempt from charity registration,[1] as explained on page 24. Conversions in Northern Ireland (see page 268) will not be possible until some time after the implementation of Northern Irish CIOs.

Table 10.1 Timescales for start of direct conversions to CIOs

Current legal form:	*Charitable company*	*Charitable CBS*	*CIC*
Conversion to E&W CIO	Expected from early 2014	Probably not before 2015	Expected from early 2014
Conversion to SCIO	From 1 Jan 2012	From 1 Jan 2012	Not possible without new legislation
Conversion to NI CIO	Probably not before 2016	Probably not before 2016	Probably not before 2016

Entities which can convert directly to CIOs

The rest of this chapter focuses on the processes applicable in England and Wales. Until final regulations are issued, however, many of the details are yet to be clarified.

The primarily legislation allows for the possibility of three types of entity being able to convert directly to a CIO:

- a charitable company;[2]
- a charitable industrial and provident society (IPS); however, as explained in chapter 1, an IPS with charitable aims will always be a

[1] While IPS charities remain exempt, they are explicitly prohibited from converting to CIOs under s. 229(2)(b) of the Charities Act 2011. So even if this section were commenced, an IPS would not be able to apply to convert while it remained exempt.

[2] Charities Act 2011, s. 228.

community benefit society (CBS), so the term 'CBS' is used in this chapter;[3]
- a community interest company (CIC).[4]

For a reminder of the acronyms, see table 1.2 on page 14, and, for more on the principles of these forms, see chapters 3 and 4.

In the case of a charitable company or charitable CBS, the body must already be a charity, and so in most cases it will, therefore, already be a registered charity; although it could previously have been excepted from registration depending on income.

In the case of a CBS, it is quite likely that the application to convert to a CIO will be made soon after CBSs cease to be exempt charities and eligible for charity registration: at that point a charitable CBS becomes an excepted charity, and registration is then required if its income exceeds £100,000 (see page 24 for more on exempt and excepted charities). In theory, a charitable CBS with an income of more than £100,000 that wishes to convert should thus apply first to register as a charity (as a CBS) and then apply to convert from a CBS to a CIO, but, in practice, it seems unlikely that the Charity Commission will require this. Also as outlined in chapter 4, many CBSs would require changes to their rules before they could be registered as charities. In such cases, if the Charity Commission agrees to allow a CBS to apply to convert to a CIO, these issues can potentially be remedied as part of the conversion.

However, a CIC is specifically not a charity[5] and so the conversion process is more fundamental as it involves the body taking on charitable purposes for the first time. At the point of conversion, the CIC's existing assets will become subject to charity law. In most cases the conversion of a CIC will involve adoption of new objects in order to be recognised as a charity, although it may occasionally be the case that the existing objects of the CIC are accepted as charitable once it gives up its CIC status. The process will clearly have parallels with the existing legislation allowing a CIC to give up its CIC status and become a charitable company.[6]

In each case the conversion involves giving up the existing status in order to become a CIO. So, a charitable company which converts to a CIO ceases

---

[3] Charities Act 2011, s. 229.

[4] Charities Act 2011, s. 234. This section does not specify a full process for conversion of CICs but simply allows the Minister to make regulations to that effect.

[5] Companies (Audit, Investigations and Community Enterprise) Act 2004, s. 26(3).

[6] Companies (Audit, Investigations and Community Enterprise) Act 2004, ss. 53–55.

to be a company and is no longer registered at Companies House (Companies House will simply retain a record of the *former* company to show that it has converted to a CIO). A CBS which becomes a CIO ceases to be an IPS, and will no longer be registered with the Financial Conduct Authority FCA).[7] A CIC which converts gives up both its status as a company *and* its status as a CIC (so it is no longer regulated by the CIC Regulator and cannot use 'CIC' in its name).

Membership of the CIO

A fundamental feature of the legislation allowing the direct conversion of other bodies is that the members of the charitable company, CIC or CBS are the same before and after the conversion.[8] This ensures that members' rights remain protected, whether the members are individuals or corporate bodies.

This does not mean the membership criteria cannot alter. In fact, the conversion to a CIO may be used in some cases to change the rules so that other people are eligible to become members. The requirement simply means that the first members of the CIO on the day after conversion will be the same persons who were the members of the company immediately before.

Bodies with share capital

Most conversions (whether of charitable companies or CICs) are likely to be cases where the existing company is limited by guarantee (i.e. a CLG where the members give a small financial guarantee, rather than holding shares).

However, all CBSs have shareholders (albeit the shares often have just a nominal value). Likewise, a CIC could have shareholders, and in rare cases even a charitable company can have shares (so long as no dividends are paid to private owners). In the case of a body with shareholders, conversion to a CIO is only possible if all shares are fully paid up, so there are no sums outstanding from shareholders.[9]

When a body with shares converts to a CIO, the shares are cancelled and former shareholders have no further rights in respect of their shares[10] (although the shareholders will continue as members of the CIO).

---

[7] Formerly the Financial Services Authority – see footnote on page 42.

[8] Charities Act 2011, s. 233(1)(c).

[9] Charities Act 2011, s. 228(2)(a) & s. 229(2)(a).

[10] Charities Act 2011, s. 233(2).

Members' guarantees

A CLG requires every member of the company to give a guarantee (usually a nominal amount such as £1 or £5) towards any outstanding liabilities if the company is dissolved. Such guarantees are possible with a CIO, but very few CIOs will want to include this.

The legislation helpfully states that if a charitable company has a members' guarantee which is no more than £10 per member, the guarantee is *extinguished* at the point of converting to a CIO.[11] This means that the complexities of a membership scheme where each member has to give a guarantee to the company are replaced by a much simpler membership arrangement in the CIO without a guarantee. However, in the rare event of a charitable company with a guarantee of more than £10 per member, it must be retained in the constitution of the CIO.[12]

The conversion process

The steps outlined below indicate how a charitable company in England and Wales will be able to convert to a CIO.

For a CIC, the process is likely to be similar. However, as explained, there may be other steps, as the CIC will not be an existing charity, and the regulations will almost certainly require the CIC Regulator to be consulted (not just the Registrar of Companies).

When conversion of CBSs is implemented, the steps will be almost the same, but involving the FCA instead of Companies House.

Planning, timescales and accounting issues

The first step if a charitable company is considering converting to a CIO is to review the advantages and disadvantages of each form, as outlined in chapter 4. Whilst the CIO form is simpler and avoids the need for a members' guarantee, the well-established status of a charitable company can have advantages in some cases. Moreover, even though a direct conversion is possible, it is still a major constitutional change and needs careful planning to ensure that the work of the charity is not disrupted. In many cases, a conversion may start to be considered when a charitable company would in any case be considering significant changes to its articles: the question would then be whether to amend the articles and

[11] Charities Act 2011, s. 228(8).

[12] Charities Act 2011, s. 228(6)&(7).

remain as a charitable company, or whether to adopt a completely new constitution as a CIO.

(It is worth noting that people often refer to the governing documents of a company as 'the memorandum and articles', but following implementation of the Companies Act 2006, a company's memorandum only contains details of the initial members. All provisions previously in a company's memorandum – including its charitable objects – are now deemed to be part of its articles.[13])

Because the direct conversion of a charitable company to a CIO does not involve creating a new entity, there is no benefit to be gained from scheduling the conversion to take place at the end of an accounting year as the conversion will not involve starting a new set of accounts. In fact, it will normally be difficult to schedule the conversion to take place on a specific date because of the communication between the Charity Commission and Companies House, as explained on page 200. It is, therefore, simplest to arrange for the conversion to take place well away from year end, preferably at a time of year which is relatively quiet in other respects, because of the need to update documents.[14]

Nevertheless, considerable time needs to be allowed for careful implementation of the steps below.

The CIO constitution

Once the trustees are agreed in principle that conversion is right, a new constitution must be prepared for the charity as a CIO, rather than as a company. This must, of course, comply with all the requirements for CIO constitutions explained in chapter 6.

One of the Charity Commission model constitutions will be useful in many cases as a starting point, but as is the case when converting an unincorporated charity, care is needed to ensure that any essential

[13] Companies Act 2006, s. 28.

[14] The draft CIO regulations published for consultation in 2008 enabling conversion of charitable companies to CIOs in England and Wales suggested that it might be necessary to prepare a financial statement at the time of applying for conversion. They also indicated that conversion might not be possible at any time when the company had passed a year end and not yet filed its accounts, which meant that for a company which took a full nine months to file its accounts after year end, conversion would only be possible in the last three months of the year. However, it is hard to see any benefit from such rules, and no requirements on these lines apply in Scotland. It is hoped that the final regulations will simply state that the company must not be in arrears with its accounts.

elements of the existing charity's governing document are reflected in the CIO constitution. Time will normally be needed for several drafts before the trustees will feel ready to table formal resolutions.

The CIO constitution may well involve a new name. Certainly, it cannot include 'Limited' if that was part of the name of the charitable company and it could be desirable to include 'CIO' in the name to make the new status clear. (However, if the former name did not contain 'Limited' and if the new name does not contain 'CIO', the name could remain unchanged; but disclosures of the status on documents will still need to be updated.)

The wording of the constitution must include the names of those who will be the first trustees of the CIO (immediately after the conversion). It would be possible to make changes of trustees as part of the conversion, if the end result will be an association CIO. But, as explained, the members cannot change as part of the conversion. So it follows that if a foundation CIO is being created from a charitable company with identical members and trustees, the trustees cannot change at that point (any trustee changes should thus take place before or after the conversion).

The resolutions

For a charitable company to convert to a CIO, two resolutions must be passed:

- to convert the company to a CIO[15] (if approved by the Charity Commission); and
- to adopt the new CIO constitution[16] (in place of the company's articles), assuming the conversion is agreed.

These are resolutions under the Charities Act but they must be passed following processes under company law. For the conversion to succeed, they must therefore be passed by the members of the company (not just by the trustees). In most cases, this will require calling a special general meeting of the company (unless this can be combined with an existing members' meeting such as an AGM).

The first of the resolutions must be passed as a special resolution.[17] This means it must gain at least a 75% majority of those present and voting, and the notice of the meeting must give the proposed wording and make clear that it is a special resolution. At least 14 clear days' notice of the

[15] Charities Act 2011, s. 228(3)(a).

[16] Charities Act 2011, s. 228(3)(c).

[17] Charities Act 2011, s. 228(4).

meeting will be needed (21 days for an AGM),[18] unless at least 90% of members agree to reduce this. Note, however, that many charitable companies have articles requiring longer notice periods for members' meetings or higher proportions of members in agreement to reduce the notice. Even in a charitable company where the members and trustees are the same people, this must be clearly called and minuted as a members' meeting (not a trustees' meeting).

Instead of calling a meeting, the members could agree these resolutions in writing, but if so the decision must be unanimous,[19] so this is only worth considering in a company with a small membership (the provisions in the Companies Act allowing written resolutions to be passed with a 75% majority do not apply to the decision to convert to a CIO which is made under the Charities Act).

Applying to the Charity Commission

Once the resolutions are passed, an application is made to the Charity Commission to approve the conversion. (Do not send anything to Companies House, as the Charity Commission will co-ordinate the process.) The application must include:

- copies of both the resolutions above;
- a copy of the proposed CIO constitution (as provisionally adopted by the second resolution);
- any other documents as specified in the regulations or which the Charity Commission requires (there will be an application form for such conversions, most probably online).

The Charity Commission then assesses the application to ensure the proposed body will still be a charity, and that the CIO constitution meets the legal requirements. It will also make sure that there is nothing objectionable about the proposed CIO name, and that removal of a members' guarantee complies with the rules outlined on page 197. It will also consider any other issues raised by the conversion regulations.[20]

At that stage, if the Charity Commission considers the essential requirements are met, it 'provisionally registers' the CIO by adding a suitable note on the Register of Charities.[21] In the case of an existing charitable company which is already a registered charity, and where the

[18] Companies Act 2006, s. 307.

[19] Charities Act 2011, s. 228(4)(b).

[20] Charities Act 2011, s. 231.

[21] Charities Act 2011, s. 232(1)(a)&(3).

proposal is to convert to a CIO without any substantive change to its objects, provisions on trustee benefits or dissolution, this stage is likely to be met fairly easily. This is similar to the well-established process for seeking Charity Commission approval for 'regulated alterations' to a company's articles.[22]

However, in the case of a company which is not currently registered as a charity, getting to the stage of provisional registration of the CIO will involve the full scrutiny involved in registration of a new charity. (Most CBS conversions are also likely to involve a new application for charity registration. A proposal to convert a CIC will certainly involve an application for charity registration, and the supporting documentation will need to focus on the future – as when registering a new CIO – because the CIC will not have been a charity in the past: see chapter 5 for further guidance.)

Once provisional registration of the CIO is reached, the Charity Commission contacts the Registrar of Companies (Companies House), or the FCA in the case of a CBS with copies of the proposed resolutions and the provisional entry in the Register of Charities showing the proposed CIO status. (It must also advise Companies House of the resolutions even if the conversion application is refused.)[23]

Companies House must then register these documents against the company's record (the resolutions are, at this stage, resolutions of a company) and it then *cancels* the registration of the company and advises the Charity Commission accordingly.

Once the Charity Commission receives confirmation from Companies House, the Register of Charities is updated to remove the 'provisional registration' status and to show that the charity is now fully constituted as a CIO. The Register entry must show the former company name and the date of conversion.[24]

The discretion on whether to allow the conversion rests entirely with the Charity Commission: once provisional registration of the CIO is reached, Companies House *must* cancel the company's registration so that the conversion becomes final (this is slightly different from the Scottish conversion process – see chapter 13). But the regulations will almost certainly require the Charity Commission to consult with Companies

[22] Charities Act 2011, s. 198.

[23] Charities Act 2011, s. 232(1)(b).

[24] Charities Act 2011, s. 232(4)–(6).

House and will set out the circumstances in which a conversion should not be allowed.

Continuing as a CIO

Once the processes above are complete, the existing company has become a CIO governed by its new constitution. All future decisions and actions by the charity must then be taken on the basis of the new status as a CIO under that new constitution.

It is vital to update all documentation promptly to show the new status as a CIO, as it would be an offence to claim to be a company when this is no longer the case. Any references, therefore, to the company number or 'company limited by guarantee' must be removed. If the new name does not include 'CIO', the documentation must clearly show the status as a 'charitable incorporated organisation'.

In the case of a company which was already a registered charity, it seems clear that no change of registered charity number will be involved, because, under the process explained, the provisional registration of the CIO relates to an existing body which is already a registered charity. However, as noted, the regulations could require additional procedures, and the Charity Commission's processes cannot be finalised until the regulations are in place.

The company's registers will need to be converted to become CIO registers (see chapter 7) and may need updating to comply with the CIO regulations.

Financial reporting after the conversion

Once converted, the next financial year end of the charity will be as a CIO, so the accounts will follow charity law, as applied to CIOs (see chapter 8) rather than company law. The accounts will be filed solely with the Charity Commission (not with Companies House, as the company's registration has been cancelled).

Unless the regulations specify otherwise, the accounts will normally cover the standard 12 months since the previous year end as a company. However, a note should be added to explain that the prior year's figures relate to a period when the charity was a company (and the current year up to the point of conversion). Nevertheless, if the CIO accounts follow the Charities SORP there should be no substantial differences in the figures. If, however, the CIO has an income of less than £250,000 and it is decided to prepare receipts and payments accounts for the CIO, the change of basis needs to be clearly explained.

The trustees' annual report must give details of the governing document and the latest amendment. So it will need to explain that the charity is constituted as a CIO (governed by a constitution effective from the date of conversion) but that it was a charitable company before that date (and if there has been a change of name that too should be explained).

Land, funding, and notifications to other parties

The conversion of a charitable company to a CIO continues the existing corporate identity and so, as explained above, there is no process of transferring staff, property and agreements with third parties. All agreements entered into by the company continue to apply to the CIO.

However, it does not follow from this that there is no need to consult staff or third parties: in particular, agreements with third parties may well stipulate that their consent is needed for any change to the company's articles, and converting to a CIO would certainly constitute a major change to the articles!

So, for example, if the charitable company has any kind of loan or mortgage, it will usually be the case that the consent of the lender is needed before converting to a CIO. In the case of a loan secured on freehold property, this security would continue after the conversion, so the lender should have no grounds to object if there are no substantial changes to the charitable objects or governance arrangements, but this will need to be checked. However, in the rare case of a charitable company having a loan secured as a floating charge on the company assets, there is no equivalent provision for registration of a floating charge over a CIO (see page 330), so the lender would almost certainly refuse.

Any agreements with funders where you were asked to supply a copy of the charity's governing documents as part of the original application will generally require notification of any change to the governing document. If the agreement stipulated that no changes can be made to the governing document without the funder's approval, you will need to obtain the funder's consent for the conversion in advance. In other cases it will normally be sufficient to advise funders and others after the conversion has taken place with a copy of the CIO constitution, but this should not be overlooked.

However, it is likely that funders, lenders, and others may be unaware of the process for converting a charitable company to a CIO – they may think that you are proposing to wind up the company and transfer assets, etc. to a CIO (as with an unincorporated charity converting to a CIO). With this in mind, stress that this is a constitutional change to an *existing* corporate charity and not a change which requires novation of agreements. But take care to follow any conditions in funding and lending agreements; otherwise, even though agreements will remain in force, the funder or lender may say that the charity has broken the terms and could take action accordingly. Similar issues are likely with landlords. Any external regulators other than the Charity Commission will also need to be advised, if applicable (for example Ofsted or the Care Quality Commission).

In case of difficulty, it may be worth drawing attention to section 233 of the Charities Act 2011 which states that the conversion of a charitable company into a CIO does not affect any liabilities it had as a company.[25] So you will be able to assure funders and lenders that the conversion will not in any way diminish the charity's obligations to deliver on its agreements and, of course, its balance sheet will be unaffected by the conversion.

If the charitable company owned freehold land, the ownership is unaffected by the change of form to a CIO. However, (assuming the land is registered) the ownership details will need to be updated with the Land Registry on form AP1 to register the change of name (since the CIO will normally have a slightly different name) and to remove the company number. At the time of writing, the Land Registry's guidance does not specifically mention CIOs: but in the meantime title could be registered as a 'non-exempt charity incorporated otherwise than under the Companies Acts'. You will need to submit a copy of the entry from the Register of Charities documenting the conversion. There is no fee to the Land Registry to register a change of name for an existing owner, but without experience it is relatively difficult to get the documentation right, and there are important additional issues for charities. Making an error could make for considerable difficulties at a later date. In practice, therefore, it will usually be sensible to use a solicitor or licensed conveyancer to register the change. (If the solicitor is not a charity specialist, make sure he or she clearly understands the nature of the conversion that has taken place – it is *not* a disposal of land from one charity to another.)

You will certainly need to advise the charity's bankers of the change. Normally this should require no more than a change of account name (if applicable) and updating of the bank mandate to make clear that the bank is acting on behalf of a CIO rather than a company. However, it is conceivable that some banks may decline to provide accounts for CIOs,

[25] Charities Act 2011, s. 233(4).

and if this were to happen, the charity could have to change banks. So, it is desirable to consult with bankers in advance (but again, make clear that you are not creating a new legal entity).

It will also be important to keep staff informed of the change – partly to reassure them that there are no changes to their contracts of employment (although the name of the employer may change) – but also to ensure that they themselves reflect the change properly in all communications with third parties. For example, staff (and volunteers if applicable) will need to be advised to switch to using new letterheads and new email signatures from the date of the change.

In most cases, the conversion will involve a change of name, and hence suppliers, freelancers and others concerned all need to be advised to update their records to show the new name (and to explain that the charity is now a CIO).

Summary: deciding whether to convert

Although the process for an existing incorporated charity to become a CIO is much simpler than for an unincorporated charity, there are still many practical issues to consider. For a large charitable company with freehold property, loans, or complex contractual funding agreements it is likely that the simplicity of the CIO form is more than outweighed by the effort of converting, and it may be preferable to remain as a charitable company.

But for smaller charitable companies with relatively simple affairs, where trustees and staff have found it challenging to comply with company law or where members want to be free of the guarantee needed in a CLG, a conversion to a CIO may provide a simple and effective way forward.

In the case of a CBS or CIC there are further issues to consider as outlined in this chapter, though the advantages may be greater. In the case of a CBS, once it becomes possible to convert to a CIO, the charity will give up its FCA registration and fees and will gain the benefits of registered charity status. In those cases where an organisation was formed as a CIC but where, on reflection, it would more appropriately be established as a charity, conversion of the CIC to a CIO following this process may be very attractive: in particular, it is likely to involve no more work than giving up CIC status to become a charitable company.

11 CIO wind-ups and mergers

Charities sometimes continue to operate for centuries with little more than the minor updating of their governing documents. Unless there are fundamental changes in charity law, it is perfectly possible that a CIO formed in (say) 2014 could still be operating in the year 2114 (long after the death of its founders) or later. As a corporate body, a CIO has a permanent existence, unless it is dissolved.

The end of a CIO

Just as there are times and reasons and processes for setting up a CIO, there may also be times when the work of a CIO comes to an end. In such cases, processes are needed to deal with the dissolution of the CIO.

Possible reasons for needing to wind up a CIO could include:

- a change in social circumstances (for example, in the needs of beneficiaries) meaning that the original rationale for the charity no longer exists;
- a positive decision by the trustees of a grant-making charity to 'spend out' the remaining assets on grants, rather than retaining funds for the future;
- an inability to attract sufficient funding to continue the work – this could be gradual, for example due to declining interest from donors, or sudden, possibly owing to the loss of a major funding source;
- a crisis where a CIO simply cannot pay its bills and has no means of addressing this: it has become insolvent;
- the loss of members or volunteers essential to the CIO's work;
- the loss of key trustees (for example, due to illness, death or moving away) where the remaining trustees no longer have the commitment or expertise to continue the CIO's work;
- a decision that the work of the CIO could be carried out more effectively by merging with another charity – typically to avoid duplication or share resources – so there is no reason to continue the CIO as a charity in its own right;

- a fundamental change which means that the CIO is no longer able to meet the definition of a charity, for example if the class of possible beneficiaries becomes so small that it no longer meets the public benefit requirement (see page 28).

In such cases, a CIO cannot simply fade away! As a corporate body, it continues to exist until it is dissolved. Moreover, there is no provision in law for a 'dormant' CIO – there may sometimes be a period of a year or more when a CIO has no income or expenditure, but it is still a body established for charitable purposes. So the trustees must meet from time to time (as required by the constitution) to agree how to advance those purposes, and they must continue to prepare and file an annual report and accounts each year. If, however, they conclude that the CIO cannot realistically continue, they must take steps to arrange for it to be wound up.

Ways in which a CIO can be wound up

Broadly speaking, there are four ways in which a CIO can be wound up:

- a solvent dissolution (where a CIO is wound up by approval of its members and trustees after settling all its liabilities and distributing all its remaining assets);
- a merger (where a CIO merges with another charity and so ceases to exist in its own right);
- an insolvent dissolution (where the CIO cannot meet its liabilities, and a process of liquidation takes place, where assets are shared between creditors);
- dissolution by the charity regulator (CCEW, OSCR, CCNI), either because the CIO has ceased to operate, or because it has ceased to be a charity.

This chapter focuses on solvent dissolutions and mergers (in particular, the very simple arrangement for one CIO to merge with another). The processes for winding up CIOs which are insolvent, inactive or no longer charitable are considered in chapter 12.

The detailed issues below apply to CIOs in England and Wales, though there are close parallels for SCIOs and CIOs in Northern Ireland (see chapters 13 and 14 respectively for more on CIO mergers and dissolutions in these jurisdictions).

Mergers of a CIO into other charities

In many cases, rather than winding up a CIO completely, it is worth exploring the possibility of a merger with another charity, if it will allow the work to continue in some form. It is worth referring to the Charity Commission's guidance on charity mergers,[1] though, at the time of writing, it does not deal with the specific legal issues for CIO mergers. If a full merger is not possible, it may still be possible for the assets to be transferred to another charity for continued use on the same basis, as explained on page 214, but the CIO itself will then be dissolved.

Many mergers are planned well ahead as a natural process of charities coming together. However, in cases of financial difficulty, merger options need to be explored as early as possible, otherwise there is a major risk of being overtaken by events, and ending up with no option other than an insolvent dissolution (see chapter 12) where creditors are left unpaid and there is huge resentment.

Merging a CIO into a non-CIO charity

If a CIO is to wind up and merge into another charity which is *not* a CIO, it has to abandon its status as a CIO. This means, in effect, following the process described below for a solvent dissolution of a CIO (see page 214).

Many of the practical issues described in chapter 9 regarding the conversion of an unincorporated charity into a CIO will apply, as the CIO's assets, staff, funding agreements, etc. have to transfer from one legal entity to another.

However, it will be rare for a CIO to wind up and transfer its assets to an unincorporated charity: in most cases, such a merger would be best done in the opposite direction, where the unincorporated charity merges with the CIO, following the process outlined in chapter 9. Either way, specialist advice will normally be needed.

On the other hand, if the existing charity which is to receive the assets of the CIO is a charitable company, it may be worth considering whether that charity could first become a CIO (as explained in chapter 10) and then the process for a CIO-to-CIO merger could be followed, as explained in the following sections.

[1] *Collaborative Working and Mergers* (Charity Commission 2009, ref CC34).

Amalgamations: CIOs merging to form a new CIO

There are simple and straightforward procedures in the Charities Act for two (or more) CIOs to merge (amalgamate) into a new CIO.[2] This amalgamation process is a more equal arrangement than the transfer process described in the next section, but it does mean dissolving both the existing CIOs.

A major feature of this process is that all property rights and liabilities of the old CIOs automatically vest in the merged CIO as a result of this process.[3] So there is no need to go through all the steps outlined in chapter 9 of transferring assets, liabilities, staff and property from one body to another. (For a CIO with staff, the provisions of the TUPE Regulations will apply, as such a merger will amount to 'a transfer of an economic entity which retains its identity'.[4] But contracts of employment will not need to be re-issued: only updated for the change of name.)

Of course the new CIO will have a new name and registered charity number, and a merger always raises plenty of practical issues to consider as two charities with different histories learn to adapt to working as one. Before the merger, each CIO will need to undertake due diligence on the other, and on the proposed new CIO, to assess the benefits and risks involved. Since the process involves a merger of liabilities as well as assets, there isn't any means to limit the risks: if the risks are too great, it may be better to accept the additional complexities of winding up one of the CIOs and transferring the assets, on the basis outlined starting on page 214.

But where an amalgamation can be agreed, in many ways the process is closer to the steps for an existing CIO making major constitutional changes rather than a traditional wind-up and merger process. There are some parallels with the process in chapter 10 of a charitable company converting to a CIO (it will still be necessary to advise the change to all affected parties and to update Land Registry records). But there is no change of status – what started as a CIO continues as a CIO.

The ability to undertake mergers on this basis vastly simplifies the traditional approach to charity mergers and is a major benefit of the CIO form (although there are similar provisions for industrial and provident societies which can facilitate CBS mergers). The CIO merger provisions

---

[2] Charities Act 2011, ss. 235–239.

[3] Charities Act 2011, s. 239(2).

[4] Transfer of Undertaking (Protection of Employment) Regulations 2006, reg. 3(1)(a).

took effect from the same date as initial CIO registrations began in England and Wales (2 January 2013) so they can be used immediately. As increasing numbers of charities are formed as CIOs, such mergers may become common. In the early years, however, it will often be the case that one partner is not a CIO, so this route will not be possible (although a charitable company could first convert to a CIO, once that route is implemented).

Once there is agreement in principle on the merger by the respective boards of trustees of the separate CIOs, a constitution must be prepared for the new CIO which will result from the merger.

The members of *both* the existing CIOs must pass resolutions approving the proposed amalgamation and agreeing to adopt the new constitution. These resolutions must be passed under the normal requirements for constitutional amendments in a CIO (see page 107); in other words, a 75% majority vote of members present at a properly convened general meeting, or unanimously if the resolution is not put to a meeting.

The constitution of the new CIO must have charitable objects which are 'substantially the same' as those of the existing CIOs; otherwise the Charity Commission could refuse the merger.[5] The same requirement applies to dissolution provisions and rules on trustee benefits. This may create a challenge if the existing CIOs have objects which are somewhat different from each other, as the objects of the merged CIO will need to be broad enough to encompass the objects of both the existing charities. In cases of doubt, it would make sense to consult the Charity Commission well in advance.

If the objects of the existing CIOs are substantially different, it would be possible in principle for each of them to make a constitutional amendment to alter their objects to a common wording prior to the merger (these would be regulated alterations requiring Charity Commission approval – see page 108).

The resolutions and proposed new constitution are submitted to the Commission using the online system for registration of a new CIO (see page 81) but selecting the amalgamation option. This will make clear that approval is sought for an amalgamation of CIOs under section 235 of the Charities Act 2011.

If the Charity Commission is satisfied that the new CIO will be properly constituted and will be a charity, and that there are no objections to the proposed name, the new CIO is created and the former CIOs are dissolved. The members of both the existing CIOs are merged to become the

[5] Charities Act 2011, s. 237(4)&(5).

members of the new CIO.[6] The initial trustees of the new CIO will need to be specified in its constitution: the existing trustee boards do *not* automatically merge. However, if the new CIO is to be a foundation CIO, where the members and trustees are the same, the members will merge, so the same will apply to the trustees. In such cases, any trustee who does *not* wish to continue will need to resign as a member and trustee of his or her existing CIO, before the merger.

All property, rights and liabilities of the previous CIOs are transferred automatically to the new CIO as a result of the amalgamation. As explained above, this approach may not, therefore, be suitable if one of the existing CIOs is exposed to major risks which the other is reluctant to accept. In other cases, however, the transfer of liabilities is very helpful as it means all contractual obligations transfer automatically. Under the amalgamation process, any gifts to the old CIOs (such as legacies) which take effect after the merger automatically pass to the new CIO.[7] Because of this provision, the merger does not need to be recorded on the Charity Mergers Register (see page 188). Indeed, the legislation for the Mergers Register does not allow CIO amalgamations or transfers to appear[8] because there was no process of winding up a former charity and transferring assets to a new entity.

Because the new CIO is a completely new body it will have its own entry on the Register of Charities and a new charity registration number. However, the Register will include a note indicating that the CIO was formed as the result of an amalgamation and giving details of the former CIOs involved. (If, on the other hand, you want to keep one of the former CIOs in existence, it would be better to use the CIO transfer process as outlined in the next section.)

The process can apply to a merger of more than two CIOs, so long as they all pass the necessary resolutions. However, these provisions in the 2011 Act only relate to CIOs registered with the Charity Commission. There are similar provisions in the Scottish and Northern Irish legislation – see chapters 13 and 14 – but there is no provision for cross-border mergers of CIOs in England and Wales with SCIOs or Northern Irish CIOs.

---

[6] Charities Act 2011, s. 239(1)(c).

[7] Charities Act 2011, s. 239(3).

[8] Charities Act 2011, s. 314.

Transfers: mergers of one CIO into another

If two charities both structured as CIOs wish to merge into one charity, rather than an amalgamation into a new CIO as described above, it will often be simpler to wind up one (normally whichever is the smaller) and merge into the other. In such cases, the Charities Act provides for a simple CIO transfer process:[9] but instead of creating a new CIO, one of the existing CIOs continues as the merged body.

This works on the same lines as the amalgamation process, with the same transfer of all property, rights and liabilities (and hence with all the associated risks), so the similar elements will not be repeated in detail. Any future gifts which may become due to the former CIO automatically transfer to the merged CIO as a result of the transfer.[10] However, as with amalgamations, this process can only be used if both charities are CIOs registered in England and Wales.

In the following explanation, the CIO which will wind up and transfer its assets is called 'the 'transferor' and the existing CIO which will become the merged charity is called 'the transferee'.

For the merger to proceed, the members of both the transferor and transferee CIOs must pass resolutions under the normal requirements for constitutional amendments; i.e. a 75% majority vote of members present at a meeting, or unanimously if the resolution is not put to a meeting.

- The members of the transferor CIO must resolve that its property, assets and liabilities be transferred to the transferee CIO (which must be named in the resolution).
- The members of the transferee CIO must resolve to agree to the transfer. (Note that even if the transferee CIO is a very large charity compared to the transferor, its members must still agree to accept the merger, because it may be taking on new liabilities.)

Both resolutions are submitted to the Charity Commission (make clear that it is an application under section 240 of the 2011 Act) and if it approves the transfer, all property, rights, and liabilities of the transferor CIO pass automatically to the transferee, and the transferor CIO is dissolved.

---

[9] Charities Act 2011, ss. 240–244.

[10] Charities Act 2011, s. 244.

Note that this process does not involve adopting a new constitution – the constitution of the transferee CIO continues to apply – so it needs to have charitable objects which are broad enough to take on the work of the transferor. However, as with amalgamations, the Charity Commission can refuse the application if it does not consider the objects, dissolution provisions and trustee benefit rules of the transferee CIO are 'substantially similar' to those of the transferor.[11]

Unlike the amalgamation process, the members of the transferor CIO do *not* automatically transfer (and similarly there is no automatic transfer of trustees). So it may be necessary to reach agreement prior to the merger that members of the transferor CIO are able to become members of the merged CIO. There may also be agreement for one or more of the trustees of the transferor to join the board of the transferee CIO.

Solvent dissolution of a CIO

In cases where the work of a CIO needs to close and it is not possible to amalgamate or agree a transfer with another CIO, the existing CIO must be dissolved using the processes set out in the CIO Insolvency and Dissolution (I&D) Regulations.[12] Provided all debts and liabilities can be settled in full, the following process allows for a solvent dissolution, which the regulations describe as a 'Dissolution otherwise than under the Insolvency Act 1986'.

A solvent dissolution may apply either in the case of the CIO merging into a non-CIO charity (see page 209) or simply where the work of the CIO has come to an end. (For insolvent dissolutions, see chapter 12.)

Remaining assets

Sometimes in such situations a charity being wound up has no assets whatsoever; for example, if the CIO is a grant-making charity, the trustees may have made grants which bring the funds down to a final balance of £nil. However, in many cases there will be some assets remaining and, in such cases, the dissolution process will then involve transferring them to another charity in accordance with the dissolution clause in the CIO's constitution.

[11] Charities Act 2011, s. 242(2)&(3).

[12] The CIO (I&D) Regulations 2012, Part 3.

So, the first step will be to look carefully at the wording of the dissolution clause and identify a suitable charity with similar objects. Other specific steps in the dissolution clause must be followed carefully, otherwise there is a serious risk of later objections and appeals that the CIO was wrongly dissolved.

If there are assets to transfer, and if the most appropriate charity to receive them is itself a CIO, it may be simpler to follow the transfer process above rather than applying for dissolution (unless this would involve transferring liabilities which are unacceptable to the transferee CIO – the advantage of a dissolution is that liabilities must be settled before any assets are transferred). But if you wish to transfer assets to a charity which is not a CIO, the solvent dissolution process will normally be appropriate.

Approval of dissolution by members and trustees

An application for dissolution of a CIO must first be approved by the members, following normal requirements for constitutional amendments (i.e. a 75% majority vote of members present at a meeting, or unanimously if decided by a written resolution).[13] The resolution must set out the proposed dissolution arrangements, including the charity or charities to receive any remaining assets. If a meeting is called, at least 14 clear days' notice must be given to all members and trustees of the CIO, with details of the proposed resolution (unless at least 90% of members agree to reduce the notice period or more if specified in the constitution). A formal decision by the members is needed even in a foundation CIO where the members and trustees are the same.

In a CIO with a large membership, it will be virtually impossible to get unanimous agreement, so a members' meeting will be needed. But if the charity is losing interest and support, it may be hard to get a quorate general meeting to make the decision. Therefore, it may be necessary to make a special case for members to attend, for example by combining it with another event. Alternatively, if the CIO constitution allows decisions to be taken by postal or electronic vote, this may be a solution.

However, where it is difficult to get a quorum of members, it is worth reviewing the membership criteria carefully to consider whether all members on the register continue to meet the requirements. If, for example, the constitution requires members to pay an annual subscription, under clause 9(4)(a)(iii) of the Charity Commission model,

[13] CIO (I&D) Regulations 2012, reg. 6(1).

membership ends if someone's subscription is more than six months overdue (and many CIO constitutions will set a shorter limit). So, any persons in this position should be removed from the register of members. Alternatively, if there is no subscription but it is clear than many members have lost interest in the charity, the trustees could take a decision (under clauses 9(4)(a)(iv) and 9(4)(b) in the model) to cancel the membership of inactive members if they believe it is in the best interests of the CIO to do so. In this case they will need to contact the members concerned and give them 21 days to make representations.

Another option, if the Charity Commission model constitution is used, would simply be to accept that the initial members' meeting will almost certainly be inquorate. The meeting is then adjourned, with members advised accordingly and the second meeting is automatically deemed quorate 15 minutes after the advertised time (see clause 11(5) in the Appendix). Alternatively, if the remaining assets have all been spent and the CIO is clearly inactive, the Commission may be willing to use its own powers to dissolve the CIO, as explained on page 234.[14] (These steps are potentially more complex, however, than with a charitable company, where a voluntary striking-off process[15] is available which can be initiated by the trustees/directors.)

Applying to the Commission for dissolution of a CIO

The normal process of seeking a solvent dissolution of a CIO simply involves an application by the trustees of the CIO to the Charity Commission requesting that the CIO be dissolved, supported by:[16]

- a copy of the resolution passed by the members;
- a declaration by the trustees that all debts and liabilities of the CIO have been settled or provided for in full;
- a statement setting out how any remaining property vested in the CIO will be applied under the dissolution process (though this will normally be specified in the resolution, so it may not need a separate document).

Care is needed before making the statement that all debts and liabilities have been satisfied. The trustees should ensure that they have up-to-date accounts, and careful enquiries should be made of staff (or former staff),

[14] CIO (I&D) Regulations 2012, regs 16–18.

[15] Companies Act 2006, ss. 1004–1005.

[16] CIO (I&D) Regulations 2012, reg. 5.

other trustees, and anyone else who may have made commitments on behalf of the CIO. It will certainly be worth waiting at least a month for any bills from suppliers which may not been received. Do not overlook commitments to beneficiaries as liabilities; for example if someone has been promised a three-year grant from the CIO and only the first year has been paid, the subsequent instalments need to be treated as liabilities. Similarly, if someone has paid in advance for services to be provided by the charity (such as advance payments for events) the costs of the services not yet provided represent a liability (unless the full advance payment is refunded).

However, if it is difficult for the trustees to make a declaration of this kind – because they are uncertain of the liabilities – it may be better to seek a 'members voluntary liquidation' of the CIO (see page 231).

By this stage, the CIO will not normally have staff in post, and if there are ongoing commitments such as utility bills for which the CIO is still responsible, there needs to be sufficient funds in the bank to cover them for the full period of the wind-up. It is a serious offence (leading potentially to an unlimited fine) to apply for a CIO to be dissolved (under the solvent dissolution process) if debts or liabilities have not been provided for, or if decisions required under the dissolution process have not been taken.[17] However, a trustee cannot be found guilty of failing to disclose liabilities of which he or she could not reasonably be aware. It is also an offence to apply on this basis if any steps have been taken towards an insolvent dissolution, as explained in chapter 12, and these have not been concluded.[18]

Also, before proceeding with the dissolution, the trustees should ensure that the CIO has received all income to which it was entitled; for example, if the CIO was receiving donations under gift aid, a final gift aid tax claim should be made in order that the maximum available assets from the CIO can be passed on to another charity. (So long as the CIO remains established, it is entitled to make such claims. If the funds are subsequently transferred to another charity, they will be applied for charitable purposes.)

---

[17] CIO (I&D) Regulations 2012, reg. 8 – applying to CIO trustees an offence under s. 1004(5) of the Companies Act 2006.

[18] CIO (I&D) Regulations 2012, reg. 9 – applying to CIO trustees an offence under s. 1005(4) of the Companies Act 2006.

In due course the Charity Commission may have a standard form for trustees applying to dissolve a CIO, but otherwise a possible wording for the declaration would be as follows.

> We, the charity trustees of . . . . CIO (regd charity no. #######) are satisfied that all debts and liabilities of the CIO have now been settled [or will be provided for] and accordingly we apply for the CIO to be dissolved.
>
> Signed: (1) . . . .
>
> (2) . . . .
>
> (3) . . . .
>
> Date: . . . .

The regulations do not require all trustees to sign individually (the declaration can be made on their behalf) but, given its importance, it would be wise to ensure that all trustees sign, or certainly a majority do so.

The dissolution process

Once the Charity Commission receives an application of this kind, it must publish a notice (typically on its website) indicating that it has received an application for the CIO to be dissolved.

Within seven days of making the application, the CIO must advise all members, employees (if still in post) and trustees of the CIO that the application for dissolution of the CIO has been made, giving the date and the names of the trustees who made the application. (In most cases, all trustees will already be aware of the application, but if any trustee was absent from the relevant meetings and did not sign the declaration, he or she must be advised). In an association CIO, all members must also be advised, as only a limited number may actually have voted on the dissolution resolution.[19]

At this stage, the CIO must not engage in any activities except as necessary for the wind-up process, and it must not incur any new debts or liabilities.[20]

It may occasionally happen that the CIO receives further assets (such as donations) after the dissolution application has been made, but before the process is complete. If so, the Charity Commission must be advised, and the application must either be withdrawn or the trustees must indicate

---

[19] CIO (I&D) Regulations 2012, regs 12 & 13.

[20] CIO (I&D) Regulations 2012, reg. 10.

plans for applying the extra income in accordance with the agreed dissolution process (in most cases it will be sensible to add it to the final amount to be transferred to the charity receiving the dissolution proceeds).[21]

If no objections are received by the Charity Commission within three months, the dissolution will take place: the Register of Charities will be updated to remove the CIO and it no longer exists (in practice, it will remain visible on the online register as a former charity). However, if valid objections are received – for example from persons who show that they are still owed money by the CIO or from a member who claims that the wind-up decision was improper – the Commission will refuse the dissolution until the objections are resolved.

There is no requirement to file a final set of accounts with the Charity Commission for a dissolved CIO. But to satisfy members and donors that all remaining funds were properly used in the final year, and that the dissolution was indeed solvent, it would be wise for the trustees to prepare final accounts. These should run from the CIO's previous year end to the date of dissolution, showing a closing balance of £nil after the final transfers of assets to the appropriate recipients of the dissolution proceeds.

[21] CIO (I&D) Regulations 2012, reg. 11.

12 CIO failures and insolvency

Sometimes the work of a CIO comes to a natural end in ways that allow for a solvent dissolution or merger with another charity, as discussed in the last chapter. That is certainly the simplest and least expensive way to wind up a CIO. But sometimes events will go badly wrong for a CIO to the point where the CIO cannot meet its financial obligations or where it falls foul of essential requirements under charity law.

If a CIO cannot meet its obligations, it is said to be insolvent. This can arise when it is unable to pay its debts as they fall due or where its assets are less than its liabilities.[1] Insolvency does not necessarily mean the end of the CIO. If the situation cannot be turned round, there may be no alternative to an insolvent dissolution – a liquidation – leading to the end of the CIO and leaving creditors unpaid, or at best partly paid. But there are also various intermediate possibilities as outlined below.

There could also be cases where a CIO is dissolved not because of insolvency but because it is inactive, or ceases to meet the definition of a charity (see page 234).

This chapter explores these issues. The explanation below relates to CIOs in England and Wales (refer to chapters 13 and 14 for a summary of the differences in Scotland and Northern Ireland respectively).

Managing financial difficulties

Even if a CIO is insolvent at a particular point in time, it may be possible to find a way forward which does not involve winding it up. For example, if a CIO has a large loan which it cannot afford to repay, it may be insolvent; but if the lender can be persuaded to write off the loan, or convert the loan to a grant, it will be solvent. Sometimes just asking creditors for a bit more time to pay may allow enough time to consider other options.

---

[1] Insolvency Act 1986, s. 123 – as applied to CIOs by reg. 3 of the CIO (I&D) Regulations 2012.

If a CIO loses a major source of income, it may well avoid insolvency by taking action quickly, although hard decisions may need to be taken. The trustees must take steps in good time, such as making staff redundant or cutting other expenditure in order to reduce the liabilities. Of course making staff redundant may increase liabilities in the short term because of redundancy payments, and it is vital to comply with employment law when considering redundancies, but if the charity simply cannot afford to keep staff in post for months ahead this may be the only option. But, if insolvency is looming, decisions should always be taken in the best interests of creditors. If the CIO has certain activities which are clearly profitable, and which could continue even if other parts of the work had to close, staff should not generally be made redundant in these areas, even if they are not seen as the most important in terms of the charity's beneficiaries. The income from such activities may help to reduce the liabilities, and even if closure is inevitable, a profitable activity could be sold as a going concern to another organisation.

However, looking simply at total assets and liabilities on the balance sheet is not a good indication of solvency in most charities, because very often substantial resources are held in restricted funds or sometimes endowment funds. This means that they are held on trust for specific purposes and they do not form part of the corporate assets of the CIO to settle claims from creditors. Proper fund accounting, therefore, is essential (see *The Charity Treasurer's Handbook*, also published in this series, for more details).

Solvency considerations must focus on the CIO's unrestricted funds. But bear in mind that if the CIO is using accruals accounting, the balance of a fund may comprise not just money but also fixed assets, debtors, and creditors. Sometimes funds can be raised quickly by selling fixed assets (such as a vehicle) but other assets may be hard to sell or may yield little – the value in the accounts is not usually a good indication of what they could achieve in a crisis. When considering debtors, knowing when the CIO is actually likely to receive payment is critical.

Assessing assets and liabilities of unrestricted funds is not always straightforward. In many CIOs, one of the biggest liabilities may be staff salaries due for payment at the end of the month. It will often be the case that certain salaries can be charged to restricted funds (because funding was received for particular posts or projects) and they do not therefore represent a liability on the unrestricted funds, whereas other salaries must be met from unrestricted funds.

If the CIO is reasonably well resourced in restricted funds but has a deficit on unrestricted funds, it would be worth negotiating with funders to see if they will agree to allow a higher proportion of the charity's general overheads to be charged to restricted projects. In some cases, this may be enough to remove the unrestricted deficit. Whilst funders would normally object to paying a large share of overheads for a restricted project, they are likely to prefer this to seeing the charity close and their funding wasted.

However, on a day-to-day basis, establishing whether the CIO can meet its debts as they fall due requires detailed cash-flow planning. If the financial expertise of staff and trustees is limited, additional expertise may be needed. In some cases an overdraft from the bank, or perhaps a short-term loan from a sympathetic supporter or funder, could allow the CIO to pay immediate commitments; but, of course, no bank will agree an overdraft to an organisation in difficulty unless there is a convincing recovery plan.

If, however, informal measures of this kind are insufficient, the trustees must be prepared to consider formal insolvency processes, as explained in the 'Formal insolvency proceedings' section, starting on page 227.

In circumstances of this kind, the trustees must also be prepared to meet much more frequently than normal in order to take decisions, and they should certainly consider the Charity Commission's guidance on managing charities through financial difficulties and insolvency.[2] However, at the time of writing, it does not deal specifically with CIOs. (For more on these issues, including more on the legal aspects, see *Managing in a Downturn* published by the Directory of Social Change.)

CIOs and insolvency: the legal framework

The Charities Act 2011 does not include any detailed framework for insolvency and dissolution of CIOs, but it allows the Cabinet Office to make regulations.[3] The provisions are in the CIO Insolvency and Dissolution Regulations 2012 (referred to in this book as the 'CIO (I&D) Regulations').[4]

The CIO (I&D) Regulations include some specific provisions for CIO dissolutions, especially solvent dissolutions (as discussed in the last chapter), but to a large extent they simply apply the company insolvency

[2] *Managing Financial Difficulties and Insolvency in Charities* (Charity Commission 2010, ref. CC12).

[3] Charities Act 2011, s. 245.

[4] The CIO (I&D) Regulations 2012 (SI 2012/2013).

framework in the Insolvency Act 1986 to CIOs in England and Wales.[5] (Note that a totally different framework applies for insolvency of SCIOs – see page 275.)

So, the CIO insolvency framework, as summarised below, is based entirely on the Insolvency Act 1986, but the regulations make many changes to the 1986 Act in order to be applicable to CIOs. The main issues are as shown in table 12.1, but there are also many other changes of detail and a number of provisions of the 1986 Act are omitted completely in cases where they would not apply to CIOs.[6]

Table 12.1: Application of Insolvency Act 1986 to CIOs – terminology[7]

Normal term in the 1986 Act (as applied to companies)	*Amended term when applied to CIOs*
Company	CIO
Directors or officers of the company	Charity trustees of the CIO
The Registrar of Companies (Companies House)	The Charity Commission
Articles of the company	Constitution of the CIO
Registered office of the company	Principal office of the CIO
Meetings of the company	General meetings (members' meetings) of the CIO
Shadow director	Not applicable to CIOs

[5] CIO (I&D) Regulations 2012, reg. 3 and Schedule.

[6] This means the 1986 Act has be read with numerous amendments, but the Cabinet Office has helpfully published an informal version of the Insolvency Act 1986 as applicable to CIOs, incorporating all these changes – available at www.gov.uk/government/uploads/system/uploads/attachment_data/file/80216/The_20Insolvency_20Act_201986_20as_20it_20will_20apply_20to_20CIOs_20-_20Nov-12.pdf

[7] CIO (I&D) Regulations 2012, Schedule, para. 1(3).

When trustees could be responsible: wrongful and fraudulent trading

A key issue when insolvency looms is whether the trustees could be liable for a charity's unpaid debts. This is where the structure of a CIO or charitable company offers many advantages over an unincorporated charity, but it does not mean the trustees could *never* be responsible.

As explained in chapter 1, a CIO has limited liability and so even if a CIO fails with unpaid creditors then the *members* of a CIO (if they are not trustees) will not be personally liable for its debts. In the rare case of a CIO with a members' guarantee (see page 100) the members would be liable for the amounts of their guarantee but not more.[8]

However, there are extreme cases where action could be taken against those in charge of running a limited liability body – in particular, against *trustees* of a CIO, and others such as senior staff – if they had acted in completely irresponsible ways.

Fraudulent trading

The offence of *fraudulent trading* under company law applies equally to CIOs.[9] Fraudulent trading arises when those running a company or CIO carry on business with the intent to defraud creditors, or for any kind of fraudulent purpose. This could include taking out loans with no means of repaying them, or ordering expensive goods or services knowing that there is no way of paying for them. Anyone who is 'knowingly a party' to such behaviour can be subject to an unlimited fine or up to ten years in prison.

But those prosecuted for fraudulent trading are typically running deliberately dishonest businesses seeking to benefit themselves by deceiving customers, lenders, or others. Of course, a CIO could be diverted into fraudulent activity by unscrupulous members or trustees and in such cases they could rightly be charged with fraudulent trading. But it is hard to imagine responsible trustees of a CIO getting into a situation where they actually *intended* to defraud creditors. Even if the trustees made unfortunate decisions which led the CIO to fail – for example investing in fundraising schemes that turned out to be

---

[8] Insolvency Act 1986, s. 74, as applied to CIOs by reg. 3 of the CIO (I&D) Regulations 2012.

[9] Companies Act 2006, s. 993, as applied to CIOs by reg. 60 of the CIO General Regulations 2012.

disastrous – it is most unlikely that they did so with the intention of defrauding others.

Wrongful trading

In less serious instances, the trustees could still face civil claims from a liquidator on behalf of creditors who are out of pocket. Insolvency law states that in certain circumstances where directors of a company have failed in their duties, the protections of limited liability no longer apply, and they could be required to contribute to the assets of a company in order to meet creditors' claims. The same could apply, in principle, to the trustees of a CIO.

The issue is known as *wrongful trading*. That is, where the directors of a company or the trustees of a CIO allow its liabilities to increase – for example, by committing to further expenditure – even though they know the company or CIO is insolvent and could not avoid insolvent liquidation (or should have known if they had applied reasonable skills and experience).[10] In such cases, where a CIO fails, the court could force the trustees to make a contribution to creditors' claims or to the wind-up expenses. The trustees could also be personally liable if the CIO goes into liquidation and they continue to make commitments under the name of CIO or a very similar name (for example if they set up a business using almost the same name so that people think they are dealing with the CIO).[11] If a CIO folds and a new organisation is formed to continue the work (whether or not it is a charity), the name must be clearly different.

Wrongful trading is sometimes confused with 'trading while insolvent'; but, as explained, it is not actually an offence to continue trading while a company or CIO is insolvent if the genuine intention is to improve the position for the creditors – for example, by seeking additional funding or cutting costs so that the CIO remains viable. However, if the CIO's day-to-day activities are incurring expenditure greater than the corresponding income, the liabilities will increase and this may well amount to wrongful trading, unless the trustees act swiftly. So, once it is clear that the CIO is insolvent and that the position cannot be resolved, the trustees must act rapidly to implement formal insolvency processes, as explained below.

---

[10] Insolvency Act 1986, ss. 214 & 215 – as applied to CIOs by reg. 3 of the CIO (I&D) Regulations 2012.

[11] Insolvency Act 1986, ss. 216 & 217 – as applied to CIOs by reg. 3 of the CIO (I&D) Regulations 2012.

However, even with commercial businesses, actions from wrongful trading are rare, and they can only be taken if the liquidator or person winding up a company or CIO specifically goes to court asking for the directors or CIO trustees to be made liable. Given the nature of a CIO where the trustees are normally unpaid, it would seem that a court would only make a declaration of this kind in the most extreme cases where trustees had clearly failed to exercise even the most basic care in their duties, and had allowed a CIO to run up totally inappropriate liabilities with no concerns for creditors. However, the court may well be harsher in cases where trustees are paid (even if this has been properly authorised), especially where trustees continue to take fees or salaries knowing that creditors will lose out.

Disqualification of trustees

In cases where CIO trustees have acted irresponsibly – for example in cases of fraudulent or wrongful trading – it is possible that the court or the Charity Commission could disqualify them as trustees of other charities more generally.[12]

Formal insolvency proceedings

If a CIO is insolvent and the position cannot be resolved informally, formal insolvency processes must be put in place. It is always best if these are instigated by the trustees, but it is also possible for a major creditor to apply to the court for the CIO to be liquidated. (A major creditor means anyone who is owed more than £750 by the CIO and who has been unpaid for more than three weeks following a written demand,[13] although in practice only a person or business owed much more than this would want to incur the expenses of such action.)

Formal insolvency arrangements always require the involvement of an authorised Insolvency Practitioner (IP), or the Official Receiver on behalf of the court. It is illegal for anyone to act who is not authorised under the 1986 Act.[14] The Insolvency Service (which is part of the government's BIS Department) maintains the register of IPs (see 'Useful addresses' on page 338) but given the particular nature of a CIO as a charity which is not

[12] Charities Act 2011, ss. 79(2) & 178.

[13] Insolvency Act 1986, ss. 122–124 – as applied to CIOs by reg. 3 of the CIO (I&D) Regulations 2012.

[14] Insolvency Act 1986, s. 389 – as applied to CIOs by reg. 3 of the CIO (I&D) Regulations 2012.

a company, and issues such as restricted funds and donated income, it is highly desirable to use an IP who is experienced with charities. The CIO's auditor or independent examiner may be able to make recommendations, and very often an IP appointed by the trustees will work closely with the auditor or examiner. It is usually best to arrange an initial meeting with the IP to explore possibilities before deciding the formal route to take, but in summary the options are as follows.

The first step is always to identify clearly all liabilities and to prepare a list of the CIO's creditors and the amounts they are owed (including employees, where applicable, and beneficiaries if there are legal liabilities to them – for more on the rights of employees see page 328). The trustees should already have this information from their initial review of the CIO's solvency position.

Most of the arrangements involve decisions by the members of a CIO (in a meeting or by written resolution), rather than just the trustees. This is because of parallels with company law where the members of a company are usually shareholders and they have a considerable financial interest, as they will be hoping to get back at least some of their share capital. In a CIO, the only financial interest of members will be in the rare case of a CIO with a members' guarantee. But even when a CIO is failing, the members have a duty to act in ways which they consider will best further its charitable purposes. They should, therefore, be looking to agree wind-up arrangements which will minimise harm to beneficiaries.[15] In a foundation CIO, the members will be the trustees, so it is not difficult to get members' approval, but in a CIO with a large membership the arrangements may require contacting all members to invite them to meetings and making the case for the insolvency process. If the members refuse to support such steps, the CIO's creditors may apply for a compulsory liquidation, which could be far more damaging.

A CIO voluntary arrangement

A 'CIO voluntary arrangement' is the CIO equivalent of a 'company voluntary arrangement' (CVA).[16] It is designed to avoid the need for liquidation or administration (as outlined in the following sections) by reaching agreement between the CIO and its creditors regarding the apportionment of debts.

---

[15] Charities Act 2011, s. 220.

[16] Insolvency Act 1986, ss. 216 & 217 – as applied to CIOs by reg. 3 of the CIO (I&D) Regulations 2012.

The trustees make a proposal to the CIO's members and creditors for 'a composition in satisfaction of its debts or a scheme of arrangement of its affairs' with an IP appointed as the supervisor of the arrangement. (In practice, the IP will support the trustees in coming up with a possible scheme.)

The nominated supervisor (the IP) must report to the court within 28 days of the proposal and state whether in his or her opinion the proposal has a chance of being accepted by the members and creditors and whether formal meetings of (a) the CIO members and (b) the creditors should be called. To be confirmed, the arrangement must be approved by the CIO's members and by at least 75% of the creditors (measured by the value of the amounts they are owed). If so, this becomes binding on all parties. If necessary, the trustees can apply for a 'moratorium', during which creditors cannot take action to recover debts, in order to allow time to agree the arrangement.

The aim is to come up with an arrangement where creditors accept less than they are due so that the CIO can continue to operate. If, however, this cannot be agreed, the creditors are likely to press for a creditors' voluntary liquidation of the CIO – a CVL (see below).

Administration

Administration involves the appointment of an 'administrator' (an IP) who takes control of the CIO in place of the trustees and seeks to run it for the benefit of the creditors.[17] An administrator can be appointed by a resolution of the CIO's trustees or members, or through an application to the court by creditors.

Once appointed, the administrator is an officer of the court. The aim is to save the CIO as a going concern by negotiation with creditors and then to bring it out of administration within a reasonable time. This may involve a CIO voluntary arrangement, as outlined above. During the period of administration, creditors cannot take action to recover their debts without the permission of the court. The administration ends automatically after a year, unless it is extended by agreement to 18 months, or it can end earlier if the administrator considers the aims have been met. Conversely, the administrator may decide that the aims are unachievable and may instigate a creditors' voluntary liquidation (CVL – see page 231). In either case the administrator advises the Charity Commission accordingly.

---

[17] Insolvency Act 1986, s. 8 & Sch. B1 – as applied to CIOs by reg. 3 of the CIO (I&D) Regulations 2012.

Where it is clear that the CIO has no property which might permit a distribution to creditors, the administrator can advise the Charity Commission, the court and the CIO's creditors that this is the case, and propose that the CIO should be dissolved without further delay. The Commission publishes this notice and the administrator's appointment then ends. If no objections are received, the CIO is automatically dissolved three months after publication of the notice.[18]

Administrative receivership

A further process involves the appointment by the court of an 'administrative receiver'[19] and the legislation allows for this in the case of CIOs. An administrative receiver has similar powers to an administrator but is appointed by holders of debentures or floating charges to recover assets. (Debentures are typically used by larger companies to raise finance by issuing their own loan instruments.) However, as there is no provision in law to protect debenture-holders in a CIO or for floating charges over a CIO to be registered (see page 330), it is most unlikely that administrative receivership would ever be used with a CIO.

Voluntary liquidations

A voluntary liquidation involves placing the CIO into liquidation by way of a resolution without involving the court, unlike a compulsory liquidation (see page 233). A liquidator is appointed who takes over the CIO's affairs and sells all its unrestricted assets for cash and then distributes the funds to creditors on a *pari passu* basis (in proportion to what they are owed – secured creditors first).[20]

Assets held on trust (which may include restricted funds) cannot be used to settle claims from creditors because they are not part of the CIO's corporate assets. But since the CIO will be wound up, it cannot continue to hold such funds. The liquidator will thus arrange for assets held on trust to be transferred to appropriate parties in accordance with the purposes for which they are held: typically by returning the funds to donors or by transfer to other similar charities.

---

[18] Insolvency Act 1986, Sch. B1, para. 84 – as applied to CIOs by reg. 3 of the CIO (I&D) Regulations 2012.

[19] Insolvency Act 1986, s. 29 – as applied to CIOs by reg. 3 of the CIO (I&D) Regulations 2012.

[20] Insolvency Act 1986, s. 107 – as applied to CIOs by reg. 3 of the CIO (I&D) Regulations 2012.

In a voluntary liquidation, an IP is appointed as liquidator and takes over all the powers of the CIO's trustees (though in the case of a members' voluntary liquidation – see below – it is possible for some powers to remain with the trustees, if the members agree). Once appointed, all activities of the CIO must cease except for the process of 'beneficial winding up' (i.e. to get the best settlement for creditors).

Members' voluntary liquidation

The members of a CIO can decide to apply for a members' voluntary liquidation (MVL) if the trustees declare that it is sufficiently solvent to pay all its debts within a year.[21] The process for getting the members' agreement is slightly different for CIOs compared to companies. A meeting of the CIO members must be called with at least 14 clear days' notice, specifying the proposed resolution, and this must be passed by a 75% majority of members voting (as for constitutional amendments). However, there is no quorum for such a meeting, so even if only a few members attend, the resolution can be passed. Alternatively, if 100% of members agree, the decision can be taken by a written resolution without a meeting.[22]

The MVL is an alternative to the solvent dissolution process described in the last chapter. The main difference is that an IP is formally appointed as liquidator by resolution of the CIO, rather than the trustees themselves managing the wind-up process (but of course the IP will incur fees).

Creditors' voluntary liquidation

If the CIO is insolvent and the trustees cannot make such a declaration, they can still ask the members to agree to liquidation on this basis, but it then becomes a creditors' voluntary liquidation (CVL). Not more than 14 days following the members' vote, a creditors meeting is held (and the creditors may appoint their own choice of IP as liquidator if they do not approve the person proposed by the members). One of the trustees (normally the Chair) must be present to preside at the creditors' meeting.[23]

---

[21] Insolvency Act 1986, s. 85 – as applied to CIOs by reg. 3 of the CIO (I&D) Regulations 2012.

[22] Insolvency Act 1986 – revised s. 84 inserted in the case of CIOs by reg. 3 of the CIO (I&D) Regulations 2012.

[23] Insolvency Act 1986, s. 99 – as applied to CIOs by reg. 3 of the CIO (I&D) Regulations 2012.

At the creditors' meeting, the choice of liquidator only needs to be approved by a majority of creditors (i.e. more than 50%, as measured by the amount owed, rather than the 75% creditor approval needed for a CVA). The creditors may appoint a 'liquidation committee' to oversee their interests as the process continues.

For either an MVL or CVL, the members' resolution must be announced within 14 days by an advertisement in the London Gazette (www.london-gazette.co.uk) so that creditors can contact the liquidator. (Advance notice of the meeting must also be given to holders of floating charges, but this is very unlikely in a CIO.)

Once the process is agreed, the liquidator then disposes of the assets as described above to settle creditors' claims *pari passu*. Any remaining assets (in the case of an MVL, but very unlikely with a CVL) are applied in accordance with the dissolution clause in the CIO's constitution. The CIO trustees must take any action required to apply the assets as the liquidator specifies.

When the CIO's affairs are wound up – when all assets have been disposed of and creditors paid to the extent possible – the liquidator draws up an account and presents this to a general meeting of the CIO (for an MVL) or a creditors meeting (for a CVL).[24] No decisions are taken at these meetings (and even if they are inquorate, the liquidator simply reports that they were called): their purpose is simply to give members and creditors a chance to consider raising objections.

The liquidator must also send a copy of the statement to the Charity Commission. The statement will, of course, show a final position where the CIO has no assets. If the liquidation takes more than a year, the liquidator must produce interim reports.

Within three months of receiving the liquidator's final statement, if there are no objections following the meetings, the Charity Commission then dissolves the CIO by removing it from the Register of Charities.[25]

The Charity Commission can also dissolve a CIO if it is being wound up, if it believes no liquidator is acting, or if no returns have been received from the liquidator for at least six months.[26]

[24] Insolvency Act 1986, ss. 94 (MVL) or s. 106 (CVL) – as applied to CIOs by reg. 3 of the CIO (I&D) Regulations 2012.

[25] CIO (I&D) Regulations 2012, reg. 18.

[26] Insolvency Act 1986, s. 201 – as applied to CIOs by reg. 3 of the CIO (I&D) Regulations 2012.

Compulsory liquidation

Where the CIO's trustees or members are unwilling to accept the need for insolvency processes (for example if they do not respond to communications) a creditor can apply directly to the court to instigate a 'compulsory liquidation' of the CIO if there is evidence that it is unable to pay its debts. This is typically a last resort and can happen without the approval of members of the CIO or of other creditors.[27] Action will take place in the High Court or the county court covering the CIO's principal office.[28] (It is in these sorts of circumstances when it is more likely that creditors may consider pressing the liquidator to bring actions for wrongful trading – see page 226 – if they feel the trustees have been deliberately making things worse.)

If the court approves the request, it makes a winding up order which is sent to the Charity Commission and entered in its records (it is likely that this will be displayed on the online Register of Charities to make clear that the CIO was in liquidation). An officer of the court, an official receiver (OR), is appointed to investigate the cause of the CIO's failure.[29]

The OR can require information from the CIO's trustees, former employees or freelance staff, and the applicants who established the CIO (if the CIO failed within a year of formation). The OR may apply to the court to 'examine in public' the trustees or anyone involved in the promotion, formation or management of the CIO.

If the OR considers that the realisable assets of the CIO are insufficient to cover the expenses of winding up and that no further investigation is needed, the OR may conclude that the CIO should be wound up right away (without attempting to distribute any remaining assets). If so, the OR just gives 28 days' notice to the CIO's creditors and contributories of the proposal to dissolve the CIO (a contributory is someone liable to contribute to the assets when the CIO is wound up, for example in the case of a CIO with a members' guarantee). Anyone wishing to object must apply to the Secretary of State (in practice, the Insolvency Service).

---

[27] Insolvency Act 1986 – revised s. 122 inserted in the case of CIOs by reg. 3 of the CIO (I&D) Regulations 2012.

[28] Insolvency Act 1986, s. 117 – as applied to CIOs by reg. 3 of the CIO (I&D) Regulations 2012.

[29] Insolvency Act 1986, ss. 131–134 – as applied to CIOs by reg. 3 of the CIO (I&D) Regulations 2012.

In other cases, the OR may act directly as liquidator, but more normally an IP is appointed as liquidator. The liquidation process then proceeds as above, although this may take some time, especially if the trustees are uncooperative and the liquidator may have to take further steps to take possession of assets. Eventually, a final meeting of creditors is called and the liquidator is released from office.[30]

In either case, at the end of the process the OR notifies the Charity Commission that the CIO should be dissolved. Within three months the Charity Commission must then dissolve the CIO by removing it from the Register of Charities, and publicises this accordingly.[31]

Dissolutions of CIOs initiated by the Charity Commission

Quite apart from the insolvency processes described above, in certain circumstances, a CIO can also be wound up by the Charity Commission.

The Commission is required to remove from the Register of Charities any institution which it considers is no longer a charity, or which has ceased to operate.[32] However, because a CIO only exists by virtue of being registered with the Commission, removing a CIO from the Register would mean that it ceases to exist: it is dissolved. It does not continue as a non-charitable body. So, special procedures apply to protect the assets if a CIO is dissolved when it is not insolvent.

A CIO ceasing to be a charity

It is important to remember that the definition of 'charity' in England and Wales (see page 21) is a body established for exclusively charitable *purposes.* Moreover, once an organisation is entered on the Register of Charities, the law states that for all purposes other than rectifying the Register it is 'conclusively presumed' to be a charity at all times when registered.[33]

Once a CIO is registered it is a corporate body established for charitable purposes. A CIO cannot cease to be a charity because, for example, the trustees use it to engage in inappropriate activities. However, the Charity

[30] Insolvency Act 1986, ss. 94 (MVL) or s. 106 (CVL) or s. 172 (compulsory liquidation) – as applied to CIOs by reg. 3 of the CIO (I&D) Regulations 2012.

[31] Insolvency Act 1986, s. 202 (early dissolution) or s. 205 (full liquidation) – as applied to CIOs by reg. 3 of the CIO (I&D) Regulations 2012.

[32] Charities Act 2011, s. 34.

[33] Charities Act 2011, s. 37(1).

Commission could use its powers to intervene and force the trustees to comply with their duties.

So there is no means in law for a CIO to 'give up' its charitable status and convert to a non-charitable body. In chapter 10 we saw how a CIC can potentially convert to a CIO, but there is no reverse of this process – a CIO could never become a CIC. This is because assets once held for charitable purposes must either be held indefinitely for such purposes, or spent in fulfilment of the charitable aim. A charity can never 'opt out' of charitable status.

Sometimes charity trustees may decide that a particular service developed by a charity would be better run by a non-charitable organisation, especially if there are concerns that access to the service may be insufficient to meet the public benefit requirement (see page 28). If so, subject to appropriate consents, the business activity and associated buildings and equipment of a CIO could be sold to a non-charitable body (including possible transfers of staff) and the CIO would receive the proceeds. In such cases, a CIO which was predominantly a service providing charity might change focus and become a grant-making charity.

But a charity cannot give away assets for non-charitable purposes: that would amount to a very serious breach of charity law. Any disposal of assets and business rights to a non-charitable body would have to involve a sale at full market value. The CIO would retain the proceeds of the sale which would be applied to its charitable aims. So, whilst certain activities might move to a non-charitable body, the CIO itself would continue.

However, it could happen that a CIO is formed and then evidence comes to light at a later stage which demonstrates that it is not in fact established for charitable purposes. This could be because of something fraudulent in the original application for registration of the CIO, or because of changes in charity law, typically as a result of future tribunal cases which clarify the meaning of public benefit as a result of changing circumstances. For example, the Charity Commission's guidance points out that for a long time the supply of cigarettes to sick people in hospital was regarded as charitable, but nowadays medical research has shown the harm caused by cigarettes would outweigh any apparent benefits from cigarettes helping to relieve patients' stress. Hence an organisation whose main purpose was to provide cigarettes to patients would not now be accepted as being established for public benefit.[34] Future changes of this kind could mean

[34] *Charities and Public Benefit* (Charity Commission 2011, ref PB1, p. 11).

that a CIO which was charitable when formed might no longer be a charity some years later.

In most cases, the way forward would be to amend the objects of the CIO to bring them up to date with later understandings of charity law, but if this was impossible, or if the members refused to change the constitution, the Charity Commission has the power to dissolve a CIO which it considers is no longer a charity.[35] It must publish a notice that it plans to dissolve the CIO, and must advise the CIO accordingly. Unless 'cause is shown to the contrary' – that is, unless evidence reaches the Commission that its understanding was wrong – it will then dissolve the CIO three months later, by removing it from the Register of Charities.

In these circumstances, the CIO is unlikely to be insolvent, and may well still have significant assets. Because these were given for charitable purposes they must continue to be applied for charitable purposes.

In practice it is likely that the Charity Commission would use its powers to ensure that any assets of the CIO were transferred to other charities before the CIO was dissolved. But if a CIO is dissolved and still has assets, they are then vested in the Official Custodian for Charities.[36] (This is different from the position for companies, where property held by a dissolved company is deemed to be *bona vacantia* – i.e. ownerless goods – and in most cases is then vested in the Crown.)

The Official Custodian is an officer of the Charity Commission who is empowered to hold charitable assets on trust, in circumstances when they cannot be held by a charity or its trustees. The Charity Commission can make an order specifying the charitable purposes for which the assets are held: these will be close to the purposes of the dissolved CIO, but may be updated for current social and economic circumstances.[37]

The Commission can subsequently make further vesting orders, transferring assets from the Official Custodian to other charities.[38] The Official Custodian can also 'disclaim' assets,[39] which means the rights revert back to others entitled to them (the rights do not return to the CIO). This may be appropriate if, for example, a CIO had property with onerous obligations which would be of no value to another charity. Special

[35] CIO (I&D) Regulations 2012, reg. 17.

[36] CIO (I&D) Regulations 2012, reg. 23.

[37] CIO (I&D) Regulations 2012, reg. 25.

[38] CIO (I&D) Regulations 2012, reg. 26.

[39] CIO (I&D) Regulations 2012, regs 27–28.

provisions apply for leasehold property and freehold property with rentcharges.[40]

A CIO which has ceased to operate

A similar process can be applied by the Charity Commission to dissolve a CIO which has 'ceased to operate'.

Every year, significant numbers of charities are removed from the Register for this reason – often the charity has made no returns nor submitted any accounts for a considerable period. The Commission would not do this, however, if it considers a charity still has significant assets. Where this is the case, considerable efforts will be made to track down trustees or to locate property.

In the case of an unincorporated charity, if there appears to be little or no remaining assets and no response to communications from the Commission, it can simply be de-registered (however, any remaining assets will still be held by the trustees as an excepted charity, and if the income goes back over £5,000 they would need to apply to re-register).

But such an approach cannot apply with a CIO: it can only be removed from the Register of Charities if it is formally dissolved. The regulations state that if the Charity Commission believes a CIO is not in operation it must write to the CIO to check the position, and if it gets no reply, a second letter must be sent within two months. The second letter will state that the Commission intends to dissolve the CIO if it does not get a reply.

If the Commission gets no response to either letter (or if it gets a reply confirming that the CIO has, in fact, closed its operations), it will publish a notice confirming its intention to dissolve the CIO (with a copy sent to the CIO – so this will be a third letter). Unless within three months the Commission receives evidence that the CIO is in operation, or will be within a reasonable period of time, the CIO is then dissolved and removed from the Register of Charities. In the event that the CIO still has assets, the assets are vested in the Official Custodian and can be transferred to other charities, as in the case of a CIO which ceases to be a charity.

Appointment of an interim manager

If the Charity Commission believes that there has been misconduct or mismanagement of a charity, and has opened a formal inquiry,[41] it can use

[40] CIO (I&D) Regulations 2012, regs 29–32.

[41] Charities Act 2011, ss. 46 & 76.

its powers to suspend trustees or to appoint an interim manager (IM).[42] The IM then takes on all the powers formerly available to the charity's trustees (under the Commission's supervision).

The appointment of an IM to a CIO does not necessarily mean that it will be dissolved, although often the IM's role will be to ensure an orderly wind-up of the charity, with viable projects and assets being transferred to other charities. However, in some cases, the IM is able to bring the charity back into normal functioning, new CIO trustees are appointed, and the IM's role then ceases.

The IM is typically an accountant, lawyer, or an insolvency practitioner specialising in charities. Although an IM can act for any type of charity, the appointment of an IM (which is made under charity law, not insolvency law) will be particularly appropriate when a CIO gets into major difficulties, given the status of a CIO as a corporate body but not subject to company law. The IM will be paid fees for the work (agreed by the Charity Commission) from the CIO's funds. So, appointment of an IM normally means substantial charity funds being spent on the process, but ultimately it may lead to charitable assets being saved and beneficiaries being protected.

As with almost all Charity Commission decisions affecting CIOs, the trustees or former trustees could appeal to the Charity Tribunal against a decision to appoint an IM (see chapter 16).

If the IM brings the CIO's affairs to a successful conclusion and all assets are disposed of, the IM will generally apply for a solvent dissolution of the CIO (see page 214). However, if it becomes clear that the CIO was not just mismanaged but also insolvent, and if the IM is unable to reach an informal agreement with creditors, the IM will initiate formal processes under the Insolvency Act, as described starting on page 227.

Restoration of a dissolved CIO

There may be instances where a CIO is dissolved, but where there are grounds for arguing that it should not have been dissolved. In such cases it is possible to apply for a dissolved CIO to be restored to the Register of Charities so that it becomes a CIO once again.[43] Any property which was vested in the Official Custodian then returns to the CIO.[44]

---

[42] Charities Act 2011, s. 78.

[43] CIO (I&D) Regulations 2012, regs 38–39.

[44] CIO (I&D) Regulations 2012, reg. 40.

The Charity Commission can itself restore a CIO which was dissolved through being inactive, or where liquidation was started but never concluded (but it is not possible to restore a CIO which had ceased to be a charity). This could be instigated either by an application from a trustee of the former CIO or by the Commission itself (so anyone who feels that a CIO was wrongly dissolved could ask the Commission to use its own powers).[45]

However, where a CIO was dissolved through liquidation under the Insolvency Act the application must be made to the court.[46] In this case, the application may be made not just by the Commission or by former trustees but by anyone with a claim against the CIO or with interests in property held by the CIO immediately before it was dissolved. In most cases, whatever dissolution process was followed, all assets of the CIO will have been disposed of before it was dissolved; so an application for restoration will normally only arise if assets were missed during the dissolution process.

A restoration can, in principle, happen any time up to six years from when the CIO was dissolved, although there is no time limit if a claim is being made against the CIO in a personal injury case.

In most cases, a CIO will be restored under its original name, but in certain cases a change of name may be required.[47] There are also special accounting rules for a restored CIO.[48]

[45] CIO (I&D) Regulations 2012, reg. 33.

[46] CIO (I&D) Regulations 2012, regs 34–36.

[47] CIO (I&D) Regulations 2012, reg. 37.

[48] CIO (I&D) Regulations 2012, reg. 41.

13 CIOs established in Scotland: the SCIO

As explained in chapter 2, charity law in the UK is treated as a devolved issue, which means that the Scottish Parliament and Northern Ireland Assembly are able to establish their own systems of charity regulation. Because of this there are a number of small but important differences in the definition and regulation of charities between the different jurisdictions of the UK. This chapter deals with the specific issues for CIOs established in Scotland, which are known as SCIOs (the acronym 'SCIO' is generally pronounced 'ski-oh'). See chapter 14 for CIOs in Northern Ireland.

But whilst charity law is devolved,[1] many other areas of law – for example company law and most areas of tax law – are 'reserved' to the Westminster Parliament, and thus operate UK-wide with very few differences.[2] Because charity law is devolved, CIOs established in Scotland (SCIOs) are subject to different legal frameworks from CIOs in England and Wales. (On the other hand, non-charitable structures, such as Community Interest Companies (see page 43) are generally subject to the same legislation UK-wide.)

Charity law in Scotland

In Scotland, the main framework of charity law is the Charities and Trustee Investment (Scotland) Act 2005 – an Act of the Scottish Parliament (abbreviated here as 'Charities & TI (Scotland) Act'). Prior to this Act, there were a number of regulations affecting charities, but there was no comprehensive system of statute law in Scotland regarding charities and

[1] Scotland Act 1998 (as amended), s. 30 and Sch. 5 (Reserved Matters). Under Part II of Sch. 5 (Specific Reservations), s. C1 makes the law of business associations a reserved matter, but charities are listed as a specific exception from this.

[2] Under the Scotland Act 2012, some tax matters will become devolved: in particular, a Scottish Land and Buildings Transactions Tax (LBTT) (from 2015 – in place of UK Stamp Duty Land Tax), and the Scottish rate of income tax (from 2016). The LBTT legislation will create a new definition of 'charity' for Scottish tax purposes.

no overall charity regulator. Although the Scottish courts had jurisdiction over charities, normally the recognition of organisations as charities was treated purely as a tax issue, under HMRC. (This differs dramatically from England and Wales, where the changes made by the Charities Act 2006 were building on more than four centuries of charity legislation, and a permanent body of Charity Commissioners had existed since 1853.)

The 2005 Act created the Office of the Scottish Charity Regulator (OSCR – generally pronounced 'Oscar') and a mandatory system of charity registration (so there is no such thing as an excepted or exempt charity in Scotland – an organisation established in Scotland which is not registered with OSCR cannot call itself a 'charity' even if it has charitable aims[3]). It includes provision for rules on charity accounting and gives OSCR a wide range of powers to supervise charities. These powers have many similarities to those of the Charity Commission for England and Wales (CCEW), but there are important differences. The Act also includes provision for a special kind of CIO, specific to Scotland, known as the Scottish Charitable Incorporated Organisation or SCIO.[4]

CIOs in all UK jurisdictions are formed through registration by the relevant charity regulator. SCIOs, therefore, are registered by OSCR.

SCIOs: the principles

Although SCIOs fall within the general principles of charitable incorporated organisations, as discussed in the earlier chapters of this book, there are some important aspects to the process of forming, operating and dissolving a SCIO which differ from CIOs under the law of England and Wales. This chapter explores the main differences.

Note that chapters 4 to 12 of this book each began with a general explanation which applies to CIOs in *all* jurisdictions – including SCIOs – so it is worth referring to those explanations. After the introductory pages, each of those chapters moved into explanations specific to CIOs established in England and Wales (E&W CIOs). However, in many cases there are close parallels with SCIOs, and much of the discussion of E&W CIOs in the earlier chapters may also be relevant to SCIOs, if you bear in mind the differences covered in this chapter.

---

[3] Charities & TI (Scotland) Act 2005, s. 13. The Act does allow in ss. 18–19 for certain cases where a body could be removed from the Scottish Charity Register but could still hold some charitable assets, but such a body would not be 'a charity'.

[4] Charities & TI (Scotland) Act 2005, Part 7 (ss. 49–64).

Timescales and guidance

SCIOs were the first type of CIOs to become eligible for registration anywhere in the UK: the regulations under the 2005 Act took effect from 1 April 2011, and the first SCIOs were registered by OSCR shortly afterwards. (This was a full 21 months ahead of England and Wales, where CIOs could only be registered from 2 January 2013.) The provisions allowing Scottish charitable companies and IPS charities to convert to SCIOs (see chapter 10 and page 268) and mergers (see chapter 11 and page 271) took effect from 1 January 2012.[5]

As soon as the implementation of SCIOs was confirmed, OSCR produced detailed guidance material to support the establishment of SCIOs. Anyone considering forming a SCIO should certainly refer to this.[6]

Figures from OSCR at the time of writing show that a third of all charity registrations in Scotland are now for SCIOs and more than 400 SCIOs were registered in the first two years.[7] Based on experience in Scotland, there was thus considerable practical understanding of the CIO concept before CIOs became law in England and Wales.

Regulations

The 2005 Act created the legal framework for SCIOs, but as in other jurisdictions, the detailed provisions are set out in regulations – in this case, regulations made under the Act by Scottish Ministers. There are two sets of regulations:

- The Scottish Charitable Incorporated Organisations Regulations 2011,[8] which deal with constitutional requirements, registers, etc.; and
- The Scottish Charitable Incorporated Organisations (Removal from Register and Dissolution) Regulations 2011,[9] which covers the requirements when a SCIO is wound up.

In the discussion below – for example in the requirements for the constitution of a SCIO – we consider the requirements in the Act itself and those in the regulations together.

---

[5] Both commencement dates were specified in The Charities & TI (Scotland) Act 2005 (Commencement No. 5) Order 2011 (SSI 2011/20).

[6] *SCIOs: A Guide – Guidance on the Scottish Charitable Incorporated Organisation for charities and their advisers* (OSCR 2011).

[7] *OSCR Management Information – March 2013.*

[8] SSI 2011/44 – abbreviated below as the 'SCIO Regulations 2011'.

[9] SSI 2011/237 – abbreviated below as the 'SCIO (RRD) Regulations 2011'.

Both sets of regulations are considerably simpler than their English equivalents: the main regulations are only 4 pages, whereas 34 pages are needed for the general regulations for E&W CIOs. Even the removal and dissolution regulations only run to 5 pages (plus a series of schedules with various forms to be used in winding up a SCIO) compared to 49 pages for insolvency and dissolution of E&W CIOs.

Legal status and extent of activities

It is important to note that a SCIO is a corporate body created under Scots law: it is a fundamentally Scottish entity. It is not just regulated by OSCR – the registration of a SCIO with OSCR leads to the creation of a new corporate entity under the laws of Scotland. It is never possible, therefore, for a charity established elsewhere to be recognised as a SCIO. Even if an E&W CIO has to register with OSCR because of its activities in Scotland (see chapter 15), its legal status remains as an E&W CIO.

However, this does not mean that the activities of a SCIO are limited to Scotland. A SCIO could advance its charitable purposes in Scotland (or a specific Scottish locality), or in England, or in Africa, or anywhere in the world.[10] For generations, many distinguished national charities have been based in Scotland, and it is perfectly possible for a charity operating UK-wide or internationally to be formed as a SCIO (see chapter 15 for more on this).

Charitable status

In order for a SCIO to be formed, it has, of course, to meet the requirements of being a charity under the Charities & TI (Scotland) Act. This includes a Scottish definition of what it means to be a charity, which is known as the 'Scottish charity test' (or just the 'charity test' in the Act itself).[11]

The Scottish charity test has many similarities to the definition of 'charity' in England and Wales – it is based on the twin requirements of exclusively charitable purposes and public benefit. However, both of these requirements differ somewhat from the English equivalents. Under the 2005 Act, OSCR is required to issue guidance on the test.[12] This is an

---

[10] The Scottish charity test makes clear that the public benefit from a Scottish charity can be 'in Scotland or elsewhere' – Charities & TI (Scotland) Act 2005, s. 7(1)(b).

[11] Charities & TI (Scotland) Act 2005, s. 7.

[12] *Meeting the Charity Test: Guidance for applicants and existing charities* (OSCR 2011).

important resource which should certainly be considered by anyone establishing a SCIO.[13]

The 2005 Act lists 16 headings of charitable purposes[14] (compared to 13 in the Charities Act 2011, applicable in England and Wales), but the increased number of headings is simply because some purposes which are brought together under one heading in England and Wales are listed separately for Scotland. However, the Scottish Act does *not* include promoting the efficiency of the armed forces or emergency services. As such, Scottish charities working in this field need to use another heading.[15]

There are also several subtle distinctions; for example, in the field of sport, the Scottish Act refers to 'the advancement of public participation in sport',[16] which is slightly different from the English purpose of 'the advancement of amateur sport'[17]. In the field of religion and belief, the Scottish Act states that the advancement of any philosophical belief (whether or not it involves belief in a god) is to be treated as analogous to the advancement of religion,[18] which is a broader approach than the definition of religion for charitable purposes in English law.[19] These small distinctions need to be considered carefully when wording the charitable objects in a SCIO's constitution.

The differences in the Scottish understanding of public benefit are more substantial. In England and Wales, the definition of public benefit is entirely linked to the purposes of the charity. Therefore, when considering whether a proposed E&W CIO will be established for public benefit, the Charity Commission is required to focus purely on the *purposes* for which it will be established. But the Scottish charity test, when considering a proposed charity (such as a SCIO), focuses on whether it 'intends to provide public benefit'.[20] So there is a central focus on the intended *activities* of a proposed SCIO, not just its purposes.

---

[13] Charities & TI (Scotland) Act 2005, s. 9.

[14] Charities & TI (Scotland) Act 2005, s. 7(2).

[15] Charities Act 2011, s. 3(1)(l). OSCR has indicated that Scottish charities in this field can be considered under Charities & TI (Scotland) Act 2005, s. 7(2)(f) – i.e. under 'the advancement of citizenship and community development'.

[16] Charities & TI (Scotland) Act 2005, s. 7(2)(h).

[17] Charities Act 2011, s. 3(1)(g).

[18] Charities & TI (Scotland) Act 2005, s. 7(3)(f).

[19] Charities Act 2011, s. 3(2)(a).

[20] Charities & TI (Scotland) Act 2005, s. 7(1)(b).

Moreover, the English legislation does not include any statutory definition of the public benefit requirement, except by reference to case law,[21] but the Scottish Act sets out specific factors to be considered in determining 'whether a body provides or intends to provide public benefit'.[22] So when an application is made to register a SCIO, OSCR must specifically consider:

- any benefits to be gained or incurred by members of the SCIO or other persons who are not beneficiaries (i.e. the issue of private benefit);
- any disbenefits likely to be incurred by the public (i.e. the issue of detriment or harm as a result of the proposed activities);
- any conditions limiting access to the benefits to be provided, including whether any charge or fee is unduly restrictive.

Whilst the issues of private benefit, detriment or harm, and fee-charging are discussed in the Charity Commission's public benefit guidance in England and Wales, these issues have greater prominence in Scotland because they are written into the Act and because OSCR is specifically empowered to consider the notion of whether a charity will actually 'provide public benefit'.

OSCR has made the point, for example, that a charity which is inactive for a long time would not be providing public benefit, so in setting up a SCIO it is important that its charitable activities can start within a reasonable period after it is formed. This does not rule out cases where several years of fundraising or building work will be needed before a SCIO can start providing benefits, as there is still a clear intention to provide benefit; but the application will need to make the timescales clear so that these issues can be considered. Likewise, if a grant-making charity is set up as a SCIO and receives a large donation soon after it is established, the trustees cannot just hold on to it as an investment for many years without making grants.

It is not possible in this book to cover in detail all the differences between the English and Scottish definitions of charity,[23] but it is worth stressing that the vast majority of charitable purposes and activities will be charitable under both legal systems. However, a SCIO can only be established if it will meet the Scottish charity test.

---

[21] Charities Act 2011, s. 4.

[22] Charities & TI (Scotland) Act 2005, s. 8(2).

[23] For more detail on this issue see, for example, O.B. Breen, P. Ford and G.G. Morgan, *Cross-Border Issues in the Regulation of Charities: Experiences from the UK and Ireland* (International Journal of Not-for-Profit Law, 11(3), 2009, pp. 5–41).

Forming a SCIO: the steps

The process of forming a SCIO is similar to the process of establishing a CIO in England and Wales, as explained in chapter 5, except that the application is made to OSCR, rather than to the CCEW. Bear in mind that, as with CIOs in all jurisdictions, a SCIO does not come into being until it is registered.

As with all CIOs, the process begins with applicants (who will become the initial members of the SCIO), initial trustees, and a proposed constitution for the SCIO.

However, an important distinction is that a SCIO must have two or more members;[24] so, unlike the E&W CIO, it is not possible to have a single-member SCIO. Moreover, whilst it is possible to add corporate members once a SCIO is formed, the initial members (the applicants) must be individuals. So if, for example, an existing charity wishes to set up a new charity as a SCIO, and wants to be able to control all the decisions made by members at an AGM, it will need to identify two (or more) individuals – for example trustees or members of staff of the existing charity – to be the initial members of the SCIO.

A SCIO must have at least three charity trustees.[25] It can be formed where the only members are the charity trustees, but even if a wider membership is planned in due course, it will often be easiest to register the SCIO with the same persons to be initial members and initial trustees.

In relation to SCIOs, it is normal to speak of a 'two-tier SCIO' (if it has a wide membership) or a 'single-tier SCIO' if the only members are the trustees. The latter term is not strictly correct because, as with all types of CIO, there is a clear legal distinction between the members of a SCIO and the charities trustees of a SCIO. Even a single-tier SCIO must hold members' meetings, for example. (However, the terms 'association CIO' and 'foundation CIO' used in the English regulations are not generally applied to SCIOs.)

The process of applying to OSCR to register a new charity (including a SCIO) is made using a form which can be downloaded from the OSCR website (www.oscr.org.uk under 'Becoming a charity'). Note that the form to apply for registration of a SCIO is different from other applications for charity registration. A separate trustee declaration form is needed (this is the same as for other charities registering in Scotland). The trustee

[24] Charities & TI (Scotland) Act 2005, s. 49(2)(c).

[25] Charities & TI (Scotland) Act 2005, s. 50(2)(b).

declaration includes a separate page for each trustee – three such pages are provided, with an instruction to make further copies as needed.

The forms are provided as PDFs for completion, but they must then be printed out, signed by those concerned (see below) and submitted to OSCR by post (together with the proposed constitution, trustee declarations and any other documents needed). At the time of writing, the main SCIO application form is provided as a PDF, in which fields can be saved, but text entered in the trustee declaration form cannot be saved without special software.

The SCIO application form is 25 pages in total, but much of this is explanatory material: only 12 pages have to be completed. The information required is very similar to what is needed when registering a CIO in England and Wales as outlined in chapter 5, but remember to answer all questions from the perspective of Scottish charity law. There is specific space to describe the activities, how they will provide public benefit, and to explain the link between the activities and purposes. There are questions about private benefit, including not only payments to trustees and connected persons, but also details of any benefits available to members of the SCIO which are not available to the wider public. There are also specific questions about the proposed beneficiaries, any fees and charges that will be required to use the charity's services, and whether a person has to become a member to benefit. The form also asks about any other restriction on those who can participate, including issues linked to the Equality Act 2010.

OSCR also requires applicants to indicate if the SCIO will be connected to other bodies, or if it will be a local charity in a federated structure, in which case details of the parent charity are required.

Many of the questions are worded in the present tense, but since the application for a SCIO is to form a body which does not yet exist, to avoid confusion, all answers should make clear that you are describing *intended* activities, *proposed* charging arrangements and *anticipated* benefits to members (if applicable). Bear in mind that, beyond the details in the constitution, nothing can be finally decided until the SCIO is formed and the trustees have held their initial meeting. However, since a Scottish charity cannot be registered unless there is clear evidence that the body *intends to provide public benefit*, try to be as precise as possible. It may well be necessary to hold preliminary meetings of the applicants and/or initial trustees to clarify plans, before submitting the application (sometimes called a 'shadow members' meeting' or a 'shadow trustees' meeting').

It is possible to give more details to any question in a separate document, and OSCR is happy to receive copies of business plans or funding bids if they will help to shed additional light on the application.

Unlike the process of registering an E&W CIO (where, at the time of writing, there is no requirement to identify the applicants to the CCEW), the SCIO form requires entry of the names (though not the addresses) of the applicants (the initial members). The form must be signed by one of the applicants on behalf of all. If the applicants are *not* the same people as the trustees, take care to ensure that these details and signatures are entered correctly.

The application to register a SCIO will thus involve submitting the following documents to OSCR:

- the completed SCIO application form, signed by one of the applicants (initial members);
- the trustee declaration form, completed and signed by *all* initial trustees;
- the proposed constitution of the SCIO;
- other documents as needed to give further details on any questions, or supplementary materials such as a business plan.

The application will be acknowledged by OSCR. As in England and Wales, there will often be a process in which OSCR raises queries, or it may even request changes to the constitution. OSCR must, of course, refuse the application if it is not satisfied that the SCIO, if formed, would meet the Scottish charity test, or if the constitution does not meet the legal requirements.[26] However, assuming all is well, you will in due course get an email confirmation and then a letter confirming that the SCIO has been formed and entered on the Scottish Charity Register.

SCIO constitutions

The legislation includes clear minimum requirements for the constitution of a SCIO. Although there are a number of parallels with the constitutional requirements for an E&W CIO, there are also some key differences as outlined below. But, more fundamentally, a SCIO is a body constituted under Scots law, and its objects must meet the Scottish charity test (see page 244). Any legal references must relate to the Charities and Trustee Investment (Scotland) Act 2005 (and to regulations made under that Act) and any mention of regulatory requirements will of course refer to OSCR, not the Charity Commission.

[26] Charities & TI (Scotland) Act 2005, s. 54(3)&(4).

So, for all these reasons, when preparing a constitution for a SCIO, it is recommended to start from a model intended for a SCIO, rather than seeking to adapt one of the Charity Commission models for E&W CIOs.

Unlike the Charity Commission, OSCR does *not* produce model constitutions. There are, however, several organisations which have produced model SCIO constitutions (with support from firms of solicitors), notably the Scottish Council for Voluntary Organisations (www.scvo.org.uk). The SCVO model is designed for two-tier SCIOs (where the membership is wider than the trustees) and SCVO helpfully provides various optional 'bolt-ons' in terms of additional clauses to cover specific situations. However, even the core SCVO model is a fairly elaborate document with 111 clauses. The SCVO website also includes a slightly simpler model for a single-tier SCIO prepared by the Edinburgh Voluntary Organisations' Council (EVOC) with 90 clauses, totalling around 4,500 words. Simpler constitutions still are possible in specific cases; for example the author prepared a constitution for a two-tier SCIO with just 15 main clauses divided into 72 sub-clauses, totalling under 3,000 words. Nevertheless, there is no point in aiming for brevity for its own sake – for instance, it is often helpful for a constitution to restate requirements which are covered by other legislation to avoid trustees having to refer to other documents.

Because OSCR does not produce its own models, there is much less pressure than in England and Wales to follow a specific model for a SCIO constitution: if you have experience in drafting constitutional documents, it is perfectly possible to start from scratch. Also, if you are proposing to establish a SCIO in a specific field of work where there is already a model constitution available for an unincorporated association, especially if there is a Scottish version, it may not be too much work to adapt that to be a constitution for a SCIO. (In many ways, the constitutional requirements of CIOs – whether a SCIO or an E&W CIO – are closer to those of unincorporated associations than to the articles of a company). Even if using an existing SCIO model, there is no need to include provisions which are not legally required, if you feel that they will be of limited help to those running the charity concerned.

In summary, the minimum legal requirements for a SCIO constitution are as follows. (In addition to the points below, you may find it helpful to refer to chapter 6 where most of these issues are discussed in more detail in relation to E&W CIOs).

Heading

As for E&W CIOs, there is no legal requirement regarding the heading of a SCIO Constitution, but it would be sensible to head the document on the following lines:

> Constitution of Scottish Charitable Incorporated Organisation
> [Name of SCIO]
> Charities and Trustee Investment (Scotland) Act 2005
> Agreed by the applicants on: [date]

– and then to update this (see chapter 6) when the SCIO is registered.

Name

The constitution must specify the name of the SCIO,[27] and this will normally be the first clause. The name of a SCIO normally includes the letters 'SCIO' at the end (or 'Scottish Charitable Incorporated Organisation' in full), although as with E&W CIOs, this can be omitted if the status is disclosed on all documents.[28]

Principal office

A SCIO must have a principal office in Scotland,[29] but because there is no choice about this, there is no requirement to state this in the constitution (in contrast to E&W CIOs, where the constitution must state whether the principal office is in England or in Wales). Nevertheless, for the avoidance of doubt, the SCVO model includes a clause stating: 'The principal office of the organisation will be in Scotland (and must remain in Scotland)'.

Charitable purposes and charity tax status

The most important part of any charity governing document is the statement of the charity's purposes and this applies equally to a SCIO. As in English and Welsh constitutions, the clause explaining the purposes is normally called 'the objects' clause. For a SCIO this must set out purposes which are charitable under Scots law, as explained above.

[27] Charities & TI (Scotland) Act 2005, s. 50(1).

[28] Charities & TI (Scotland) Act 2005, s. 52.

[29] Charities & TI (Scotland) Act 2005, s. 49(2)(a).

However, as well as meeting the Scottish charity test, a SCIO will normally want to benefit from the various tax reliefs available to charities. But, as explained at the start of this chapter, most aspects of tax law are not devolved. The definition of a 'charity' under UK tax law is linked to the definition for England and Wales in the Charities Act 2011, so it is possible in theory that a purpose could be charitable under Scots law but fall just outside the English definition. So, to be sure that a SCIO is established only for purposes which are charitable under UK tax law, it can be helpful to add at the end of the objects clause a statement such as:

> PROVIDED that nothing in this Constitution shall authorise the application of property or funds of the Charity for any purpose unless that purpose is exclusively charitable both under the Charities and Trustee Investment (Scotland) Act 2005 and under United Kingdom tax legislation.

Powers

The Charities & TI (Scotland) Act states:

> *Subject to anything in its constitution, a SCIO has the power to do anything which is calculated to further its purposes or is conducive or incidental to doing so.*[30]

So, as with an E&W CIO, there is no specific requirement to include a powers clause in the constitution of a SCIO. However, most SCIO constitutions include this phrase (for the avoidance of doubt) and you may also wish to add specific powers such as the power to borrow if you feel lenders may want this.

The powers can, if necessary, be restricted to make them narrower than this.[31] As in England and Wales, this may occasionally be needed for ethical reasons where the founders wish to exclude certain activities.

Organisational structure

One specific requirement in the constitution of a SCIO (which has no direct equivalent for E&W CIOs) is to make provision about 'the organisational structure of the SCIO'.[32] The term is not defined, but even if the constitution has clear details regarding the members and the trustees of the SCIO, OSCR considers that the regulations require a specific clause explaining this. A possible wording would be:

[30] Charities & TI (Scotland) Act 2005, s. 50(5).
[31] SCIO Regulations 2011, reg. 2(a).
[32] SCIO Regulations 2011, reg. 2(b).

The structure of the organisation consists of:

(1) *the members* – who have the right to attend members' meetings (including any annual general meeting) and have important powers under the constitution; in particular, the members appoint people to serve as trustees and take decisions on changes to the constitution itself; and

(2) *the trustees* – who hold regular meetings, and generally control the activities of the organisation; for example, the trustees are responsible for monitoring and controlling the financial position of the organisation.

Members

The constitution of a SCIO must make provision about who is eligible for membership, how someone becomes a member,[33] and processes for withdrawal and removal of members.[34]

As explained on page 247, a SCIO must always have at least two members, and the initial members (the applicants) must be individuals.

As with E&W CIOs, the legislation gives specific duties to the members of the SCIO. These duties do not have to be stated in the constitution, but it may be helpful to do so. The 2005 Act states that one of the key duties of charity trustees is also applicable to members who are *not* trustees[35] – in other words:

> *members must seek in good faith to ensure that the charity acts in a manner which is consistent with its purposes.*

The Act also states that this does not exclude any obligations under other laws, and that any breach of this duty is to be treated as misconduct in the administration of the charity.[36]

The SCIO's constitution must also include procedural rules for convening meetings, records of meetings, voting rights, quorums and how resolutions are passed.[37] These requirements are less specific than for E&W CIOs, but it will clearly be necessary to make provision for 'general meetings' of members – including an AGM – and issues such as the procedure for calling such meetings (such as giving notice), the quorum, and the procedures for decision-making. Under the regulations, a members' meeting must be held not later than 15 months after the SCIO is registered, and not less than every 15 months thereafter. At least 14 days' notice of such

---

[33] Charities & TI (Scotland) Act 2005, s. 50(2)(a).

[34] SCIO Regulations 2011, reg. 2(d).

[35] Charities & TI (Scotland) Act 2005, s. 51.

[36] Charities & TI (Scotland) Act 2005, s. 66(1)(b), (3)&(4) – as applied to members of a SCIO by s. 51.

[37] SCIO Regulations 2011, reg. 2(c).

meetings must be given to members and trustees[38] (you may wish to specify a longer notice period, but the constitution would be invalid if it allowed members' meetings to be called with fewer than 14 days' notice). However, the Scottish regulations do not refer to 'clear days', so it is possible in principle to give notice for a meeting to take place exactly two weeks later.

The regulations do not refer specifically to electronic communications, postal voting or similar issues, but it is perfectly possible to include such provisions if needed (certainly most SCIOs will want to allow for the possibility of giving notice of meetings by email where members have provided email addresses).

The regulations state that membership in a SCIO must be non-transferable,[39] so it is helpful to mention this is the constitution.

Trustees

The constitution of a SCIO must make provision for the appointment of charity trustees (never fewer than three) and any conditions of eligibility for becoming a trustee.[40] It must also specify processes for withdrawal and removal of trustees.[41]

This clause will typically include a provision allowing trustees to be elected by members at an AGM, and possibly for other trustees to be co-opted, and (in some cases) provision for certain *ex officio* trustees or trustees nominated by an external person or organisation. However, the regulations are very broad, and the constitution could specify any appropriate means for appointing trustees.

On the issue of eligibility to be a trustee, in a two-tier SCIO you may wish to specify that someone must be a member before he or she can become a trustee. Some organisations may also wish to include requirements regarding professional qualifications or commitments to statements of values or beliefs. It is helpful to state that anyone disqualified from being a charity trustee under the Charities and Trust Investment (Scotland) Act 2005 is automatically excluded.

It is worth noting that the 2005 Act includes a clear statement of the duties of charity trustees – this applies equally to a SCIO's trustees and to those of other Scottish charities. These duties apply whether or not they are stated in the constitution, but you may wish to refer to them.[42]

---

[38] SCIO Regulations 2011, reg. 8.

[39] SCIO Regulations 2011, reg. 7.

[40] Charities & TI (Scotland) Act 2005, s. 50(2)(b).

[41] SCIO Regulations 2011, reg. 2(d).

[42] Charities & TI (Scotland) Act 2005, s. 66.

Benefits to trustees and conflicts of interest

The rules relating to trustee benefits and conflicts of interest are slightly different in Scotland compared to charities in England and Wales.

The normal position in Scotland, as elsewhere, is that charity trustees serve voluntarily: they are entitled to be reimbursed expenses but cannot normally receive remuneration. However, the Charities & TI (Scotland) Act includes broad-ranging provisions under which payments to trustees or connected parties can be authorised by other trustees, provided all the required four criteria are followed. Moreover (unlike the position in England and Wales) this can even include authorising a trustee to have a contract of employment with the charity, or to receive payment for normal duties as a trustee.[43]

In many cases this may be considered too broad, but the regulations allow the constitution of a SCIO to restrict these arrangements.[44] It is important to include such wording if you do not want the full provisions of the 2005 Act regarding trustee remuneration to apply. It is worth bearing in mind that some funders will refuse to support charities which have powers to pay trustees for their normal duties.

A SCIO constitution *must* include procedures for dealing with any conflict of interest,[45] and it would be sensible to incorporate (as a minimum) the provision in the 2005 Act which applies to trustees of all Scottish charities.[46] Whilst the Act only refers to conflicts between the charity and 'a person responsible for the appointment of the charity trustee', it is helpful to apply the Act's provision to any kind of conflict with external interests. The following wording would achieve this:

> In circumstances capable of giving rise to a conflict of interest between the charity and other persons or organisations, the trustee must:
>
> (i) put the interests of the charity before those of the other person or organisation, or
>
> (ii) where any other duty prevents the charity trustee from doing so, disclose the conflicting interest to the charity and refrain from participating in any deliberation or decision of the other charity trustees with respect to the matter in question.

---

43 Charities & TI (Scotland) Act 2005, s. 67.

44 SCIO Regulations 2011, reg. 2(e).

45 SCIO Regulations 2011, reg. 2(f).

46 Charities & TI (Scotland) Act 2005, s. 66(1)(c).

Dissolution

A SCIO's constitution must contain a dissolution clause, specifying purposes as similar as possible to those of the SCIO to which any surplus assets will be applied if the SCIO is dissolved.[47]

Amending the constitution of a SCIO

Once a SCIO has been formed, its constitution can be amended by means of a members' vote.[48] The process has similarities to the process outlined in chapter 6 for an E&W CIO, but there are key differences.

Normally such amendments will be made at a general meeting of members of the SCIO. Bear in mind that even in a single-tier SCIO where the members and trustees are the same this must be called as a members' meeting rather than a trustees' meeting, so be sure to give sufficient notice as specified in the constitution (see under 'Members', page 253). In such cases, a two-thirds majority is needed (including postal and proxy votes, if allowed) for the resolution to be passed (but note that this is less than the three-quarters majority needed to amend the constitution of an E&W CIO).

However, amendments can also be made by a *unanimous* resolution of members without calling a meeting (for example by means of a written resolution, or a resolution agreed by email if the constitution allows for this).

Unlike the position for E&W CIOs, there is no special regime for registration of SCIO amendments by OSCR: so, except in the case of amendments which explicitly need OSCR's consent, they take effect as soon as they are agreed by the SCIO's members (unlike E&W CIOs where constitutional amendments only take effect when registered by the Charity Commission – see page 114).

However, the 2005 Act includes general provisions for *all* types of charities seeking to amend their governing documents which apply equally to SCIOs.[49] As in England and Wales, there is a distinction between changes which need the regulator's consent (OSCR's consent in the case of a SCIO) and other changes (although the term 'regulated alteration', used in the Charities Act 2011, see page 108, is not actually used in Scottish charity law).

[47] SCIO Regulations 2011, reg. 2(g).

[48] Charities & TI (Scotland) Act 2005, s. 63.

[49] Charities & TI (Scotland) Act 2005, s. 16 & 17.

Any constitutional change which would affect the charitable purposes of the SCIO must be notified to OSCR at least 42 days before the date on which the change is to take effect (so the wording of the resolution will need to specify that a certain change is to take effect from a specified date, at least six weeks ahead). After receiving notice, OSCR must advise the charity within 28 days if it objects to the change, or it can require the charity to put the issue on hold for up to six months. However, if no objection is received from OSCR within 28 days, the change goes ahead (but in general OSCR will respond positively if it is happy to consent to the change).

The legislation only mentions constitutional change to charitable purposes as needing OSCR's consent, but it could be argued that any change to clauses regarding benefits to trustees, or regarding the application of assets on dissolution of the SCIO, could amount to a change of charitable purposes. So it would be wise to consult OSCR regarding any proposed changes of this kind in order that consent could be sought if necessary.

Other constitutional changes must simply be notified to OSCR within three months of when they take effect: as explained (unlike the position for E&W CIOs) there is no delay awaiting registration of changes before they take effect. Of course, it is wise to notify OSCR of any change as swiftly as possible so that records are up to date, rather than waiting three months.

There is no explicit provision in the Scottish legislation for a SCIO with entrenched provisions in its constitution (see page 103 for an explanation of the concept). It is, of course, possible to include provisions in the constitution that no changes can be made without the consent of an external person, but the members could vote by a two-thirds majority to remove this (removing such a provision would not usually affect the charitable purposes, so it would not need OSCR's consent).

Designated religious charities in Scotland

There is no system in Scotland of exempt or excepted charities (unlike the situation in England and Wales where many churches are currently excepted from registration with the Charity Commission unless their income exceeds £100,000). In any case, CIOs, wherever they are established, must be registered with the relevant charity regulator.

However, the Charities & TI (Scotland) Act includes a category of 'designated religious charities' (DRCs). These are registered with OSCR in the normal way and included on the Scottish Charities Register, and they fall under most of the provisions of the Act, but many of the regulatory requirements are lighter (in the sense that OSCR's powers are more limited) compared to other Scottish charities.[50] It is possible in principle that a SCIO in the religious charity sector could fall in this category.

A DRC does not require OSCR's consent for a wind-up or merger, and OSCR cannot direct the trustees to take specific actions.[51] The normal criteria which could disqualify someone from being a trustee do not extend to DRCs.[52] Whilst OSCR can still conduct an inquiry into a DRC, it cannot suspend trustees or restrict transactions that the charity can undertake,[53] and similar restrictions apply even if OSCR believes there has been mismanagement and applies to the Court of Session.[54]

There are effectively two levels of DRC classification. The OSCR decision on designation is normally applied to a 'parent charity' (although this term is not used directly in the legislation). If agreed, the designation extends to all the 'component elements' of the parent charity, which could include local parishes and congregations constituted as charities in their own right and other charities under the oversight of the parent (even if not established for religious purposes).

To be designated as a DRC in its own right (i.e. to be a 'parent DRC') the charity must have the advancement of religion as its principal purpose, hold regular public worship, have been established in Scotland for at least ten years, and have at least 3000 members (aged 16 or over) in Scotland. It must have an 'internal organisation' which includes authorities in

[50] Charities & TI (Scotland) Act 2005, s. 65.

[51] Charities & TI (Scotland) Act 2005, ss. 16 & 28 – partly disapplied in the case of DRCs by s. 65(4).

[52] Charities & TI (Scotland) Act 2005, s. 69 – disapplied by s. 65(4).

[53] Charities & TI (Scotland) Act 2005, s. 31 – partially disapplied by s. 65(4).

[54] Charities & TI (Scotland) Act 2005, s. 34 – partially disapplied by s. 65(4).

Scotland that exercise 'supervisory and disciplinary functions' in relation to its component elements. It must also have accounting rules (although DRCs must still comply with the accounting requirements under the 2005 Act, as explained on page 262). The essence of DRC status is that the supervisory function within the religious body concerned makes it appropriate to dispense with some of OSCR's powers.

So, if establishing a SCIO in the religious field, it is worth considering whether it should be classed as a DRC. For a completely new individual SCIO to achieve DRC 'parent charity' status it would need to have been established for at least ten years with at least 3000 members (so, even if the SCIO was formed in 2011 it would need to be proactive in enrolling members and, even so, the earliest possible classification as a DRC would be 2021). But a SCIO could be a 'component element' under an existing DRC parent – such as a new local congregation – and hence be designated immediately. If this status is sought, be sure to give details of the parent charity when applying to register the SCIO. However, the legislation also states that a new charity constituted by 'members who have removed themselves' from an existing DRC immediately beforehand can be designated. So, for example, if a local church which was previously classed as a DRC restructures as a SCIO, the SCIO could ask OSCR to recognise it immediately as a DRC.

At the time of writing, only the following Christian denominations are designated:[55]

- The Church of Scotland;
- The Free Church of Scotland;
- The United Free Church of Scotland;
- The two Roman Catholic Archdioceses of Scotland (and some of the individual dioceses are also DRCs, though the designation of the Archdioceses effectively covers all Roman Catholic charities in Scotland).

So any local charity within these denominations – regardless of its structure – is a treated as DRC. (The online Scottish Charity Register includes a field showing if a charity is a DRC, but this only applies to the parent DRC.)

[55] 'Designated Religious Charities Named' [web news article], www.oscr.org.uk, OSCR Reporter, 3 October 2007, accessed October 2007. The announcement said there would be a review of DRCs seven to ten years from that date – i.e. some time in the period 2014–2017.

Of course, many church charities are established under other legislation and, as explained on page 165, they cannot simply vote to wind up and convert to a SCIO. But the provisions could be relevant where an existing church establishes a new charity as a SCIO to do additional work; for example where a new charity is created for a special building appeal or outreach project.

Records and registers

As discussed in chapter 7, CIOs in all jurisdictions must keep proper registers of members and trustees. In the case of a SCIO, the regulations are slightly different from the equivalent provisions for E&W CIOs.

Register of trustees

Every SCIO must maintain a trustees' register,[56] which records the following details for each trustee:

- name;
- address;
- date of becoming a trustee of the SCIO;
- any office held (such as chair, treasurer or secretary).

(It is possible in principle to have SCIO trustees which are corporate bodies rather than natural persons – see page 51 – though a minimum of three trustees must still be specified in the constitution.[57] For corporate SCIO trustees, further information is needed in the register, but in this book we only consider charity trustees who are individuals.)

The register must also contain the names of past charity trustees and the date on which they ceased to be trustees, going back at least six years.

The register must be kept up to date as trustees join or leave or change address. Any change must be recorded within 28 days, but there can be real problems if the information on trustees is out of date, so in practice changes should be recorded immediately.

Anyone at all can ask for a copy of the register of trustees. This is part of the general principle that anyone should be able to find out who is governing a charity, and in any case the names of the trustees will normally be disclosed each year in the trustees' report, which is a public document. If the request comes from someone who is not a trustee, it is sufficient to provide the information with the addresses

[56] SCIO Regulations 2011, reg. 3.

[57] Charities & TI (Scotland) Act 2005, s. 50(2)(b).

removed (so you would just provide the names and date of joining); but trustees are, of course, entitled to each other's full details. For an external request, you can even refuse to provide trustees' names if it would put them in personal danger or would lead to identification of premises which need to remain confidential, but you would still need to provide the number of trustees, and how long each of the anonymous trustees had served.

Register of members

A register of members of the SCIO is only needed where the members are *not* also all charity trustees (generally this means it will only be needed in two-tier SCIOs). The register must contain (as a minimum) the following information for each current member:[58]

- name;
- address;
- date of becoming a member of the SCIO.

Where a member is not a natural person (i.e. is a corporate member) the register must also record:

- any other names used (such as a working name if different from the legal name of the member organisation);
- principal contact details;
- registered charity number and/or company number if applicable.

The register must also contain the names of past members and the date on which they ceased to be members, going back at least six years. The register must be kept up to date as members join or leave or change address, and any change must be recorded within 28 days.

Any member can ask for a copy of the register of members – so a member has the right to know who the other members are – but if the request comes from members who are not trustees, the information can be provided with the addresses removed (so you would just provide the names and date of joining).

[58] SCIO Regulations 2011, reg. 5.

Accounting and reporting by SCIOs

The broad principles of charity accounting and reporting as discussed in chapter 8 – for example, the requirement to keep proper accounting records and to produce year-end financial statements – apply to all charities, including SCIOs. But it is very important to appreciate that the charity accounting framework under the Charities & TI (Scotland) Act 2005 has a number of differences from the regime applicable to charities in England and Wales.

The detailed requirements are contained in regulations made under the 2005 Act,[59] and OSCR publishes various guidance documents to assist in their application.[60] The framework for Scottish charity accounting is also explained in the *Charity Treasurer's Handbook*, also published in this series.

The good news is that are no special provisions for accounting by SCIOs over and above the normal accounting requirements for Scottish charities. In particular, because a SCIO is *not* a company, there is no statutory requirement to prepare accruals accounts until the income reaches the threshold of £250,000, so smaller SCIOs are free to prepare their accounts on the receipts and payments (R&P) basis if the trustees consider this appropriate.

A summary of the requirements is shown in table 13.1, but remember that these are simply the *minimum* requirements in the Act and regulations. Donors, funders, the SCIO's own constitution, or the SCIO trustees could in some cases stipulate more than the minimum.

---

[59] The Charities Accounts (Scotland) Regulations 2006 (SSI 2006/218) – made under s. 44 of the Charities & TI (Scotland) Act 2005. Note that the 2006 regulations were amended in 2007, 2008 and 2010 by the following orders and regulations (the 2010 amendments make the key changes to thresholds):

- The Charities Accounts (Scotland) Amendment Regulations 2007 (SSI 2007/136);
- The Companies Act 2006 (Consequential Amendments, etc.) Order 2008 (SI 2008/948) Sch. 1 para. 35; and
- The Charities Accounts (Scotland) Amendment Regulations 2010 (SSI 2010/287).

[60] See in particular *Scottish Charity Accounts: An Updated Guide to the 2006 Regulations* (OSCR 2012).

Table 13.1 Financial thresholds for SCIOs (see text in this chapter or chapter 8 for an explanation of abbreviations)

GROSS INCOME OF SCIO	MINIMUM REQUIREMENTS FOR *PRESENTATION* OF THE ACCOUNTS	MININUM REQUIREMENTS FOR *SCRUTINY* OF THE ACCOUNTS
£0 to £250,000	Receipts and payments accounts with a statement of balances	Independent examination (lay examiner permitted if accounts are on the R&P basis)
£250,000 to £500,000	Accruals accounts (SOFA, balance sheet and notes) prepared in accordance with the Charities SORP, subject to certain simplifications)	Independent examination (professionally qualified examiner)[61]
Over £500,000	Accruals accounts (SOFA, balance sheet and notes) prepared in accordance with the Charities SORP, applied in full)	Audit

Firstly, a key difference to note (in comparison to an E&W CIO – see table 8.1 on page 139) is that there is no lower band where the accounts can be approved purely by the trustees. Every Scottish charity, no matter how low the income, must have at least an independent examination of its accounts.

[61] In the rare case of a charity preparing accruals accounts having under £500,000 income but more than £3.26 million assets, an audit is needed even though the income is below the audit threshold (Charities Accounts (Scotland) Regs 2006 *as amended*, reg. 10(1)(b)). However, Lord Hodgson's review of the Charities Act 2006 has recommended dropping this in England and Wales, and similar changes could follow in Scotland.

Secondly, a Scottish charity must use a professionally qualified independent examiner in all cases where the accounts are on the accruals basis (not just if the income is greater than £250,000). This means that for SCIOs with incomes of less than £250,000, the choice of R&P or accruals accounts is not only a matter of which presentation will be most effective but also affects who can act as independent examiner. The prescribed professional qualifications[62] are essentially the same as in England and Wales (although in the case of the Association of Charity Independent Examiners (ACIE) the regulations allow an ACIE Member (rather than a Fellow) to be the independent examiner in the case of accruals accounts for a charity whose income is less than £250,000).

The reporting duties of IEs under the Scottish regulations[63] are the same as for IEs in England and Wales. There is no direct equivalent to the Charity Commission's Directions to IEs, but OSCR has issued guidance to IEs[64] which, though non-statutory, should certainly be followed.

However, the requirements for Scottish charity accounts on the R&P basis are laid down in the regulations[65] (unlike the position in England and Wales where the Charity Commission provides guidance but there is no general detail in law regarding R&P accounts).[66] So this gives R&P accounts a firmer basis in Scotland. In particular, an independent examiner has ample grounds for raising concerns on inadequate R&P accounts. So, unless the charity has members or funders who specifically expect SORP accounts, the R&P basis is likely to be sufficient for the majority of SCIOs with incomes of less than £250,000.

The statement of assets and liabilities (SOAL) provided with R&P accounts in England and Wales is replaced in Scotland with a 'statement of balances'. However, the requirement remains essentially the same: to give a summary of all balances held by the charity at year end. Given the status of a SCIO as a corporate body with limited liability, this provides the key snapshot of its financial position, which is very important for banks and other external parties.

If the accounts are prepared on the accruals basis, the regulations give general principles but, in essence, the SCIO must follow the Charities

---

[62] Charities Accounts (Scotland) Regulations 2006 *as amended,* reg. 11(2).

[63] Charities Accounts (Scotland) Regulations 2006, reg. 11.

[64] *Independent Examination: OSCR Guidance for Charities and Independent Examiners* (OSCR 2009).

[65] Charities Accounts (Scotland) Regulations 2006, reg. 9 and Sch. 3.

[66] However, as explained in chapter 8, the CIO Regulations 2012 introduce a small additional requirement for E&W CIOs using R&P accounts (see page 146).

SORP[67] (see page 148 for more details). The SORP is a common standard for charity accounting throughout the UK, so there are no specific differences for SCIOs. (The SORP Committee is nowadays convened jointly by the CCEW and OSCR.)

The accounts of a SCIO, like other Scottish charities, must be accompanied by a trustees' annual report (TAR), which is on similar lines to a TAR for an E&W CIO (see page 142). For R&P accounts, the requirements for the annual report are set out in the regulations,[68] but for accruals accounts, the regulations simply refer to the annual report requirements in the SORP. There is no specific requirement in the Scottish regulations at the present time for public benefit reporting in the TAR, though the report must explain the main activities of the charity and OSCR is very keen that the TARs of Scottish charities should make clear how the activities lead to the provision of public benefit.

Like other Scottish charities, a SCIO must file its annual report and accounts with OSCR each year, and the deadline for this is nine months after year end[69] (as compared to the ten months allowed for filing charity accounts in England and Wales). These must of course be signed by the trustees and by the auditor or independent examiner. The SCIO's entry on the online register is clearly marked if the accounts are late, which can damage its reputation.

However, unlike the CCEW, OSCR does not currently make charities' accounts available on its website (although this is being considered). As such, currently the only way anyone can obtain the accounts of a SCIO is to contact the SCIO directly. This could be a disadvantage, as the accounts of an E&W CIO can be obtained from the CCEW website, and the accounts of a Scottish charitable company can be obtained (on payment of a fee, which is currently £1) from the Companies House website. However, the OSCR register provides a link to the charity's own website (where applicable) – so, if the SCIO has a website, it is thus very helpful to provide the final accounts each year as a PDF on the site (typically this would be on an 'About us' page or similar).

If a SCIO has a subsidiary, the rules on consolidated accounts[70] are almost identical to the requirements in England and Wales (see page 154). Also, if an auditor or examiner of a SCIO uncovers serious issues which are likely

---

[67] Charities Accounts (Scotland) Regulations 2006, reg. 9 and Sch. 2.

[68] Charities Accounts (Scotland) Regulations 2006, reg. 8 and Sch. 1.

[69] Charities Accounts (Scotland) Regulations 2006, reg. 5.

[70] Charities Accounts (Scotland) Regulations 2006, reg. 6.

to be of material relevance to OSCR's regulatory functions, then there is a whistleblowing duty to OSCR[71] (similar to the duties on whistleblowing to the CCEW – see page 152).

Third parties dealing with SCIOs

The issues for banks, funders and others dealing with CIOs in any jurisdiction are discussed in chapter 17. However, in the case of SCIOs, it is worth noting that OSCR has produced an attractive booklet called *Working with SCIOs* to assist such discussions.[72]

Converting unincorporated charities to SCIOs

The process of converting an unincorporated Scottish charity into a SCIO is essentially as described in chapter 9: the SCIO must first be formed, and then the old charity is wound up with its assets and activities transferred to the SCIO.

However, OSCR has a number of processes which help to simplify this. In particular, it is willing to allow the new charity (the SCIO) to keep the same registration number on the Scottish Charity Register if there is an instant transfer – i.e. if there is no period when the old and new charities are running in parallel.

Since there is no lower limit for charity registration in Scotland, the existing charity should always be on the Scottish Charity Register at the start of the process. However, as OSCR's guidance confirms, it is possible that it could be a cross-border charity (see chapter 15), for example an unincorporated charity in England and Wales which is also registered in Scotland. As a result of the conversion, all the assets would be transferred to the SCIO and would become subject to Scots law, and it would then be registered solely with OSCR (a SCIO cannot be registered with the CCEW).

For a conversion of this kind, rather than using the normal form to register a new SCIO, two separate OSCR forms are used at different stages – both are called 'Change to SCIO Application' (i.e. an application from an existing charity to change its form to that of a SCIO). Each form has guidance notes which should be followed carefully (the forms are available from the section of the OSCR website named 'Making changes to your charity').

---

71 Charities & TI (Scotland) Act 2005, s. 46.

72 *Working with SCIOs: A new form of charity* (OSCR 2011).

The Stage 1 form is concerned with applying for formation of the new SCIO. As when registering a brand new SCIO with no link to an existing charity (see page 247), you must comply with the proposed constitution, trustee declarations and details of how the SCIO will carry out its work. In addition you must provide:

- a copy of the governing document of the *existing* charity;
- minutes of the meeting of the existing charity agreeing to wind up and convert to a SCIO (in a charitable association this requires a resolution by members, not just by the trustees);
- any outstanding accounts for the existing charity (OSCR will not allow the process to proceed if there are accounts outstanding).

The form also asks for details of the assets and liabilities that will need to be transferred: for example, bank balances, equipment, property, debtors and creditors. Since you do not yet know the date of transfer, you cannot know the exact balances of all these, but it is helpful to give an estimate. (In a complex case it would be worth attaching a schedule.) You are also asked if there are any obstacles which would prevent the transfer, such as covenants on property.

OSCR then reviews the Stage 1 application, raises queries as appropriate, and if all is well it confirms that the process can proceed. However, this is only an approval in principle – the SCIO is not created until Stage 2.

The Stage 2 form is the formal request by the old charity to be removed from the Register with assets transferred to the SCIO. At this stage, it is possible to advise OSCR of any changes to trustee information or the principal office for the SCIO, or any changes to the assets to be transferred. The form also asks for an indication of the timescale (a) for the transfer and (b) for the wind up of the old charity.

If you are looking to avoid the two charities existing in parallel, and hence to keep the same Scottish charity number, it is necessary for the SCIO to be formed, the assets transferred and the old charity wound up all on the same day. So careful planning is needed, as explained in chapter 9. At this stage, you will be in touch with OSCR staff and it is usually possible to agree a specific date (it must be a working day) when the SCIO will be formed and hence when the transfer will take place (OSCR will need at least a week's notice after it receives the Stage 2 form).

However, it is not always desirable to aim for the SCIO formation and transfer all on the same date: sometimes you will want to form the SCIO some time ahead of the actual transfer so that proper provision can be made for transfer of property, for example. So, in complex cases, a period of parallel operations with the old and new organisations can be helpful.

Bear in mind that, even with a same day transfer, the SCIO is a new legal entity and so a new set of accounts must be started. Final accounts must be prepared for the old charity, ending on the date of transfer. In many cases this will *not* be the charity's normal year end, so remember to notify OSCR of the change of financial year, otherwise there is a risk of accounts being submitted late. (Unlike the position in England and Wales, where the Charity Commission treats the old and new charities as completely separate entities, and the old charity is removed from the Register, OSCR is keen to maintain continuity where possible when a charity converts to the SCIO. So filing the last accounts for the old charity is extremely important, or the SCIO will show as being in arrears with its accounts.)

Converting charitable companies and CBSs to SCIOs

It is possible for a charitable company to convert directly to a SCIO (i.e. without winding up the existing charity) following the general process outlined in chapter 10. The same principles allow an Industrial and Provident Society (IPS) which is a charity to become a SCIO – as explained in chapter 4, a charitable IPS will be always be a community benefit society (CBS).

Moreover, these provisions took effect from 1 January 2012 (unlike the position in England and Wales, where such conversions will not be possible before 2014). The conversion requirements are set out in the 2005 Act.[73] OSCR has produced an application form for such conversions which includes extensive guidance on points to consider (the form is called *Conversion into a SCIO*, available from the OSCR website under 'Making changes to your charity').

However, there are a number of important differences in the conversion process to become a SCIO as opposed to an E&W CIO. In particular, the legislation for England and Wales assumes the conversion process will involve an application for charity registration, but the Scottish legislation only applies to a company or CBS which is already a charity[74] (this means a Scottish charity, so it must already be registered with OSCR).

Also there is no provision for direct conversion of a community interest company (CIC) to a SCIO, even if the CIC is established in Scotland. So a Scottish CIC wishing to convert would first need to give up its community interest status and become a normal company with charitable aims, that

[73] Charities & TI (Scotland) Act 2005, ss. 56–58.

[74] Charities & TI (Scotland) Act 2005, s. 56(1).

company would need to register with OSCR as a Scottish charity, and only then could an application be made for conversion to a SCIO.

Although the company or CBS must already be registered as a charity in Scotland, the 2005 Act does not seem to require that it is actually established in Scotland. So, in principle, an English charitable company registered with OSCR because of activities in Scotland (see page 303) could apply. However, it would need to establish a principal office in Scotland (as a charity, not as a company) before converting.

As explained in chapter 10, the process of converting an existing corporate body (company or CBS) directly to a CIO requires that the members remain the same before and after the conversion. Since a SCIO must have at least two members, only a company with two or more members can convert.[75] (However, as this is not an application to form a new SCIO, the members could in principle be corporate bodies rather than individuals.) In the case of a body with shareholders, any shares must be fully paid up so that there are no sums outstanding from shareholders[76] (but this is unlikely to be a problem, as a charitable company will not normally have shareholders at all and a charitable CBS will normally only have shares of a nominal value).

The broad steps are as explained in chapter 10. First of all, a new constitution must be prepared for the charity as a SCIO, rather than as a company or IPS. This must of course comply with all the requirements for SCIO constitutions explained above (see page 249). In the case of a company, two resolutions must be passed under company law: to convert the company to a SCIO and to adopt the new SCIO constitution. OSCR helpfully provides templates for these resolutions (available from the same webpage as the application for conversion). The suggested wording of the resolution on the constitution allows for changes to be made in negotiations with OSCR without needing to take a fresh decision by members of the company. Similar resolutions are needed by the members of a CBS seeking to convert.

The application form includes most of the information which OSCR requests for a new charity registration, but this appears to be solely in order that OSCR can verify that the body will still be a charity (the original charity recognition may have been many years ago, possibly even before the 2005 Act). The provisions in the Act relating to new charity registrations do *not* apply to conversions of charitable companies and CBSs,[77] although OSCR must be satisfied that, once converted, the body

[75] Charities & TI (Scotland) Act 2005, s. 56(2)(b).

[76] Charities & TI (Scotland) Act 2005, s. 56(2)(a).

[77] Charities & TI (Scotland) Act 2005, s. 56(4).

would continue to meet the charity test. The form requires the names of the members of the company or CBS who will become the members of the SCIO. If there is already a large membership, it may be necessary to attach a separate list.

The application is made by submitting the form to OSCR together with the proposed SCIO constitution, the existing constitution (i.e. the articles of the company or the rules of the CBS), copies of the resolutions and a declaration form signed by all the charity trustees (as used for new charity registrations).

OSCR initially verifies that the documentation is complete, and then undertakes an assessment to ensure the proposed SCIO constitution meets the legal requirements, to make sure there is nothing objectionable about the proposed SCIO name, and to be satisfied that the proposed SCIO will continue to meet the charity test.

At that stage, if there are no concerns, OSCR adds a note to the existing entry on the Scottish Charity Register indicating that the charity is proposing to convert to a SCIO. OSCR then contacts Companies House (if a company is seeking to convert) or the Financial Conduct Authority (FCA),[78] in the case of a CBS, to check if there are any objections to the conversion. It sends copies of the resolutions which will be registered by Companies House or the FCA, as required under company law or IPS law.[79] (It may also consult other parties if it feels this is necessary; for example, if the charitable company was previously registered with the CCEW and has only recently moved its base to Scotland, OSCR may wish to consult the CCEW.)

There is nothing in the Act or the regulations regarding the grounds on which Companies House or the FCA can object to the conversion, although the guidance states that OSCR has agreed with them a list of reasons which would be likely to lead to a refusal.[80] These include cases where the company or CBS proposing to convert is:

- overdue on filing its accounts or annual returns;
- subject to enforcement action by the existing regulator (Companies House or the FCA), for example if it has late filing penalties which are unpaid;
- attempting to avoid enforcement or prosecution by converting;

[78] Formerly the Financial Services Authority – see footnote on page 42.

[79] Charities & TI (Scotland) Act 2005, s. 57.

[80] *SCIOs: A Guide – Guidance on the Scottish Charitable Incorporated Organisation for charities and their advisers* (OSCR 2011, s. 4.2).

- already in a process of voluntary dissolution, or is in liquidation or administrative receivership; or
- where the existing regulator is aware that a proposed trustee of the new SCIO is disqualified from being a charity trustee.

Assuming that Companies House or the FCA has no objections, it cancels the registration of the company or CBS and advises OSCR. OSCR then updates the Scottish Charity Register to show that the conversion to a SCIO is complete. The former charitable company or charitable CBS is now a SCIO and is governed by its new SCIO constitution. The SCIO keeps the same entry in the Scottish Charity Register as the former company or CBS, and hence the same Scottish charity number.

At the time of writing, a small number of charitable companies have successfully made this conversion to SCIOs and no doubt it will become more popular in due course as awareness of this option increases.

There are a number of further practical issues to consider, but these are not specific to SCIOs and would also apply when companies or CBSs convert in any jurisdiction – see chapter 10 for further details.

OSCR's guidance suggests that companies or CBSs wishing to convert should allow around three months for the whole process, but, as explained on page 197, there is no need to try to tie up the conversion with a financial year end. It would be much simpler to avoid a year-end conversion. It is also important to make sure that the conversion does not take the company or CBS into a point where its accounts are overdue with Companies House or the FCA, so it will often be easiest to complete the conversion during the first nine months of a financial year. Once converted, the next set of accounts will cover the standard 12 months since the previous year end, but will be prepared purely as charity accounts for the SCIO, with no references to company or IPS law (although details of the conversion will need to be explained in the TAR).

Winding up, mergers and insolvency of SCIOs

As explained in chapters 11 and 12, a CIO may well come to the end of its life for a variety of reasons. But as a corporate body – a legal entity – it cannot simply cease to operate. It must be formally dissolved or amalgamated into another body.

Although the processes for transfers and amalgamations are similar to those in England and Wales, the procedure for dissolution of SCIOs is one area where the Scottish legislation differs substantially from the dissolution and insolvency arrangements for E&W CIOs. It is thus imperative that anyone dealing with the dissolution of a SCIO is fully conversant with the SCIO dissolution regulations.[81] There are four types of wind up to consider.

1. Amalgamations: SCIOs merging to form a new SCIO

There are simple and straightforward procedures in the 2005 Act for two SCIOs to merge (amalgamate) into a new SCIO.[82] These closely mirror the equivalent arrangements for England and Wales (see page 210 for more on the implications). These provisions took effect from 1 January 2012, and as more and more charities are formed as SCIOs, such mergers may become common. This amalgamation process is a more equal arrangement than the transfer process outlined in the next section, but it does mean dissolving both existing charities.

A constitution is prepared for the new SCIO which will result from the merger, and the members of *both* the existing SCIOs must pass resolutions approving the proposed amalgamation and agreeing to adopt the new constitution. These resolutions must be passed under the normal requirements for constitutional amendments in a SCIO (see page 256) – i.e. a two-thirds majority vote of members present at a meeting, or unanimously if the resolution is not put to a meeting. If OSCR agrees, the old SCIOs are dissolved and all property, rights and liabilities of the previous SCIOs are transferred automatically to the new SCIO.[83]

The process can apply to a merger of more than two SCIOs, so long as they all pass the necessary resolutions. However, it is specific to SCIOs. It is not possible to amalgamate in this way if either of the existing charities is not a SCIO (so it is not possible for E&W CIOs to amalgamate into a SCIO under this process).

2. Transfers: mergers of one SCIO into another

If two charities, both structured as SCIOs, wish to merge into one charity rather than an amalgamation, it will often be simpler to wind up one (normally whichever is the smaller) and merge into the other. In such cases, the 2005 Act provides for a simple SCIO transfer process,[84] again following largely the same processes as applicable in England and Wales

[81] The Scottish Charitable Incorporated Organisations (Removal from Register and Dissolution) Regulations 2011 (SSI 2011/237).

[82] Charities & TI (Scotland) Act 2005, ss. 59–60.

[83] Charities & TI (Scotland) Act 2005, s. 60(3).

[84] Charities & TI (Scotland) Act 2005, s. 61.

(see page 213). As with amalgamations, this process can only be used if both charities are SCIOs.

Resolutions must be passed by the members of both SCIOs and submitted to OSCR. If OSCR approves the transfer, all property, rights and liabilities of the former SCIO pass automatically to the continuing SCIO, and the old SCIO is dissolved.

3. Solvent dissolutions

Sometimes a charity comes to the end of its natural life: it is not insolvent, but for practical reasons it is clear that its work cannot continue. In the case of a SCIO, there is a simple procedure to apply to OSCR for it to be dissolved and removed from the Scottish Charity Register (see chapter 11, page 214, for more on the general principles of solvent dissolutions).

Sometimes there are situations where a charity has no assets whatsoever; for example, if the SCIO is a grant-making charity, the trustees may have made grants which bring the funds down to a final balance of £nil. However, in many cases there will be some assets remaining and, in such cases, the dissolution process will then involve transferring them to another charity in accordance with the dissolution clause in the SCIO's constitution.

If there are assets to transfer, and if the most appropriate charity to receive them is itself a SCIO, it may well be simpler to follow the transfer process above rather than applying for dissolution (though this will transfer liabilities as well as assets). But, if you wish to transfer assets to a charity which is not a SCIO, the solvent dissolution process will normally be appropriate.

To dissolve a SCIO in this way, the members must vote:[85]

- to wind up its affairs;
- to transfer any surplus assets (after all debts and liabilities are settled) to a named body;
- to be removed from the Scottish Charity Register and dissolved.

As for other proceedings of this kind, the resolution must be passed by a two-thirds majority vote of members present at a meeting, or unanimously if the resolution is not put to a meeting. In a two-tier SCIO with a wide membership but where the SCIO has become inactive, considerable efforts may be needed to get a quorate meeting of members – see page 215 for possible solutions.

---

[85] SCIO (RRD) Regulations 2011, reg. 3(2).

The resolution must be submitted to OSCR within 21 days,[86] accompanied by:

- the signature of at least two-thirds of the trustees confirming the resolution (or one trustee can sign on behalf of all if authorised to do so);
- a declaration of solvency, signed by at least two-thirds of all the trustees (or one trustee on behalf of all) stating: 'We, the charity trustees of the above named SCIO hereby affirm that as of this date the SCIO is solvent, being able to pay its debts as they become due and having a surplus of assets over liabilities'
- a copy of the current SCIO constitution;
- a copy of the SCIO's register of trustees;
- a statement explaining the proposed dissolution arrangements – this must explain how liabilities will be settled (including details of any funds that must be returned to funding bodies).[87]

A SCIO solvent dissolution form (with extensive guidance notes) is provided by OSCR for the purpose of providing all this information (available under 'Making changes to your charity' on the OSCR website).

The SCIO must then immediately write to all known creditors explaining the proposal (and in practice it would be sensible to settle any outstanding liabilities immediately, otherwise creditors may object to the dissolution). Care may be needed to identify all persons who could be creditors awaiting payments from the SCIO; this could include employees, freelance staff, beneficiaries, suppliers, funders, lenders, etc.

In the meantime, OSCR will publish the dissolution notice on its website within 14 days of receiving the application, and a 28-day period follows during which anyone can raise objections (however, an objection does not necessarily mean OSCR will refuse the request).

Within 21 days after the end of the period, OSCR must decide either to allow the dissolution (possibly with conditions) or to refuse it. A refusal may well result if, for example, it became clear that creditors could not be paid in full, meaning that an insolvent dissolution is needed.

If OSCR agrees to the dissolution, the remaining assets must be transferred to the body specified in the resolution (subject to any conditions in the resolution). The SCIO advises OSCR when this has

---

[86] SCIO (RRD) Regulations 2011, reg. 3(3).

[87] SCIO (RRD) Regulations 2011, reg. 3(4).

been done, and OSCR then removes the SCIO from the Register and it is dissolved.[88]

There is no requirement in the regulations to produce a final set of dissolution accounts, though OSCR may require a final set of accounts as part of its conditions to approve the dissolution.

Overall, this process will take around three months (including time to call a meeting of the SCIO members, the notification to OSCR, the 28-day notice period, the 21-day period for OSCR to reach a decision, the distribution of the final assets, and the removal from the Register). However, whilst some of the steps require considerable administrative care, it should not be a difficult process.

4. Insolvent dissolution

As explained in chapter 12, a corporate body can sometimes find itself in a position where it cannot meet its liabilities: it is insolvent. Unless an urgent injection of resources can be found, a SCIO in this position will have to go into an insolvent dissolution. This means the SCIO will be wound up without creditors being paid in full.

However, unlike E&W CIOs, where insolvencies are handled under provisions in the Insolvency Act 1986, a completely different process applies for SCIOs under the Bankruptcy (Scotland) Act 1985 (as amended) where the dissolution is handled by a Scottish officer called the Accountant in Bankruptcy (AIB). The AIB is more often involved in administering personal bankruptcies, but it also records corporate insolvencies in Scotland (see www.aib.gov.uk).

A SCIO which finds itself in this position will normally want to seek help from a Scottish insolvency practitioner specialising in charities.

The insolvent dissolution process involving the AIB can only be used if a SCIO has outstanding debts of at least £1,500.[89]

The regulations do not specify any process for dissolving a SCIO which is insolvent with debts of less than £1,500, but in practice it is unlikely that creditors would wish to engage with the AIB process for debts below this level. So, for a SCIO which is insolvent but only with very modest debts, it will probably be best to negotiate with creditors to pay what the SCIO can afford from its remaining assets, and then ask them to write off what remains. If they agree, the SCIO will have settled its debts,

[88] SCIO (RRD) Regulations 2011, reg. 3(11).

[89] SCIO (RRD) Regulations 2011, reg. 4.

and can follow the solvent dissolution process outlined above. If they do not agree, the SCIO will almost certainly have to incur further expenses on the wind-up process, and the debts are likely to rise beyond £1,500 (but this will mean that the creditors will get even less, so it is not in their interests to object to writing off a small debt).

For dissolution with debts that are greater than £1,500, the SCIO trustees can make an application to OSCR for the estate of the SCIO to be sequestrated by the AIB – this means the AIB would take over all the assets for the benefit of creditors. This also requires a fee (currently £100) to be paid to the AIB: this can be paid out of remaining funds held by the SCIO, as it is ultimately for the creditors' benefit.

As for other SCIO wind ups, an application for an insolvent dissolution requires a resolution passed by a two-thirds majority vote of members present at a meeting, or unanimously if the resolution is not put to a meeting. The declaration must then be signed by two-thirds of the charity trustees (or one trustee if authorised to sign for others). The resolution must specify another charity to receive any remaining assets, although of course it is most unlikely that there would be any assets left after settlement of debts if the SCIO is insolvent. Assets will only remain if creditors decide not to seek settlement of liabilities.

A form to apply for insolvent dissolution of a SCIO, incorporating all the required declarations both for OSCR and for the AIB is provided by OSCR (available under 'Making changes to your charity' on the OSCR website). The form covers 35 pages in all, with extensive guidance notes, in order to ensure that all information required is provided, as specified in the regulations.[90] The form requires a statement of the SCIO's assets and liabilities, and answers to a wide range of questions regarding the SCIO's financial resources and liabilities. If the SCIO has obligations to beneficiaries which it has not met, the beneficiaries concerned should be listed as creditors.

Other documents to be supplied include the current constitution of the SCIO and trustees' register (as for a solvent dissolution).

OSCR reviews the form and within 14 days publishes a notice on its website indicating that the SCIO has applied for dissolution and sequestration. If OSCR is satisfied that the application complies with the regulations, it forwards the application to the AIB and notifies the SCIO, and the £100 fee to the AIB must then be paid within 21 days from the OSCR notification.

[90] SCIO (RRD) Regulations 2011, regs 5&6.

The AIB reviews the application and, if satisfied that the SCIO is insolvent with debts of at least £1,500, it awards sequestration of the SCIO's estate and OSCR publishes a notice on its website to that effect. The AIB then appoints a Trustee in Bankruptcy who takes control of all of the SCIO's assets and arranges a meeting of creditors if he or she thinks it appropriate. If the SCIO is still active and has staff in post, for example, this means that the Trustee in Bankruptcy takes over the duties of the charity trustees on operational issues. However, unless the charity has a profitable venture which could be sold as a going concern, it is almost certain that activities will be ceased and staff made redundant. The charity trustees of the SCIO may well be required to provide information to assist the process. The AIB will review the creditors listed in the application and will arrange a settlement which gives a fair distribution between them of whatever assets remain. In general, this process will take at least 15 months.

Once all payments to creditors have been made, the AIB transfers the remaining assets (if any) to the body specified in the original resolution, prepares a final account and notifies OSCR that the sequestration is complete. OSCR then removes the SCIO from the Register and it is dissolved.

It is also possible to have an insolvent dissolution requested by creditors, rather than by the SCIO itself. For example, if a bank has made substantial loans to a SCIO and realises it is unlikely to get full repayment, the bank could apply to the Sheriff Court for sequestration of the estate of the SCIO.[91] Such an application can only be made if the creditor is owed at least £3,000. The creditor must give notice to OSCR and to the SCIO itself at least 7 days (but not more than 14 days) before the application (the petition) is made. This gives the SCIO a chance to object if, for example, there has been a misunderstanding, or if the SCIO actually has effective plans to settle the debt.

It is then up to the court to decide whether to award sequestration; and the court may, of course, require further financial information from the SCIO before reaching a decision. If sequestration is awarded, the court appoints a Trustee in Bankruptcy, as outlined above, and OSCR publishes a notice on its website. The process of settling with creditors then proceeds, and when the sequestration is complete, OSCR is advised and the SCIO is dissolved.

[91] SCIO (RRD) Regulations 2011, reg. 7.

Even in the case of an insolvent dissolution, the members of the SCIO cannot be compelled to meet its debts, because it is a limited liability body. The same would apply to the SCIO's trustees (whether or not they are members). However, in cases of reckless behaviour – where, for example, the trustees deliberately allowed the SCIO to enter into commitments which it could never meet – it is possible that they could face prosecution (see page 225 for more on the principles involved).

SCIOs no longer meeting the charity test

The situation could arise with a SCIO where OSCR considered that it met the charity test at the time of registration, but where subsequently it ceases to do so. This could happen if its activities change to the extent that it no longer 'provides public benefit' as required by the 2005 Act. It could also arise if the SCIO was inactive for a long period.

This raises fundamental problems because a SCIO is, by definition, a charity. OSCR cannot, for example, just remove it from the Register if it no longer meets the charity test.

If problems of this kind arise, OSCR will normally offer informal guidance to the SCIO's trustees, but if they do not respond, OSCR can use its statutory powers to open an inquiry into the charity and make directions to the trustees.[92] It could, for example, require them to apply for a reorganisation scheme[93] for the SCIO, which could involve transferring all its assets to another charity, or it could require them to apply for the SCIO to go through the process of a solvent dissolution (as outlined above), including transferring the remaining assets to another charity.[94]

If the trustees still fail to act, OSCR can apply to the Court of Session, which then has the power to make further orders or to 'deal with the SCIO and its charity trustees in any way the court thinks fit'.[95]

It follows that anyone thinking of establishing a SCIO and then diverting its assets or activities for non-charitable purposes can face the full force of the law. Using these powers, OSCR can compel a SCIO either to operate for its established purposes, or to face dissolution, with its assets transferred to another charity.

[92] Charities & TI (Scotland) Act 2005, s. 28.

[93] Charities & TI (Scotland) Act 2005, s. 39.

[94] SCIO (RRD) Regulations 2011, reg. 8(1),(2)&(5).

[95] SCIO (RRD) Regulations 2011, reg. 8(3)&(4).

14 CIOs established in Northern Ireland

In the last chapter we considered the specific differences for CIOs established in Scotland – known as SCIOs. This chapter focuses on CIOs established under the law of Northern Ireland.

There is no special acronym for a Northern Irish CIO – the name normally ends with the letters 'CIO' as in England and Wales. However, the abbreviation 'NI CIO' is used in this book to make clear when we are talking specifically about CIOs established in Northern Ireland.

Charity law is devolved in Northern Ireland (as in Scotland), which means that the Northern Ireland Assembly is able to legislate on issues of charity regulation.[1] However, tax law is 'reserved' to the Westminster Parliament, so Northern Irish charities seeking charitable tax reliefs – including NI CIOs – are subject to normal UK-wide tax law.

Charity law in Northern Ireland

In Northern Ireland, the main framework of charity law is the Charities Act (Northern Ireland) 2008 – an Act of the Northern Ireland Assembly. Some details (particularly the definition of public benefit) were amended by the Charities Act (Northern Ireland) 2013, but the 2008 Act remains the primary legislation.

There had been earlier Charities Acts for Northern Ireland, notably in 1964 (which had parallels with the Charities Act 1960 for England and Wales), but there was no comprehensive legislative framework for charity accounting and no overall charity regulator. Although the Northern Irish courts recognised bodies as being established for charitable purposes, this followed the English definition under tax law. In most cases, as in Scotland, the recognition of organisations as charities was treated purely as a tax issue, under HMRC.

The 2008 Act created the Charity Commission for Northern Ireland (CCNI) and a mandatory system of charity registration, so once the Act is fully in

[1] Northern Ireland Act 1998 (as amended), s. 4 – charities are not included in the list of reserved or excepted matters and are thus a transferred matter, on which the NI Assembly is able to legislate.

force there will be no such thing as an excepted or exempt charity in Northern Ireland. All organisations established in Northern Ireland for charitable purposes will be required to register with CCNI.[2] The Act includes provision for rules on charity accounting and gives CCNI a wide range of powers to supervise charities.

These powers have many similarities to those of the Charity Commission for England and Wales (CCEW) – but there are also important differences. However, the Northern Ireland legislation follows the English legislation very closely – large portions of the Charities Act (NI) 2008 and the Charities Act 2011 have identical wording. So the differences in Northern Ireland (as compared to England and Wales) are much less than the differences in Scotland.

The 2008 Act also includes provision for a special kind of CIO, established under the laws of Northern Ireland, registered and regulated by CCNI.

Implementation timescales

Whilst the CCNI is established and has considerable regulatory powers over charities operating in Northern Ireland, much of the 2008 Act has yet to be implemented at the time of writing. The new definition of 'charity' under the 2008 Act applies to CCNI's regulatory powers, but the registration of charities under this definition by CCNI is only due to start from autumn 2013. Other provisions, such as the rules on charity accounting, are unlikely to begin until 2014, and NI CIOs may not take effect until 2015.

During the transitional period, CCNI has been given powers to regulate bodies on the 'deemed list' of charities for Northern Ireland. This is the list of organisations established in Northern Ireland which were previously recognised as charities by HMRC up to 18 February 2011[3] (it is available on the CCNI website, but it is not legally a register of charities). It is possible that further orders will add charities recognised by HMRC since that date. However, bodies on this list will all have to apply individually for charity registration with CCNI – there is no equivalent to the arrangement in Scotland where charities on the former HMRC list were transferred directly to the Scottish Charity Register.

For those setting up new charities in Northern Ireland it is helpful to consider three timescales.

---

[2] Charities Act (NI) 2008, s. 16(2).

[3] Charities Act 2008 (Transitional Provisions) Order (Northern Ireland) 2011, reg. 2 (NISR 2011/12).

(a) Until CCNI begins its registration role, it is possible to set up a new charity in Northern Ireland and seek tax recognition from HMRC (but it cannot technically be added to the 'deemed list' unless the regulations are updated, so it would remain purely recognised for tax purposes with no oversight by CCNI). Such a charity could use any of the existing structures (for example a charitable trust, charitable association, charitable company or CBS) so long as the governing document makes clear that it is established under or subject to the laws of Northern Ireland.
(b) Once the new definition of charity for Northern Ireland is implemented and CCNI begins its registration function (expected from autumn 2013) new charities will apply directly to CCNI to be registered. However, only the existing structures can be used at this stage, because the legislation for NI CIOs will not yet be implemented.
(c) In due course – probably from 2015 – regulations will be made for NI CIOs and the provisions in the 2008 Act for NI CIOs will be implemented. New charities will then be able to be formed as NI CIOs, and in due course existing charities will be able to convert.

As in England and Wales, the legislation allows for companies, community benefit societies (CBSs) and community interest companies (CICs) to convert directly to CIOs, but as in Scotland and in England and Wales, the conversion provisions will not be implemented until some months after the initial registration of NI CIOs begins.

If it is known that a new charity definitely wishes to become an NI CIO in due course, it is probably best in the short term to establish it as a Northern Irish charitable company (see page 54 for more on charitable companies). Whilst this means taking on the additional demands of company law in the short term, it will be able to convert directly to an NI CIO in due course, rather than having to wind up and start afresh, which would be the case if it is established as an unincorporated charity.

Northern Irish CIOs: the principles

Although NI CIOs fall within the general principles of charitable incorporated organisations, as discussed in the earlier chapters of this book, there are some differences compared to England and Wales. However, the differences between NI CIOs and E&W CIOs are very limited as the underlying legislation is identical in most respects.

The main differences are simply that an NI CIO must meet the definition of a charity under the Charities Act (NI) 2008 (rather than the English definition) and it is regulated by CCNI rather than CCEW.

However, because (at the time of writing) CIOs have yet to be implemented in Northern Ireland, it is not possible to give as much detail as we could offer in earlier chapters for E&W CIOs and SCIOs. In particular, detailed regulations have not been made for NI CIOs, so it is not possible to comment on the full constitutional requirements and insolvency arrangements. It is, however, likely that the regulations for NI CIOs will closely follow those for E&W CIOs, given the common wording of the legislation.

Note that chapters 4 to 12 of this book each began with a general explanation which applies to CIOs in *all* jurisdictions – including NI CIOs – so it is worth referring to those explanations. After the introductory pages, each of those chapters moved to a point where the text stated that the remaining explanations were specific to CIOs established in England and Wales (E&W CIOs). However, in many cases, there are close parallels with NI CIOs, and much of the discussion of E&W CIOs in the earlier chapters may also be relevant to NI CIOs, if you bear in mind the differences covered below.

Legal status and extent of activities

It is important to note that an NI CIO is a corporate body created under the laws of Northern Ireland: it is fundamentally a Northern Irish entity. It is not just regulated by CCNI – the registration of an NI CIO with CCNI leads to the creation of a new corporate entity under the laws of Northern Ireland.

So, it is never possible for a charity established elsewhere to be recognised as an NI CIO. Even if an E&W CIO has to register with CCNI because of its operations in Northern Ireland its legal status remains as an E&W CIO. Note, however, that charities formed elsewhere but operating in Northern Ireland will not be added to the main CCNI register, but only to a supplementary register, widely referred to as the 'Section 167 Register' (see chapter 15 for details). The Section 167 Register is not likely to start until the main CCNI Register is largely complete.

However, this does not mean that the activities of an NI CIO are limited to Northern Ireland. An NI CIO could advance its charitable purposes in Northern Ireland (or a local area within Northern Ireland), or in England, or in the Republic of Ireland, or Latin America, or anywhere in the world. Indeed, it is perfectly possible for a charity operating UK-wide or internationally to be based in Northern Ireland and formed as an NI CIO (see chapter 15 for more on this).

Regulations

The 2008 Act creates the legal framework for NI CIOs,[4] but, as in other jurisdictions, the detailed provisions will be set out in regulations – in this case, regulations made under the Act by the Department for Social Development (the part of the Northern Ireland Executive responsible for charities). There are likely to be three sets of regulations along the following lines:

- 'general regulations' for NI CIOs, dealing with constitutional requirements, registers, etc.;[5]
- 'insolvency and dissolution regulations' for NI CIOs, covering the requirements when an NI CIO is wound up;[6]
- regulations for the conversion of charitable companies, IPS charities, and probably also CICs into CIOs[7] (these are likely to take effect at a later date than the initial regulations if the process used in Scotland and in England and Wales is followed).

There will also need to be a 'commencement order' bringing the relevant provisions of the 2008 Act into effect, and possibly also a 'consequential amendments order' if changes to other legislation are needed to allow for NI CIOs. Most of the regulations will require formal approval by the Northern Ireland Assembly before they can take effect.[8]

Charitable status

In order for an NI CIO to be formed, it has, of course, to meet the requirements of being a charity under the Charities Act (NI) 2008. There is no reference to a 'charity test' (as in Scotland) but simply to 'charitable purposes'[9] (as in England and Wales).

The Northern Irish definition of 'charity' under the 2008 Act has many similarities to the definition of 'charity' in England and Wales – it is based on the twin requirements of exclusively charitable purposes and public benefit.

---

[4] Charities Act (NI) 2008, ss. 105–122 and Sch. 7.

[5] Made primarily under ss. 179(5) & 122 of the 2008 Act.

[6] Made primarily under s. 119 of the 2008 Act.

[7] Made primarily under ss. 119 & 122(1) of the 2008 Act.

[8] Charities Act (NI) 2008, s. 119(4) & s. 179(2)(b).

[9] Charities Act (NI) 2008, s. 2(2).

The 2008 Act lists 12 headings of charitable purposes[10] (compared to 13 in the Charities Act 2011 applicable in England and Wales). The Northern Irish Act does *not* include promoting the efficiency of the armed forces or emergency services,[11] so Northern Irish charities working in this field need to use other headings (including possibly the category of other purposes previously recognised as charitable under existing charity law).

There are also a few subtle distinctions within some of the 12 headings as compared to England and Wales. In the field of religion and belief, the Northern Irish Act states that 'religion' includes any analogous philosophical belief (whether or not it involves belief in a god).[12] This is similar to the position in Scotland, but is a broader approach than the definition of religion for charitable purposes in England and Wales[13].

The 2008 Act also states specifically that 'the advancement of peace and community relations' is included within heading (h) (the advancement of human rights, conflict resolution or reconciliation etc.).[14] This, of course, is an important field for many existing Northern Irish charities. So it would be possible to register an NI CIO with objects specifically referring to peace and community relations, whereas the CCEW might argue that objects expressed in these terms were not necessarily charitable under English law.[15]

The final heading which refers to existing purposes that have previously been accepted as charitable is also worded slightly differently from that in England and Wales. It refers to 'existing charity law' (rather than 'the law relating to charities in England and Wales') and it makes an explicit reference to charitable purposes recognised under the Recreational Charities Act (Northern Ireland) 1958.[16]

These small distinctions need to be considered carefully when wording the charitable objects in the constitution of an NI CIO.

---

[10] Charities Act (NI) 2008, s. 7(2).

[11] Charities Act 2011, s. 3(1)(l).

[12] Charities Act (NI) 2008, s. 3(3).

[13] Charities Act 2011, s. 3(2)(a).

[14] Charities Act (NI) 2008, s. 2(3)(e).

[15] In practice, it is understood that the CCEW is prepared to register charities with objects of this kind, by considering them under s. 3(1)(m) of the Charities Act 2011 (analogous purposes) provided it is satisfied that they are established for public benefit.

[16] Charities Act (NI) 2008, s. 2(2)(l) & s. 2(4).

However, following the amendments by the 2013 Act, the definition of the public benefit in the Charities Act (NI) 2008[17] is now identical to that in England and Wales (except that it refers to 'public benefit as that term is understood for the purposes of the law relating to charities in Northern Ireland' (rather than 'in England and Wales'). In practice, however, it is doubtful if this makes any difference, because most Northern Irish cases over the years concerning whether or not a body is a charity have been tax law cases, and hence were decided in relation to the English definitions (as tax law has never been devolved).

As with CCEW, one of the objectives of CCNI is 'to promote awareness and understanding of the public benefit requirement'.[18] The CCNI is given similar powers to CCEW to issue guidance on the public benefit requirement and trustees of Northern Irish charities are required to 'have regard' to this guidance.[19] Draft guidance was published for consultation in spring 2013 and, once revised, the full guidance is expected to take effect from summer 2013, with the first charity registrations to follow soon after (though not initially for CIOs).

It should be noted that, based on the consultation draft, CCNI's guidance on public benefit will differ considerably from the guidance issued by CCEW, even though most of the underlying legal principles are the same. To some extent, CCNI has benefited from the experience of CCEW and OSCR before preparing its own guidance and issues such as the interaction between charity law and equality law have been incorporated from the outset. (However, it must be noted that Northern Irish equality legislation – which encompasses a wide range of laws – has many differences in comparison to the Equality Act 2010 which provides the framework for England, Wales and Scotland.)

It is important that trustees of NI CIOs – and applicants wishing to establish an NI CIO – carefully consider the CCNI's guidance on public benefit.

Forming an NI CIO: the steps

In terms of the legislation, the process of forming an NI CIO is very similar to the steps for establishing a CIO in England and Wales, as explained in chapter 5, except that the application is made to CCNI, rather

[17] Charities Act (NI) 2008, s. 4 as amended by the Charities Act (NI) 2013.

[18] Charities Act (NI) 2008, s. 7.

[19] Charities Act (NI) 2008, s. 4.

than to the CCEW. Bear in mind that, as with CIOs in all jurisdictions, an NI CIO does not come into being until it is registered.

As with all CIOs, the process begins with applicants (who will become the initial members of the NI CIO), initial trustees, and a proposed constitution for the NI CIO.

As with an E&W CIO, an NI CIO only has to have one or more members[20]. (unlike the position in Scotland). The legislation does not specify a minimum number of charity trustees, but, in practice, three trustees will generally be the minimum for effective working.

And, as with CIOs elsewhere, an NI CIO can be formed with a 'two-tier' structure (if it has a wide membership) or as a 'single-tier CIO', if the only members are the trustees. (It is not yet clear whether the terms 'association CIO' and 'foundation CIO' used by the CCEW will be used with NI CIOs.)

Because CCNI has not yet started registering charities at all, it is far from clear exactly what forms and procedures will be needed to register an NI CIO. However, it is unlikely that the steps for registering an NI CIO will be substantially different, but, as with CCEW and OSCR, some of the questions for registering a CIO are likely to alter because an application to register an NI CIO will, of necessity, relate to a proposed charity, rather than seeking registration of a body which already exists. Remember, too, that as with all CIOs the application for registration is made by the applicants (the initial members).

Nevertheless, it is clear than an application to register an NI CIO will involve submitting the following documents to CCNI in some form (all submitted online unless there are exceptional reasons):[21]

- a completed application form;
- a trustee declaration form, completed and signed by *all* initial trustees;
- the proposed constitution of the NI CIO;
- other documents as needed to give further details on any part of the application, in particular to explain the charitable purposes and how they will be carried out for public benefit within the definitions of Northern Irish charity law.

As in England and Wales and in Scotland, there is likely to be a process in which CCNI raises queries, or it may request changes to the constitution. CCNI must, of course, refuse the application if it is not satisfied that the

[20] Charities Act (NI) 2008, s. 105(5).

[21] Charities Act (NI) 2008, s. 110(2).

NI CIO, if formed, would be a charity under the laws of Northern Ireland or if the constitution does not meet the legal requirements.[22] CCNI can also refuse applications where the proposed name would be unacceptable.[23]

However, assuming all is well, you will in due course receive confirmation that the registration is approved. On the date when it is entered on the Northern Ireland Charity Register, the CIO comes into being as a corporate body and, from that moment, it is a registered charity in Northern Ireland.

NI CIO constitutions

The 2008 Act includes clear minimum requirements for the constitution of an NI CIO,[24] which are almost identical to those for an E&W CIO. However, as explained on page 283, the Act allows for further constitutional requirements to be set down in regulations,[25] so until the regulations are made, it is impossible to be precise about the full constitutional requirements.

Nevertheless, since the primary legislation for NI CIOs is almost identical to that for E&W CIOs, it seems likely that the regulations will be similar. Hence, the constitutional requirements for an NI CIO are expected to be very close to the constitutional requirements for an E&W CIO (see chapter 6).

Whilst the constitution of an NI CIO may look very similar to that of an E&W CIO, it is crucial to remember that an NI CIO is a corporate body under Northern Irish law, and its objects must meet the Northern Ireland definition of charity as laid down in the 2008 Act as amended (see page 279). Any legal references must relate to the Charities Act (Northern Ireland) 2008 (and to regulations made under that Act) and any mention of the regulator will of course refer to the Charity Commission for Northern Ireland, not the CCEW.

---

[22] Charities Act (NI) 2008, s. 110(3), s. 121 & Sch. 7. (Note that unlike the Charities Act 2011, where all the CIO provisions are included in the sections of the Act, a number of the requirements for NI CIOs are in Schedule 7 to the 2008 Act. This is because it follows the original English drafting of the Charities Act 2006 before the consolidation process which led to the Charities Act 2011.)

[23] Charities Act (NI) 2008, s. 110(4).

[24] Charities Act (NI) 2008, s. 106(2).

[25] Charities Act (NI) 2008, s. 106(3).

It is not yet known whether the CCNI will produce model constitutions for NI CIOs in the way that the CCEW has done. However, if it does not, the closeness of the legal framework for CIOs in England and Wales on the one hand and Northern Ireland on the other, means that it should not be particularly difficult to adapt one of the CCEW model constitutions for use in Northern Ireland.

Whilst some of the final constitutional requirements cannot be known until the regulations are made, it is possible to set out certain minimum legal requirements for an NI CIO constitution as follows. (In addition to the points below, you may find it helpful to refer to chapter 6 where most of these issues are discussed in more detail in relation to E&W CIOs).

Heading

As for E&W CIOs, there is no legal requirement regarding the heading of an NI CIO Constitution, but it would be sensible to head the document on the following lines:

> Constitution of Charitable Incorporated Organisation in Northern Ireland
> [Name of CIO]
> Charities Act (Northern Ireland) 2008
> Agreed by the applicants on: [date]

– and then to update this (see chapter 6) when the CIO is registered.

Name

The constitution must specify the name of the CIO[26], and this will normally be the first clause. The name of an NI CIO will normally include the letters 'CIO' at the end (as in England and Wales).

There is no requirement to include any specific reference to Northern Ireland in the name – but because there is no direct equivalent to the 'SCIO' abbreviation in Scotland, you may wish to include 'Northern Ireland' or 'NI' in the name if you wish to ensure it is not confused with an E&W CIO. (The abbreviation 'NI CIO' is used in this book simply to distinguish Northern Irish CIOs from others – it is not a legal term.) As with E&W CIOs, the letters 'CIO' can be omitted if the status is disclosed on all documents.[27]

---

[26] Charities Act (NI) 2008, s. 106(a).

[27] Charities Act (NI) 2008, s. 107.

A CIO established in Northern Ireland which is carrying out work across the island of Ireland may simply wish to include 'Ireland' in its name – there should be no confusion because at the present time there is no provision for CIOs in the Charities Act 2009 in the Republic of Ireland. However, it is important to remember that CCNI can refuse to register a CIO if it considers the name is misleading.

Principal office

An NI CIO must have a principal office in Northern Ireland,[28] but because there is no choice about this, there is no requirement to state this in the constitution (in contrast to E&W CIOs, where the constitution must state whether the principal office is in England, or in Wales). Nevertheless, for the avoidance of doubt, it would help to include a clause (along the lines of models used for SCIOs) saying: 'The principal office of the organisation will be in Northern Ireland (and must remain in Northern Ireland.)'

Charitable purposes – and charity tax status

The most important part of any charity governing document is the statement of the charity's purposes and this applies equally to an NI CIO. As in other charity constitutions, the clause explaining the purposes is normally called 'the objects' clause. For an NI CIO this must set out purposes which are charitable under Northern Irish law, as explained in the 'Charitable status' section on page 283.

However, as well as meeting the Northern Irish definitions of charity, an NI CIO will normally want to benefit from the various tax reliefs available to charities. But, as explained at the start of this chapter, tax law is not devolved. The definition of a 'charity' under UK tax law is linked to the definition for England and Wales in the Charities Act 2011, so it is possible in theory that a purpose could be charitable under Northern Irish law but fall just outside the English definition. To be sure, therefore, that an NI CIO is established only for purposes which are charitable under UK tax law it could be helpful to add at the end of the objects clause a statement such as:

> PROVIDED that nothing in this Constitution shall authorise the application of property or funds of the Charity for any purpose unless that purpose is exclusively charitable both under the Charities Act (Northern Ireland) 2008 and under United Kingdom tax legislation.

[28] Charities Act (NI) 2008, s. 105(4).

Powers

The Charities Act (NI) 2008 states:

> *Subject to anything in its constitution, a CIO has the power to do anything which is calculated to further its purposes or is conducive or incidental to doing so.*[29]

So, as with an E&W CIO, there is no specific requirement to include a powers clause in the constitution of an NI CIO. However, it will generally be helpful for NI CIO constitutions to include this phrase (for the avoidance of doubt) and you may also wish to add specific powers such as the power to borrow, if you feel lenders may want this.

The powers can, if necessary, be restricted to make them narrower than this.[30] As in England, this may occasionally be needed for ethical reasons where the founders wish to exclude certain activities.

Members

As with an E&W CIO, the constitution of an NI CIO must make provision about who is eligible for membership and how someone becomes a member,[31] and the regulations will no doubt require processes for withdrawal and removal of members.

As in England and Wales, an NI CIO can be formed with just a single member if needed. Also, as with an E&W CIO, even the initial member(s) can be corporate bodies – there is no requirement (as in Scotland) stating that the initial members (the applicants) must be individuals.

As with E&W CIOs, the 2008 Act gives specific duties to the members of the NI CIO. These do not have to be stated in the constitution, but it may be helpful to do so. It states:[32]

> *It is the duty of every member of the CIO to exercise powers in the way the member decides, in good faith, would be most likely to further the purposes of the CIO.*

An NI CIO's constitution must also include procedural rules for convening general meetings of members[33] and the regulations will almost certainly

---

[29] Charities Act (NI) 2008, Sch. 7, para. 1(1).

[30] Charities Act (NI) 2008, Sch. 7, para. 1(1).

[31] Charities Act (NI) 2008, s. 105(2)(a).

[32] Charities Act (NI) 2008, Sch. 7, para. 9.

[33] Charities Act (NI) 2008, Sch. 7, para. 11(3).

extend this to include records of meetings, voting rights, quorums and how resolutions are passed.

It is almost certain that the regulations will allow NI CIOs to make provision for electronic communications, as this possibility is mentioned in the Act.[34]

Trustees

The constitution of an NI CIO must make provision for the appointment of charity trustees and any conditions of eligibility for becoming a trustee.[35] No doubt the regulations will also require inclusion of processes for withdrawal and removal of trustees.

This clause will typically include a provision allowing trustees to be elected by members at an AGM, and possibly for other trustees to be co-opted, and (in some cases) provision for certain trustees to be nominated by an external person or organisation.

It is helpful to state that anyone disqualified from being a charity trustee under the Charities Act (Northern Ireland) 2008 is automatically excluded.

It is worth noting that the 2008 Act includes a clear statement of the duties of charity trustees of NI CIOs.[36] The requirement is the same as for E&W CIOs (see page 73), although the drafting in the legislation is not so clear, as the duties of members and trustees are combined in one paragraph in the Act. These duties apply whether or not they are stated in the constitution, but you may wish to refer to them.

Benefits to trustees and conflicts of interest

The rules for NI CIOs relating to trustee benefits and conflicts of interest[37] are the same as for E&W CIOs.

Trustees of an NI CIO are entitled to be reimbursed for expenses which they have legitimately incurred.[38] But beyond this, if there are any circumstances in which it is intended that trustees may receive benefits from the CIO, this must be stated explicitly in the constitution. For example, if the trustees want to be able to use the provisions in sections 88 to 90 of the Charities Act (NI) 2008 under which the other trustees can, in

---

[34] Charities Act (NI) 2008, s. 122(2)(b).

[35] Charities Act (NI) 2008, s. 106(2)(b).

[36] Charities Act (NI) 2008, Sch. 7, para. 9.

[37] Charities Act (NI) 2008, Sch. 7, para. 11.

[38] Charities Act (NI) 2008, Sch. 7, para. 12.

exceptional cases, agree to pay a fee to a trustee for work outside his or her trustee duties (see page 31), the regulations will almost certainly require this to be stated explicitly.

Dissolution

The regulations will almost certainly require the constitution of an NI CIO to contain a dissolution clause, specifying purposes as similar as possible to those of the CIO to which any surplus assets will be applied if the NI CIO is dissolved.

Amending the constitution of an NI CIO

Once an NI CIO has been formed, its constitution can be amended by means of a members' vote.[39] The requirements in the 2008 Act are identical to those for E&W CIOs, and hence the processes explained in 'Amending a CIOs constitution' on page 107 will apply.

As with an E&W CIO, a 75% majority vote is needed for members to agree a constitutional amendment at a general meeting (rather than the two-thirds majority which suffices in Scotland), or 100% of members must agree if no meeting is called.[40]

As with E&W CIOs, it will be necessary for amendments to the constitution of an NI CIO to be registered by CCNI before they take effect[41] (unlike the position in Scotland). The 2008 Act makes a distinction on the same lines as the English framework between regulated alterations (which require the prior permission of CCNI) and unregulated alterations which can simply be decided by the members and notified to CCNI.[42]

Designated religious charities in Northern Ireland

Once charity regulation with CCNI is fully in force, Northern Ireland (like Scotland) will have no system of charities not required to register (unlike the situation in England and Wales where many churches are currently excepted from registration with the Charity Commission unless their income exceeds £100,000). In any case, CIOs, wherever they are established, must be registered with the relevant charity regulator.

---

[39] Charities Act (NI) 2008, Sch. 7, paras 14–15.

[40] Charities Act (NI) 2008, Sch. 7, para. 14(2).

[41] Charities Act (NI) 2008, Sch. 7, para. 15.

[42] Charities Act (NI) 2008, Sch. 7, para. 14(6).

However, the Charities Act (NI) 2008 includes a category of 'designated religious charities' (DRCs), similar to the provisions in Scotland (see page 258). These are registered with CCNI in the normal way and included on the Northern Ireland Register of Charities, and they fall under most of the provisions of the Act. But many of the regulatory requirements are lighter (in the sense that CCNI's powers are more limited) in comparison with other Northern Irish charities.[43] It is possible in principle that an NI CIO in the religious charity sector could fall in this category.

In a DRC, CCNI cannot suspend trustees or members, give orders regarding application of property, appoint an interim manager or direct the trustees to take specific actions.[44]

As in Scotland, there are effectively two levels of DRC classification. The CCNI decision on designation is normally applied to a 'parent charity' (although this term is not used directly in the legislation). If agreed, the designation extends to all the 'component elements' of the parent charity, which could include local parishes and congregations constituted as charities in their own right and other charities under the oversight of the parent (even if not established for religious purposes).

To be designated as a DRC in its own right (i.e. to be a 'parent DRC') the charity must have the advancement of religion as its principal purpose, hold regular public worship, and must have been established in Northern Ireland for at least five years (shorter than the ten years required in Scotland, and unlike Scotland there is no requirement to have a specific number of members). It must also have an 'internal organisation' which includes authorities in Northern Ireland that exercise 'supervisory and disciplinary functions' in relation to its component elements. It must also have accounting rules (although DRCs must still comply with the accounting requirements under the 2008 Act as explained on page 295). The essence of DRC status is that the supervisory function within the religious body concerned makes it appropriate to dispense with some of CCNI's powers.

So, if establishing an NI CIO in the religious field, it is worth considering whether it should be classed as a DRC. For a completely new individual NI CIO to achieve DRC 'parent charity' status it would need to have been established for at least five years (so, even if the NI CIO was formed in, say, 2015, the earliest possible classification as a DRC would be 2020). But an NI CIO could be a 'component element' under an existing DRC parent –

[43] Charities Act (NI) 2008, ss. 165–166.

[44] Charities Act (NI) 2008, ss. 33–36 – disapplied in the case of DRCs by s. 165(1).

for example a new local congregation – and hence be designated immediately. However, as in Scotland, the legislation also states that a new charity constituted by 'members who have removed themselves' from an existing DRC immediately beforehand can be designated. So, for example, if a local church which was previously classed as a DRC restructures as an NI CIO, the NI CIO could ask CCNI to recognise it immediately as a DRC.

At the time of writing, the charity registration provisions of the 2008 Act have yet to be commenced, so no Northern Irish charities have yet been recognised as DRCs. It is not yet clear, therefore, which religious groupings will be covered. The trustees of the parent charity have to make an application to CCNI if they wish it to be classified as a DRC. But it is worth noting that in Scotland not all Christian denominations applied (in any case, those with a high degree of congregational independence were unlikely to qualify and this is likely to be the same in Northern Ireland). Moreover, some religious charities may wish to forgo the DRC status rather than be seen to be opting out of certain aspects of charity regulation in Northern Ireland.

However, many church charities are established under other legislation and, as explained in on page 165, they cannot simply vote to wind up and convert to an NI CIO. But the provisions could be relevant where an existing church establishes a new charity as an NI CIO to do additional work, for example where a new charity is created for a special building appeal or outreach project.

Records and registers

Much of the detail for registers will only be determined once the regulations are made. However, it will clearly be the case that an NI CIO will need to maintain a register of members and a register of trustees, and the requirements are likely to be either identical or very similar to those for E&W CIOs, as explained in chapter 7.

It is worth noting that, as with E&W CIOs, CCNI has the power to determine the membership of a charity, which could be useful if there are disputes about who is actually a member of an NI CIO.[45]

[45] Charities Act (NI) 2008, s. 50.

Accounting and reporting by NI CIOs

The broad principles of charity accounting and reporting as discussed in chapter 8 concerning accounting records and year-end financial statements will apply equally to NI CIOs. But it is crucial to appreciate that the charity accounting framework under the Charities Act (NI) 2008 has a number of differences from the regime applicable to charities in England and Wales.

The detailed requirements will be contained in regulations made under the 2008 Act, and no doubt CCNI will produce guidance to assist in their application, but regulations are not expected to take effect before 2014. However, it is almost certain that the accounting regulations will come into force *before* the provisions for NI CIOs, so an NI CIO will be subject to the accounting framework under the Act from the outset. The general framework for charity accounting in Northern Ireland is also explained in the *Charity Treasurer's Handbook* (published in this series).

The good news is that the Act adds no special provisions for accounting by NI CIOs over and above the normal accounting requirements for other charities established in Northern Ireland, although it is possible that minor additions could be made in regulations, as for receipts and payments (R&P) accounts with E&W CIOs (see page 146). But because an NI CIO is *not* a company, there is no statutory requirement to prepare accruals accounts until the income reaches the threshold of £100,000, so smaller NI CIOs are free to prepare their accounts on the R&P basis if the trustees consider this appropriate. (Note that this threshold is lower than the £250,000 upper limit for R&P accounts in England and Wales and in Scotland; however, it is possible that the Northern Irish threshold could be altered before the accounting regulations are implemented.)

A summary of the requirements is shown in table 14.1, but remember that these are simply the *minimum* requirements in the Act and regulations. Donors, funders, the NI CIO's own constitution, or the NI CIO trustees could in some cases stipulate more than the minimum.

Table 14.1 Financial thresholds for NI CIOs (see text in this chapter or chapter 8 for explanation of abbreviations)

GROSS INCOME OF NI CIO	MINIMUM REQUIREMENTS FOR *PRESENTATION* OF THE ACCOUNTS	MININUM REQUIREMENTS FOR *SCRUTINY* OF THE ACCOUNTS
£0 to £100,000	Receipts and payments accounts with a statement of assets and liabilities	Independent examination (lay examiner)
£100,000 to £500,000	Accruals accounts (SOFA, balance sheet and notes) prepared in accordance with the Charities SORP, subject to certain simplifications)	Independent examination (professionally qualified examiner)
More than £500,000	Accruals accounts (SOFA, balance sheet and notes) prepared in accordance with the Charities SORP, applied in full)	Audit

A key difference to note (compared to an E&W CIO – see table 8.1 on page 139) is that there is no lower band where the accounts can be approved purely by the trustees. Every Northern Irish charity, no matter how low the income, must have at least an independent examination of its accounts, as is the case in Scotland. (However, there is no equivalent to the Scottish requirement to use a professionally qualified independent examiner in all cases where the accounts are on the accruals basis, even though this could be good practice. In Northern Ireland, as in England and Wales, the legal requirement for a qualified independent examiner only applies when the income reaches the threshold shown.)

Unlike the provisions in England and Wales and in Scotland, there are no assets thresholds at which an audit can be triggered: all the requirements are based on income, which is a helpful simplification. The prescribed professional qualifications[46] for IEs are essentially the same as in England

[46] Charities Act (NI) 2008, s. 65(4)&(5) – as amended by Charities Act (NI) 2013.

and Wales (although in the case of the Association of Charity Independent Examiners (ACIE), the Act allows allow an ACIE Member (rather than a Fellow) to be the independent examiner for charities with incomes greater than £100,000, although ACIE's own regulations would require the examiner to be a Fellow if the income was more than £250,000).

Because detailed accounting regulations for Northern Ireland have yet to be issued, the precise reporting duties of IEs are not yet certain, but since common reporting duties apply in England and Wales and in Scotland, it seems very likely that the same provisions will apply in Northern Ireland. The CCNI is given power (like CCEW, but unlike OSCR) to issue mandatory Directions to IEs.[47]

As in England and Wales (unlike Scotland) the 2008 Act does not provide for detailed regulations to be made for Northern Irish charity accounts on the R&P basis, but no doubt the CCNI will issue non-statutory guidance. Because of the importance of the published accounts of a CIO for external parties (see chapter 17), NI CIOs preparing R&P accounts are strongly recommended to follow this. The assets statement for Northern Irish R&P accounts is called a 'statement of assets and liabilities',[48] as in England and Wales (rather than using the Scottish term 'statement of balances').

It seems almost certain that when the accounts of a Northern Irish charity are prepared on the accruals basis the regulations will apply the Charities SORP (see page 148 for more details) as elsewhere in the UK. If so, there will be no specific differences for NI CIOs.

The accounts of an NI CIO, as is the case for other Northern Irish charities, will need to be accompanied by a trustees' annual report (TAR).[49] The regulations have not yet been made, but it seems likely that the requirements will be similar to those for an E&W CIO (see page 142).

Like other Northern Irish charities, an NI CIO will have to file its annual report and accounts with CCNI each year, and the deadline for this is ten months after year end[50] (as in England and Wales, but longer than the nine-month limit for charitable companies and for SCIOs). These must, of course, be signed by the trustees and by the auditor or examiner.

It is not yet certain whether the CCNI will make charity accounts available online in the manner of the CCEW (unlike the approach of OSCR following implementation of the charity accounting regime in Scotland).

---

[47] Charities Act (NI) 2008, s. 65(9)(b).

[48] Charities Act (NI) 2008, s. 64(3).

[49] Charities Act (NI) 2008, s. 68.

[50] Charities Act (NI) 2008, s. 68(3)(a).

However, it is very much to be hoped that this will be done, especially for NI CIOs, so that external parties can readily access their accounts.

If an NI CIO has a subsidiary, the statutory framework for consolidated accounts[51] is identical to the requirements in England and Wales, so it is likely the regulations will take a similar approach in terms of thresholds (i.e. group accounts will almost certainly be compulsory if the consolidated income of the group is more than £500,000). Also, if an auditor or examiner of an NI CIO uncovers serious issues which are likely to be of material significance for CCNI's regulatory functions, then there is a whistleblowing duty to CCNI[52] (similar to the duties on whistleblowing to the CCEW). See page 152 for more on these issues.

There is nothing in the Act stating that the accounts of Northern Irish charities have to be in pounds sterling (nor in fact for CIOs elsewhere). So, unless the regulations stipulate otherwise, if an NI CIO is operating Ireland-wide and keeps most of its internal accounts in euro it could in theory prepare its year-end accounts in euro and file them accordingly with CCNI, as long as all the presentation requirements comply with the Act and regulations (including SORP compliance if they are on the accruals basis). Only the totals would need to be converted to sterling equivalents for the charity's annual return to CCNI. However, the accounts of a charity must relate to the whole organisation. So the practice which has sometimes been used by charities in the past – of producing two separate sets of accounts in sterling and euro for their affairs north and south of the border – would not be possible with an NI CIO. If all the affairs are conducted through one charity structured as an NI CIO (rather than having a separate charity established in the Republic of Ireland), the accounts would have to be combined into an overall account in one currency for the charity as a whole. (However, an alternative structure would be to establish a charity in the Republic of Ireland to operate Ireland-wide, and then to register in Northern Ireland purely on the Section 167 Register, but it could not be a CIO unless CIO legislation were enacted south of the border.)

Converting unincorporated charities to NI CIOs

The process of converting an unincorporated Northern Irish charity into an NI CIO is essentially as described in chapter 9: the NI CIO must first be

[51] Charities Act (NI) 2008, ss. 64(8), 72 & Sch. 6.

[52] Charities Act (NI) 2008, s. 67.

formed, and then the old charity is wound up with its assets and activities transferred to the NI CIO.

It is not yet clear whether CCNI will produce any special application forms for such cases (as used by OSCR), but the legal framework follows the same approach as in England and Wales. In particular, for unincorporated charities without wind-up powers, the trustees can resolve to transfer all assets to an NI CIO without a limit on the income of the charity[53] (as under the English legislation). In the case of transfers of permanent endowment, regulations will need to be made similar to those in England and Wales, if trustees are to be able to make their own pre-merger vesting declaration[54] to transfer permanent endowment (see page 174).

Since there is no lower limit for charity registration in Northern Ireland, the existing charity should already be registered with CCNI.

Converting charitable companies, CBSs and CICs to NI CIOs

It is possible for a charitable company to convert directly to an NI CIO (i.e. without winding up the existing charity) following the general process outlined in chapter 10. The same principles allow an Industrial and Provident Society (IPS) which is a charity (i.e. a community benefit society – CBS) to become an NI CIO. As in England and Wales, the 2008 Act allows for this to be extended by regulations to allow conversion of Community Interest Companies (CICs).[55]

These provisions are unlikely to be implemented until some time after the registration of NI CIOs begins; nevertheless, the underlying legal framework is the same as for conversion to an E&W CIO, so the processes will no doubt be almost the same. However, in the case of a CBS conversion, it should be noted that IPS law in Northern Ireland[56] has a number of differences from the framework applicable in Britain, so there could be slight differences in the conversion regulations.

---

[53] Charities Act (NI) 2008, s. 123–123(1)(a) is disapplied in the case of transfers to an NI CIO by s. 120.

[54] In E&W, such a declaration can be made under Charities Act 2011, ss. 310–313 as amended for CIOs by reg. 61 of the CIO General Regulations 2012. It would be helpful if the NI CIO Regulations made similar amendments to ss. 163–164 of the Charities Act (NI) 2008.

[55] Charities Act (NI) 2008, ss. 112–115.

[56] Industrial and Provident Societies Act (Northern Ireland) 1969.

Winding up, mergers and insolvency of NI CIOs

As explained in chapters 11 and 12, a CIO may well come to the end of its life for a variety of reasons. But as a corporate body – a legal entity – it cannot cease to operate. It must be formally dissolved, or amalgamated into another body.

However, the details will not become certain until regulations are made under the 2008 Act for insolvency and dissolution of NI CIOs.[57]

The procedures are, however, likely to be very similar to those in England and Wales (see chapter 12) given the similarity of the legal framework for NI CIOs and E&W CIOs. In particular, it is likely that the insolvency framework will follow corporate insolvency law, rather than following the bankruptcy framework in Scotland. However, there may be some differences, as insolvency law in Northern Ireland is governed by the Insolvency (Northern Ireland) Order 1989 which has a number of differences from the Insolvency Act 1986 as applied in England and Wales.

The Charities Act (NI) 2008 has provisions directly equivalent to those in England and Wales for mergers of NI CIOs, either by transfer or amalgamation[58] (see page 209 for details). However, these can only be used where all the parties are already established as NI CIOs – they could not be used for cross-border mergers with E&W CIOs or SCIOs, for example.

Dissolution of NI CIOs which are inactive or no longer charities

It seems likely that the insolvency and dissolution regulations for NI CIOs will make similar provisions to those for E&W CIOs (see chapter 11) allowing CCNI to dissolve an NI CIO which is not in operation or which has ceased to be a charity. If the CIO appears still to have charitable assets, CCNI will no doubt use its regulatory powers to force these to be transferred to another charity before the CIO is dissolved.

[57] Charities Act (NI) 2008, s. 119.

[58] Charities Act (NI) 2008, ss. 116–118.

15 CIOs operating UK-wide

So far in this book we have focused on CIOs established and operating in just one of the three UK jurisdictions:

- CIOs established in England and Wales – E&W CIOs – registered and regulated by the Charity Commission for England and Wales (CCEW);
- CIOs established in Scotland – SCIOs – registered and regulated by the Office of the Scottish Charity Regulator (OSCR);
- CIOs established under the laws of Northern Ireland which (when implemented) will be registered and regulated by the Charity Commission for Northern Ireland (CCNI).

Many CIOs operating solely in particular towns and regions – or perhaps across a single country but not further – can focus purely on the requirements of charity law in the jurisdiction where they are established without worrying about other regulators. This is described as the 'home jurisdiction'. But many other CIOs may be operating UK-wide, or even internationally.

This book cannot consider the impact of charity and not-for-profit law on CIOs operating outside the UK, but within the UK a CIO may well need to consider the impact of more than one system of charity law and may need to be registered with more than one regulator. This chapter summarises these issues.

This is not just an issue for very large charities. Many charities working in specialist fields, even with quite a modest income, but with groups and events across the UK are 'cross-border charities' and are frequently therefore registered with more than one regulator. (Also, whilst the discussion in this chapter focuses on CIOs, it is worth noting the requirements for registration with more than one regulator to any type of cross-border charity.)

The points below consider the issues in each jurisdiction for *external CIOs* – that is, a charity established as a CIO in another part of the UK. At the end of the chapter is a summary of the relative advantages of where to establish a CIO operating UK-wide.

In almost all cases, a CIO will require recognition as a charity for tax purposes (by HMRC) as well as being registered by the relevant charity regulator. So, potentially, a CIO could have four regulators to consider: CCEW, OSCR, CCNI and HMRC. However, issues of charity tax recognition were considered previously (in chapters 5, 13 and 14) and are not repeated here. But, unlike a charitable company, a CIO is never subject to further regulation by Companies House; so, even for a cross-border CIO, the arrangements are simpler than for a charitable company.

External CIOs operating in England and Wales

The position for external charities operating in England and Wales is very simple: there is no system of registration with CCEW for external charities. Apart from a few issues concerning charitable property in England and Wales held on behalf of Scottish charities,[1] the Charities Act 2011 has no direct impact on a SCIO or NI CIO operating in England and Wales, other than the definition of 'charity' for tax purposes. Operating in England and Wales does not generate any additional accounting issues.

A SCIO or NI CIO operating in England and Wales therefore cannot register with the CCEW even if it wishes to do so.

However, it is an offence to claim to be fundraising on behalf of a registered charity if this is not the case[2] (and the term 'registered charity' is defined in terms of registration with CCEW). So it is very important that SCIOs and NI CIOs operating UK-wide do not simply put 'Registered charity no #######' on their literature; rather, it is essential that they make clear *where* they are registered.

External CIOs operating in Scotland

Scotland has the strictest system for external charities. The general principle is that *any* body operating in Scotland which claims to be a charity must be included on the Scottish Charity Register through registration with OSCR, except in the cases explained in the following section.[3]

---

[1] Charities Act 2011, s. 87.

[2] Charities Act 1992, s. 63.

[3] Charities & TI (Scotland) Act 2005, s. 13.

Many charities operating across England, Wales and Scotland are now, therefore, 'dual registered'; for example, a CIO with its principal office in London will have its main registration with CCEW, but it will also be registered with OSCR. All literature must then show:

- Registered charity in England and Wales no. ####### and in Scotland no. SC*******.

So, an E&W CIO is formed by registration with the CCEW, but it must *also* be registered with OSCR if it has significant activities in Scotland (see the following section for details).

In such cases, the CIO will have a normal constitution as an E&W CIO with objects that are charitable under the Charities Act 2011, but it is important to make certain that the objects are worded in such a way as to ensure it is *also* a charity under the laws of Scotland, as defined in the Charities & TI (Scotland) Act 2005. (Otherwise it would be unable to register with OSCR at all and could not therefore describe itself as a charity in relation to any of its activities in Scotland.)

However, when an E&W CIO becomes registered with OSCR in this way, it does *not* become a SCIO. Only CIOs *formed* by registration with OSCR, established under Scots law, can be SCIOs. The charity will remain an E&W CIO (and if the name includes 'CIO' this is unchanged). However, all literature will need to show both charity registration numbers as above.

The same requirements would apply to an NI CIO operating in Scotland: unless the exceptions below apply, it will need to register with OSCR as well as CCNI.

Exceptions from registration with OSCR

There are some limited exceptions to the rules requiring external charities to register with OSCR. If an external charity such as an E&W CIO or an NI CIO:

(a) does not occupy any land or premises in Scotland; and
(b) does not carry out activities in any shop, offices or similar premises in Scotland,

then it does not have to register with OSCR, *provided* all its literature makes clear where it is established, so there is no confusion with Scottish charities.[4]

[4] Charities & TI (Scotland) Act 2005, s. 14.

So, an E&W CIO can have members or donors in Scotland without having to register with OSCR, provided all its literature clearly shows 'Registered charity in England and Wales no. #######'; but it would be committing an offence if the words 'England and Wales' were omitted. However, it cannot occupy premises or hold regular activities in Scotland (except possibly in someone's home). OSCR has indicated that it is not concerned about very occasional activities in Scotland, but if an E&W CIO establishes a Scottish branch which is regularly hiring rooms in Scotland, or if it opens a charity shop in Scotland, it certainly needs to register with OSCR (and similarly for an NI CIO).

Implications of registration with OSCR

Once an external charity is registered with OSCR it becomes subject to almost all the provisions of Scottish charity law. In particular, it must make annual returns to OSCR and comply with the Scottish charity accounting rules (see page 262 for further details).[5]

In many respects, the Scottish charity accounting requirements are stricter than those in England and Wales, and these may affect many smaller CIOs operating UK-wide. It is usually best, therefore, to start from the Scottish requirements, even if most of the CIO's work is outside Scotland. In particular, for charities on the Scottish Register, there is no lower limit for independent examination of accounts (in England and Wales, independent examination is not needed until the income of a charity reaches £25,000) and there are slightly stricter rules for receipts and payments accounts, and on when an independent examiner must be professionally qualified. (There are fewer differences for charities with incomes greater than £500,000 which are subject to audit.) The trustees' report must also refer specifically to activities in Scotland.

For an E&W CIO which is also registered with OSCR, the report of the auditor or independent examiner must explain that the scrutiny was conducted in accordance with *both* the Charities Act 2011 *and* the Charities and Trustee Investment (Scotland) Act 2005. So it is important to use an auditor or independent examiner who is familiar with both regimes. Also, the deadline for submission of year-end accounts to OSCR is nine months after year end, whereas an E&W CIO could (if needed) take up to ten months to file its accounts with CCEW.

[5] Charities & TI (Scotland) Act 2005, s. 44.

The same issues will apply to an NI CIO operating in Scotland: its accounts would have to comply with the Northern Irish charity accounting requirements (under the 2008 Act) and with the Scottish requirements.

OSCR has a memorandum of understanding with CCEW regarding cross-border charities established in England and Wales: in general, if major concerns arise, CCEW will take the lead in any investigations. Further details for cross-border charities are available on the OSCR website. However, OSCR has extensive powers to intervene in any charity on the Scottish Register, even if it is established outside Scotland.

External CIOs operating in Northern Ireland

The requirements for external charities in Northern Ireland under the Charities Act (Northern Ireland) 2008 are a compromise between the arrangements in England and Wales on the one hand, and those in Scotland on the other.

An external charity – such as an E&W CIO or a SCIO – is not required to register on the main Northern Ireland Register of Charities, but (when implemented) it will need to join a simpler register of external charities operating in Northern Ireland.[6] This is currently referred to as the 'Section 167 Register' (though it may have a clearer name when it comes into effect). This will include any institution which is not a Northern Irish charity, but which operates for charitable purposes in or from Northern Ireland. (However, the Section 167 Register is not likely to be implemented for several years until CCNI has registered charities established in Northern Ireland itself. By that time, NI CIOs are also likely to be established.)

An E&W CIO or SCIO on the Section 167 Register does not have to meet the full Northern Irish charity accounting requirements, but it will need to prepare a financial statement and a statement of activities for CCNI summarising its operations in Northern Ireland. The details of this will depend on regulations still to be made, but for any E&W CIO or SCIO planning to operate in Northern Ireland, it would be worth structuring the accounting records in such a way that income and expenditure relating to activities in Northern Ireland can be separated easily.

[6] Charities Act (NI) 2008, s. 167.

Where to establish a CIO operating UK-wide

From the descriptions above, it is clear that there is little symmetry between the three jurisdictions, with Scotland having the most demanding requirements for external charities, and England and Wales the lightest.

For most charities operating UK-wide, the largest amount of income and expenditure will be in England because of the much larger populations. So, to establish a CIO operating UK-wide, it may seem logical to form it in England and Wales through registration with CCEW and then register in Scotland and Northern Ireland if needed.

Minimising regulation

However, for those seeking to minimise the total burden of charity regulation, this is *not* the simplest approach. As shown in table 15.1, the simplest approach is to form the charity as a SCIO through initial registration with OSCR.

Table 15.1 Implications of establishing a UK-wide CIO in each jurisdiction

Legal form	E&W CIO	SCIO	NI CIO
Home regulator (which forms the CIO)	CCEW	OSCR	CCNI
Other registrations needed if operating UK-wide	OSCR CCNI (s. 167 only)	CCNI (s. 167 only)	OSCR
Charity accounting requirements	England & Wales Scottish NI brief report (s. 167)	Scottish NI brief report (s. 167)	Northern Irish Scottish
Total number of regulators (counting s. 167 registration in NI as a half regulator)	2.5	1.5	2

As long as there is *some* work in Scotland and so long as it is possible to give an address in Scotland as the principal office, a charity can be structured as a SCIO even if most of its work is in England. Of course, it may be necessary to give some explanation to supporters, but there have long been a number of highly respected UK charities originally founded in Scotland (but with much of their work in England), and hence they are registered with OSCR but *not* with CCEW. However, if this approach is taken, the charity trustees should ensure that they have appropriate professional advice for a Scottish body but with extensive operations in England.

Comparison of the three forms of CIO

For those seeking the least complex regulatory arrangements, the SCIO may, therefore, be the form of choice for UK-wide charities which have elected to work using the CIO structure.

However, it is important to remember that E&W CIOs, SCIOs and NI CIOs are not just the same entities registered with different regulators. They are fundamentally different bodies, subject to different legal frameworks, corresponding to the three different legal systems, and established under different definitions of 'charity'. There are different procedures for constitutional amendments, mergers and insolvency.

Table 15.2 summarises some of the differences – for more on these issues and for clarification of the terms, see chapters 5 to 12 in relation to E&W CIOs, chapter 13 for SCIOs and chapter 14 for NI CIOs.

In general, the legal framework of the SCIO is the simplest of the three options. So for those seeking to run a charity with the minimum legal complexities, the SCIO is very attractive. But because the regulations for E&W CIOs are more extensive (and in some respects slightly closer to company law) the E&W CIO could be considered more robust. It is too early to speculate about the details for NI CIOs, although the legal framework is closer to that for E&W CIOs than to SCIOs (though the Northern Irish legislation is slightly harder to follow because of major provisions in a schedule). But, given that NI CIOs may not be implemented for some time, in the short term, most UK-wide bodies will choose the E&W CIO or SCIO.

Table 15.2 Summary of major features of CIOs in each jurisdiction

Legal form	E&W CIO	SCIO	NI CIO
Central feature	Corporate body with limited liability and registered as a charity under the English definition	Corporate body with limited liability and registered as a charity under the Scottish definition	Corporate body with limited liability and registered as a charity under the Northern Irish definition
Primary legislation	Charities Act 2011, ss. 204–250	Charities & TI (Scotland) Act 2005, ss. 49–64	Charities Act (Northern Ireland) 2008, ss. 105–122 & Schedule 7
Secondary legislation	CIO General Regulations 2012 CIO (I&D) Regulations 2012 (Total: 83 pages)	SCIO Regulations 2012 SCIO RR&D Regulations 2012 (Total: 10 pages excluding sample forms)	Not yet made
First established	2 Jan 2013	1 April 2011	Awaited
Minimum number of members	One	Two	One
Insolvency framework	Follows Insolvency Act 1986 (adapted for CIOs)	Similar to framework for personal bankruptcy in Scotland under AIB	To be confirmed
Regulatory approval needed for constitutional amendments	Regulated alterations need approval by CCEW – others just agreed by members	Regulated alterations need approval by OSCR – others just agreed by members	Regulated alterations need approval by CCNI – others just agreed by members

Legal form	E&W CIO	SCIO	NI CIO
Proportion of votes needed to agree constitutional amendments at a general meeting of members	75%	Two-thirds	75%
Process of implementing constitutional amendments	Do not take effect until registered with CCEW	Must be advised to OSCR, but amendments take effect immediately	Do not take effect until registered with CCNI
Access to register of members	Any member can request *names and addresses* of all members – though members can use service addresses	Any member can request *names* of all members, but access to *addresses* can be limited to trustees	To be confirmed
Retention of past information in registers	Formers members' details kept for 10 years. Former trustees' details kept indefinitely	Details of former members and trustees kept for 6 years	To be confirmed

16 Appealing CIO decisions made by charity regulators

When deciding to establish a CIO, or when making changes to an existing CIO, the relationship with the relevant regulator (CCEW, OSCR or CCNI) will hopefully go smoothly.

It is worth bearing in mind, for example, that in England and Wales the Charity Commission has statutory objectives which include: promoting the effective use of charitable resources, promoting compliance by trustees with their legal obligations, and enhancing the accountability of charities.[1] So, if you are looking to establish a CIO for purposes which are genuinely charitable, or looking to convert an existing charity to a CIO in order to enable it to be administered more effectively, the Commission should be on your side. Similar principles apply with OSCR and CCNI.

However, there can be cases where decisions made by charity regulators go against what you are seeking. The most obvious case is when an application to register a CIO is refused. In serious cases, regulators also have powers to intervene in charities directly, for example to open a statutory inquiry, restrict the transactions which a charity can undertake, freeze assets, suspend trustees, and even to appoint an 'interim manager' in place of all the trustees (see page 237).

If a CIO (or applicants looking to establish a CIO) find themselves in any of these situations, the obvious question is: what can we do to challenge the regulator's decision? The answer is that in all three jurisdictions (England and Wales, Scotland, and Northern Ireland) a system of independent tribunals or panels exist, which allow many decisions by a regulator to be challenged.

This chapter outlines very briefly how these tribunal processes work and the situations where it may be appropriate to consider appealing decisions affecting CIOs.

[1] Charities Act 2011, s. 14.

The tribunals

As noted, there are three separate tribunal systems – each established under the same legislation which created CIOs.

- Decisions regarding CIOs in England and Wales (decisions by the CCEW) can be appealed to the *First-tier Tribunal (Charity)* and then, if necessary, to a second-tier tribunal, the *Upper Tribunal (Tax and Chancery).*[2] The Upper Tribunal has the status of a 'superior court of record', meaning that its decisions can be cited with authority in other cases. The major cases in 2011 concerning the public benefit requirement[3] were heard in the Upper Tribunal (although they were not specifically about CIOs).
- Decisions regarding SCIOs (decisions taken by OSCR) can be appealed to the *Scottish Charity Appeals Panel* (SCAP).[4] In 2010, the SCAP was suspended as a staffed body, as only two appeals were received in three years. But, to date, it has not been abolished and appeals can still be lodged. However, recent reviews of the Scottish Tribunals system may lead to a new structure in due course.
- Once CIOs are implemented in Northern Ireland, it will be possible for decisions by CCNI to be appealed to the *Charity Tribunal for Northern Ireland.*[5] (This has already started operating in relation to appeals from existing Northern Ireland charities.)

The First-tier Tribunal (Charity) in England and Wales was originally created as the 'Charity Tribunal' (under the Charities Act 2006) and that name is still widely used informally and in the following discussion. Although the Scottish appeal body is technically a 'panel' rather than a 'tribunal', the three appeal bodies are described in this chapter as the 'charity tribunals'.

In each case it is possible to appeal further, from the tribunals to the courts, if necessary (although in England and Wales, and in Northern Ireland, this is only possible on a point of law). Each of the tribunals is administered as part of the courts service and is completely independent of the charity regulators. Contact information for the tribunals is given under 'Useful addresses' (see page 338).

All three tribunals became operational prior to the implementation of the new definition of charity in each jurisdiction (well before the first

[2] Charities Act 2011, ss. 315–331.

[3] See footnote 13 on page 28.

[4] Charities & TI (Scotland) Act 2005, ss. 75–78.

[5] Charities Act (NI) 2008, ss. 12–15.

registrations of CIOs). Therefore, any decisions affecting CIOs can be appealed from the outset.

Whether to appeal

While at first sight it may be tempting to file a tribunal appeal as soon as a decision concerning a CIO goes against what you were seeking, it is important to remember that appealing any decision by a charity regulator will take considerable time and resources.

Although the charity tribunals are intended to be more informal than the courts and it is possible, in principle, to make an appeal without using lawyers, the tribunal procedures are laid down by regulations which mirror court practices.[6]

You will, of necessity, find yourself and your fellow applicants or trustees in an adversarial situation against the charity regulator (CCEW, OSCR or CCNI). You will be 'the appellants' and the regulator will be 'the respondent'. The regulator is likely to be represented at least by a qualified lawyer from its own legal team, or possibly by a specialist barrister. Often the arguments will hinge on the issues of what is and is not a charity, and the regulator is likely to cite case law in support of its position, to which you will have to respond. Whilst the tribunal judges will do all that they can to ensure you get a fair hearing even without having legal representation, in practice, you are unlikely to win a case without legal advice. Some decisions are taken purely on paper, but if there is an oral hearing, you may well want legal representation at the hearing. So this could mean a considerable investment of resources.

However, only in the most exceptional cases where someone had acted unreasonably would a tribunal award costs to the other party, so (unlike cases which go to court) you are not normally at risk of having to meet the regulator's legal costs if you lose (but equally you will not be able to recover your own costs if you win).

Any tribunal hearing is a public event which could mean dealing with press enquiries and reports. While there are still relatively few appeals to the charity tribunals, even the initial notice of appeal may create interest. (It may be possible to ask a tribunal to allow certain witnesses to give

[6] For appeals regarding CIOs in England and Wales see The Tribunal Procedures (First-tier Tribunal) (General Regulatory Chamber) Rules 2009 (SI 2009/1976) – rules 25–31 deal specifically with charity cases. For Scotland and Northern Ireland, see The Scottish Charity Appeals Panel Rules 2006 (SSI 2205/571) and The Charity Tribunal Rules (Northern Ireland) 2010 (NISR 2010/77).

evidence without it being made public, but because a charity is established for public benefit there will be very few instances where a tribunal will allow the entire case to be heard in private.)

Steps short of an appeal

In practice, therefore, the first step is always to consider whether a different approach to the regulator could achieve what you are seeking without the need for an appeal. For example, if an application to register a CIO was refused, examine carefully the reasons given. It may be possible to word the charitable objects differently or make other changes to the proposed CIO constitution and re-apply. It may be that other information submitted with the application was insufficiently clear as to how the public benefit requirement would be met.

If you are convinced that the application was correct, but was in some way misinterpreted by a particular member of staff, all three regulators operate a process allowing to you to request an internal 'review' of a decision. This means that it will be reconsidered by a senior member of staff or board member who was not involved in the original decision. In Scotland, the process for seeking reviews by OSCR is included in the Act, and you cannot take a case to the Scottish Charity Appeals Panel unless this review process has first been invoked.[7] Such a request must be made to OSCR within 21 days of the original decision.

Appeal timescales and outcomes

If, however, an appeal is to be made, the procedural rules for each tribunal (see footnote on page 313) lay down strict timetables which must be followed.

In England and Wales the appeal must be filed with the First-tier Tribunal (Charity) within six weeks (42 days) of the regulator's decision which is being appealed (in the case of an appeal by the applicants, trustees, or others directly involved), unless the Tribunal agrees that there are reasons for allowing more time. (For appeals made by others, the six weeks run from the date when the decision was made public.) In Scotland the time limit is four weeks (28 days).

The rules then lay down timescales for the regulator to respond, and for further responses by each party, and a possible oral hearing, before the tribunal reaches a decision.

---

[7] Charities & TI (Scotland) Act 2005, s. 74.

Many appeals end up being withdrawn, but if a case goes through the full process, it will typically take up to 30 weeks (seven months) to reach a decision by the tribunal (although cases can take considerably longer). At that stage, the tribunal may confirm or vary the regulator's decision, or substitute its own decision. So, for example, it could direct that a CIO must be registered, even though the regulator initially rejected the application. However, even if the tribunal finds that the regulator made an error, it is more likely to send the application back to the regulator to reconsider, which will take further time.

Issues which may be the subject of an appeal

Only a *decision* by a charity regulator can be appealed. So, for example, if you are applying to register a new CIO and the regulator refuses registration, that decision can be appealed to the relevant charity tribunal. But there are no grounds for appeal while the application remains under consideration (and in complex cases where the regulator has other demands, an application to register a new charity can take many months or even years before you get a decision). Similarly, you cannot appeal a general policy decision made by a regulator – it has to be a decision affecting a specific CIO or proposed CIO (although in England and Wales and in Northern Ireland, the Attorney General can refer more general questions to the charity tribunals).

Who can appeal?

The legislation in each jurisdiction specifies those persons or bodies which are allowed to appeal in different circumstances.

Generally, appeals can only be made by persons who are 'affected by' a decision – this would include the CIO itself as a corporate body (if registered), its members or trustees. If an application to register a CIO was refused, the proposed CIO cannot appeal (because it does not exist) but an appeal can certainly be brought by the applicants (the proposed members). Moreover, beneficiaries (service users) or potential beneficiaries, and members of staff may also be able to argue that they are affected. In cases where the Charity Commission decides to dissolve a CIO, the CIO itself no longer exists, but an appeal can be made by the former trustees.

In some cases, appeals could come from parties who have no direct involvement in the CIO, if they can show that they are affected. And bear in mind that decisions by regulators can, in most cases, be appealed either way. So, for example, it could happen that a CIO is registered but other people object: perhaps on the grounds that they consider the name of the

CIO to be misleading and that it would end up attracting donations properly intended for another charity. If so, they could ask the relevant tribunal to overthrow the registration decision.

Decisions that can be appealed: England and Wales

In England and Wales, the decisions, directions and orders of the Charity Commission which can be appealed to the Tribunal are set out in a Schedule to the Charities Act.[8]

The most common grounds for appeal are likely to be a refusal to register a CIO, but there are many other cases in the life of a CIO where there could be a case for challenging a decision. The list of Charity Commission decisions *specific* to CIOs which can be a basis for appeal are as follows (but refer to the legislation for details):

- registration of a CIO or refusal of registration (see chapter 5);
- refusal to register a CIO constitutional amendment (see chapter 6);
- refusal of an application for a charitable company or CBS to convert to a CIO – and the final regulations will no doubt also allow appeals against refusal of a conversion application by a CIC (see chapter 10);
- approval or refusal of an application of CIO merger applications whether by amalgamation or transfer (see chapter 11);
- approval or refusal of an application for dissolution of a CIO (see chapters 11 and 12);
- decision to dissolve a CIO which is being wound up (see chapter 12);
- decision by the Charity Commission to dissolve a CIO which it believes is not in operation or which it believes is no longer a charity (see chapter 12);
- order made for application of the property of a CIO which has been dissolved – for example, an order that all assets of a former CIO are to be transferred to another charity (see chapter 12);
- order made to vest former CIO assets in the Official Custodian for Charities (see chapter 12);
- decision by the Charity Commission to restore (or not to restore) a former CIO which has been dissolved (see chapter 12).

This list summarises issues specific to CIOs. However, it is also possible to appeal a range of Charity Commission decisions[9] that could affect a CIO

[8] Charities Act 2011, Sch. 6, as amended by article 8 of the Charitable Incorporated Organisations (Consequential Amendments) Order 2012 (SI 2012/3014).

[9] Some decisions are decisions to do something and some are to refuse to do something: see Charities Act 2011, Sch. 6.

but which could also relate to any type of charity, for example a decision to suspend a trustee or employee.[10] It should be noted that where a charity, including a CIO, or other person affected is aggrieved at the opening of an inquiry by the Charity Commission, the process is not strictly an appeal (where the Tribunal may substitute its own decision for that of the Commission) but an application for review[11] (where the Tribunal examines the legality of the decision).

Decisions that can be appealed: Scotland and Northern Ireland

The range of decisions by OSCR regarding SCIOs which can be challenged in the Scottish Charity Appeals Panel largely follow similar issues but refer to the 2005 Act for details.[12] However, those affected must first ask OSCR to review its original decision:[13] an appeal can only be made against OSCR's final position following an internal review.

Nevertheless, there are important differences as compared to England and Wales because, as explained in chapter 13, constitutional amendments by SCIOs do not have to be registered by OSCR before they take effect. Also, the dissolution process for SCIOs is very different from that for CIOs in England and Wales.

It is not yet possible to confirm the full range of situations which will present grounds for appeal against CCNI decisions regarding CIOs: a number of instances are listed in the 2008 Act,[14] but, as in England and Wales, the final regulations may add to these. However, as in England and Wales, there are issues relating to charities which take other legal forms on which the Tribunal has heard appeals, which may also be of relevance to CIOs.

[10] Charities Act 2011, s. 46 & ss. 79–80.

[11] For the list of 'reviewable matters' see Charities Act 2011, s. 322.

[12] Charities & TI (Scotland) Act 2005, ss. 71 & 76.

[13] Charities & TI (Scotland) Act 2005, ss. 74 & 76(1).

[14] Charities Act (NI) 2008, Sch. 3.

17 Banks, funders, employees: rights of third parties dealing with CIOs

Most of this book has looked at CIOs from the perspective of those seeking to carry out charitable work through a CIO. But no charity operates in isolation: most charities need donors, funders and suppliers. Many also need workers (employees, freelancers, volunteers), premises, and, in some cases, loan finance. CIOs are only effective if other parties dealing with a CIO have confidence in the agreements they make with a CIO.

This chapter looks briefly at some specific provisions in law to protect those entering into agreements with CIOs. An external person dealing with an organisation (whether an individual or a corporate body) is generally referred to in law as a 'third party', so banks, funders, employees, other charities, and so on, are all third parties in their relationships with a CIO. Unless otherwise stated, the points in this chapter apply to CIOs in all three jurisdictions: England and Wales, Scotland (SCIOs) and Northern Ireland.

A corporate body with limited liability

A CIO is a corporate body with limited liability, established for charitable purposes. This means anyone entering into an agreement with a CIO is making an agreement with the CIO as a corporate body. It is not an agreement with individual trustees or members of the CIO.

In most cases this is attractive. Third parties are generally more comfortable having agreements with corporate bodies rather than with groups of individuals, because if anything goes wrong, action is taken against a single body. Also, whilst it will always be distressing for trustees if their CIO is the subject of legal action, the fact that the action is against the CIO, rather than the trustees personally, keeps a sense of 'distance' between the action and the trustees.

But third parties will also be aware that the CIO has limited liability. If the CIO has made a financial commitment and does not pay, it can be sued, and if the action is successful, the courts can force the CIO to make settlement. Alternatively, the creditor could go to court to force a liquidation of the CIO, as explained in chapter 12 (see page 233). But these rights are of little use unless the CIO has sufficient assets to settle the liability. Because it is a limited liability body, a third party cannot take action against the CIO's trustees, even if they were foolish to have made the commitment in the first place (except in the extreme cases where 'wrongful trading' may have occurred – see page 226 – but this requires an explicit order of the court).

So, a third party dealing with a CIO (as when dealing with any limited liability body) needs to consider this and make a sensible judgement of the risks they are accepting.

Guarantees of liabilities

Banks and businesses offering substantial levels of credit to small commercial limited companies often ask the directors to give personal guarantees. Then, if the company fails, the directors become personally liable (thus wiping out many of the benefits of limited liability, but this may be acceptable in the early years to get a business established). However, it would rarely be appropriate for CIO trustees, who are normally serving on a voluntary basis, to give personal guarantees.

There may, however, be some circumstances where a major funder might be prepared to give guarantees; for example, if a new CIO is awarded funding for a major building project, the funder will probably only wish to hand over funds to the CIO as the project proceeds, so at any time the CIO's assets will be modest. But the funder (who will be keen to see the project built) may be willing to enter into a guarantee with the builder to meet the remaining costs of the project if the CIO were to fail. In return, however, the funder may insist on taking a charge over the land being used (see page 329).

Funding arrangements: grants versus contracts

Most discussion in text books of third-party relationships assumes a third party having a contractual relationship with the body concerned. A contract is a two-way agreement: 'If you do X, I will do Y': for example, 'If you deliver these goods, we will pay you £200'.

Many funding agreements with charities involve a purchase of services from the CIO (procurement) which means they are contracts. Similarly, agreements with suppliers will be contracts, as are contracts of employment (though subject to many protections under employment law). A contract can be enforced under contract law by suing the other party.

However, many third-party relationships with charities are not contractual but are subject to trust law. Indeed, traditionally, all support to charities was given on trust. When a donor gives money or assets to a charity, the donor is entrusting the charity with a gift (albeit possibly subject to conditions). If it is a larger amount, it may be called a grant rather than a donation, but the same principle applies (so long as it is genuinely a grant – occasionally a so-called 'grant agreement' is really a contract).

A donation or grant may be given for the general work of the charity (held as unrestricted funds) or may be given on trust for specific purposes (and is then held in a restricted or endowment fund). If the charity abuses the grant or donation, for example by failing to use it within the terms for which it was given, the donor or funder may be able to take action for breach of trust (for instance, by requiring the gift to be repaid, or asking the court to force the charity to apply it for the specified purposes). But under a trust law relationship, the funder cannot sue for breach of contract. Likewise, the charity cannot sue if a promised gift does not materialise (unless the donor entered into a *deed* to make the gift legally binding even though nothing was expected in return; for example, a gift under a will is a gift by deed, so it is a binding commitment if all the conditions in the will are met).

In the case of a CIO which is itself a grant-making charity, grants (whether to other charities or individuals) will normally be given on trust: so recipients do not have contractual rights in the event that the CIO cannot pay a promised grant.

In considering the rights of third parties in any issue with a CIO, it is therefore crucial to consider whether the relationship with the CIO is a contractual relationship, or purely a relationship of trust. These differences are also very important for accounting purposes (see *The Charity Treasurer's Handbook*, also published in this series, for more details).

Constitutional capacity: when third parties can rely on a CIO

A CIO is not free to do anything its members or trustees may wish to do – it is bound by its constitution. In particular, all resources must be used either:

- directly to advance the charitable objects specified in the constitution; or
- in ways that, taking account of the CIO's powers, are 'conducive or incidental' to advancing the objects[1] (see page 96). This can include, for example, employing staff, renting premises, investing in fundraising, and all kinds of other expenses which help to further the objects, even though these do not directly transfer resources from the CIO to the beneficiaries.

Whilst these requirements are vital to ensure a CIO keeps to its charitable aims, they could cause problems for third parties, because whenever a CIO enters into an agreement, the third party might ask: 'Am I sure this is a valid agreement – did the CIO really have the power to make this commitment?'

Also, a CIO can only take decisions by following the procedures specified in its constitution; for example, any decision to spend funds can only be taken by a properly convened trustees' meeting, or under powers delegated by the trustees to sub-committees or individuals. So, whenever a CIO makes an agreement, the third party might ask: 'Did the CIO go through all the required processes to make this commitment?'

If a CIO entered into a commitment which was outside its objects and powers, or which had not been approved by its trustees, it would be acting outside its 'constitutional capacity'. This could be a minefield for anyone dealing with a CIO, as there could be constant uncertainties as to whether the CIO was acting within its constitutional capacity and hence whether an agreement was legally binding.

---

[1] Charities Act 2011, s. 110; Charities & TI (Scotland) Act 2005, s. 50(5); Charities Act (NI) 2008, Sch. 7, para. 1(1).

Fortunately, in order to protect third parties from such uncertainties, the legislation for CIOs specifically addresses this issue, in all three jurisdictions.[2] The English wording states that:

> .... *the validity of an act done (or purportedly done) by a CIO is not to be called into question on the grounds that the CIO lacked constitutional capacity*[3]
> ... *the power of the charity trustees of the CIO to act as to bind the CIO (or to authorise others to do so) is not to be called into question on the grounds of any constitutional limitations on their powers.*[4]

However, these provisions are subject to two very important conditions:[5]

(a) the action or agreement is only binding if the person gives 'full consideration in money or money's worth', so it does not apply to a gift or grant, or a contract where the third party paid less than a commercial price; and

(b) it is only binding if the third party did not know that the act was beyond the CIO's constitutional capacity or the powers of the trustees – so if the person *knew* the arrangement had not been properly approved it cannot be enforced.

But third parties are not required to delve into these issues, because the Act also states that:

> *A party to an arrangement or transaction with a CIO is not bound to inquire (a) whether it is within the CIO's constitutional capacity or (b) as to any constitutional limitations on the powers of its charity trustees as to bind the CIO or authorise others to do so.*[6]

It also states that even if a CIO transfers property to a third party when it was outside the CIO's capacity, it does not affect the title of a person who acquires the property for 'full consideration'.[7] So if, for example, the CIO sells a vehicle to someone, and the purchaser paid a commercial price, the purchaser retains legal ownership even if the CIO should not have agreed the sale in the first place. If, however, the CIO gave the vehicle away (as a charitable gift) or sold it at much less than a commercial price, and it then

---

[2] Charities Act 2011, ss. 218–219; Charities & TI (Scotland) Act 2005, s. 62; Charities Act (NI) 2008, Sch. 7, para. 5.

[3] Charities Act 2011, s. 218(1).

[4] Charities Act 2011, s. 218(2).

[5] Charities Act 2011, s. 218(3).

[6] Charities Act 2011, s. 218(4).

[7] Charities Act 2011, s. 218(5).

turned out that it had no authority to do so, it would be possible in principle for the CIO to regain possession of the vehicle.

However, these provisions are only for the protection of third parties dealing with a CIO not to have to spend time checking the validity of decisions. They certainly do not authorise the CIO's trustees or staff to act outside the CIO's constitutional powers and capacity and the Charity Commission has extensive powers to take action if this happens. Action could also be brought by others – for example by members of a CIO – if they became aware that trustees were acting outside the terms of the constitution.[8]

Formalising agreements

If third parties are to be able to rely on a CIO to honour its agreements, they must be properly made in order to be legally binding. Likewise, the CIO itself needs to be sure it can rely on agreements made with others.

Disclosure of the CIO's status

It is essential that anyone dealing with a CIO realises that they are entering into agreement with a CIO. All documents must show the full legal name of the CIO. If the name does not include 'CIO', 'SEC' (a Welsh CIO), or 'SCIO' (as applicable), its status as a charitable incorporated organisation must be clearly stated elsewhere on the document.[9] This applies to all letters, order forms, donation forms, cheques, fundraising appeals, emails, websites, etc. However, sometimes a complex agreement is drafted by a funder (for example), or goods are ordered using a standard order form from a supplier, and the CIO status must be clearly added somewhere, if it is not part of the name.

It is also a requirement to show the status of the CIO as a registered charity.[10] Technically this is not compulsory in England and Wales for a CIO with an income of less than £10,000, but in practice it is sensible to show the registered charity number in all cases (or at least the abbreviation 'regd charity' if there is no room for the full number). (It could be argued that showing the abbreviation 'CIO', 'SEC' or 'SCIO' in the name is sufficient to show that it is a registered charity since all CIOs

---

[8] Charities Act 2011, s. 219.

[9] Charities Act 2011, ss. 211–212; Charities & TI (Scotland) Act 2005, s. 52; Charities Act (NI) 2008, s. 107.

[10] Charities Act 2011, s. 39; Charities & TI (Scotland) Act 2005, s. 15; Charities Act (NI) 2008, s. 19.

are registered charities, but it is much clearer to state this explicitly.) In the case of a CIO registered with OSCR as well as CCEW or CCNI (see page 302), both registrations must be shown.

Where a former charity has converted to a CIO, make sure all documents are clearly updated (or use stickers) to ensure that the new status is clear.

Written and electronic agreements

Binding agreements cannot be made with a CIO (or anyone else) by email, telephone or other electronic means unless each party agrees to this. In practice, this can normally be assumed for small agreements – for example, emailing a firm of printers to order some more leaflets – but major agreements should be in writing unless there is clear evidence that all parties are agreeing to make a legally binding agreement by other means. However, documents can be signed electronically if a party has made a statement agreeing to this.[11]

In other cases, you may wish to circulate drafts electronically, but they should then be printed and signed by each party and a signed copy sent to the other party. (In most cases it is best to have two copies of any agreement, where both copies are signed by both parties, as in the event of a dispute it is hard to get access to any agreement which is only held by the other party.)

Making a binding agreement

A corporate body such as a CIO can only enter into an agreement by a human agent or officer acting on its behalf. For CIOs in England and Wales, the regulations specify how such agreements may be made, as follows.[12] There are no directly equivalent regulations for SCIOs (and regulations are yet to be made for NI CIOs) but if a SCIO follows the normal provisions of Scots law with regard to agreements it is unlikely to face difficulties.

It is possible in principle for a corporate body to have a seal to execute documents, but since 1989 the use of seals has been optional. The regulations allow for a CIO to have a seal (and, if necessary, different seals for use abroad) but few companies nowadays have a seal and it is unlikely that many CIOs will want a seal, so the points below omit this option.

[11] Electronic Communications Act 2000, s. 7.

[12] CIO General Regulations 2012, regs 19–24.

A straightforward contract with a CIO can be made by any person acting under the CIO's authority. So, for example, a member of staff acting within his or her duties as agreed by the trustees can place orders on behalf of the CIO, and the CIO is then legally obliged to pay for the goods or services received.[13] Such an agreement could even be made verbally, as explained above, if all parties are happy. An individual signing a contract on behalf of the CIO signs in his or her own name, but the document should make clear that the person is signing on behalf of the CIO. If in doubt, add after the signature 'For and on behalf of XYZ CIO'.

However, there can always be doubts as to whether an individual signing in this way has legal authority to make a commitment on behalf of the CIO (for example, it is unlikely that the most junior staff would be given such authority). So, for any kind of major agreement, the other party will normally want it to be 'executed' formally by the CIO.

Assuming the CIO has at least two trustees, a document can be formally executed by the signature of at least two trustees.[14] If a document purports to be signed by two trustees, then, unless it can be shown to be a fraud, it is legally binding and commits the CIO (even if the other trustees were not involved). However, the trustees who sign should of course take care not to execute any document unless they have the clear authority to do so, for example from a properly convened trustees' meeting where a majority voted in favour. (Note that there is no equivalent to a company secretary in a CIO, so there is no option for a secretary to sign who is not a trustee – two trustees are needed.)

Some documents must be executed as deeds – the same procedures apply (signatures by two trustees) but the document must make clear that it is a deed.[15] Transactions involving transfers of land must be executed as deeds. However, a charity in England and Wales or Northern Ireland must not dispose of land without following specified legal processes (see page 331).

Also, if the CIO wishes to make a legally binding agreement for a situation which is not recognised in law as a contract, it may be necessary to use a deed (see page 321). For example, if a CIO promises a grant to another charity, and the recipient needs to be sure that the grant is legally payable even if the CIO goes into liquidation, the grant agreement should be written as a deed.

---

[13] CIO General Regulations 2012, reg. 19.

[14] CIO General Regulations 2012, reg. 20.

[15] CIO General Regulations 2012, reg. 21.

In the case of agreements between two or more charities which have trustees in common, the trustees should sign separately on behalf of each charity. The same applies for agreements with businesses or non-charitable organisations where trustees are involved; but such agreements must not be made if they would lead to unauthorised private benefits (see page 30).

Banking arrangements

A person or organisation depositing funds at a bank is lending money to the bank, and then asking the bank to accept instructions either in making payments to third parties or returning the deposit when requested. In the case of a current account, the person or organisation has the right to withdraw the funds on demand, although other accounts may require notice. In some cases interest may be paid on deposits. Banking law ensures that only certain institutions are permitted to take deposits on this basis.

In the case of a CIO, it is the CIO as a corporate body (not the individual trustees) which is making a deposit and asking the bank to accept its instructions, though since a corporate body cannot speak, the bank will require arrangements whereby the CIO's instructions are communicated via the trustees or via persons authorised by the trustees. Normally two trustees must sign cheques, or give electronic authorisation for payments (though the trustees could agree that smaller amounts could be authorised by one trustee or even a member of staff – see *The Charity Treasurer's Handbook* for more on financial controls).

These arrangements require a legal arrangement with the bank which is usually called a 'mandate' – the depositor (the CIO) is mandating the bank to act on its instructions. Banks are free to choose who they accept as customers. A CIO can only, therefore, maintain a bank account with a bank which is prepared to accept a mandate from a CIO.

Banks which offer special accounts for charities are generally keen to offer accounts to CIOs, but others may be cautious. The vast majority of bank accounts are maintained either for:

- individuals; or
- groups of individuals such as a couple, a business partnership, a trust, or an unincorporated society or charity; or
- companies formed under the Companies Act 2006.

A CIO does not fit any of these categories as it is a corporate body but not formed under company law (although there are many other possible legal forms). However, if visiting a local bank branch where the staff are not charity specialists, you need to be prepared to spend time explaining the nature of a CIO, if your CIO is one of the first in the area.

It is vital, therefore, in the early stages of establishing a CIO – or converting an existing charity to a CIO – to check that the intended bankers will be happy to operate an account for a CIO. If not, it would be worth looking elsewhere to banks which specialise in charity accounts.

If a bank is prepared to open an account for a CIO but does not have forms ready for a CIO mandate, a company mandate can be adapted; but make clear that the body is an E&W CIO, SCIO, or NI CIO as appropriate, show the registered charity number, delete any reference to company number, and change any references to 'directors' to 'charity trustees'.

If a bank asks for a 'certificate of incorporation' to open an account for a CIO (as usually needed for a company), the equivalent information is a copy of the entry on the Register of Charities. For an E&W CIO it is also possible, once a new charity has received its password for access to the Charity Commission's online system, to download a certificate of charity registration. In the case of a CIO, the date of charity registration is also the date of incorporation. The bank may also, of course, ask for a copy of the CIO's constitution (which is equivalent to the articles for a company).

Employees

It is important to remember that an employee of a CIO is an individual who has an agreement with the CIO. Hence an employee is a 'third party' for the purposes of the issues in this chapter.

So, for example, a contract of employment must be properly signed on behalf of the CIO and the employee in order to be binding. (In law, the employer can just give the employee a 'statement of terms' – there does not have to be a contract signed by both parties – but most CIOs will want a signature from the employee accepting the terms of employment.)

Some employees may be authorised by the trustees to sign contracts of employment and other agreements (up to specified levels), but no one should sign a contract on behalf of the CIO where they are the other party! Employment contracts with senior staff should thus be signed by at least one trustee (on behalf of the CIO) and by the employee.

If employees are not paid their salaries or wages, they can take action against the CIO in the same way as other creditors; although if a CIO becomes insolvent, employees' wages (up to a limit) and accrued holiday pay are given priority over ordinary unsecured debts. However, if a CIO becomes insolvent and they are made redundant, legislation provides special protection for employees (for more on insolvency see chapter 12, page 228). Subject to limits, their outstanding wages up to the day they are laid off (including holiday pay due) are guaranteed by the government's BIS Department from the National Insurance Fund (at the time of writing, the maximum is eight weeks at £450/week). Statutory redundancy pay (depending upon their age and length of service) and certain amounts of compensatory notice pay can also be claimed. Payments are made by the Redundancy Payments Office, which then claims as a creditor against the insolvent CIO.[16] However, employees may need to claim directly against the CIO for other amounts due such as pay in lieu of notice, salaries in excess of the statutory limits, or unpaid claims for travel expenses.

Lenders

It is perfectly possible for a CIO to borrow funds if the trustees consider it appropriate and if the lender agrees. The general power of a CIO to do anything which is 'conducive or incidental' to advancing the objects is sufficient to authorise borrowing where the trustees consider it would help to advance the objects. There can be a case, however, for including a specific power to borrow in a CIO's constitution, as some lenders prefer to see this (see chapter 6 and clause 4(1) of the Charity Commission's model constitution in the Appendix).

Anyone lending to a CIO (or to any other party) has to consider whether they are willing to take the risk of an unsecured loan, or whether to require security. The lender must bear in mind the status of the CIO as a limited liability body, which means that they will not normally be able to pursue anyone else if the CIO folds and the loan is not repaid. Where security is taken, the lender is given a 'charge' over certain assets: this means that if the loan is not repaid, the lender can take possession of the asset concerned.

Unsecured loans

Unsecured loans include most bank overdrafts and other loan agreements (often fixed-term loans) agreed without security. Charities may also receive loans from donors or supporters which are usually unsecured.

If a CIO has a clear business plan for a worthwhile project which requires start-up funding or working capital, it may well be possible to raise unsecured loans, particularly from lenders with social objectives sympathetic to the CIO. Often this may be classed as a 'social

[16] See *Redundancy and Insolvency: A Guide for Employees* (Insolvency Service/BIS 2009).

investment' or a social enterprise loan, supporting the development of social enterprise (in this case, as an activity within a CIO). Many projects of this kind succeed and the loan is repaid.

If a CIO fails and becomes insolvent with loans outstanding, the various processes explained in chapter 12 may apply – the lender becomes an unsecured creditor, seeking to recover a share of the assets. However, an unsecured lender may be open to arrangements such as a CIO voluntary arrangement, rather than seeking liquidation of the CIO.

Secured loans

A lender advancing substantial sums to a CIO may be unwilling to lend on an unsecured basis. A lender may want more certainty of getting their money back rather than having to sue the CIO and possibly then ranking alongside other unsecured creditors if the CIO fails.

If the CIO has valuable assets, the solution could be to take a charge over the assets concerned: for example a property, particular equipment, stocks, book debts, or a 'floating charge' over the unrestricted assets as a whole. All of these are widely used for lending to companies, but there is an important difference with a CIO. Any charge against the assets of a company must be registered within 21 days at Companies House and is available on the public register of companies for anyone to check. So a lender can easily check whether, for example, a company already has existing charges, which avoids the same assets being charged to two lenders. It also means that in the event of the company becoming insolvent, the evidence on a public register of all charges makes it clear which debts of the company are secured creditors and which are unsecured.

There is no equivalent of a public charges register for CIOs: the charity regulators do not have any powers to keep registers of that kind. Without a public register allowing lenders to check whether a CIO has any existing charges, they may be more cautious. Nevertheless, all CIOs must file accounts with the relevant charity regulator and SORP accounts must always disclose details of loans and security given. For CIOs in England and Wales this even applies if the accounts are on the receipts and payments basis[17] (see page 146). So any charges against CIO assets would become public when accounts are published (but this could be as long as 22 months after a charge was agreed).

---

[17] CIO General Regulations 2012, reg. 62.

The lack of a public charges register does not, however, mean that no one would ever undertake secured lending to a CIO, because there are other ways of securing a loan. In particular, where the CIO owns land and buildings, it is possible to enter into a mortgage agreement, which is then registered at the Land Registry (for land in England and Wales – other registers apply for Scotland and Northern Ireland). It is thus impossible for anyone to sell the land without repaying the loan secured by the mortgage, or the mortgagee (the lender) can take possession of the land if the terms of the mortgage are not met.

Note, however, that a charity in England and Wales or Northern Ireland cannot make a 'disposition' of land without complying with procedures laid down in law.[18] (This includes selling the land, giving it away, leasing it for more than seven years, or allowing it to be mortgaged.) In particular, under charity law, entering into a mortgage requires that the trustees must obtain independent advice on the necessity of the loan, the terms of repayment, and the ability of the charity to repay.[19] The advice must be given by someone who has no financial interest in the loan and who has practical experience in financial matters. In some charities there may be a member of staff who could do this, but often it will be appropriate to seek advice from the charity's auditor or independent examiner.

Lenders may also be willing to take security over certain other CIO assets, for example vehicles, or office equipment such as computers and photocopiers. Such lending is normally arranged through the firm which supplied the item, so there is little chance of the same item having charges in favour of two lenders. If payments are not made, it is generally not too difficult for the lender to recover the item. Loans of this kind are frequently made to individual sole traders and partnerships where there is no equivalent of a company charges register. Alternatively, the trustees may decide it would be better for the CIO to lease such items (under an 'operating lease') which means that the items remain owned by a leasing company and the CIO pays a rental.

Sometimes the only way a charity can raise working capital (for example, to finance services paid for in arrears) is if the trustees are prepared to accept a floating charge over all the assets. This is sometimes used by charitable companies, in which case the floating charge is publicly registered at Companies House. In principle, a lender could agree a floating charge with a CIO, but without a public charges register, a lender may be reluctant to agree this (details of the charge will still be published

[18] Charities Act 2011, Part 7 (ss. 117–129); Charities Act (NI) 2008, Part 7 (ss. 57–62).

[19] Charities Act 2011, s. 124; Charities Act (NI) 2008, s. 60.

in the CIO's accounts, but the lender may feel this is insufficient). So, where a charity clearly needs to raise finance by accepting floating charges, a charitable company may well be more appropriate than a CIO. However, even in charitable companies, trustees will often be very cautious about agreeing floating charges because, if the charity becomes insolvent, the entire assets (apart from any assets held on special trusts – see page 222) could be taken by the lender. Also, if donors realise a charity may be getting into difficulties and discover it has a floating charge, they may withdraw their support, making the financial position worse, as any further donations could well be claimed by a lender.

Security for grant funding

Increasingly, funders of major charitable building projects are asking for security over the land, even when the funding is by way of a grant rather than a loan. This is so that if the charity were to fold, the funder can gain possession of the building and perhaps enable it to be used for another charity, rather than just being sold commercially to pay creditors.

Provided the trustees agreed such an arrangement is appropriate, a CIO can certainly accept funding on this basis. As a corporate body, the CIO itself holds the title to the land. The CIO then grants the funder a mortgage over the land which is a registered charge (in the same way as for a loan even though no repayments are due). In England, Wales and Northern Ireland the same processes apply as outlined above – the trustees must obtain independent advice on the terms of the grant.

Trustees should not, however, accept grants on terms which require them to mortgage the charity's land, unless they are satisfied that it is in the interests of the charity, bearing in mind the independent advice. In particular, funders may want rights allowing the building to be reclaimed in a wide range of circumstances over a long period of time, which could hamper the flexibility of the CIO to use the building in different ways in the future. Careful negotiation is therefore needed: beware of announcing to supporters that the funding for the CIO's new building has been received until agreement has been reached on such conditions.

18 CIOs: the future

The CIO will not be appropriate in every situation where a new charity is to be formed – the advantages and disadvantages were introduced in chapter 4 and developed further as detailed aspects were introduced in subsequent chapters.

However, the simplicity of the CIO is that it is a corporate form of organisation governed entirely by charity law, regulated only by a charity regulator (CCEW, OSCR or CCNI), and which is incorporated and registered as a charity at the same moment.

Origins

It was in 2002, in the report *Private Action, Public Benefit*,[1] that the government first formally recognised the benefits which CIOs could offer. It pointed out that the UK had no specific corporate form for charities, and listed five reasons why companies limited by guarantee were less than ideal.

A box in that report set out the basic features of a CIO, which corresponded almost exactly to the final reality (see table 1.1 on page 4). The report made many other recommendations to improve the legal framework for charities and social enterprises: these included the creation of CICs, reforms to IPS law, updating the definition of 'charity', increasing the charity audit threshold, and much else – virtually all of these were implemented well ahead of CIOs.

The report initially proposed the implementation of CIOs solely in England and Wales, leaving the devolved governments in Scotland and Northern Ireland to make their own decisions, but in the end all three jurisdictions enacted legislation for CIOs: in Scotland in 2005,[2] England and Wales in 2006,[3] and Northern Ireland in 2008.[4]

---

[1] *Private Action, Public Benefit: A Review of Charities and the Wider Not-For-Profit Sector* (Cabinet Office Strategy Unit Report 2002, pp. 57–58).

[2] Charities & TI (Scotland) Act 2005, ss. 49–64.

[3] Charities Act 2006, now consolidated in Charities Act 2011, ss. 204–250.

[4] Charities Act (NI) 2008, ss. 105–122 & Sch. 7.

Implementation

Implementation came first in Scotland with SCIOs available from April 2011, nearly two years earlier than the implementation in England and Wales in January 2013. Implementing the whole framework for charity registration in Northern Ireland has taken longer than hoped, largely owing to amendments to the public benefit requirement,[5] but it seems certain that CIOs in Northern Ireland will be implemented in due course.

It will, of course, take some time for CIOs to be clearly understood by banks, landlords, public sector funders, and even by other organisations in the third sector. However, to date, reported problems have been few, even though the CIO structure has been operational in Scotland (SCIOs) since April 2011. By March 2013, two years after their advent, more than 400 SCIOs had been registered, and OSCR reported that a third of all new charity registrations in Scotland are for SCIOs, so the form is certainly proving popular.

In England and Wales, the Charity Commission registered more than 170 CIOs in the first four months to April 2013, even though the phasing of applications meant that only a very few existing charities wishing to incorporate had been able to establish a CIO by then. This initial volume suggests that CIOs will account for a significant proportion of the roughly 5000 new charities registered in England and Wales each year.

The report *Private Action, Public Benefit* raised the possibility that developments in company law, especially to comply with European law, might make companies less suitable for charities in the longer term, and suggested that three years after the introduction of CIOs the government would consider whether forms of incorporation other than CIOs should continue to be available for charities. In the event, a five-year review was built into the Charities Act 2006: Lord Hodgson of Astley Abbotts was appointed in November 2011 and reported in summer 2012.[6] At the time of his review, CIOs had still not been implemented in England and Wales, so the idea that other forms might be phased out was not considered (and now seems unlikely). However, in terms of bringing CIOs in England and Wales into reality, Lord Hodgson reported assurances he received that they would not be delayed much further: in the end, regulations were finally tabled in Parliament in November 2012.

---

[5] Charities Act (NI) 2013, s. 1.

[6] Lord (Robin) Hodgson, *Trusted and Independent – Giving charity back to charities: Review of the Charities Act 2006*, presented to Parliament July 2012.

Under the Conservative/Liberal Democrat Government elected in 2010, the Minister for Civil Society, Nick Hurd MP, stated that one of his prime objectives was 'to make it easier for people to set up and run a charity'. Similar points had been made by Labour ministers. Implementing CIOs, which by then were already on the statute book, was a very obvious way to support this aim. It thus seems extraordinary that, when it had already taken four years from *Private Action, Public Benefit* to get CIOs enacted for England and Wales in the Charities Act 2006, it then took a further six years for them to be implemented (although there were certainly some complex issues to address in regulations, particularly the insolvency framework).

Voluntary sector advisors had seen the benefits of the CIO from the earliest days and were keen to help new groups establish themselves as charities using this form; considerable resources were invested in training.

In the meantime, some charities wishing to incorporate as CIOs gave up waiting and converted to charitable companies, others remained unincorporated (with all the associated liabilities) for much longer than intended.

The significance of CIOs

In terms of modernising the framework of charity law, and enabling charities to be run sensibly in the 21st century, CIOs were, in my judgement, the single most important feature in the Charities Act 2006. I would argue that, in terms of practical impact for those running charities, they were more important even than the updating of the definition of 'charity' and the renewed focus on public benefit, which took up huge amounts of Parliamentary time, and then created a massive workload for the Charity Commission in issuing guidance and dealing with Tribunal hearings.

Charitable companies will continue to be popular for the largest charities, but for the 95% of charities with incomes below the £500,000 audit threshold (and for a good number above this), the simplicity of the CIO is likely to prove more attractive than the established framework of company law, even though the latter may have greater benefits in certain cases (see table 4.1 on page 62). This will be particularly so for charities with a wide membership, where an association CIO offers much greater simplicity in terms of membership rights and obligations than in a body with a large membership subject to company law.

This does not mean that the CIO legislation will work perfectly for all. As indicated in various parts of this book, there are aspects of the primary legislation and regulations which create slightly bureaucratic processes which could perhaps have been framed differently. It is unfortunate that CIOs in England and Wales had not been implemented prior to Lord Hodgson's 2012 Review of the Charities Act 2006, which would have provided a very good opportunity to identify minor improvements needed, although there will surely be opportunities for tweaks to the framework in due course. But for those who find the E&W CIO framework to be over-complex, the SCIO is well worth considering if the organisation is in a position to have a principal office in Scotland.

The way forward: CICs and CIOs?

CIOs, along with community interest companies (CICs), have brought the UK into line with many other countries in having specific legal forms for non-profit organisations. As time goes on, I believe that fewer and fewer people will be willing to set up new charities on an unincorporated basis, given that a CIO can be formed and registered with no more effort than a charitable trust or association.

For non-charitable organisations, the CIC has proven very effective, and my prediction is that new third sector organisations will largely be formed as CICs or CIOs depending on whether or not they are charitable. The fact that a CIO is *always* a charity and a CIC is *never* a charity makes for simplicity in this respect.

Implications

The implementation of CIOs does not mean that existing charities will rush to convert: the time has to be right for a charity to make major constitutional changes. But for many unincorporated charities, which have waited until now to incorporate, CIOs will certainly be popular. A number of smaller charitable companies will probably also choose to convert. Organisations established as CICs when they should have been charities will no doubt value the anticipated route for conversion to CIOs. In due course, I expect that charitable CBSs, rather than attempting to register as charities in the current form, will readily opt to become CIOs.

For advisors, the challenge may be to persuade those establishing new charities *not* to opt automatically for a CIO, but to consider the alternatives carefully and make an informed choice (the summaries in chapter 4 may help). But it seems likely that once advisors have set up a few CIOs, they will soon consider them as the norm for new charities, except in complex situations. However, for charities operating over large parts of the UK, there are also important decisions as to which form of CIO to use (see chapter 15). As explained, there are substantial legal differences between SCIOs and CIOs in England and Wales which affect their suitability for different situations: these go beyond the geographical location of the charity's work.

Of course, the real proof of CIOs may not come for some years. Ironically, it will need a few CIOs to fail, and for the insolvency frameworks to be followed through, before other stakeholders will feel fully confident in establishing major contracts with CIOs, or providing loan finance from multiple sources. But many unincorporated charities already have such arrangements without the benefit of a corporate form: contracting with a CIO is almost always clearer.

The sector has waited a long time for CIOs. For many charities, certainly new ones, I am convinced that CIOs are the prime structure for the future.

Useful addresses

Charity regulators

Charity Commission for England and Wales (CCEW)

PO Box 1227, Liverpool L69 3UG
Tel: 0845 300 0218
Email: enquiries@charitycommission.gsi.gov.uk
Website: www.charitycommission.gov.uk

Office of the Scottish Charity Regulator (OSCR)

OSCR, 2nd Floor, Quadrant House, 9 Riverside Drive, Dundee DD1 4NY
Tel: 01382 220446
Email: info@oscr.org.uk
Website: www.oscr.org.uk

Charity Commission for Northern Ireland (CCNI)

257 Lough Road, Lurgan, Craigavon BT66 6NQ
Tel: 028 3832 0220
Email: admin@charitycommissionni.org.uk
Website: www.charitycommissionni.org.uk

Charity tribunals etc.

First-tier Tribunal (Charity) (for England and Wales)

Tribunals Operational Support Centre, PO Box 9300, Leicester LE1 8DJ
Tel: 0300 1234504
Email: CharityTribunal@hmcts.gsi.gov.uk
Website: www.justice.gov.uk/tribunals/charity

Scottish Charity Appeals Panel

1st Floor, Bothwell House, Hamilton Business Park, Caird Park, Hamilton ML3 OQA
Tel: 01698 390000
Email: scap@scotland.gsi.gov.uk
Website: www.scap.gov.uk

Charity Tribunal of Northern Ireland

Tribunals Hearing Centre, 3rd Floor, Bedford House, 16–22 Bedford Street, Belfast BT2 7FD
Tel: 028 9072 4892
Email: tribunalsunit@courtsni.gov.uk
Website: www.courtsni.gov.uk/en-GB/Tribunals/CharityTribunal

Other regulators

HM Revenue and Customs (Charities Division)

PO Box 205, Bootle L69 9AZ
Tel: 0845 302 0203
Website: www.hmrc.gov.uk/charities

Companies House

Crown Way, Cardiff CF14 3UZ
Tel: 0303 1234 500
Email: enquiries@companies-house.gov.uk
Website: www.companieshouse.gov.uk

Regulator of Community Interest Companies (CICs)

CIC Regulator, Room 3.68, Companies House, Crown Way, Cardiff CF14 3UZ
Tel: 029 2034 6228
Email: cicregulator@companieshouse.gov.uk
Website: www.bis.gov.uk/cicregulator

Financial Conduct Authority

Mutual Societies Registration Team (*Formerly Financial Services Authority until 1 April 2013*)
25 The North Colonnade, Canary Wharf London E14 5HS
Tel: 0845 606 9966
Email: mutual.societies@fsa.gov.uk
Website: www.fsa.gov.uk/doing/small_firms/msr

The Insolvency Service

4 Abbey Orchard Street, London SW1P 2HT
Tel: 0845 602 9848
Website: www.bis.gov.uk/insolvency

Appendix: A CIO Model Constitution

The Charity Commission's model constitution for a CIO with a voting membership (in addition to the charity trustees)

The following wording is taken from the text of the Model Constitution published by the Charity Commission in December 2012 for an 'Association CIO' – that is a CIO where the members of the CIO are *not* identical to the CIO's charity trustees.

A slightly simpler model – for a 'Foundation CIO' where the members and trustees are the same people – is available from the Charity Commission's website. For more on CIO constitutions and the use of these models, see chapter 6.

This model only applies to CIOs established in England and Wales – see chapters 13 and 14 for more on SCIOs and Northern Irish CIOs.

This appendix only includes the text of the Constitution itself, *not* the Charity Commission's guidance notes which appear alongside in the Commission's published version. These notes distinguish what **must** be included from points which the Commission considers **should** be included or which **may** be helpful and they also give further guidance on many points. If you plan to use this model, it is strongly recommended to download the full document from the Charity Commission's website with these explanations.

Adjustments to the model for this book

The Commission's model includes a number of options – where multiple options are included here, the alternatives are shown in square brackets. In general cross-references to other clauses are also in square brackets because the inclusion or omission of options may affect the numbering of clauses.

However, the text below focuses on options most likely to be used: *it does not reproduce every option*, so it is essential to refer to the full Charity Commission document if these are needed. In particular, in the wording below:

- the option of a CIO where members have to give a financial guarantee (as in a charitable company) – which can be used in clause 8 – is *not* included

- the option of adding informal non-voting membership categories in clause 9 (for people who are not actual members of the CIO) is *not* included
- in clauses 12 and 13 (charity trustees) the wording below is based on the Commission's 'option 1' where all trustees are elected by the members up to a specified limit – alternative wordings are available to allow for addition of ex-officio trustees and/or trustees nominated by external bodies, or where there is no limit to the number of trustees
- the optional additions for proxy and/or postal voting are *not* included
- however the optional provisions for electronic communications *are* included.

Also, the Commission's model assumes that the initial trustees will be directly listed in clause 12(4) but the text below has been adapted to include them in a schedule.

Model Constitution for an Association CIO

1. Name

The name of the Charitable Incorporated Organisation ("the CIO") is

. . . .

2. National Location of Principal Office

The CIO must have a principal office in England or Wales. The principal office of the CIO is in [England][Wales].

3. Object[s]

The object[s] of the CIO [is][are]

. . . .

. . . .

Nothing in this constitution shall authorise an application of the property of the CIO for the purposes which are not charitable in accordance with [section 7 of the Charities and Trustee Investment (Scotland) Act 2005] and [section 2 of the Charities Act (Northern Ireland) 2008].

4. Powers

The CIO has power to do anything which is calculated to further its object[s] or is conducive or incidental to doing so. In particular, the CIO's powers include power to:

(1) borrow money and to charge the whole or any part of its property as security for the repayment of the money borrowed. The CIO must comply as appropriate with sections 124 and 125 of the Charities Act 2011 if it wishes to mortgage land;

(2) buy, take on lease or in exchange, hire or otherwise acquire any property and to maintain and equip it for use;

(3) sell, lease or otherwise dispose of all or any part of the property belonging to the CIO. In exercising this power, the CIO must comply as appropriate with sections 117 and 119–123 of the Charities Act 2011;

(4) employ and remunerate such staff as are necessary for carrying out the work of the CIO. The CIO may employ or remunerate a charity trustee only to the extent that it is permitted to do so by clause 6 (Benefits and payments to charity trustees and connected persons) and provided it complies with the conditions of those clauses;

(5) deposit or invest funds, employ a professional fund-manager, and arrange for the investments or other property of the CIO to be held in the name of a nominee, in the same manner and subject to the same conditions as the trustees of a trust are permitted to do by the Trustee Act 2000.

5. Application of income and property

(1) The income and property of the CIO must be applied solely towards the promotion of the objects.

(a) A charity trustee is entitled to be reimbursed from the property of the CIO or may pay out of such property reasonable expenses properly incurred by him or her when acting on behalf of the CIO.

(b) A charity trustee may benefit from trustee indemnity insurance cover purchased at the CIO's expense in accordance with, and subject to the conditions in, section 189 of the Charities Act 2011.

(2) None of the income or property of the CIO may be paid or transferred directly or indirectly by way of dividend, bonus or otherwise by way of profit to any member of the CIO. This does not prevent a member who is not also a charity trustee receiving:

(a) a benefit from the CIO as a beneficiary of the CIO;

(b) reasonable and proper remuneration for any goods or services supplied to the CIO.

(3) Nothing in this clause shall prevent a charity trustee or connected person receiving any benefit or payment which is authorised by Clause 6.

6. Benefits and payments to charity trustees and connected persons

(1) *General provisions*

No charity trustee or connected person may:

(a) buy or receive any goods or services from the CIO on terms preferential to those applicable to members of the public;

(b) sell goods, services, or any interest in land to the CIO;

(c) be employed by, or receive any remuneration from, the CIO;

(d) receive any other financial benefit from the CIO;

unless the payment or benefit is permitted by sub-clause (2) of this clause, or authorised by the court or the Charity Commission ("the Commission"). In this clause, a "financial benefit" means a benefit, direct or indirect, which is either money or has a monetary value.

(2) *Scope and powers permitting trustees' or connected persons' benefits*

(a) A charity trustee or connected person may receive a benefit from the CIO as a beneficiary of the CIO provided that a majority of the trustees do not benefit in this way.

(b) A charity trustee or connected person may enter into a contract for the supply of services, or of goods that are supplied in connection with the provision of services, to the CIO where that is permitted in accordance with, and subject to the conditions in, section 185 to 188 of the Charities Act 2011.

(c) Subject to sub-clause (3) of this clause a charity trustee or connected person may provide the CIO with goods that are not supplied in connection with services provided to the CIO by the charity trustee or connected person.

(d) A charity trustee or connected person may receive interest on money lent to the CIO at a reasonable and proper rate which must be not more than the Bank of England bank rate (also known as the base rate).

(e) A charity trustee or connected person may receive rent for premises let by the trustee or connected person to the CIO. The amount of the rent and the other terms of the lease must be reasonable and proper. The charity trustee concerned must withdraw from any meeting at which such a proposal or the rent or other terms of the lease are under discussion.

(f) A charity trustee or connected person may take part in the normal trading and fundraising activities of the CIO on the same terms as members of the public.

(3) *Payment for supply of goods only – controls*

The CIO and its charity trustees may only rely upon the authority provided by sub-clause (2)(c) of this clause if each of the following conditions is satisfied:

(a) The amount or maximum amount of the payment for the goods is set out in a written agreement between the CIO and the charity trustee or connected person supplying the goods ("the supplier").

(b) The amount or maximum amount of the payment for the goods does not exceed what is reasonable in the circumstances for the supply of the goods in question.

(c) The other charity trustees are satisfied that it is in the best interests of the CIO to contract with the supplier rather than with someone who is not a charity trustee or connected person. In reaching that decision the charity trustees must balance the advantage of contracting with a charity trustee or connected person against the disadvantages of doing so.

(d) The supplier is absent from the part of any meeting at which there is discussion of the proposal to enter into a contract or arrangement with him or her or it with regard to the supply of goods to the CIO.

(e) The supplier does not vote on any such matter and is not to be counted when calculating whether a quorum of charity trustees is present at the meeting.

(f) The reason for their decision is recorded by the charity trustees in the minute book.

(g) A majority of the charity trustees then in office are not in receipt of remuneration or payments authorised by clause 6.

(4) In sub-clauses (2) and (3) of this clause:

(a) "the CIO" includes any company in which the CIO:

(i) holds more than 50% of the shares; or

(ii) controls more than 50% of the voting rights attached to the shares; or

(iii) has the right to appoint one or more directors to the board of the company;

(b) "connected person" includes any person within the definition set out in clause [30] (Interpretation);

7. Conflicts of interest and conflicts of loyalty

A charity trustee must:

(1) declare the nature and extent of any interest, direct or indirect, which he or she has in a proposed transaction or arrangement with the CIO or in any transaction or arrangement entered into by the CIO which has not previously been declared; and

(2) absent himself or herself from any discussions of the charity trustees in which it is possible that a conflict of interest will arise between his or her duty to act solely in the interests of the CIO and any personal interest (including but not limited to any financial interest).

Any charity trustee absenting himself or herself from any discussions in accordance with this clause must not vote or be counted as part of the quorum in any decision of the charity trustees on the matter.

8. Liability of members to contribute to the assets of the CIO if it is wound up

If the CIO is wound up, the members of the CIO have no liability to contribute to its assets and no personal responsibility for settling its debts and liabilities.

9. Membership of the CIO

(1) Admission of new members

(a) Eligibility

Membership of the CIO is open to anyone who is interested in furthering its purposes, and who, by applying for membership, has indicated his, her or its agreement to become a member and acceptance of the duty of members set out in sub-clause (3) of this clause.

A member may be an individual, a corporate body, or [an individual or corporate body representing] an organisation which is not incorporated.

(b) Admission procedure

The charity trustees:

(i) may require applications for membership to be made in any reasonable way that they decide;

(ii) [shall, if they approve an application for membership, notify the applicant of their decision within [21 days];]

(iii) may refuse an application for membership if they believe that it is in the best interests of the CIO for them to do so;

(iv) shall, if they decide to refuse an application for membership, give the applicant their reasons for doing so, within [21 days] of the decision being taken, and give the applicant the opportunity to appeal against the refusal; and

(v) shall give fair consideration to any such appeal, and shall inform the applicant of their decision, but any decision to confirm refusal of the application for membership shall be final.

(2) Transfer of membership

Membership of the CIO cannot be transferred to anyone else [except in the case of an individual or corporate body representing an organisation which is not incorporated, whose membership may be transferred by the unincorporated organisation to a new representative. Such transfer of membership does not take effect until the CIO has received written notification of the transfer].

(3) Duty of members

It is the duty of each member of the CIO to exercise his or her powers as a member of the CIO in the way he or she decides in good faith would be most likely to further the purposes of the CIO.

(4) Termination of membership

(a) Membership of the CIO comes to an end if:

(i) the member dies, or, in the case of an organisation (or the representative of an organisation) that organisation ceases to exist; or

(ii) the member sends a notice of resignation to the charity trustees; or

(iii) any sum of money owed by the member to the CIO is not paid in full within six months of its falling due; or

(iv) the charity trustees decide that it is in the best interests of the CIO that the member in question should be removed from membership, and pass a resolution to that effect.

(b) Before the charity trustees take any decision to remove someone from membership of the CIO they must:

(i) inform the member of the reasons why it is proposed to remove him, her or it from membership;

(ii) give the member at least 21 clear days notice in which to make representations to the charity trustees as to why he, she or it should not be removed from membership;

(iii) at a duly constituted meeting of the charity trustees, consider whether or not the member should be removed from membership;

(iv) consider at that meeting any representations which the member makes as to why the member should not be removed; and

(v) allow the member, or the member's representative, to make those representations in person at that meeting, if the member so chooses.

(5) *Membership fees*

The CIO may require members to pay reasonable membership fees to the CIO.

10. Members' decisions

(1) *General provisions*

Except for those decisions that must be taken in a particular way as indicated in sub-clause (4) of this clause, decisions of the members of the CIO may be taken either by vote at a general meeting as provided in sub-clause (2) of this clause or by written resolution as provided in sub-clause (3) of this clause.

(2) *Taking ordinary decisions by vote*

Subject to sub-clause (4) of this clause, any decision of the members of the CIO may be taken by means of a resolution at a general meeting. Such a resolution may be passed by a simple majority of votes cast at the meeting [(including votes cast by postal or email ballot, and proxy votes)].

(3) *Taking ordinary decisions by written resolution without a general meeting*

(a) Subject to sub-clause (4) of this clause, a resolution in writing agreed by a simple majority of all the members who would have been entitled to vote upon it had it been proposed at a general meeting shall be effective, provided that:

(i) a copy of the proposed resolution has been sent to all the members eligible to vote; and

(ii) a simple majority of members has signified its agreement to the resolution in a document or documents which are received at the principal office within the period of 28 days beginning with the circulation date. The document signifying a member's agreement must be authenticated by their signature (or in the case of an organisation which is a member, by execution according to its usual procedure), by a statement of their identity accompanying the document, or in such other manner as the CIO has specified.

(b) The resolution in writing may comprise several copies to which one or more members has signified their agreement.

(c) Eligibility to vote on the resolution is limited to members who are members of the CIO on the date when the proposal is first circulated in accordance with paragraph (a) above.

(d) Not less than 10% of the members of the CIO may request the charity trustees to make a proposal for decision by the members.

(e) The charity trustees must within 21 days of receiving such a request comply with it if:

(i) The proposal is not frivolous or vexatious, and does not involve the publication of defamatory material;

(ii) The proposal is stated with sufficient clarity to enable effect to be given to it if it is agreed by the members; and

(iii) Effect can lawfully be given to the proposal if it is so agreed.

(f) Sub-clauses (a) to (c) of this clause apply to a proposal made at the request of members.

(4) *Decisions that must be taken in a particular way*

[(a) Any decision to remove a trustee must be taken in accordance with clause [15(2)].]

(b) Any decision to amend this constitution must be taken in accordance with clause [28] of this constitution (Amendment of Constitution).

(c) Any decision to wind up or dissolve the CIO must be taken in accordance with clause [29] of this constitution (Voluntary winding up or dissolution). Any decision to amalgamate or transfer the undertaking of the CIO to one or more other CIOs must be taken in accordance with the provisions of the Charities Act 2011.

11. General meetings of members

(1) *Types of general meeting*

There must be an annual general meeting (AGM) of the members of the CIO. The first AGM must be held within 18 months of the registration of the CIO, and subsequent AGMs must be held at intervals of not more than 15 months. The AGM must receive the annual statement of accounts (duly audited or examined where applicable) and the trustees' annual report, and must elect trustees as required under clause [13].

Other general meetings of the members of the CIO may be held at any time.

All general meetings must be held in accordance with the following provisions.

(2) *Calling general meetings*

(a) The charity trustees:

(i) must call the annual general meeting of the members of the CIO in accordance with sub-clause (1) of this clause, and identify it as such in the notice of the meeting; and

(ii) may call any other general meeting of the members at any time.

(b) The charity trustees must, within 21 days, call a general meeting of the members of the CIO if:

(i) they receive a request to do so from at least 10% of the members of the CIO; and

(ii) the request states the general nature of the business to be dealt with at the meeting, and is authenticated by the member(s) making the request.

(c) If, at the time of any such request, there has not been any general meeting of the members of the CIO for more than 12 months, then sub-clause (b)(i) of this clause shall have effect as if 5% were substituted for 10%.

(d) Any such request may include particulars of a resolution that may properly be proposed, and is intended to be proposed, at the meeting.

(e) A resolution may only properly be proposed if it is lawful, and is not defamatory, frivolous or vexatious.

(f) Any general meeting called by the charity trustees at the request of the members of the CIO must be held within 28 days from the date on which it is called.

(g) If the charity trustees fail to comply with this obligation to call a general meeting at the request of its members, then the members who requested the meeting may themselves call a general meeting.

(h) A general meeting called in this way must be held not more than 3 months after the date when the members first requested the meeting.

(i) The CIO must reimburse any reasonable expenses incurred by the members calling a general meeting by reason of the failure of the charity trustees to duly call the meeting, but the CIO shall be entitled to be indemnified by the charity trustees who were responsible for such failure.

(3) Notice of general meetings

(a) The charity trustees, or, as the case may be, the relevant members of the CIO, must give at least 14 clear days notice of any general meeting to all of the members, and to any charity trustee of the CIO who is not a member.

(b) If it is agreed by not less than 90% of all members of the CIO, any resolution may be proposed and passed at the meeting even though the requirements of sub-clause (3)(a) of this clause have not been met. This sub-clause does not apply where a specified period of notice is strictly required by another clause in this constitution, by the Charities Act 2011 or by the General Regulations.

(c) The notice of any general meeting must:

(i) state the time and date of the meeting:

(ii) give the address at which the meeting is to take place;

(iii) give particulars of any resolution which is to be moved at the meeting, and of the general nature of any other business to be dealt with at the meeting; and

(iv) if a proposal to alter the constitution of the CIO is to be considered at the meeting, include the text of the proposed alteration;

(v) include, with the notice for the AGM, the annual statement of accounts and trustees' annual report, details of persons standing for election or re-election as trustee, or where allowed under clause [22] (Use of electronic communication), details of where the information may be found on the CIO's website.

(d) Proof that an envelope containing a notice was properly addressed, prepaid and posted; or that an electronic form of notice was properly addressed and sent, shall be conclusive evidence that the notice was given. Notice shall be deemed to be given 48 hours after it was posted or sent.

(e) The proceedings of a meeting shall not be invalidated because a member who was entitled to receive notice of the meeting did not receive it because of accidental omission by the CIO.

(4) *Chairing of general meetings*

The person nominated as chair by the charity trustees under clause [19](2) (Chairing of meetings), shall, if present at the general meeting and willing to act, preside as chair of the meeting. Subject to that, the members of the CIO who are present at a general meeting shall elect a chair to preside at the meeting.

(5) *Quorum at general meetings*

(a) No business may be transacted at any general meeting of the members of the CIO unless a quorum is present when the meeting starts.

(b) Subject to the following provisions, the quorum for general meetings shall be the greater of [5]% or [three] members. An organisation represented by a person present at the meeting in accordance with sub-clause (7) of this clause, is counted as being present in person.

(c) If the meeting has been called by or at the request of the members and a quorum is not present within 15 minutes of the starting time specified in the notice of the meeting, the meeting is closed.

(d) If the meeting has been called in any other way and a quorum is not present within 15 minutes of the starting time specified in the notice of the meeting, the chair must adjourn the meeting. The date, time and place at which the meeting will resume must [either be announced by the chair or] be notified to the CIO's members at least seven clear days before the date on which it will resume.

(e) If a quorum is not present within 15 minutes of the start time of the adjourned meeting, the member or members present at the meeting constitute a quorum.

(f) If at any time during the meeting a quorum ceases to be present, the meeting may discuss issues and make recommendations to the trustees but may not make any decisions. If decisions are required which must be made by a meeting of the members, the meeting must be adjourned.

(6) *Voting at general meetings*

(a) Any decision other than one falling within clause [10(4)] (Decisions that must be taken in a particular way) shall be taken by a simple majority of votes cast at the meeting. Every member has one vote [unless otherwise provided in the rights of a particular class of membership under this constitution].

(b) A resolution put to the vote of a meeting shall be decided on a show of hands, unless (before or on the declaration of the result of the show of hands) a poll is duly demanded. A poll may be demanded by the chair or by at least 10% of the members present in person or by proxy at the meeting.

(c) A poll demanded on the election of a person to chair the meeting or on a question of adjournment must be taken immediately. A poll on any other matter shall be taken, and the result of the poll shall be announced, in such manner as the chair of the meeting shall decide, provided that the poll must be taken, and the result of the poll announced, within 30 days of the demand for the poll.

(d) A poll may be taken:

(i) at the meeting at which it was demanded; or

(ii) at some other time and place specified by the chair; or

(iii) through the use of postal or electronic communications.

[(e) In the event of an equality of votes, whether on a show of hands or on a poll, the chair of the meeting shall have a second, or casting vote.]

(f) Any objection to the qualification of any voter must be raised at the meeting at which the vote is cast and the decision of the chair of the meeting shall be final.

(7) Representation of [organisations and] corporate members

A[n organisation or a]corporate body that is a member of the CIO may, in accordance with its usual decision-making process, authorise a person to act as its representative at any general meeting of the CIO.

The representative is entitled to exercise the same powers on behalf of the [organisation or] corporate body as the [organisation or] corporate body could exercise as an individual member of the CIO.

(8) Adjournment of meetings

The chair may with the consent of a meeting at which a quorum is present (and shall if so directed by the meeting) adjourn the meeting to another time and/or place. No business may be transacted at an adjourned meeting except business which could properly have been transacted at the original meeting.

12. Charity trustees

(1) Functions and duties of charity trustees

The charity trustees shall manage the affairs of the CIO and may for that purpose exercise all the powers of the CIO. It is the duty of each charity trustee:

(a) to exercise his or her powers and to perform his or her functions as a trustee of the CIO in the way he or she decides in good faith would be most likely to further the purposes of the CIO; and

(b) to exercise, in the performance of those functions, such care and skill as is reasonable in the circumstances having regard in particular to:

(i) any special knowledge or experience that he or she has or holds himself or herself out as having; and

(ii) if he or she acts as a charity trustee of the CIO in the course of a business or profession, to any special knowledge or experience that it is reasonable to expect of a person acting in the course of that kind of business or profession.

(2) *Eligibility for trusteeship*

(a) Every charity trustee must be a natural person.

(b) No one may be appointed as a charity trustee:

- if he or she is under the age of 16 years; or
- if he or she would automatically cease to hold office under the provisions of clause [15(1)(f)].

(c) No one is entitled to act as a charity trustee whether on appointment or on any re-appointment until he or she has expressly acknowledged, in whatever way the charity trustees decide, his or her acceptance of the office of charity trustee.

[(d) At least one of the trustees of the CIO must be 18 years of age or over. If there is no trustee aged at least 18 years, the remaining trustee or trustees may act only to call a meeting of the charity trustees, or appoint a new charity trustee.]

(3) *Number of charity trustees*

(a) There must be at least [three] charity trustees. If the number falls below this minimum, the remaining trustee or trustees may act only to call a meeting of the charity trustees, or appoint a new charity trustee.

(b) The maximum number of charity trustees is [12]. The charity trustees may not appoint any charity trustee if as a result the number of charity trustees would exceed the maximum.

(4) *First charity trustees*

The first charity trustees of the CIO are the persons listed in the Schedule to this constitution.

13. Appointment of charity trustees

[(1) At the first annual general meeting of the members of the CIO all the charity trustees shall retire from office;]

(2) At every [subsequent] annual general meeting of the members of the CIO, one-third of the charity trustees shall retire from office. If the number of charity trustees is not three or a multiple of three, then the number nearest to one-third shall retire from office, but if there is only one charity trustee, he or she shall retire;

(3) The charity trustees to retire by rotation shall be those who have been longest in office since their last appointment or reappointment. If any trustees were last appointed or reappointed on the same day those to retire shall (unless they otherwise agree among themselves) be determined by lot;

(4) The vacancies so arising may be filled by the decision of the members at the annual general meeting; any vacancies not filled at the annual general meeting may be filled as provided in sub-clause (5) of this clause;

(5) The members or the charity trustees may at any time decide to appoint a new charity trustee, whether in place of a charity trustee who has retired or been removed in accordance with clause [15] (Retirement and removal of charity trustees), or as an additional charity trustee, provided that the limit specified in clause [12(3)] on the number of charity trustees would not as a result be exceeded;

(6) A person so appointed by the members of the CIO shall retire in accordance with the provisions of sub-clauses (2) and (3) of this clause. A person so appointed by the charity trustees shall retire at the conclusion of the next annual general meeting after the date of his or her appointment, and shall not be counted for the purpose of determining which of the charity trustees is to retire by rotation at that meeting.

14. Information for new charity trustees

The charity trustees will make available to each new charity trustee, on or before his or her first appointment:

(a) a copy of this constitution and any amendments made to it; and

(b) a copy of the CIO's latest trustees' annual report and statement of accounts.

15. Retirement and removal of charity trustees

(1) A charity trustee ceases to hold office if he or she:

(a) retires by notifying the CIO in writing (but only if enough charity trustees will remain in office when the notice of resignation takes effect to form a quorum for meetings);

(b) is absent without the permission of the charity trustees from all their meetings held within a period of six months and the trustees resolve that his or her office be vacated;

(c) dies;

(d) becomes incapable by reason of mental disorder, illness or injury of managing and administering his or her own affairs;

(e) [is removed by the members of the CIO in accordance with sub-clause (2) of this clause;] or

(f) is disqualified from acting as a charity trustee by virtue of section 178–180 of the Charities Act 2011 (or any statutory re-enactment or modification of that provision).

[(2) A charity trustee shall be removed from office if a resolution to remove that trustee is proposed at a general meeting of the members called for that purpose and properly convened in accordance with clause [11], and the resolution is passed by a [two-thirds] majority of votes cast at the meeting.

(3) A resolution to remove a charity trustee in accordance with this clause shall not take effect unless the individual concerned has been given at least 14 clear days' notice in writing that the resolution is to be proposed, specifying the circumstances alleged to justify removal from office, and has been given a reasonable opportunity of making oral and/or written representations to the members of the CIO.]

16. Reappointment of charity trustees

Any person who retires as a charity trustee by rotation or by giving notice to the CIO is eligible for reappointment. [A charity trustee who has served for [three] consecutive terms may not be reappointed for a [fourth] consecutive term but may be reappointed after an interval of at least [three years].]

17. Taking of decisions by charity trustees

Any decision may be taken either:

- at a meeting of the charity trustees; or
- by resolution in writing or electronic form agreed by all of the charity trustees, which may comprise either a single documentor several documents containing the text of the resolution in like form to each of which one or more charity trustees has signified their agreement.

18. Delegation by charity trustees

(1) The charity trustees may delegate any of their powers or functions to a committee or committees, and, if they do, they must determine the terms and conditions on which the delegation is made. The charity trustees may at any time alter those terms and conditions, or revoke the delegation.

(2) This power is in addition to the power of delegation in the General Regulations and any other power of delegation available to the charity trustees, but is subject to the following requirements –

(a) a committee may consist of two or more persons, but at least one member of each committee must be a charity trustee;

(b) the acts and proceedings of any committee must be brought to the attention of the charity trustees as a whole as soon as is reasonably practicable; and

(c) the charity trustees shall from time to time review the arrangements which they have made for the delegation of their powers.

19. Meetings and proceedings of charity trustees

(1) Calling meetings

(a) Any charity trustee may call a meeting of the charity trustees.

(b) Subject to that, the charity trustees shall decide how their meetings are to be called, and what notice is required.

(2) Chairing of meetings

The charity trustees may appoint one of their number to chair their meetings and may at any time revoke such appointment. If no-one has been so appointed, or if the person appointed is unwilling to preside or is not present within 10 minutes after the time of the meeting, the charity trustees present may appoint one of their number to chair that meeting.

(3) Procedure at meetings

(a) No decision shall be taken at a meeting unless a quorum is present at the time when the decision is taken. The quorum is [two] charity trustees, or the number nearest to [one third] of the total number of charity trustees, whichever is greater, or such larger number as the charity trustees may decide from time to time. A charity trustee shall not be counted in the quorum present when any decision is made about a matter upon which he or she is not entitled to vote.

(b) Questions arising at a meeting shall be decided by a majority of those eligible to vote.

[(c) In the case of an equality of votes, the chair shall have a second or casting vote.]

(4) *Participation in meetings by electronic means*

(a) A meeting may be held by suitable electronic means agreed by the charity trustees in which each participant may communicate with all the other participants.

(b) Any charity trustee participating at a meeting by suitable electronic means agreed by the charity trustees in which a participant or participants may communicate with all the other participants shall qualify as being present at the meeting.

(c) Meetings held by electronic means must comply with rules for meetings, including chairing and the taking of minutes.

20. Saving provisions

(1) Subject to sub-clause (2) of this clause, all decisions of the charity trustees, or of a committee of charity trustees, shall be valid notwithstanding the participation in any vote of a charity trustee:

- who was disqualified from holding office;
- who had previously retired or who had been obliged by the constitution to vacate office;
- who was not entitled to vote on the matter, whether by reason of a conflict of interest or otherwise;

if, without the vote of that charity trustee and that charity trustee being counted in the quorum, the decision has been made by a majority of the charity trustees at a quorate meeting.

(2) Sub-clause (1) of this clause does not permit a charity trustee to keep any benefit that may be conferred upon him or her by a resolution of the charity trustees or of a committee of charity trustees if, but for clause (1), the resolution would have been void, or if the charity trustee has not complied with clause 7 (Conflicts of interest).

21. Execution of documents

(1) The CIO shall execute documents either by signature or by affixing its seal (if it has one).

(2) A document is validly executed by signature if it is signed by at least two of the charity trustees.

(3) If the CIO has a seal:

(a) it must comply with the provisions of the General Regulations; and

(b) it must only be used by the authority of the charity trustees or of a committee of charity trustees duly authorised by the charity trustees. The charity trustees may determine who shall sign any document to which the seal is affixed and unless otherwise determined it shall be signed by two charity trustees.

22. Use of electronic communications

(1) *General*

The CIO will comply with the requirements of the Communications Provisions in the General Regulations and in particular:

(a) the requirement to provide within 21 days to any member on request a hard copy of any document or information sent to the member otherwise than in hard copy form;

(b) any requirements to provide information to the Commission in a particular form or manner.

(2) *To the CIO*

Any member or charity trustee of the CIO may communicate electronically with the CIO to an address specified by the CIO for the purpose, so long as the communication is authenticated in a manner which is satisfactory to the CIO.

(3) *By the CIO*

(a) Any member or charity trustee of the CIO, by providing the CIO with his or her email address or similar, is taken to have agreed to receive communications from the CIO in electronic form at that address, unless the member has indicated to the CIO his or her unwillingness to receive such communications in that form.

(b) The charity trustees may, subject to compliance with any legal requirements, by means of publication on its website –

(i) provide the members with the notice referred to in clause 11(3) (Notice of general meetings);

(ii) give charity trustees notice of their meetings in accordance with clause 19(1) (Calling meetings); [and

(iii) submit any proposal to the members or charity trustees for decision by written resolution or postal vote in accordance with the CIO's powers under clause 10 (Members' decisions), 10(3) (Decisions taken by resolution in writing), or [[the provisions for postal voting] (if you have included this optional provision, please insert the correct clause number here)].

(c) The charity trustees must:

(i) take reasonable steps to ensure that members and charity trustees are promptly notified of the publication of any such notice or proposal;

(ii) send any such notice or proposal in hard copy form to any member or charity trustee who has not consented to receive communications in electronic form.

23. Keeping of Registers

The CIO must comply with its obligations under the General Regulations in relation to the keeping of, and provision of access to, registers of its members and charity trustees.

24. Minutes

The charity trustees must keep minutes of all:

(1) appointments of officers made by the charity trustees;

(2) proceedings at general meetings of the CIO;

(3) meetings of the charity trustees and committees of charity trustees including:

- the names of the trustees present at the meeting;
- the decisions made at the meetings; and
- where appropriate the reasons for the decisions;

(4) decisions made by the charity trustees otherwise than in meetings.

25. Accounting records, accounts, annual reports and returns, register maintenance

(1) The charity trustees must comply with the requirements of the Charities Act 2011 with regard to the keeping of accounting records, to the preparation and scrutiny of statements of accounts, and to the preparation of annual reports and returns. The statements of accounts, reports and returns must be sent to the Charity Commission, regardless of the income of the CIO, within 10 months of the financial year end.

(2) The charity trustees must comply with their obligation to inform the Commission within 28 days of any change in the particulars of the CIO entered on the Central Register of Charities.

26. Rules

The charity trustees may from time to time make such reasonable and proper rules or bye laws as they may deem necessary or expedient for the proper conduct and management of the CIO, but such rules or bye laws must not be inconsistent with any provision of this constitution. Copies of any such rules or bye laws currently in force must be made available to any member of the CIO on request.

27. Disputes

If a dispute arises between members of the CIO about the validity or propriety of anything done by the members under this constitution, and the dispute cannot be resolved by agreement, the parties to the dispute must first try in good faith to settle the dispute by mediation before resorting to litigation.

28. Amendment of constitution

As provided by clauses 224–227 of the Charities Act 2011:

(1) This constitution can only be amended:

(a) by resolution agreed in writing by all members of the CIO; or

(b) by a resolution passed by a 75% majority of votes cast at a general meeting of the members of the CIO.

(2) Any alteration of clause 3 (Objects), clause [29] (Voluntary winding up or dissolution), this clause, or of any provision where the alteration would provide authorisation for any benefit to be obtained by charity trustees or members of the CIO or persons connected with them, requires the prior written consent of the Charity Commission.

(3) No amendment that is inconsistent with the provisions of the Charities Act 2011 or the General Regulations shall be valid.

(4) A copy of any resolution altering the constitution, together with a copy of the CIO's constitution as amended, must be sent to the Commission within 15 days from the date on which the resolution is passed. The amendment does not take effect until it has been recorded in the Register of Charities.

29. Voluntary winding up or dissolution

(1) As provided by the Dissolution Regulations, the CIO may be dissolved by resolution of its members. Any decision by the members to wind up or dissolve the CIO can only be made:

(a) at a general meeting of the members of the CIO called in accordance with clause [11] (Meetings of Members), of which not less than 14 days' notice has been given to those eligible to attend and vote:

(i) by a resolution passed by a 75% majority of those voting, or

(ii) by a resolution passed by decision taken without a vote and without any expression of dissent in response to the question put to the general meeting; or

(b) by a resolution agreed in writing by all members of the CIO.

(2) Subject to the payment of all the CIO's debts:

(a) Any resolution for the winding up of the CIO, or for the dissolution of the CIO without winding up, may contain a provision directing how any remaining assets of the CIO shall be applied.

(b) If the resolution does not contain such a provision, the charity trustees must decide how any remaining assets of the CIO shall be applied.

(c) In either case the remaining assets must be applied for charitable purposes the same as or similar to those of the CIO.

(3) The CIO must observe the requirements of the Dissolution Regulations in applying to the Commission for the CIO to be removed from the Register of Charities, and in particular:

(a) the charity trustees must send with their application to the Commission:

(i) a copy of the resolution passed by the members of the CIO;

(ii) a declaration by the charity trustees that any debts and other liabilities of the CIO have been settled or otherwise provided for in full; and

(iii) a statement by the charity trustees setting out the way in which any property of the CIO has been or is to be applied prior to its dissolution in accordance with this constitution;

(b) the charity trustees must ensure that a copy of the application is sent within seven days to every member and employee of the CIO, and to any charity trustee of the CIO who was not privy to the application.

(4) If the CIO is to be wound up or dissolved in any other circumstances, the provisions of the Dissolution Regulations must be followed.

30. Interpretation

In this constitution:

"**connected person**" means:

(a) a child, parent, grandchild, grandparent, brother or sister of the charity trustee;

(b) the spouse or civil partner of the charity trustee or of any person falling within sub-clause (a) above;

(c) a person carrying on business in partnership with the charity trustee or with any person falling within sub-clause (a) or (b) above;

(d) an institution which is controlled –

 (i) by the charity trustee or any connected person falling within sub-clause (a), (b), or (c) above; or

 (ii) by two or more persons falling within sub-clause (d)(i), when taken together

(e) a body corporate in which –

 (i) the charity trustee or any connected person falling within sub-clauses (a) to (c) has a substantial interest; or

 (ii) two or more persons falling within sub-clause (e)(i) who, when taken together, have a substantial interest.

Section 118 of the Charities Act 2011 applies for the purposes of interpreting the terms used in this constitution.

"**General Regulations**" means the Charitable Incorporated Organisations (General) Regulations 2012.

"**Dissolution Regulations**" means the Charitable Incorporated Organisations (Insolvency and Dissolution) Regulations 2012.

The "**Communications Provisions**" means the Communications Provisions in Part 9 of the General Regulations.

"**charity trustee**" means a charity trustee of the CIO.

A "**poll**" means a counted vote or ballot, usually (but not necessarily) in writing.

Schedule – First Trustees

The first charity trustees of the CIO are:

. . . .

. . . .

. . . .

. . . .

. . . .

Index

For references to legislation and cases, please see table at the front of the book starting on page xv.

Pages where a concept is defined or discussed in detail are shown in bold.